ARCHITECTURE AND IDENTITY

ARCHITECTURE AND IDENTITY

Responses to cultural and technological change

Second edition

160101

Chris Abel

With a foreword by Suha Ozkan

Architectural Press
OXFORD AUCKLAND BOSTON JOHANNESBURG MELBOURNE NEW DELHI

Architectural Press
An imprint of Butterworth-Heinemann
Linacre House, Jordan Hill, Oxford OX2 8DP
225 Wildwood Avenue, Woburn, MA 01801-2041
A division of Reed Educational and Professional Publishing Ltd

A member of the Reed Elsevier plc group

First published 1997
Second Edition 2000

British Library Cataloguing in Publication Data
Abel, Chris
Architecture and identity: responses to cultural and technological change. – 2nd ed.
1. Architecture – Environmental aspects
I. Title
720.4'7

ISBN 0 7506 4246 7

Library of Congress Cataloguing in Publication Data
A catalogue record for this book is available from the Library of Congress

Composition by Scribe Design, Gillingham, Kent
Printed and bound in Great Britain

CONTENTS

Foreword by Suha Ozkan		*vii*
Preface to second edition		*xi*
Preface to first edition		*xiii*
Acknowledgements		*xv*
Part One	**Science and Technology**	**1**
1	Ditching the dinosaur sanctuary	3
2	Urban chaos or self-organization?	15
3	Design method and new science	27
4	Return to craft manufacture	37
5	Visible and invisible complexities	48
6	The Bio-Tech Architecture Workshop	68
Part Two	**Critical Theory**	**79**
7	Architectural language games	81
8	Role of metaphor in changing architectural concepts	97
9	Function of tacit knowing in learning design	106
10	The essential tension	114
11	Tradition, innovation and linked solutions	131
Part Three	**Regionalism and Globalization**	**139**
12	Architecture as identity	141
13	Living in a hybrid world	151
14	Regional transformations	163
15	Prime objects	178
16	Localization versus globalization	190
17	Towards a global eco-culture	198
18	Asian urban futures	211
Notes and references		235
Index		263

FOREWORD

Those who studied architecture in the 1960s London-centric architectural world went through a completely different experience from their peers elsewhere in the West. At that time, architects in the US were still holding the Modern Movement close to their chest, mindful of securing a safe nook in corporate architecture. Fearful of being marginalized themselves, most ignored the offbeat examples set by Paolo Soleri and Bruce Goff. Continental Europeans were likewise stuck with their own orthodoxies. The Germans were struggling to revive Bauhaus thinking at the Hochschule für Gestaltung at Ulm, while the French, absorbed with Le Corbusier and standardization, were busy creating endless megablocks in the new towns outside Paris.

The concerns of such as John Turner, Charles Correa and Balkrishna Doshi with the larger world beyond with its pressing problems of human habitat and urban degradation were generally ignored by the mainstream. Theorists fared little better. Christopher Alexander impressed academics with his cool, Platonic logic and mathematical rigour but was felt to be too sophisticated and remote for the common architect then, trained as he was to rely on catalogue searches and other humbler methodologies. Neither theoretical speculation nor urgent problems of shelter seemed relevant to the profession at large.

London was different. Archigram was in active search of both a new language and a new mythology for architecture for the masses. On the one hand, Peter Cook and Ron Herron projected an aggressive Brave New World in their 'Plug-in' and 'Walking Cities', rivalling the contemporary visions of Japanese Metabolists. On the other, David Greene hinted at a gentler, decentralized future, fit for both the electronics revolution and nature, with his 'roc plug' and 'log plug'. Many of the group's ideas on new technologies were also influenced by the innovative writings and projects of Reyner Banham and Cedric Price respectively. All then taught or lectured at the Architectural Association School in London along with other radical thinkers, creating a hotbed of insurrection. The same School, through its Tropical Architecture Department under Otto Koenigsberger, presented a window to a still wider world of commitments, and a magnet to students from developing countries everywhere.

Concurrently, the influential journal *Architectural Design* (*AD*), with Monica Pidgeon as editor, was exploring new frontiers of architectural discourse and expanding into other, little known fields of knowledge.

Towards the end of the decade, almost every issue of the journal featured a novel input to architectural thought. Far from remaining aloof from social and political developments, Pidgeon consistently lent *AD*'s voice to philosophical and interdisciplinary concerns in architecture. Other schools eventually followed suit, modifying their curricula and opening them up to other professionals to contribute and to participate.

First as a prominent student at the Architectural Association and then immediately after as a youthful contributor to *AD*, Chris Abel was one of the few to help shape the interdisciplinary discourse of architecture at this time. From these early days, he has pursued an academic career marked by a dogged concern to understand and explain the complexities of his subject, often repositioning himself in different parts of the world in a restless search for answers and new questions. The same concern has kept him firmly in the theoretical realm of architecture for the past thirty years or so.

The main sources of interdisciplinary thinking to emerge in the 1960s were general system theory (GST), semiotics, or the theory of signs, and Thomas Kuhn's theory of scientific paradigms. From these early explorations one thing became clear to any who were prepared to accept it: there is no simple axiomatic entity in architecture from which a singular theory could evolve. On the contrary, architecture addresses itself from the outset to the diversity and complexity of cultural and psycho-sociological existence. While generalized and abstract theories such as GST may increase the scope for theory, they may also reduce the meaning content of the subject. The dilemma for any architectural theorist is therefore to strike an acceptable balance between scope and content, generality and specificity – an exercise which resists the imposition of any simplistic or exclusive framework. It is therefore perfectly legitimate to pursue, as Chris Abel has done, an approach based on selected concepts and cases as opposed to striving after all-encompassing theories.

The essays presented here cover an unusual range of topics. It is extremely exciting to see, in 1969, a young architecture graduate committed to the problems of the general population and spelling out for the first time the potential impact on building production of computerized manufacturing systems – what is now called Post-Fordism. In so doing, he also rejected his former teachers' obsessions with mass production and signalled a turning point in the way architecture can be made. It is even more intriguing to see the same person go on to delve into the foggy area of architectural experience and meaning. Rarely among theorists, Chris Abel has consistently avoided the trap of dogmatism and has embraced all three lines of thinking from the Sixties, emphasizing one or the other or weaving them together as appropriate to the topic under discussion. Consequently, his approach is not constituted of a linear body of assertions, but resembles more a collage of theoretical discursions and case studies, the evolution of which he has built into his discourse. When the pieces are read in their original chronological order, they not only reflect his mode of thinking at the time of writing, but also contain substantial undertones of the state-of-the-art of architectural theory at the time.

The identity theme recurs throughout the book, along with other related themes and ideas. However, it is not a single concept the way 'space' is for Bruno Zevi, 'type' is for Aldo Rossi, 'tectonic' is for Kenneth Frampton, or various semantic categories are for Charles Jencks, but is rather an intellectual commitment to increase the meaning and responsiveness of architecture. It surfaces in various guises – customized production methods, language games, user participation, or regionalism – according to the case in question and which approach the writer is taking. This is unusual in itself, since it brings a richness devoid of the usual strait-jackets. It also allows the author to compensate in subsequent chapters for over-stressing one aspect at the expense of another, as he does with his related discussions of 'rational design' and 'tacit knowing', without the need to force everything into the same deductive framework. Each chapter has an integrity and consistent logic of its own. The connections between the chapters on the other hand are relatively open, which makes the writer's carefully balanced assertions all the more sympathetic and persuasive.

The commitment to complexity and the evident desire to avoid over-simplification in architecture is closer to Robert Venturi's thinking than to orthodox Modernism. However, though distancing himself from the latter, Abel nevertheless eschews the Postmodern label, and is fiercely critical of Venturi and other Postmodernists – not to mention Deconstructionists – for their fixation on form for its own sake. Instead, he propagates a liberal and outward-looking Modernism, open to other disciplines, to regional differences, and to constant experimentation in the best spirit of both the sciences and the arts. This inclusion of elements of both Modern and Postmodern thinking makes Abel's work all the harder to pin down to any single idea or movement.

In addition to the identity theme and the language analogy, the most repeated idea or method is metaphor and analogical thinking itself, which is used, explicitly or implicitly, in nearly every chapter, and is frequently the subject of analysis. As Abel notes, the main problem arises when analogies are taken too literally, and users forget the limitations of the borrowed idea. In architectural theory the use of metaphor generally applies to selected aspects of architecture, as in the popular analogy between architecture and music. At their most useful, metaphors and analogies are creative tools to instigate thought, to structure research and to compare the 'unknowns' of one problem area with the 'knowns' of another. The most fruitful analogies in the social sciences, such as the application of 'laws of gravity' to population movements, may generate sufficient testable propositions and empirical research that the validity of the original idea becomes largely irrelevant. So long as the analogy produces valid assertions it does the job. The ends justify the means. The use of metaphor and analogy in architectural theory is more problematic than in the sciences though. It is worth noting, for example, that, as with the music analogy, analogies in architecture are rarely reciprocated. While architects do not hesitate to describe their work as 'frozen music', musicians are not known to call their work 'fluid architecture'. This may be due to the very complexity and multiplicity of architectural phenomena, which do not lend themselves readily as a source of valid assertions from which other fields might benefit. The same reasons place architecture beyond the explanatory range of any one analogy, which if used carelessly may bring with it as much irrelevant as relevant baggage from the source idea.

Abel's own treatment of analogy acknowledges these difficulties, not only by his refusal to be bound by any single analogy or line of thinking, but also by his self-conscious and reflective dissection of the method of thought itself. In the key chapter on 'Architecture as identity', he is careful to differentiate his own preferred relativistic model of language from the more familiar structuralist model which dominated architectural theory into the Eighties. Building on the known evidence of the links between language and cultural identities, he goes on to assert similar links in architecture and proposes that colonial architecture might provide hard evidence of a sort, involving the recreation of cultural identities in an 'alien' environment. In the following chapter, 'Living in a hybrid world', he takes up his own challenge and pursues the idea with detailed analyses of the colonial architecture of Malaysia, writing, among other cases, of the 'Palladian' villas of the region, and the related trade-offs between imported and local building forms.

The studies of colonial architecture are accompanied by a host of other case studies and examples of both historical and contemporary architecture from the Asian Pacific and Middle East, as well as from Western countries. The diverse examples substantiate the need for a heterogeneous approach to a heterogeneous subject. Architects hoping for clear-cut images of national identity will find small comfort in the ambiguous picture presented here of the cross-cultural influences and transformations that go to make up regional architecture. Architectural elitists who place their faith in the star system and its trickle-down effects will likewise find little support, though stars as well as lesser known designers do feature in these pages. What counts most to the author is the cultural and technological base for architectural production. In the penultimate chapter, Abel sketches the outlines of a broad-based 'eco-culture', which might encompass cultural as well as biological diversity, despite acknowledged global trends to the contrary. Like much else in this book, the idea contains contradictory elements of both idealism and down-to-earth realism, indicative of its author's cautious optimism and awareness of the problems involved in achieving any general improvement in environmental quality. More of an analysis of selected cultural and technological developments of a positive nature, nothing could be further from the totalizing prescriptions usually favoured by architectural theorists than this essentially pragmatic and open-ended vision.

It is not easy to span an array of concerns from robotics through the psycho-sociological aspects of architecture to philosophy, but Chris Abel does so with conviction. He has studied low-, medium- and high-tech building modes with the same depth of understanding and sympathy, while his knowledge of human science has been reinforced by his own researches in the field. He has been exposed to and tested his ideas against a vast range of cultural and geographical situations across both the developed and developing world. His experience and insights are invaluable.

Suha Ozkan

PREFACE TO SECOND EDITION

Although it has been a fairly short time since the first edition of this book was published, some omissions have become apparent which need addressing. In particular, whilst I had formerly observed (see Chapter 4) that information technology called for radically new approaches in architectural education as well as in practice, nothing was said about what shape educational reform might actually take. When the editors at Architectural Press suggested last year that I might like to consider a second expanded edition rather than a straightforward reprint I therefore welcomed the opportunity to include fresh material on these and other matters.

The essay in Chapter 6 describes a series of experimental design studios I conducted at the University of Nottingham School of Architecture between 1993 and 1997, culminating in the Bio-Tech Architecture Workshop, which was purposefully conceived as a new model for design education. The reader may also trace the roots of the Workshop in the concerns expressed in earlier essays dating back to the late 1960s, on the need for architects to grasp the opportunities that computer-based methods present to create a more responsive and diverse Modern architecture. Much has happened since those early years but I underestimated the time it would take for the innovations in production technologies discussed in those essays to work their way through into the construction industry and related professions. The rarefied situation in architectural education has not helped any and is aggravated by the growing divide between the academic values and criteria which now dominate university-based schools everywhere, and the conflicting values and criteria which every architecture graduate must face up to upon entering practice. It is no coincidence that all of the individual architects described in these pages who are working at the technological cutting edge of design and production are essentially self-taught. This does not mean that what they learnt at university has no value, but simply that the collaborative methods and interdisciplinary skills which define their common approach and distinguish their work from that of other architects were only acquired after they left school, and only then by breaking with customary practice and professional prejudice.

It will no doubt be argued that the current proliferation of computer-based media courses signals a positive change of direction, but my impression is that such courses, which are mainly focused on techniques of visualization, will not in themselves break the mould. In other words, such techniques are mostly being used to help students do better what they have always been taught to do, which is to explore traditional issues of form, space and appearance, leaving equally important aspects of fabrication and performance to others. While the experiments reported here do not represent a complete agenda they do suggest the outlines of an alternative approach which integrates these neglected aspects into a more soundly based programme in tune with the technological era. The attached brief 'manifesto' also sketches in the wider dimensions of the exercise, to be spelt out in future publications in hand.

The new concluding essay on 'Asian urban futures', which is published here for the first time (Chapter 18), takes up some of the discussions on the relative merits of planned and unplanned urban growth which first appeared chronologically in Chapter 2's essay in a developed world context and again much later in the essays in Chapters 16 and 17 in a developing world context. Written in 1969, several years before the first oil shortage impacted on architects' awareness, the earlier polemic was both a reaction to the rigid masterplanning which still dominated urban theory and design at the time, and a call for planners to embrace uncertainty and change, which dispersed and incremental growth allows for. Thirty years on, the ideological pendulum has swung firmly in the other direction and it is now fashionable to reject any form of planned intervention as unrealistic and doomed to failure. There has also been much misunderstanding regarding the meaning of concepts of 'self-organization' originally derived from systems theory, or what is now generally called complexity theory. Self-organization, it needs to be stressed, does not mean 'no organization', but describes systems of human activity which can swiftly adapt to changes in an unpredictable world. As the recent financial crisis in the Far East dramatically demonstrated, these may call for new global institutions no less than for new local institutions or less formal procedures. Readers of the first edition may already have noted an adjustment in my position towards a more balanced relation between so-called 'top down' and 'bottom up' decision-making structures in my discussions on the prospects for a global eco-culture. The concept of the 'development city' advocated in the new essay, which also embodies a theory of 'parallel development' I have elaborated elsewhere, takes these arguments further into the realms of physical and social planning, building on the ideas and experience of several accomplished Asian architect-planners. As with the previous essays and discussions, however, the responsibility for the interpretation of these ideas and any related concepts of urbanization and development is entirely my own.

Making space for the new essays while keeping both the size and cost of the book within reasonable limits necessitated the sacrifice of at least one chapter from the first edition. My choice reluctantly fell upon my 1979 essay on 'Rationality and meaning in design', since it has already been republished several times. Other changes include a new subtitle for the book which better reflects the scope of its contents. The previous subtitle, 'Towards a global eco-culture', is now used as the title for Chapter 17, from which essay the concept and phrase were originally taken.

Chris Abel,
Gharghur, Malta,
1999.

PREFACE TO FIRST EDITION

The essays collected here record a personal search for the principles of an architecture for our time, as true to the diversity of human culture and the natural environment as it is to their universal values. That same search has taken many forms itself, covering both a wide timespan and a catholic range of approaches, factors which present special problems of selection. How to weed out those subsidiary exercises which might detract from the main theme, whilst still retaining the open spirit of the exploration which has been the main motivation and reward? At the same time, how to bring out the essential links between the essays without covering over the internal dialogue which has been such a vital part of the investigation?

The division of the book into three distinct sections offers a convenient compromise which encompasses both divergent and convergent lines of thought. Whilst chronological sequence is generally respected within each part, it is therefore broken across the book in favour of a grouping of chapters on similar approaches and topics (Chapter 17 was moved out of strict sequence for purposes of summary). Beyond these divisions in the subject matter and related shifts in perspective, it may be noted that whilst one idea or approach may be set aside for a time in favour of other ideas and approaches, it invariably crops up again in some revived form in a later essay. The grouping into like topics and methods of analysis therefore pays respect to the persistence of these key concepts over long periods of time which might otherwise be obscured in a straightforward chronology.

Part 1 focuses on new ideas in science and technology which are enlarging our understanding of the complexities of human behaviour, and which are reshaping our technical capacity to deal with those complexities. It includes the very earliest essays from the late 1960s, as well as the most recent. They appear in their original form save for Chapter 2, which is a compendium of two separate but closely related publications from the same period. Some new passages have also been added to the same chapter from my 1968 Architectural Association dissertation on biological models and systems theory, which was the original source of all these early essays. The fact that the same writings on self-organizing systems and flexible production techniques appear to be gaining rather than losing their relevance or topicality, has in turn encouraged me to resist further changes.

Part 2 opens with a selection of essays from the late 1970s and early 1980s, concerned with the nature of architectural theory and criticism, and with their relations to other disciplines and ways of thought. Whilst the essays in Part 1 draw heavily on other fields of knowledge in an enthusiastic but relatively unselfconscious way, Part 2 offers a closer examination of the analogical reasoning underlying such approaches and its role in the innovation of ideas. A key issue in these chapters is the identity and integrity of architecture itself as a culture-form, and the particular problems and contradictions this raises in any interdisciplinary or analogical approach to the subject. In the chapter on language games I have outlined a middle road between objectivism and extreme relativism, which I call critical relativism, which proffers a general solution to some of these problems.

Part 3 contains essays written from the early 1980s onwards, which expand the geographical and cultural ground, a result of various overseas teaching appointments and travels throughout that decade. Common themes running through this section are the dual processes of globalization and localization, themes first broached in Chapter 2 in the context of the interaction between global communications and urban decentralization. The idea also first proposed in that chapter – that there might be some kind of self-organizing or evolutionary factor underlying these reciprocal processes – is raised again in these final chapters in the context of architectural regionalism and ecologically based models of development.

The individual philosophers and other thinkers most often referred to in this book are not drawn from any one school of thought but are those which I have discovered for myself as most relevant to the specific questions and issues raised in each essay. Their repeated appearance does however signify common threads of thought which may help the reader in turn to thread his or her own way through these pages (in the notes and references for each chapter I have indicated which other chapters in the book may be consulted for these and other supporting arguments). One such thinker is Thomas Kuhn, whose work on scientific paradigms has been a major influence in this book. In recognition of that influence I have adopted the title 'The essential tension' from a collection of Kuhn's own essays for Chapter 10, for which it is eminently fitting. I take full responsibility though for my interpretation of Kuhn and other writers and for the ideas presented in these essays.

Many of my friends and former colleagues who have observed my struggles with this book over the years say that it is long overdue. I hope that they will find the final result worthwhile, as I hope the general reader will.

Chris Abel,
Gharghur, Malta,
1996.

ACKNOWLEDGEMENTS

Any work spanning a period as long as this book carries an equally ancient burden of debt to all those generous persons who have lent encouragement and support along the way. First thanks, then, go to those who played their part at the very beginning of my career in opening up new avenues of enquiry or creating other opportunities. Special thanks go to Roy Landau, who as Third Year teacher at the AA School introduced me to urban and regional planning and helped me to see architecture as part of a broader spectrum of environmental issues. Just a few years later, as guest editor of two special issues of *Architectural Design* (*AD*) on complexity theory, Roy published some of my first writings on the subject, reproduced here in Chapter 2. Thanks are also due to Melvin Webber who gave me some of his precious time on a visit to London and passed on some invaluable advice on how to best pursue my obsession with biological analogies. I spent the next year following up Webber's tips in the British Museum Library, poring over hitherto unknown scientific papers on systems theory. Webber's own seminal works on urban decentralization were also a formative influence on my studies at the time. Especially warm thanks go to the late Gordon Pask who, first as external tutor during my final year at the AA School and later at Brunel University where I took a course with him on cybernetics, taught me what I know of that subject. Gordon also guided me in my later research into interpersonal communication and arranged for me to work with the Architecture Machine Group at Massachusetts Institute of Technology as visiting scholar in 1973–74. I deeply regret that Gordon is no longer here to see his student's work. I am also most grateful to Nicholas Negroponte who, as Director of that Group, gave me free reign and support to create the ARCHITRAINER program reported in Chapter 3, and who invited me back for a return visit to complete my work on that experiment.

Editors also play a vital role in the career of any writer and I have been fortunate to have been exceptionally well served in these early stages. My deepest gratitude goes to Monica Pidgeon and Robin Middleton who, as Editor and Technical Editor respectively of *AD*, published the first essay in this book, giving it front cover treatment to boot, as well as others not included here. I have already mentioned the part later played by Roy Landau as guest editor for the same journal. Also not forgotten are my former colleagues from Portsmouth Polytechnic School of Architecture in the 1970s, Tomas Llorens and James Powell. In their extra-curricular roles as editors and consultants on various academic publications, both were instrumental in publishing some of the theory essays written just before and after I left the United Kingdom.

My next round of thanks goes to those good persons who came onto the scene at a later stage, and who either gave me the opportunity to work outside the UK or else published the results of those experiences. First recipient in this category is Angela Schweitzer, who arranged my first visit and lecture tour outside the northern hemisphere, to South America, and so changed my perspective on the world at large. Second is Ray Kappe who, as Founder-Director of the Southern California Institute of Architecture (SCIARCH) in Los Angeles, appointed me as visiting lecturer there in the spring of 1979. It was during this time, which was also one of the most enjoyable teaching experiences of my career, that I was able to put together my thoughts on linguistic analogies and some of the other topics which were eventually published in the essays of this period. Next is Fawiza Lucas who, as Dean of the Department of Architecture at the Science University of Malaysia in Penang, appointed me as associate professor at that University in 1981. In so doing Fawiza opened up another fascinating part of the world for me, with which I have been absorbed ever since. Warm thanks also go to Saleh Al-Hathloul who, as Dean and Head of the Department of Architecture at King Saud University, gave me my next appointment and opened the gateway to the Middle East for me, and with it access to an infinite source of architectural wealth. I am especially grateful for his support for my efforts to assimilate Islamic traditions into the education programme, about which I have written elsewhere. As Editor of *The Architectural Review*, Peter Davey published the first products of these experiences, and has been publishing my work ever since. I cannot thank Peter enough for his cheerful faith and support, some of the fruits of which are reproduced here in Chapters 5, 14 and 16. I am also indebted to Toshio Nakamura as Editor of *A+U* for publishing the essay in Chapter 10, and for taking the trouble to translate it into Japanese himself.

Special thanks are also due to David Nicholson-Cole at Nottingham University School of Architecture for the computing skills and unstinting support he contributed to the Bio-Tech Architecture Workshop described in Chapter 6. My gratitude also goes to Farhang Daemi, former Director at the Centre for Medical and Industrial Informatics, and to all those many persons in other departments around the Nottingham campus who collaborated on the Workshop, and most importantly, lent us access to their advanced and costly research and production facilities. Not least, my warmest thanks go to the students involved for all their hard work – which far exceeded any mandatory requirements – in making the Workshop and the preceding experimental studios such a success.

The last group of persons to whom I owe appreciation includes all those architects who have been generous and patient enough to give me many hours, and frequently more, of their personal time to explain their firm's work to me, and who have kindly made their resources available for my researches. They include many of those architects featured in this book, but especially Sir Norman Foster, Henning Larsen, Mike

Davies, Richard England, Charles Correa, Ken Yeang, Jimmy Lim, Ruslan Khalid, Liu Thai Ker, Tay Kheng Soon and Sumet Jumsai. I am very happy to count some of these very gifted people as friends as well as fellow architectural junkies.

Special thanks also go to Suha Ozkan, both for his generous introduction to this book and for his equally kind encouragement over the many years of our acquaintance. First as Deputy Secretary General and later as Secretary General, Suha has involved me in the work of the Aga Khan Award for Architecture on a number of occasions, from which vantage point I have been able to observe the Award's multiple activities and positive impact. Though our routes have differed widely I hope that Suha and his colleagues at the Award, especially Jack Kennedy and Farrokh Derakhshani, will accept this book as a contribution towards the same ultimate goals.

Final and heartfelt thanks go to the team at Architectural Press who have toiled so patiently to bring this book into the world: to former publisher Neil Warnock-Smith, Diane Chandler, Zoë Youd and Sarah Leatherbarrow, who all worked on the first edition; to Mike Cash, who took over from Neil and got the second edition on its way, and especially to Marie Milmore, who as associate editor saw it expertly through to production.

PART ONE

SCIENCE AND TECHNOLOGY

'In the electric age, when our central nervous system is technologically extended to involve us in the whole of mankind and to incorporate the whole of mankind in us, we necessarily participate, in depth, in the consequences of our every action.'

Marshall McLuhan, 1964

1 DITCHING THE DINOSAUR SANCTUARY

First published in *Architectural Design*, August 1969.

Few would claim that the building industry has yet come of age as a manufacturing concern, in even the common meaning of the term. Compared with other industrial sectors, building production seems permanently mired in outdated practices, unable to respond to new technologies or production methods.

For most architects concerned with the issue, the way forward is clear. Raymond Wilson's mock report on the 'Ideal Building Corporation'[1] provides a good illustration of the commonly accepted formula. Published shortly after John Kenneth Galbraith's Reith Lectures on 'The new industrial state',[2] Wilson's account of the conditions conducive to the success of his dream enterprise is well stocked with fallout from Galbraith's analysis. Central to these conditions is acceptance of the determinate nature of mass production and rejection of the myth of consumer orientation and the role of the market. The complexities of conventional mass production meant that each product was necessarily preplanned, sometimes years in advance of consumption. Once launched on the market, the rigid disciplines of the mass-production line, with its enormous investment in capital, afforded next to no room for variation without drastic and costly overhaul of the whole operation. So we have the ready made assumption that industrialization must mean the design of a product for large serial production, and with it the design of components related through standardization. However, while this Galbraithian view may be valid for industrialization in its widespread form, it does not hold true for many emergent sectors of post-industrial production.

Among the factors likely to affect architects and other designers in the future will be the general 'use of automation and cybernation in management and production'.[3] Qualifications for post-industrial status will entail new approaches to design and manufacture, including those applicable to the building industry.

PERFORMANCE CRITERIA

Although efforts have been made to modernize the industry, little has been achieved so far. Both designers and builders have failed to master the fundamentals of industrialized production. It is worth trying to understand why. For although many of the structural features of post-industrial manufacture will differ from conventional processes, performance

1.1.
Conventional mass production line.
Courtesy of Ford Motor Company, UK.

criteria will still be comparable. It is important therefore to see how these criteria have been interpreted by architects and others within their own industry.

Doubts of one kind on the objective of the industrialized building movement as portrayed by Wilson have been voiced by Reyner Banham, who, together with a handful of designers, distinguishes a genuine mass-production aesthetic from the 'universal' architectural vernacular.[4] But the observation seems to have had little effect. The literature on industrialized building rarely deviates from the gospel of modular coordination and standardization.[5] We have been constantly assured that these twin principles have their rationale in the mass-production process. In fact, this was never the case. They are the product, as Banham implied,

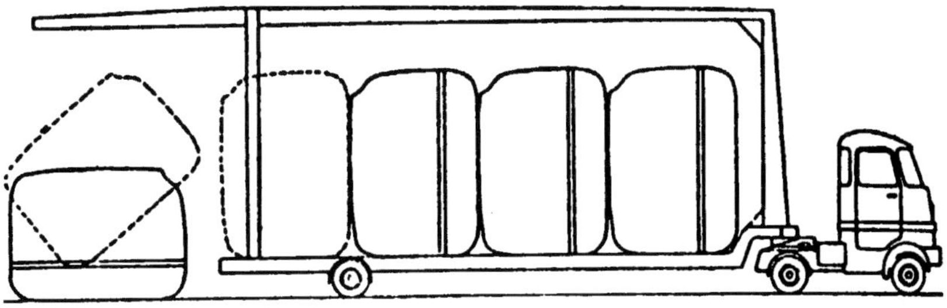

1.2a.
Plastic motel units and delivery truck system, 1956. Architect: Ionel Schein, with Magnant and Coulon. From the catalogue to the International Exhibition of Experimental Architecture, Folkestone, 6–30 June, 1966.

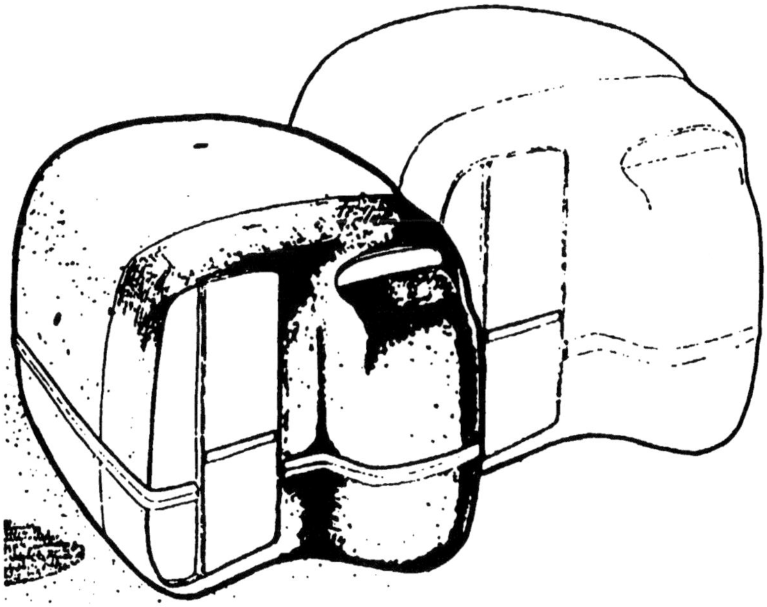

1.2b.
Motel units have genuine mass-production aesthetic. From the exhibition catalogue, 1966.

not of the manufacturing industry, but of a way of thinking – the ultimate goal, a 'unity of style'. That way of thinking is conditioned by an architectural tradition that holds that order in the built artefact is achieved through geometrical discipline. The attitude was typified by the classical scholar P. H. Scholfield, who held that:

In a building where all the parts are of different shapes, the visual effect is one of the greatest possible disorder, indeed, chaos. Order can be introduced by the repetition of similar shapes, and the highest degree of order results when comparatively few shapes are used, repeated as often as possible'[6] [my emphasis].

The same view was rationalized as a means of systematizing the design of components for mass production by the doyen of the IB movement, Ezra Ehrenkrantz. In his *Modular Number Pattern*, Ehrenkrantz[7] laid down rules for the industrialization of building: standardization – with a limited number of sizes selected for their combinatorial value; and modular coordination – providing a numerical measure for determining those standard sizes. It was claimed that only in this manner could the variety be achieved which could facilitate mass production. Acceptance of such standards throughout the building industry is generally believed to make possible interchangeability of components and therefore increase the choice available to the designer.

MYTHS AND MISCONCEPTIONS

This popular notion of standardization reveals a gross misrepresentation of manufacturing processes. J. F. Eden[8] argues that the rules of dimensional coordination as intepreted by IB enthusiasts indicate 'little authentic contact with engineering'.[9] Eden points out that the aims of modular coordination are not implicit in the engineering history of dimensional control. While some control over tolerances is essential to enable sets of components to be interchanged and replaced, such control does not necessitate any standardization of sizes: 'Interchangeability has been achieved in mechanical engineering *without the module*[10] [my emphasis].'

Other ideas on standardization prevalent in the building industry would seem to be founded on similar myths and misconceptions. The most common among them is the simple notion that the more that can be produced of any one component, the more economical it is going to be for mass production. Hence the idea of securing the largest possible market for building components by coordinating the needs of a wide range of building types.

Again, this effort, enshrined for many years as government policy among ministerial building programmes for schools and other types, makes industrial nonsense. Although there is a minimum scale of production needed to justify such methods, it is not a sliding scale of costs continually decreasing with the number of components produced. Mass-production manufacture is constrained by factors other than just the number of components coming off a production line. Once the heavy investments needed for setting up the purpose-built machinery are repaid, there is a sharp levelling off of general costs due to depreciation of equipment and running expenses. After the first sharp fall in costs, the level of savings is strictly determined by any economies achieved in the initial design of the product through a more efficient use of materials or raising some other performance criterion. Performance specification and design are therefore far more important determinants of the economics of any one product than the numbers produced above the minimum figure.

Appropriate conditions for efficient design are nonetheless slow in forthcoming from IB propagandists. The desire to open the production of building components to the widest possible application, and the need to achieve the requisite performance of individual structures, leads to an inevitable conflict of aims. It is one of the basic principles of manufacture that if a product is to be designed for maximum efficiency, then its constituent parts must be integrated together in the manner that most closely approximates the desired performance specification for the whole. This is likely to remain as true of post-industrial production as it is for conventional production. Yet this principle has been virtually ignored by IB enthusiasts, obsessed as they are with open systems.

A distinguished exception is Jean Prouvé.[11] As one of the very few architectural designers who have committed themselves wholeheartedly to studying manufacturing at first hand, Prouvé's work perfectly expresses his own maxim: 'Machines are seldom built with parts selected from various sources; they are aggregately designed.'[12] The lesson is: where interchangeability occurs in manufactured products, it occurs within a limited family of components. Further, such components owe their compatibility, not to any size range, but because they are designed together as an integrated set.

For this reason it has always been advantageous for manufacturers to exercise as much control over the total process of design and production as possible. This authority serves industrialists doubly. It enables them to attain the desired maximum efficiency from integral design and to change their products whenever it suits them – a vital strategy that may dictate a firm's continued success. It is a truism to say that technology has a habit of making advances in unpredictable directions. But if manufacturers did not retain control over their own production, they could not respond to such changes. Even within present conditions, the power of change resting with individual firms is exercised as far as the current range of technology permits.

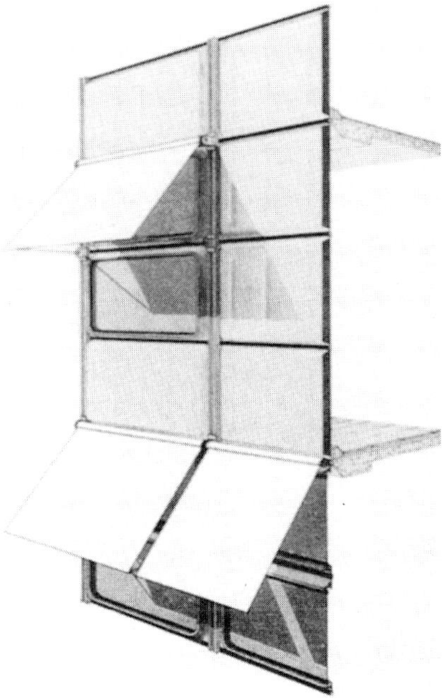

1.3.
Metal wall panel system for school in St-Egrève, 1963. Architect: Jean Prouvé with Belmont, Periller, Silvy. From Prouvé, 1965.

However, if architects' preferred universal standards are adhered to, then it will not be possible to make any rapid changes to any components that would fall outside of those standards. Pursued to its logical conclusion, no component could be seriously modified unless like changes were performed on all other related components in the entire industry. This is no exaggeration. The aims of orthodox Modernists are explicitly designed to secure a strict uniformity throughout the building industry, and the European Market into the bargain. Yet the attainment of this Nirvana would mean stagnation within the original range of standards, for the effort involved in a total changeover would severely discourage innovation, technological or otherwise. Such a conception of standardization could lead the building industry to commit itself to just one kind of technology, and still a very crude one at that, when, as we shall see, other industries are gearing themselves to continual change, both in technology and in consumer demand.

VARIABLE PRODUCTION

The tools of post-industrial production will facilitate precisely the integration of design for specific performance that IB enthusiasts have so far failed to comprehend. Until recently, industrial manufacture has relied upon two distinct scales of production, mass production and batch production. The former traditionally centres on the automated transfer line, a multi-station machine in which components to be machined remain fixed throughout the sequence of operations, and are moved automatically from station to station between each stage of machining.[13] Transfer machines of this sort make up the backbone of the mechanization of industry, familiarly known as automation, and provide Galbraith and other analysts with their model of the mass-production process. By its nature, mechanization of this kind invariably involves special-purpose machinery: machines which can produce only one component each, or at best, one family of components.

At the other end of the scale is production of a variety of components in limited quantities, carried out by batch-production methods. The

1.4.
Section of an automated transfer line for mass-production of engine blocks. Courtesy of Ford Motor Company, UK.

process typically involves a large number of manually operated, simple machines, each performing a limited, discrete operation, with manual transfer of components between machines.

These alternatives are now proving insufficient to meet the requirements of industry's fast changing and highly variable production needs. Consumer goods manufacturers who used to have large batch sizes of continuous production of identical parts are finding their products splitting up into ever smaller batches offering a wider variety. It is a trend that is steadily having its effect in most areas of production, not least in the automobile factory. It is equally apparent that the usual method of batch production, with its ponderously slow rate of output, is not going to cope.

Into the conventional two-sided picture then, a new dimension is now being introduced in the form of production machinery that is both automatic *and* variable. In the rapidly growing application of these machines, flexibility and sophistication of performance differ widely according to the sector of industrial production at which a particular machine is aimed. Thus many types will perform a large variety of operations on one kind of product only, for example in the cutting and shaping of sheet materials. Others may perform a wide variety of operations in a large number of entirely different product ranges.

Of the latter type, the most spectacular is the industrial robot.[14] Such robots are programmable, and incorporate advanced control techniques and memory systems. When a job becomes obsolete, the robot may be taught a new one, and if necessary, is easily transported to another part of the factory. Most robots perform operations analogous to those carried out by human arms and hands and they can, when equipped with grippers or special handling attachments, hold and operate conventional hand tools, spray guns, welding guns and power tools. Unlike the human

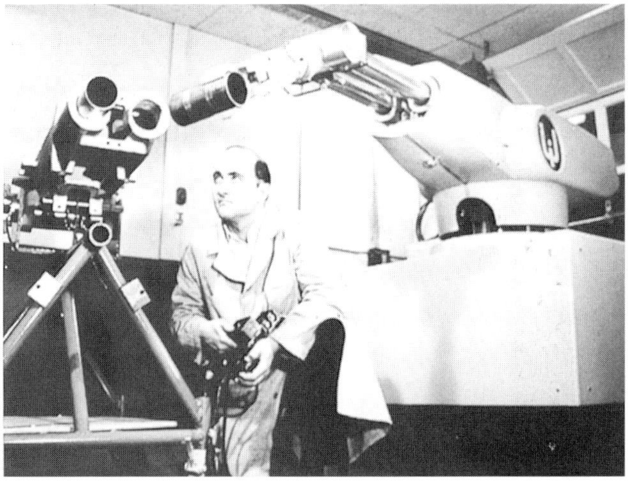

1.5a.
Unimate robot being taught to assemble an identical robot. Courtesy of GKN Machinery.

1.5b.
Unimate robot at work. Courtesy of Versatile Technology.

operator though, the robot is relatively insensitive to a hostile environment and not at all subject to fatigue or boredom. Already performing a multitude of different tasks in diverse industries, such robots are quickly earning their description as 'universal transfer devices'.

Even the sophisticated robots, however, have their limitations. Essentially, they apply variable automation to just one section of a whole series of operations that go to make up the total production process. Single variable machines of this type may help to ease a bottleneck or relieve manual workers of an unpleasant and dangerous job, but they go very little way toward ensuring integration of more than a limited sequence of tasks. While improving on flexibility, the volume and overall efficiency of production will still be determined by the cumulative effect of the firm's combined operations.

To go beyond this point, it is necessary to have some means of controlling flexible machinery in an integrated and continuously variable production process. Here the machine tool industry is setting the pace. The cutting and shaping of metal components by machine tools forms a major part of industrial manufacture, and is still carried out generally in the conventional techniques of batch production. In its most advanced state, however, the machine tool industry offers a model of an approach to variable production that augurs of the shape of the fully automated factory.

Basic to these advances is the adaptation of the machine tool to numerical control.[15] In the numerically controlled (NC) machine, all machine tools operate in terms of numerical information derived from the dimensions of the workpiece itself, and this can be fed back to control the machine's movements, which include automatic tool changing for different operations. The complexity of motion that is possible – and hence the complexity of shape that is produced – is described in terms of the number of axis on which the machine can operate: 2-axis, 3-axis, and so on, up to as many as 6-axis machines. Such machines are inherently flexible, able to cope with a variety of operations at high speed and handle complexities in component shape where the human operator would be a limiting factor. The same milling machine may produce gas-turbine blades one minute, wave guides for radar the next.

Though highly flexible in themselves, individual NC machines still cannot make much of an impression on the overall rate of components flowing through the factory. Furthermore, by combining operations of varying degrees of complexity within the same machine, the full potential of the more complex and expensive machines is often tied up on relatively simple tasks. The real breakthrough came with the idea of linking together a number of different NC machines with complementary performance capabilities into a numerically controlled 'machining complex' of the kind pioneered by Molins Machine Company with System 24. The brainchild of D. T. N. Williamson,[16] Molins' System 24 is a fully integrated, flexible manufacturing system designed – as the name implies – to run 24 hours a day without interruption. Hitherto restricted to such process industries as petro-chemicals and steel-making, the new approach brings continuous process control theory directly into manufacturing. Connected by an automated transfer line and controlled by an on-line computer, the combination achieves, in effect, a flexible, automatic transfer line. A six-machine system, for example, is capable of producing between 2000 and 20 000 parts per day, with wide variation in both configuration and size. The result is a revolutionary system that combines the high-volume, high-speed characteristics of mass production with a vastly increased variety of components.

1.6.
'System 24' computer controlled production line. Model. Courtesy of Molins Machine Company in the UK.

TOWARD THE CYBERNETIC FACTORY

The capacity to vary production in this manner puts firms at an altogether different level of control over the production process than was possible with previous techniques. The extension of this capacity from the shop floor into the governing mechanisms of the industrial corporation has been the chief preoccupation of the British cybernetician, Stafford Beer.[17] Beer sees the conventional industrial concern as a clumsy phenomenon, dependent for its survival on paying advertising agencies enormous sums, 'to make less mutable an environment to which the (industrial) organism cannot adapt. If the dinosaur can no longer live in the world, the world must be turned into a dinosaur sanctuary.'[18]

Beer's comment matches Galbraith's analysis well enough, but whereas Galbraith assumes consumerism is irrevocably tied to mass production and all its strictures, Beer offers a radically different vision. Beer's alternative lies in the application of cybernetics to the factory as a whole, lifting the manufacturing concern finally out of the industrial into the post-industrial era: 'the cybernetic factory seeks a more

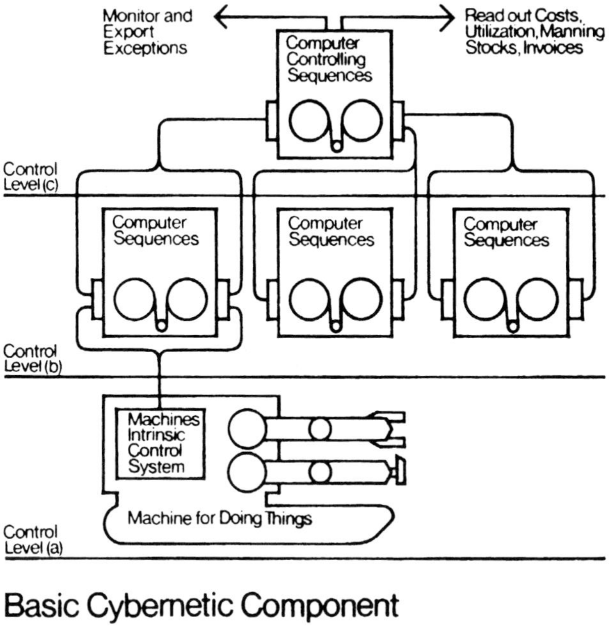

1.7a.

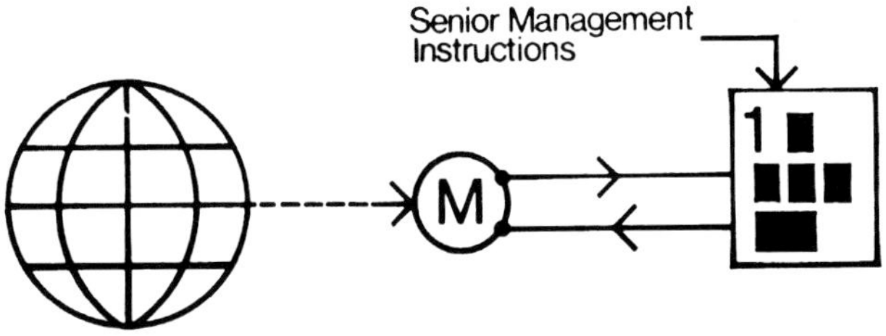

1.7b.

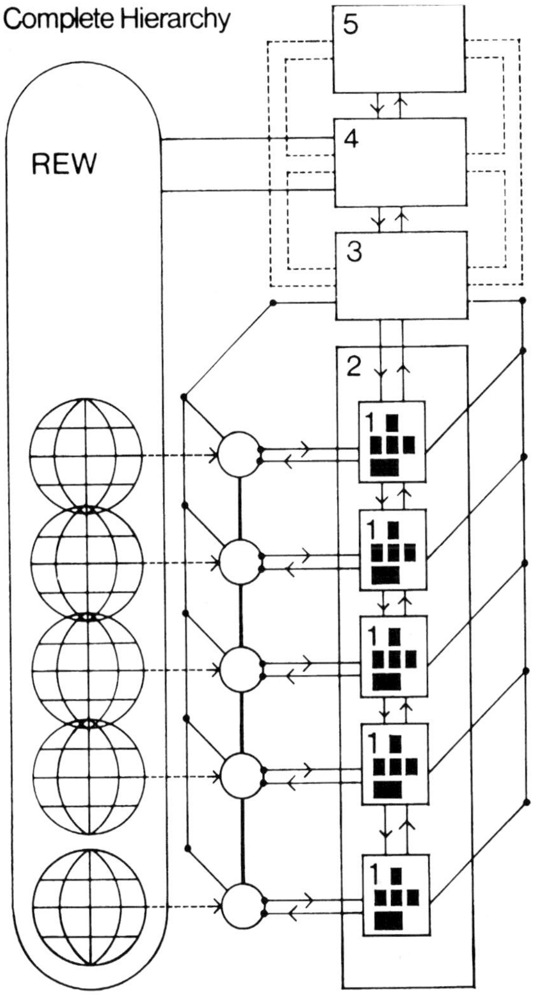

1.7c.

adaptive, more readily responsive, automatic system which would be capable of controlling any kind of company'.[19]

Beer's conception of the adaptive industrial organism is that of a 'nervous system' of control functions that applies automation, not only at the shop-floor level, but extends it in an integrated series of computer-aided operational techniques throughout the firm's organization, right up to the boardroom. Beer posits a five-level hierarchy to fulfil the cybernetic industrial structure, based on the flexible transfer line as the 'basic cybernetic component'.[20] This first complex in itself already contains a three-level hierarchy of command, making up the 'System One Controller'. Thus the NC production machine is monitored by the computer which produces its control tape, which is in turn controlled by another computer which coordinates a number of such machines, and which monitors the inputs and outputs connecting the process with the larger industrial organization. This last connection is made through the divisional management, which relates that particular production line to the demands and constraints of the market, so completing 'System One'. At each further level a more complex control function is established. Thus the 'System Two Controller' maintains a balance of demand

1.7a.
System One Controller (after Beer, 1968). The basic component of the cybernetic factory involves a three-level hierarchy of command consisting of a set of 'doing machines', a set of sequencing controls, and finally, controls which sequence the sequencers.

1.7b.
Cybernetic factory (after Beer, 1968). System One is used by the management (M) to maintain control of the company as it responds to its own relevant external world (globe on the left).

1.7c.
Cybernetic factory (after Beer, 1968). The complete five-level hierarchy of command shows a number of System One Controllers each responding to its own relevant external world (REW), coordinated through four higher levels of control.

on resources between the different basic components or divisions that go to make up a large corporation. 'System Three' will shift that balance in whatever direction overall company policy dictates. 'System Four' and 'System Five', respectively, provide information on the external environment as it affects the company as a whole, and information on what the future effects of alternative policies are likely to be.

Every company management must perform these control functions to some extent or other if it is to survive. But what Beer has done is to show that, through their formalization into mathematical terms, they can each be translated into operational problems which can be solved with the aid of a computer. The functions of each control level have their parallel in existing operational research techniques. Cybernetics shows us how these techniques may be coordinated to provide an integrated framework of control for the company as a whole. The result is to provide management with an extraordinarily sensitive mechanism to aid it in making its decisions, and which will provide continuous, updated information on the effects of those decisions on diverse aspects of company behaviour.

CHANGING HUMAN ROLES

Parallel changes are also taking place in the roles of worker and manager alike to match the changes in technology. For all its revolutionary consequences, the impact of cybernation on the workshop is nevertheless unlikely to result in the extinction of manual work. For better or worse, there will remain many tasks of assembly which will be uneconomic to automate. These more intricate tasks will remain the prerogative of the human operator. Here, too, traditions are undergoing reappraisal. A new approach that could match the variable production line is indicated in the changeover to team assembly. The flow-line method of assembly for mass production has meant the degradation of human operators and their restriction to repetitive, non-creative roles as slaves of the production line. Each operator performs only a limited task before the product moves on to the next stage, where another operator performs a different but also limited task, and so on. As pioneered by the aptly named American company, Non-Linear Systems, the idea of team assembly emerges in direct opposition to the flow line. Assembly is carried out by a number of small teams (anything from one to ten operators, depending upon the product), each team being responsible for the manual assembly of the product from start to finish. The new method has been found to boost morale and to improve both the rate and the quality of output – including fewer rejects – over flow-line standards. Its success derives from the increase in scope given to the human operators' most valuable asset, their natural heuristic talents. Assembly for the more limited quantities of batch and medium batch production puts those qualities at a premium. Close control over the total assembly also enables the assembly operator to understand and adapt to changes in his or her task more easily and so better control any variations in the product.

Like changes are also affecting the way managers operate. If management now has the means to make it more aware of the interrelation of its different responsibilities, it would seem perfectly reasonable to expect that that awareness would be reflected in the management role proper. Another questionable feature of the Galbraithian thesis is that management of the large corporation must involve specialization; all decisions are group decisions made by specialists. This approach alone does little to ensure that the broader problems of the firm will be appreciated. As with the specialized line worker, it also seriously curtails any individual's ability to respond to the increasing rate of change in the industrial environment. The methods of operational research employed in the cybernetic company structure, on the other hand, imply in themselves an approach that relates more to the generalist than to the specialist.[21] The post-industrial factory will require a more flexible management role if it is to make the most of the new techniques at its command. Just as we have seen the beginnings of changes in the kind of human labour and skills needed for the variable production workshop, so new directions are appearing in management methods. Indicative of the new approach is the 'free form management' advocated by some consultants. Designed to ease the specialist manager and engineer out of their narrow confines, the approach aims at introducing the concept of the generalist into industrial management. Free form management combines the hitherto disjointed tasks of policy making, production operation, and general administration into one flexible management role.

UNIVERSAL MACHINES FOR SPECIALIZED MARKETS

We now have the responsive tools of production, and the responsive organization and human skills for their control, that can together release manufacturing industries from their present constraints. Given the highly flexible nature of the machines described here, manufacturers need no longer rely on passive markets to ensure justification for efficient production lines. Efficient production to particularized performance specifications can be achieved without the standardization entailed by conventional mass production.

With variable technologies supplemented by the increased information and sensitivity made possible by computer analysis and control at all levels, we have the heart of post-industrial production. Manufacturers are able to improve their control over production processes, but relinquish it over consumers. Rather than the universal standard and the one-product machine aimed at a tame general market, we now have the universal machine – and by 'machine' we now include the factory as a whole – capable of adjusting to the vagaries of specialized and rapidly changing markets.

The post-industrial, cybernetic factory effectively reverses the present relationship of manufacturing concerns to the social systems they are meant to serve. It is a characteristic of social systems, as it is of all evolving systems, that in order to survive they may adopt one of two main strategies. The system can either respond to environmental pressures by a process of mutual give and take, reorganization, and the learning of new patterns of behaviour, or it can seek to dominate the environment as far as it can, and so trim external pressures to its own demands. The latter method, we have learnt, accurately describes classic consumerism. Dinosaur sanctuaries may not be hard to find in any social sphere, but while they may be able to contain divergent pressures for a time, they tend to be unreliable in the longer term.

Notwithstanding such drawbacks, the mass-production line has been upheld as a panacea for a backward building industry. It is a sad comment on any design profession that it should be so eager to embrace a technological strait-jacket in order to impose its own dubious ideas of a visual order onto consumers. It is also very short-sighted. Instead of tuning the consumer to the machine, we can now tune the machine to the consumer. Even assuming that architectural designers will eventually adjust successfully to mass-production technologies, it would be a misguided reconciliation. Designers for a manufactured environment are liable to find they have come to terms with the wrong animal.

2 URBAN CHAOS OR SELF-ORGANIZATION?

Based on 'Evolutionary planning'. *Architectural Design*, December 1968, and 'Urban chaos or self-organization', *Architectural Design*, September 1969.

A telling example of the preconceptions and prejudices underlying architects' urban visions is the recurrent enthusiasm among the avant-garde for utopian urban schemes, frequently demonstrated in the form of so-called 'megastructure' projects. Though nominally propagating new technologies, change and flexibility, they are actually rooted in relatively static and well-worn concepts of the ideal city. Usually, they feature an articulated general-purpose supporting structure, which also acts as the servicing and circulation system, into which are placed a variety of subsystems and components, all closely integrated with and dependent upon the supporting megastructure. The overall appearance is that of a high density, closely knit urban form virtually comprising a continuous, all-in-one structure. Archigram's Plug-in City project and the completed extension to Berlin Free University by Candilis Josic and Woods, are two of the most influential of these schemes. Moshe Safdie's Habitat for the Montreal Expo represents another, more static conception. At their best, the designs represent an attempt to cope with adaptation according to predetermined rates of obsolescence. At worst, they constitute a system of parts where change in any one part is severely limited by its multiplied effects on other parts. Radical change cannot be accommodated without a drastic overhaul of the whole system.[1]

UNITARY FRAMEWORK

In reality, the megastructure concept has been strongly conditioned by a vision of the urban environment as an ordered formal experience. Such visions are not unusual. Urban theorists Melvin Webber[2] and Donald Foley[3] argue that architects typically approach the city within a unitary conceptual framework in which physical artefacts are spatially distributed and activity locations are geometrically arranged. The approach is apparent in almost all planned urban development, most notably in new towns in the UK and elsewhere, and in the redeveloped central business districts and centres of larger American and European cities. Whether megastructure or new town, the dominant conception is invariably that of a static spatial arrangement. The design for Cumbernauld New Town central area on its hilltop site presents the commonly favoured image of a dense, multi-layered urban centre, reminiscent of mediaeval cities. The designer's vision is absolute, with no room whatever for innovation or ambiguity. Similar parallels might be

2.1.
Commuter country: low density, semi-rural 'exurbia' in Westchester County, New York State, twenty miles north of midtown Manhattan. Photo: Fairchild Aerial Surveys.

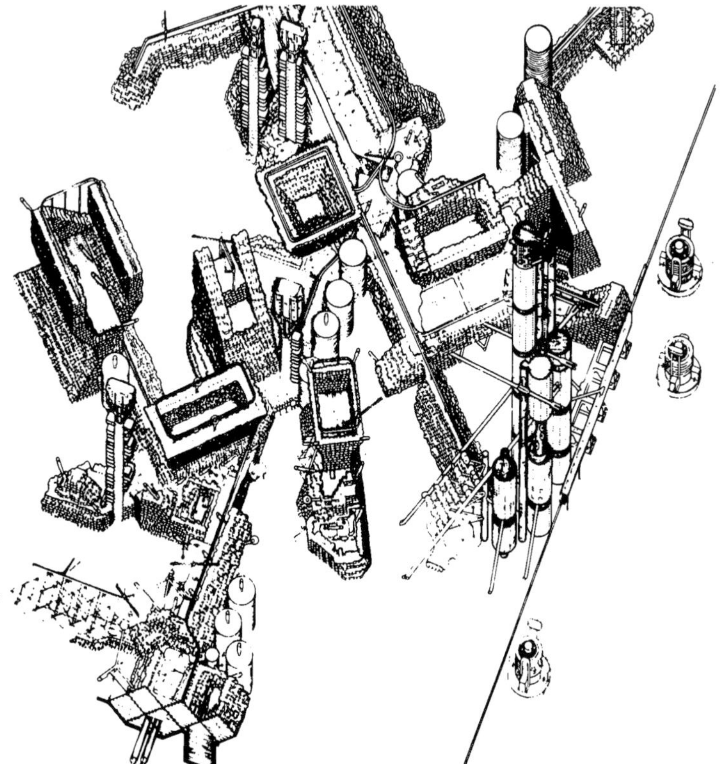

2.2.
Plug-in City, 1964. Architect: Peter Cook. From Roy Landau, *New Directions in British Architecture*, 1968.

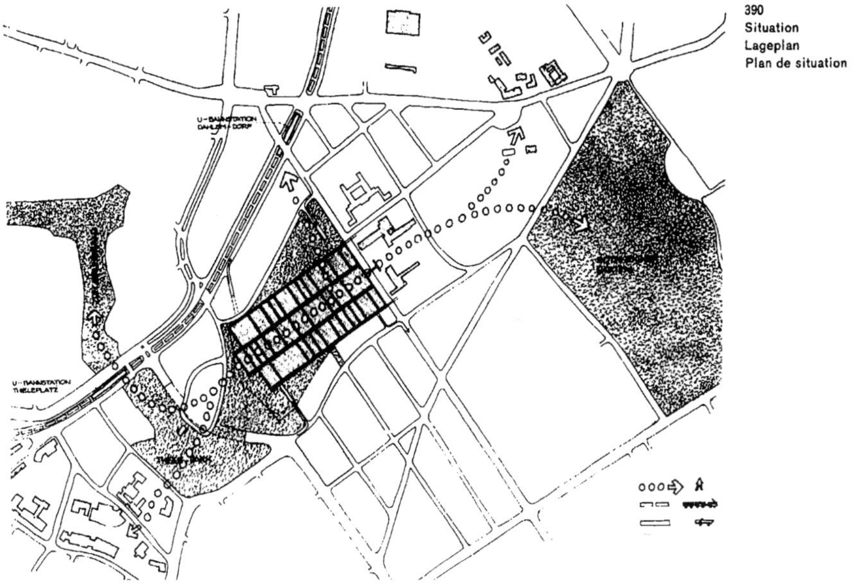

2.3a.
Berlin Free University, 1963. Situation plan. Architect: Candilis Josic Woods with Manfred Schiedhelm. From *Candilis Josic Woods*, 1978.

2.3b.
Berlin Free University. Ground floor plan. Architect: Candilis Josic Woods with Manfred Schiedhelm. From *Candilis Josic Woods*, 1978.

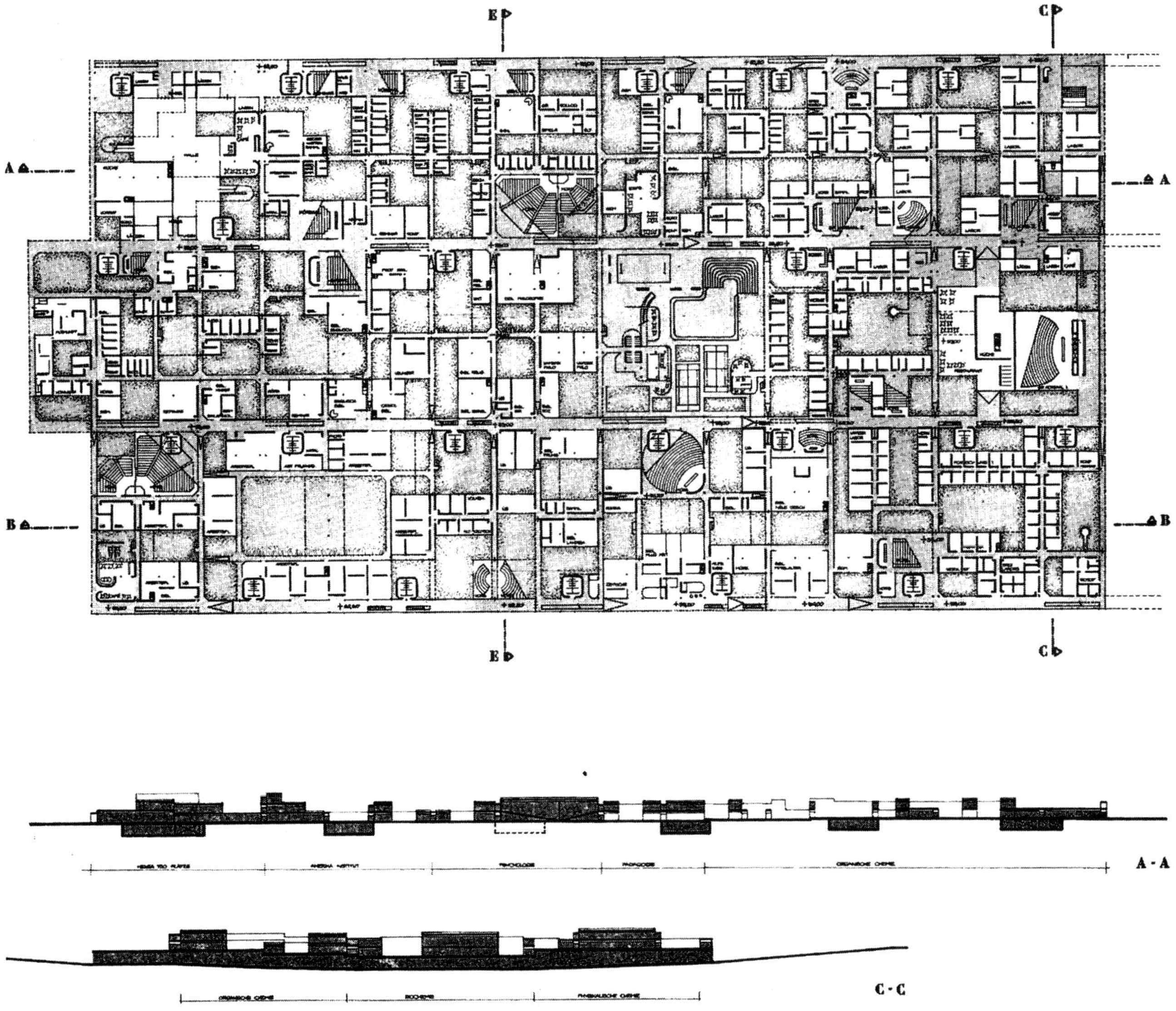

2.4.
Cumbernauld New Town Centre, 1958–68. Perspective of central area and megastructure. Architect: L. Hugh Wilson, D. R. Leaker and Geoffrey Copcutt. From *Domus*, December 1963.

drawn between the Berlin Free University and fortified cities. Like the older urban form, the Berlin complex presents a compact urban island standing in an open landscape. Even Archigram's Plug-in City has its static formal precedents and bears marked similarities to the solid, reinforced concrete masses of John Andrew's Scarborough College at Toronto. For all the megastructure's trumpeted flexibility, the overwhelming desire of its designers to control the process of change is ultimately self-defeating; the capacity for change is an illusion. The designer seems to say to us: 'change, yes – but *my* way'.

FRAGMENTATION OF URBAN STRUCTURE

In contrast to these unitary visions of a physically integrated and coherent environment, postwar urban growth appears to be heading in wholly different directions. It is now widely accepted that advances in telecommunications, information technologies and high-speed travel are rapidly creating a 'global village' where decisions taken on one side of the globe are instantly known and may have instant repercussions on the other.[4] This massive trend towards integration on the grand scale is paralleled by forces which are having an equal and opposite effect on the environment. That effect is one of a general fragmentation of urban structure and form into relatively independent subsystems and components. It has been most apparent in the dispersal and decentralization of cities,[5] and while many aspects of these trends are well documented, the discussion to date has been mostly skin deep and centred on form. Especially, little attention has been paid so far to the nature of the evolutionary processes underlying the growth and development of urban form. If

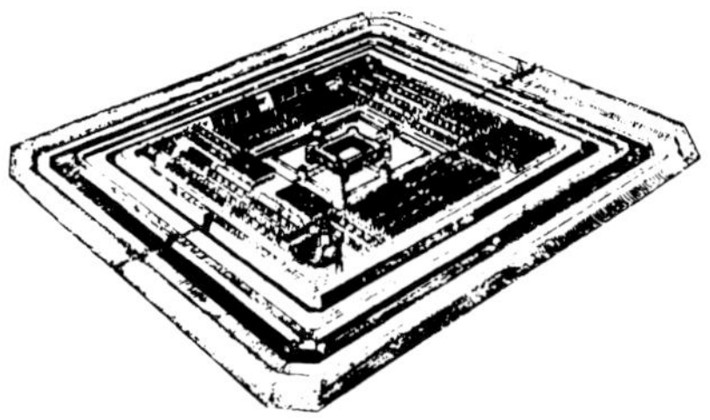

2.5.
Fortified 'ideal city', 1527. Architect: Albrecht Durer. From Giulio Argan, *The Renaissance City*, 1969.

there is to be any advance in understanding these processes, then cities need to be examined as organic systems subject to the same laws governing all complex systems.

COMPLEXITY

Evolutionary or organic analogies in themselves are not new to architecture or planning. However, recent studies in cybernetics[6] and general systems theory[7] based on biological models lend such analogies a renewed relevance and authority.

The new sciences themselves represent a radical break with previous scientific thought. While most scientists are concerned with breaking nature down into its constituent components or parts, systems theorists and cyberneticians are more interested in the relations between the parts. In particular, they are concerned with how those relations change over the life cycle of an organism. A familiar and recurring example is the complementary role played by the dual processes of anabolism and catabolism in building up and breaking down complex organic substances in the human body. Arthur D. Hall[8] claims that similar processes of integration and fragmentation are characteristic of the growth of all organic or living systems. He distinguishes between two kinds of fragmentation: the first corresponds to the loss of information, or entropy[9] and decay, with parts breaking down and no longer behaving as a system; the second corresponds to the growth of organic systems. In the latter, a system spontaneously changes in the direction of increasing division into subsystems and sub-subsystems, or differentiation of functions, typical of creative or evolutionary processes.

Table 2.1

Information	*Entropy*
Knowledge	Uncertainty
Negentropy	Entropy
Signal	Noise
Accuracy	Error
Form	Chaos
Regularity	Randomness
Pattern or form	Lack of pattern or formlessness
Order	Disorder
Organization	Disorganization
Regular complexity	Irregular simplicity
Heterogeneity	Homogeneity
Improbability (only one alternative correctly describes the form)	Probability (more than one alternative correctly describes the form)
Predictability (only one alternative correctly describes the form)	Unpredictability (more than one alternative correctly describes the form)

The idea that life simultaneously exhibits processes leading to both order and disorder (Table 2.1. After Miller, 1965) is one of the great paradoxes of modern science. In classical physics, the Second Law of Thermodynamics holds that an isolated or closed system in an inhomogeneous state will most probably be found sometime in the future in a more homogeneous state. The Second Law is in this sense a law of increasing entropy or decay of structure and was until recently interpreted pessimistically as heralding inevitable and universal decline of information and energy. However, in a landmark paper, Ludwig von Bertalanffy,[10] the founder of general systems theory, pointed out that while the Second Law held for all closed systems, it did not hold for open systems which exchange energy and materials continuously with their environments. In an open system such as a living organism, not only does entropy increase due to irreversible processes, burning up of energy and so on, but: '...the organism "feeds", to use an expression of Schrodinger's, "from negative entropy", importing complex organic molecules, using their energy, and rendering back the simpler end products to the environment'. Thus: 'Though the second law is not violated, or more precisely, though it holds for the system plus the environment, it does not hold for the system itself.'[11]

Entropy may therefore decrease in open systems, which may in turn develop toward states of greater heterogeneity and complexity. While in the inanimate world there appears to be a tendency toward maximum disorder and a chaotic state, in organic development and evolution there is a tendency towards states of ever higher order and differentiation:

Now certain processes associated with life seem to go counter to this current (of increasing entropy). Within living organisms proteins are synthesized as well as broken down or denatured; gradients are established as well as neutralized; specific structures are created; behaviour tends to go from random to specific in many learning processes, and on the grand scale biological evolution seems to give rise to ever-increasing ordered complexity in the development of higher species[12] [my emphasis].

SELF-ORGANIZING SYSTEMS

A corollary of these evolutionary principles is that the appropriate degree of internal organization or connectivity of any living system will be relative to its environment. The linkage between system and environment is crucial. According to Ross Ashby,[13] one of the pioneers of cybernetics, the issue can affect our understanding of even so highly organized a system as the human brain. He asks:

Is it not good that a brain should have its parts in rich functional connection? I say no – not in general; *only when the environment is itself richly connected. When the environment's parts* are *not richly connected (when it is highly reducible, in other words), adaptation will go on faster if the brain is also highly reducible, i.e. if its* connectivity *is small.*[14] Thus the degree of organization can be too high as well as too low[15] [my emphasis].

It follows that 'only variety can destroy variety'.[16] Winning a game of football against a skilled team, for example, requires at least an equal number of equally skilled players with equally imaginative tactics. A living system can therefore only be judged successful when it generates organizational levels and constraints which are appropriate to the changing environment in which it lives. The less organized, or more chaotic and unpredictable the environment, then the more adaptable should the living system itself be, which may require an equivalently loose organization. When the system achieves this correspondence, it is self-organizing;[17] when it does not, we may conclude that those self-organizing processes have broken down. Stafford Beer[18] notes of such systems – which he calls 'cybernetic systems' – that their inherent complexity and spontaneous behaviour preclude any arbitrary imposition of order from without:

A cybernetic system is recognizable by three outstanding characteristics. It is exceedingly complex; to the point where its interconnectivity is indefinable in detail. It is exceedingly probabilistic; to the point where its structure though complex becomes undifferentiated, and every trajectory is equiprobable. It is unreal to suppose that any such system can be controlled by the imposition of rules from outside; because the system by definition defies analysis, and therefore no start can be applied by which the adequacy of the rules can be judged. The third characteristic it displays is generated from within: it is self-organizing[19] [my emphasis].

DECENTRALIZATION

Such arguments suggest that the apparent 'chaos' of postwar urban growth may be at least in part due to underlying processes of self-organization. The major forces of urbanization over the last few decades have meant a steady breakup of the traditional city form into the dispersed and fragmented pattern with which we are now familiar. Moreover, these forces show no sign of abatement. They stem from fundamental changes in technology, income levels, family status and consumer taste – changes compounded by an ever-increasing mobility of the population. The ability, particularly that of middle-class Americans, to afford decentralized residential locations, private gardens and automobiles as their incomes have risen has strengthened an overwhelming trend towards urban dispersal. The most significant impact of technological changes on urban locations or structure has been to reduce densities and decentralize or disperse activities.[20] Telecommunications, mass air travel, containerization, mechanized methods of materials handling, continuous processing, do-it-yourself deliveries, automation – all connote recent technological changes that have reinforced decentralization of job opportunities. The resultant form of the modern urban conurbation is that of a loose patchwork of farms and built-up areas with no clear demarcation between rural and urban land. The only connection between the scattered clusters of buildings is the tenuous network of communications, the thin lines of the roads on the ground and the invisible telecommunications of the air.

By contrast, at regional, national and supranational levels, many urban systems are becoming increasingly structured and centralized. The

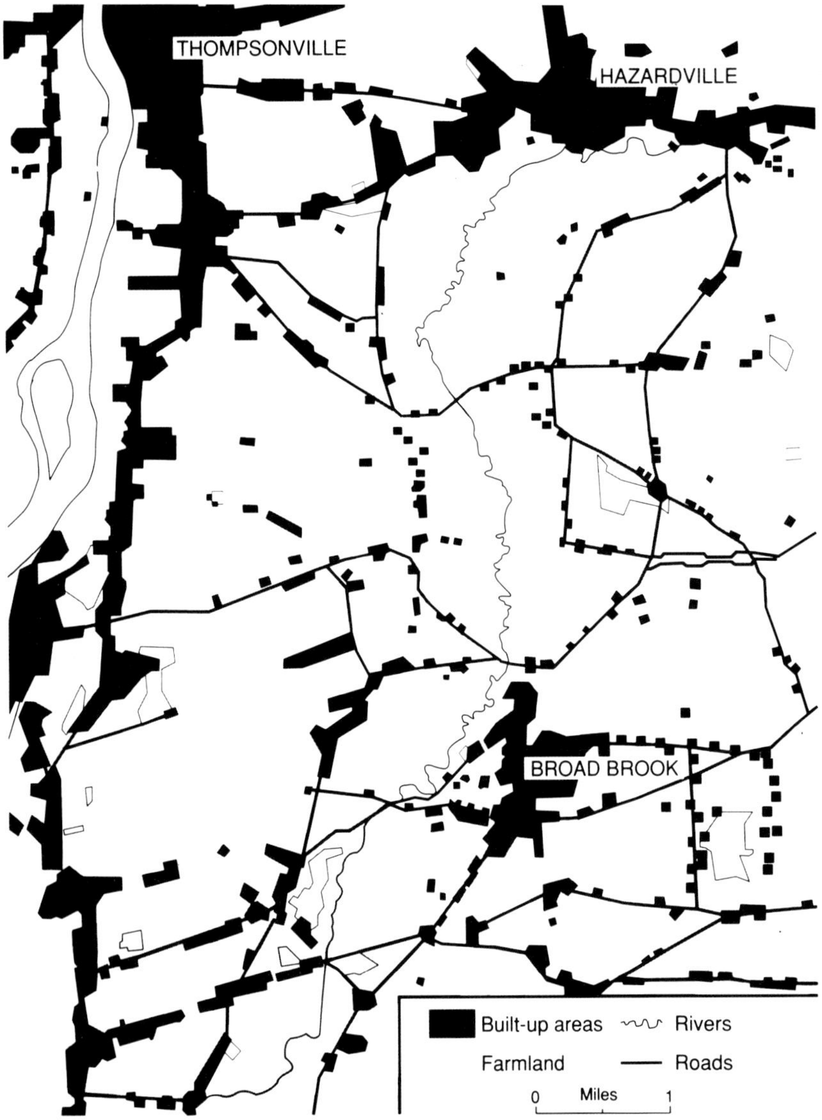

2.6.
Land use plan, Windsor, Connecticut. The plan shows a complex mixed use pattern of linear urban development, farmland and woodland (white areas). After a map by the Graduate School of Geography, Clark University. From Chris Abel, *Adaptive Urban Form: A Biological Model*, Dissertation, 1968.

development of regional planning agencies and the general increase in federal control in the US, the integration and merging of industries, the growth of multi-national corporations and the control systems for telecommunications networks, are all instances of this process.[21] All these developments demonstrate a high degree of centralization and integration of the environment at the macroscale and are balanced by the trend towards decentralization and fragmentation at the local level.[22]

In favour of decentralization at the local level, Webber[23] argues that physical coherence, particularly with regard to the distribution of activities in space, is actually unnecessary to the healthy functioning of cities. On the contrary, it may even be a disadvantage, interfering with a city's natural evolution. The success of an urban system may depend more on its communications systems than on any spatial distribution of activities. For example, research into household activity patterns in the US substantiates the hypothesis that most residents of American cities do not have any particular consciousness of areas of a scale between their immediate and local environment, and an area whose population would be measured in hundreds of thousands.[24] Further, they are liable to locate their friends and spend their time just about anywhere in the larger region. The reasons advanced for this tendency include changing economic and social conditions which have led to a breakdown of the extended family system and the rise of the nuclear family, and social mobility resulting in new and wider associations being made at numerous stages of a family's career. Such factors in turn imply that associates are scattered over a wide area, even across country. Further, people tend towards indifference to time–distance considerations below some value of the order of magnitude of a quarter to a half hour (though this factor varies considerably with circumstances). It seems reasonable to suggest then, that what makes this kind of pattern work is the availability of efficient and flexible communications channels – the automobile and the telephone are the most obvious and significant of the direct links – and most important, a shared community of interests among people, whatever their location.

A change in emphasis from spatial organization to the direct and indirect or institutional channels of communication implies a major revision in attitudes as to what determines behavioural interaction in a city. Social scientists such as Herbert Gans[25] have shown us that even in the much lauded, multi-functional city centre, diverse social and ethnic groups mixed up together in a small area in reality have little to do with each other, but tend to move only within their own social circles. The popular identification of cross-cultural fertilization with the high density, multi-activity city centre is based on a myth. As Gans shows, social integration is not so much a function of space as a function of social class, the norms that govern the different classes, and the institutions that exist to arbitrate between them. In the same vein, Gans argues that physical planning will not induce cohesion or identification within a community; this can only come about through political measures inducing acceptance of a pluralistic society. Gans's pioneering social surveys into the behaviour and attitudes of American suburbanites indicate that the majority lead active and contented lives, and that this is primarily a reflection of the population mix that they encounter in the suburban environment.[26] Given suitable means of communication, social integration will therefore occur in even the most dispersed patterns of settlement – provided the norms of society allow it.

Los Angeles represents the most extreme example of this kind of loose urban structuring: its elements physically separate, if not distant from each other, mixed up in an almost haphazard fashion, knit together within an intensive, evenly distributed network of several hundred miles of freeways. Both in the nature and scale of its development, the sprawling megalopolis has profoundly shaken some of the most cherished notions of what a city is supposed to be about.[27] Beginning at the north-eastern end of LA County, the Los Angeles metropolitan area stretches over seventy miles to the south, thrusting part way through neighbouring Orange County – more than 5000 square miles of mountains, plains, valleys and beaches, with the city proper surrounded by an encircling ring of militantly independent communities. Essential services are dispersed throughout the area, with decentralized civic government,

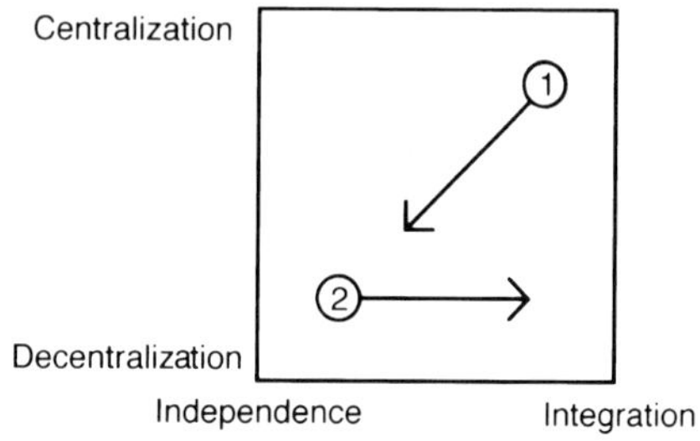

2.7.
Diagram of relations between urban processes: arrow (1) corresponds to the fragmentation occurring at the local or micro-level and arrow (2) corresponds to the centralization occurring at the regional or macro-level (it may be noted that the degree of centralization is constant at the macro-level to indicate the balance with decentralization at local levels). From Chris Abel, *Adaptive Urban Form: A Biological Model*, Dissertation, 1968.

2.8.
Fragmented urban sprawl connected by freeways in Nassau County, Long Island. Photo: Fairchild Aerial Surveys.

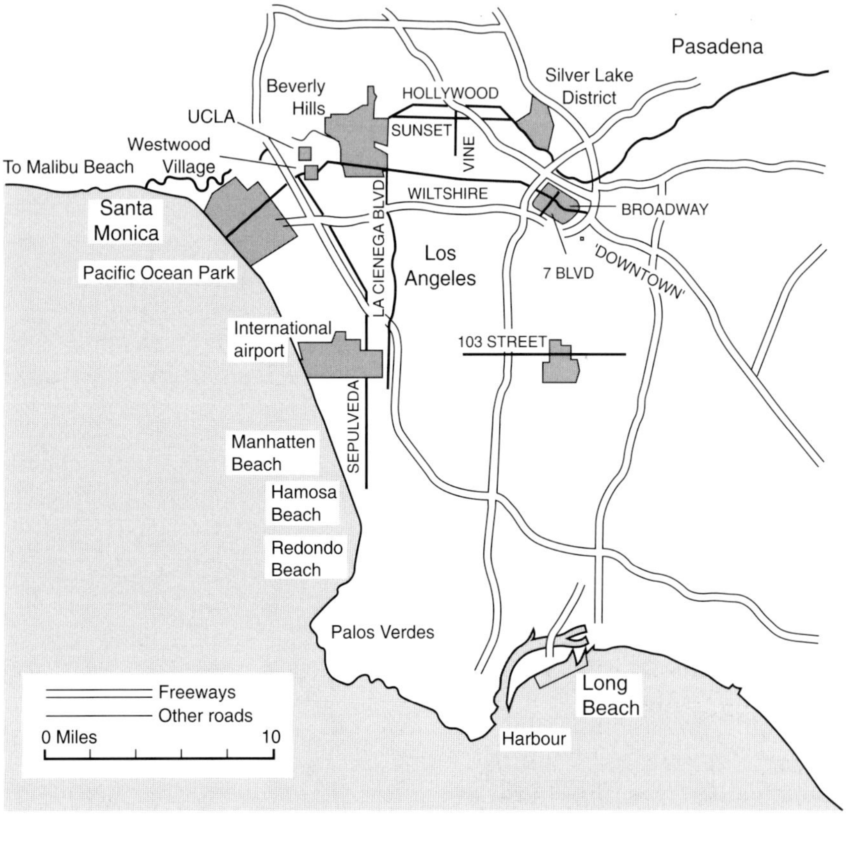

2.9.
Map of Los Angeles showing main freeways and districts. From Chris Abel, *Adaptive Urban Form: A Biological Model*, Dissertation, 1968.

decentralized banking and retailing, and, not least, a decentralized media serving a multitude of different communities and interest groups.[28] The essence of this polynucleated conurbation is summed up by a member of the LA planning staff:

The prophets of the future show that if you have complete dependence on the automobile it can lead to nothing but change. As long as you are orientated toward the automobile, any location is subject to reorganization or redevelopment according to how the driver can exert pressure – for shopping centres or apartment houses. As long as unbridled fluidity exists, there can be no permanent pattern.[29]

EVOLUTIONARY PLANNING

The dispersed urban structure exemplified by Los Angeles not only facilitates change and adaptation, it actively encourages it. Cohesion in the fragmented conurbation is provided, not by the proximity of physical elements as in the megastructure and other dense city concepts, but by the city's communications systems. The merging of institutions and the growing of new links through communication and data networks is a part of the evolution toward greater heterogeneity and complexity. Whereas the traditional unitary city is therefore characterized primarily by its fixed spatial and formal configuration and major civic buildings, the dispersed, adaptive city is characterized primarily by its communications systems and other interactive social channels.

A convincing interpretation of how these interactive channels function in situations of great uncertainty, and how diverse interests are represented, has been presented by Charles E. Lindblom[30] in his seminal essay, 'The science of "muddling through"'. As a faithful account of urban policy making in the US, it follows the self-organizing model

2.10.
Los Angeles, looking across the low density 'garden city' towards the downtown area. Photo: Chris Abel.

remarkably closely. According to Lindblom, the decision-making process of urban administration is a largely responsive process, but still by no means directionless. Policies decided upon by representatives of different interests are treated as 'successive approximations' of limited problem areas, to be continually modified as new problems are encountered. As each decision maker will be acting on different motives and values from any other decision maker, the only test for each policy can be agreement among the decision makers on the policy itself. Similarly, objectives and means are identified together as policies, there being no realistic manner in which the two can be separated due to the closeness of their interaction. The overall effect of such a system is a restriction of interests, or, in other words, a fragmentation of problem areas. Policy evolves through a complex series of incremental responses to each problem area as it impinges on a number of particular interest groups. In essence, it is a process of adaptation to change through negotiation between self-interested parties with different value systems.

This essentially evolutionary process is characteristic of an urban system – in marked contrast to architects' unitary visions – exhibiting relatively little internal restraint. In terms of self-organization, we can say that the institutions and techniques for controlling the dispersed urban region reflect in their own flexible order the low degree of order and predictability inherent in modern, fast-changing social systems. For 'fragmented and disorganized environment', we can now substitute 'fragmentation of normative values, and incremental growth and response'. Evolutionary planning might not suit many architects and others with grander schemes in mind, but it is more in tune with the self-organizing cities of today.

3 DESIGN METHOD AND NEW SCIENCE

Presented to the 1980 Design Research Society Conference, Portsmouth, 14–16 December, under the title 'Vico and Herder: origins of methodological pluralism'. First published under the same title in R. Jacques and J. Powell (eds). *Design: Science: Method.* Westbury House, Guildford 1981.

A common perception of the value of scientific knowledge, as differentiated from any other form of knowledge, is that it is systematic: the scientist traditionally aims to abstract general laws from the minutiae of observational data, whether these be laws of nature or universal principles of human behaviour.[1] Thus a scientific theory is evaluated according to what it may add to the unity of our knowledge of the natural and human world. The language and methodology of all branches of the sciences have likewise evolved according to systemic criteria special to science as a culture-form.[2] It follows that, ultimately, orthodox science recognizes no methodological divisions between the study of natural phenomena and the study of man.

Since the beginning of the design methods movement in the 1960s, science has provided design researchers with their prime model for theory and research method. Thus design research is invariably aimed at the derivation of general principles of design applicable to all forms of design activity. In an early paper on the subject, Bruce Archer, one of the founders of the systems design movement, presents a typical view: 'No distinction is drawn between architectural design, engineering design, graphic design and industrial design. This paper embodies the premise that the design act is logically identical in all these fields.'[3]

In so far as the approach conforms to the orthodox canons of science as they have just been described, then the design methods movement represents a concerted effort to make the activity of architecture over into a science. There are, however, implicit in the movement a number of premises founded on fundamental misconceptions concerning the current state of the art of human science. It is also questionable whether architecture, with all its special concerns with place and context, may ever be adequately understood solely in terms of any general model of the design process.

ORIGINS

The new picture of human science now emerging has its origins in the historical and cultural relativism introduced by Giovanni Batista Vico (1688–1744) and Johann Gottfried Herder (1744–1803) in the eighteenth century. Between them, these two philosopher–historians brought about a revolution in thought concerning the nature of human science and culture, the full effects of which are only now beginning to be felt in the changing conduct of scientists.

In his biographical study, *Vico and Herder*, Isaiah Berlin[4] explains that it was largely as a result of the overwhelming dominance of Cartesian thought during the same period that recognition for the two thinkers has been so long in coming. According to the prevailing wisdom of that day, rational, i.e. scientific, thought and method was equated with the strictly logical procedures of mathematical deduction. Thus true knowledge was established on the basis of immutable truths, from which, proceeding step by logical step, conclusions were derived, which, being logically deduced from true premises, must also be true. There was therefore only one kind of true science, and any form of knowledge that did not conform to the model was disregarded as an 'unscientific hotch-potch of sense perception, rumour, myth, fable, travellers' tales, romances, poetry, and idle speculation'.[5]

Neither the Cartesian model for true knowledge nor the disparaging attitude toward human culture generated by the Enlightenment were acceptable to Vico or Herder. They proceeded instead to construct an alternative theory of knowledge based upon a profound respect for the variety and integrity of human culture in all its manifestations. For both writers, it was the form of human culture itself, and not some abstract and idealized logical model of rationality, that was to be taken as the measure for valid knowledge. The result in the theory of knowledge and human culture is not unlike a gestalt switch, where what was once deemed worthless is now seen to be of the greatest value.

Among his most important ideas, it was Vico who sowed the first seeds for what we now call linguistic relativism, or the theory that there exists some positive link between the specific language form spoken by a people and their 'thought world', or *Weltanschauung*. This one theory in itself would have earnt Vico a place in the history of ideas, since it refutes all the basic canons of Descartes, in particular the view, still widely held by linguists to this day, that all human languages are cut to the same universal pattern.[6] But for Vico, the relation between language, thought and reality for each culture was unique. The evolving pattern of history was likewise unique for every culture. Whereas Descartes held that the history of all cultures could be traced back to the same ideal primitive state, Vico contested that there was no single blueprint for history, and that each people followed their own path and carved their own destiny.

Vico's views on the nature of knowledge and science – how we come to know the natural and human world – were no less radical for his time, or for that matter, our own. According to Vico, human beings can understand themselves and their own cultural milieu in a way that they could never come to know that which is already given in nature, and for which they have no responsibility. The natural scientist, Vico states, can never be more than a detached observer. He or she can record, classify and generalize, but the essence of what is nature can never be grasped in the same way that the scientist can know the results of his or her own artifice. In contrast to the student of nature, the student of humankind 'enters into' the phenomena and products of human behaviour in a fashion quite different from the detached posture of the natural scientist. This is what Vico meant by 'understanding'. Human culture can only be understood from 'within', from the point of view of the human agents under study. This the student of human behaviour achieves by act of imagination, which Vico called 'Fantasia'. Against the logical modes of reasoning employed by the natural scientist, it is 'fantasia' which enables the human scientist to understand the culture of another time and place and to perceive the motivations of others. Thus, for the first time, a sharp distinction had been drawn between the methods and goals of *Naturwissenschaft* and *Geisteswissenschaft* – natural science as against human studies – between *Wissen* and *Verstehen* (knowing and understanding).

Herder's fame rests primarily on his reputation as the formidable opponent of the French *philosophes* of the Enlightenment and their German disciples. Herder is known for his virulent criticism of rationalism, scientific method, and the Cartesian concept of the universal authority of intelligible laws. In the process of such criticism, he also acquired the reputation of being the chief propagandist for the growth of particularism, both national and literary, and religious and political irrationalism. Thus Herder has come to be identified by some historians with the emergence of European nationalism, including that German movement which was eventually to prove so troublesome in later times. But, as Berlin explains, the picture is an inaccurate one and oversimplified. For Berlin, Herder's originality lies in giving form to three key ideas and movements which eventually came to shape modern culture:

Populism: *the belief in the value of belonging to a group or a culture, which, for Herder at least, is not political, and is indeed, to some degree, anti-political, different from, and even opposed to, nationalism.*

Expressionism: *the doctrine that human activity in general, and art in particular, expresses the entire personality of the individual or the group, and is intelligible only to the degree that it does. Still more specifically, expressionism claims that all the works of men are above all voices speaking, are not objects detached from their makers, are part of a living process of communication between persons and not independently existing entities, beautiful or ugly, interesting or boring, upon which external observers may direct the cool and dispassionate gaze with which scientists – or anyone not given to pantheism or mysticism – look on objects of nature.*

Pluralism: *the belief not merely in the multiplicity, but in the incommensurability, of the values of different cultures and societies, and, in addition, in the incompatibility of equally valid ideals, together with the implied revolutionary corollary that the classical notions of an ideal man and of an ideal society are intrinsically incoherent and meaningless.*[7]

As with Vico, there are too many ideas contained even in this abbreviated description deserving of attention for any summary to do justice, but the following may suffice to indicate the more important methodological implications of Herder's position *vis à vis* the science of his day, and indirectly, ours.

For Herder, as with Vico, the production of cultural artefacts could never be understood by the detached process of rational analysis common to the natural scientist's approach to his studies. What is required is a process of indentification with the life and sensibility of the group, that which Herder called *Einfühlen*, a word approximating with the English word 'empathy'. As Berlin puts it, Herder had a great sense of place,[8] an intense appreciation for the natural 'genius' of a people and their culture. Rather than seeking to impose some ideal concept of uniformity on the diversity of human culture, the human scientist, according to Herder, ought to take such diversity as the very material of his studies and to tailor his method accordingly. For example, since each culture had its own 'centre' and was guided by its own purposes, there could be no universal standards of judgement, either scientific or moral, applicable to all cultures. Hence there could be no standard methodology of research or universal language of analysis and description for human studies. Each culture, each group, must be understood by its own internal criteria, logic and purposes. Thus, Herder denies the possibility of absolute and universal standards of scientific investigation and evaluation, at least for human cultures and man-made artefacts.

Not only did Vico and Herder therefore challenge the prevailing doctrine, then as now, that human science should be modelled on natural science, they also challenged still-prevailing assumptions concerning the superiority of scientific knowledge over other forms. Underlying the arguments of both writers lies an appeal to scientists to respect and try to understand human behaviour and culture as it 'really is', and not to attempt always to squeeze their observations into some preconceived scientific mould originally devised for purposes other than the study of human nature. Both argue that the different forms of human culture and their products are each valid in their own right and can only be comprehended through sympathetic insight. Accordingly, a specifically human science, by necessity, if it is to be at all productive of knowledge of the human condition, would be a much more flexible tool for research than that which scientists, as well as non-scientists, are generally accustomed to think of as 'scientific'. Furthermore, since human culture is so varied, we should not begin with any presumptions concerning the possibility of being able to generalize from one culture to the next, but should be prepared instead to comprehend and accept each culture in its own terms.

'NEW PARADIGM' HUMAN SCIENCE

Though Vico and Herder wrote so long ago, it is only recently that a 'new paradigm' human science conforming to their doctrines is at last emerging as a viable alternative to the still dominant Cartesian model of a unitary scientific rationality. Among the most influential new schools of thought the 'symbolic interactionist' group of social scientists,[9] who take their lead from George Herbert Mead's works,[10] typify the new attitude. In particular, Herbert Blumer's criticisms[11] of orthodox social scientists for their fondness for using standardized methods of observation and evaluation in the face of complex and varied forms of human behaviour are very much in accord with the views propounded by Vico and Herder. Blumer argues that orthodox scientists' observations of human behaviour typically owe more to the characteristics of the particular methodology favoured by the scientist than to the intrinsic nature of the human phenomena under study. In a fashion reminiscent of the two earlier thinkers, as well as Mead, Blumer recommends that the scientist take the role of his human subjects and 'enter into' the world of reality as it is perceived by those subjects, and not by the scientist. Thus a truly empirical science of human studies is that which produces knowledge of the empirical world as it is interpreted by fallible human beings, which does not necessarily conform to the orthodox scientist's preconceptions of the rational order of things.

The conversational methodology originated by Jean Piaget[12] for the study of cognitive development has been much elaborated by Gordon Pask[13] in his studies of learning styles. Both stress the role of the 'participant observer' and the need to adapt the psychologist's observational frames of reference to the subject's own natural and preferred learning strategies. In both Piaget's and Pask's work the scientist converses with the subject in a language of tasks and forms of expression which both subject and observer (and not merely the observer, as in orthodox learning experiments) have determined in mutual response to each other's actions.

In the same spirit, R. D. Laing's interpersonal psychology and methodology[14] makes explicit the reciprocal perspectives on shared problems held by different people, thereby encouraging each party to a conflict to identify with the other's point of view, and so move towards mutual understanding. Similarly, George Kelly's personal construct theory[15] and methodology is aimed at elucidating the world as viewed by individuals, and is concerned more with self-understanding than with 'results'. Yet again, sympathetic insight into the world as it is perceived by the human agents themselves is one of the significant features of Erving Goffman's dramaturgical model of social behaviour,[16] which lays its emphasis on the variations in human role playing according to the different situations in which people find themselves.

In the philosophy of science, the natural heirs to Vico and Herder are Thomas Kuhn[17] and Paul Feyerabend,[18] both of whom stress the relativity of scientific paradigms. Feyerabend explicitly bases his own approach on the linguistic relativism of Benjamin Whorf,[19] which was derived in turn from the same Italian and German origins. Both philosophers reject the idea that there can be any suprarational criteria by which competing paradigms may be evaluated. Both stress instead the importance of historical process in the evolution of scientific ideas, and the social and ideological factors which influence their success.

For all that, the relativism of Kuhn and Feyerabend, and especially of Feyerabend, is not the same extreme relativism of Vico and Herder, and should not be confused as such. As expounded by the two earlier thinkers, relativism rejects any possibility of evaluating any cultural system or set of beliefs by any criteria other than those which have evolved *within* the culture. But by stressing the competing role of alternative paradigms as sources of *external* criteria of evaluation, Kuhn and Feyerabend adopt a brand of critical relativism, which allows for criticism by analogy; that is to say, the findings of one scientific paradigm are evaluated in the terms of another.[20] But whereas Kuhn stresses the role of external criteria only during times of crisis or periods of 'revolution' in science, Feyerabend argues that the evidence we need to refute a theory can often only be obtained with the help of an incompatible alternative. Accordingly, scientists should always proceed counter-inductively, and introduce and elaborate hypotheses which are inconsistent with well-established theories.

ENVIRONMENTAL DIALOGUES

For all their radical approach, none of these emergent concepts or positions de-emphasizes the value of empirical observation. On the contrary, respect for the empirical facts of human behaviour, that is, as it is actually experienced, might be said to be the hallmark of the new relativistic human science. For example, Harold Proshansky,[21] one of the more creative figures in the emergent environmental sciences, recommends that in order to understand the specific nature of the relations between people and the buildings they use, scientists need to leave behind their preconceived concepts and methods, most of which, he argues, originated in the quite different and irrelevant context of the controlled laboratory experiment. Instead, they should get to grips as closely as possible with the behaviour of people in their natural context. The consequence, Proshansky claims, is a quite different pattern of research in environmental studies from that which still predominates:

We worry far less about the experimental controls in doing our research and far more about what, when, and how to describe ongoing events [my emphasis], *an approach that is possible because we are not looking for the usual independent–dependent variable relationships. We are looking in contrast for patterns of relationships between the observed and described properties of physical settings and similarly observed and described reactions of people in these settings. It is our contention that it is these patterns of relationships that provide the only meaningful theoretical and empirical terms for understanding human/physical environment adaptations. Such an approach necessarily divorces itself from a concern with how one isolated variable causes effects in another.*[22]

Proshansky goes on to indicate that one of the results of this new approach is that human scientists' traditional concerns with looking for 'immutable general principles' with respect to how people relate to the physical environment are now jettisoned in favour of a more descriptive approach which concentrates upon the time and place-related characteristics of human behaviour:

...whatever generalizations emerge must be viewed in the context of the social structure and social process that defines our present society. As that context changes, not only will those so-called general principles no longer be applicable, but future researchers will have to identify the essential characteristics of the changed society in order to derive a new set of principles. For me, environmental psychology is a socio-historical behavioural science [my emphasis]. *What it finds today may have little consequence for our society 100 years from now.*[23]

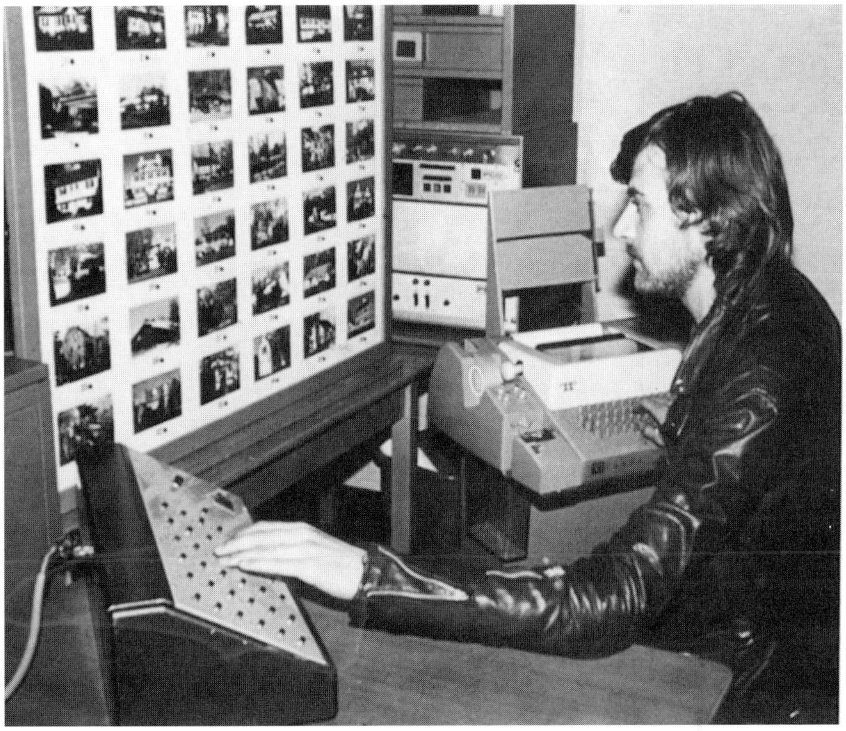

3.1.
ARCHITRAINER: an interactive computer game devised by the author in 1973–74, uses techniques derived from interpersonal psychology and computer-aided instruction (CAI) to simulate 'dialogues' between student architects and hypothetical clients. The program incorporates a client model based on a real subject's personal construct system, linked to a display board showing a variable array of architectural examples. Acting on structured clues based on the client model, the student architect (right) is invited to emphathize with the client and predict how he or she differentiates one form of architecture from another. Photo: Chris Abel.

New approaches in environmental psychology have also been applied to the problem of design participation. A group of architects and computer scientists at the Massachusetts Institute of Technology is experimenting with various forms of computer-based participatory design methods which challenge conventional role models and break down professional barriers between architects and non-architects.[24] As part of these experiments, an interactive computer program called ARCHITRAINER has been devised which simulates a dialogue between an architect and a

Table 3.1. Hierarchy of perspectives on environmental topic (E) as viewed by architect (A) and client (C).

A → (E) ← C	Direct perspective
A → C → (E) ← A ← C	Meta perspective
A → C → A → (E) ← C ← A ← C	Meta-meta perspective

Table 3.2. Model of communication between architect and client in which the architect strives to understand the client's viewpoint on topic (E).

A → [(E) ← C]	The client model
[A → C → (E)] ← A ← C	The architect model
A → C → A → [(E) ← C ← A ← C]	The teaching model

hypothetical client, in which the architect is challenged to 'enter into' the thought processes of his or her client and to see the built world as he or she sees it.[25] Structured in a fashion similar to Laing's hierarchy of reciprocal perspectives, the program leads the architect through a series of guided steps like an exercise in computer-aided instruction, until such point as he or she achieves sufficient understanding of the other's viewpoint and values to be able to assimilate them into his or her own design approach. It is envisaged that such interactive games will eventually play a normal part in architectural design, opening up previously closed design processes to wider access, even at the expense of professional authority and control.

EMPATHY IN SCIENCE AND DESIGN

Given the early Modern Heroes' fascination for the science of their day, it was understandable that they and their current followers in the design methods movement should reject the specificity of architecture in favour of a universal design process commensurate with the orthodox scientific ideal of a universal rationality. But the human science of our day is a very different science from that which predominated in the first half of the century. And if factors such as socio-historical context, meaning, individual interpretation and place relatedness are all defining attributes of specifically human, as opposed to natural, phenomena, then it is the new paradigm – which takes such factors into account – which is the more genuine human science, rather than Cartesian science, which does not.

The concept of empathy[26] is therefore central to both an interpretation of the role of an architect and to the new science. The architect empathizes with a people and the place in which they live in order to *give form* to that identity. The human scientist empathizes with his subjects in order to understand, describe, and *explain* that identity. That the new human scientist should be disposed to 'enter into' a particular situation and culture bodes well for the study of an architecture concerned as much with the differences between places and peoples as with their more common attributes.

ADDENDUM

The client in ARCHITRAINER is simulated from information obtained in interview with a real person involved in the topic area, using the repertory grid technique devised by George Kelly to test his personal construct theory. Kelly's theories are particularly appropriate for an exercise of this kind because his whole emphasis is on the individuality of each person. The repertory grid technique was accordingly designed to elicit information about the subject's outlook on the world in the subject's own terms and not in the usually preconceived terms of the psychologist.[27] Asked to discriminate like from unlike among a set of architectural photographs, the subject forms as many distinct sets of examples as he or she can, naming each set by whichever description fits the similarity or contrast in his or her own words. Following each selection, the subject is then asked to rate each

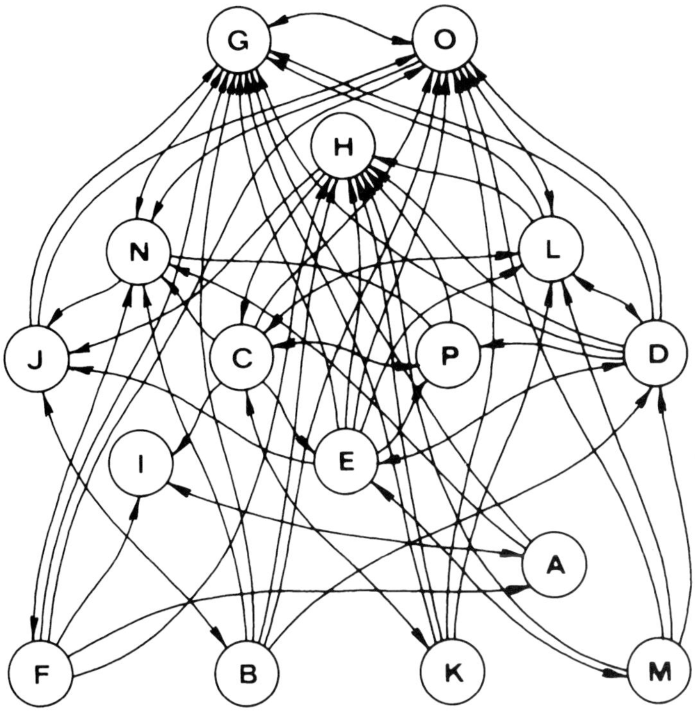

3.2a.

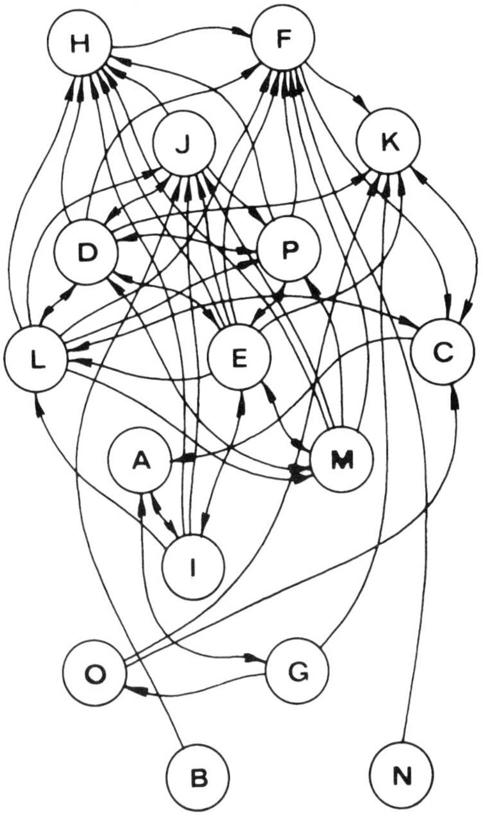

3.2b.

example on a five-point scale, indicating effectively how that person actually uses that construct in everyday life to structure their world. The result is a matrix of scores denoting where each photograph lies on each construct scale. While a particular construct may resemble another person's construct in some way, the system of numerical relations among the entire set will be unique to that person. A computer-based psychological model built from this information provides the instructional material for the game.[28]

A follow-up series of tests was also designed to test the interpersonal skills of an architect in understanding the outlook and values of his test subject.[29] Kelly's sociality corollary states: 'To the extent that one person construes the construction processes of another, he may play a role in a social process involving that person.'[30] By the same token, a professional architect's social role is at least in part defined by his ability to construe his client's construction processes. It was further noted that related research in social perception had found significant correlations in the relation between cognitive complexity and predictive behaviour; i.e. the more differentiated a person's construct system was, the more accurate a person was in predicting another's behaviour in a given situation. Put another way, the greater the number of distinct construct dimensions a person has available to him or her, then the better the possibility that person has of finding room for and interpreting another person's constructs.[31]

A pilot test involving members of a local authority architectural and planning board was carried out to verify whether or not the same

3.2a.
'Cognitive profile' devised by the author shows hierarchical structure of relations between personal constructs, indicating cognitive rigidity. In the graph, constructs (nodes) are ordered vertically according to the number of links (arcs) implied by other constructs. The greater the number of implications the more important the construct, and the more 'resistant to change'. From Abel, 1975.

3.2b.
'Cognitive profile' taken from a different case study shows looser, heterarchical structure, indicating greater cognitive complexity and flexibility. From Abel, 1975.

hypothesis applied to problems of interpersonal communication in multidisciplinary situations.[32] The test consisted of each person in the team being shown how another person discriminated similarities and contrasts among a given set of architectural examples, and then being asked to predict the way that person might use the same construct on a different set of examples, this time with no clues being offered. The team member's accuracy of performance was then compared with the actual results of the test subject's construct system, as recorded previously in his or her repertory grid test. Accuracy of prediction was then in turn compared with cognitive complexity. In addition to the standard measures, a graphical method of illustrating cognitive structure, the 'cognitive profile', was specially devised for the test. Based on results obtained from other tests related to the repertory grid, a cognitive profile was obtained for each architect, planner or administrator doing the interpersonal test. The less complex a person's construct system was, the more hierarchical the cognitive structure was, suggesting that that person's construct system was dominated by relatively few, or even a single construct dimension. By contrast, the more complex cognitive profiles resembled a loose heterarchy, indicating a number of alternative mental pathways along which a person could search in order to find the most effective means of accessing and predicting another person's constructs.

As might be expected from the above hypothesis, there was a significant correlation between accuracy of prediction and both the statistical and graphical measures of cognitive complexity.[33] Beyond this observation, it may be noted that, on a more general level, the respective operational flexibility or rigidity of the two structural forms supports the observations made elsewhere (see Chapter 2) on the relative advantages of loosely ordered organizational structures in changing and unpredictable environments. That similar observations can be made regarding phenomena as diverse as cognitive and urban systems is of no small interest. While it would be unwise to draw any definite conclusions from such a limited study (supported by related studies), it is tempting to speculate that the same self-organizing processes that adjust a city's level of order to suit its regional environment, may also play a role in adjusting individual cognitive structures to handle unpredictable and complex social environments.

4 RETURN TO CRAFT MANUFACTURE

First published under the title 'Ditching the dinosaur sanctuary: seventeen years on' in *CAD and Robotics in Architecture and Construction.* Proceedings of the 1986 Joint International Conference at Marseilles, 25–27 June, Kogan Page, London, 1986.

Ever since the nineteenth century, when mechanization began to have a serious impact on the building industry, architects have been increasingly distanced from the systems of production by which buildings and their parts are made. The English Arts and Crafts Movement was a nostalgic reaction to this development, which was recognized by William Morris and others as symptomatic of the more general trend towards human alienation in an industrialized society.[1] Walter Gropius later saw the problem differently, and tried for a more constructive approach in the Bauhaus School. Even Gropius's approach though was based in part on expediency, having to reconcile the early craft orientation of Bauhaus teaching with the emphasis on industrial design which the School came later to represent.[2] In a deft compromise aimed at bridging the gap, he described the continuing need for craft training as follows:

The teaching of a craft is meant to prepare for designing for mass production. Starting with the simplest tools and least complicated jobs, he gradually acquires ability to master more intricate problems and to work with machines, while at the same time he keeps in touch with the entire process of production from start to finish.[3]

The implication is that both craft and industrialized production methods belong together on the same scale, ranging from simple to complex tools of production. The basic idea was correct for what it promised, but at the time the statement was made it glossed over some enormous differences, not just in the scale of production, but in the degree of human control the designer had over mass-production processes, and not least in the degree of individuality that could then be achieved in the end product.

BRIDGING THE GAP

It was many years before architects were to take up the challenge again and get to grips with manufacturing technologies. For a short time, the spirit of Gropius's educational programme was revived at the Hochschule für Gestaltung at Ulm in southern Germany, where students were encouraged to develop working prototypes of product designs intended for large-scale production.[4] Few designs reached the commercial market, however, and none of the housing prototypes, which

4.1.
'Z' Building Construction System. Architect: Bernd Meurer with 3rd Year students at the Hochschule für Gestaltung, Ulm, 1959/60: Testing of structural prototype. Courtesy of the Hochschule für Gestaltung, Ulm.

remained wedded to prewar concepts of standardization and mass production, were realized. The mass housing systems that eventually came to dominate the market involved relatively crude, heavyweight technologies and bore little relation to the sophisticated methods of industrialized manufacture that had motivated Gropius and other Modernist visionaries.

Not until the late Sixties, with the emergence of more flexible, computer-based production systems, did the possibility of any true reconciliation between craft and factory production become feasible.[5] Now, the extraordinary thing about the new 'cybernetic factory' is that the incongruities previously inherent in Gropius's vision disappear, and the scale from craft tools to automated tools reflects a true continuum. For now we can produce factory-made components that are also tailor-made – a previous contradiction in terms – according to specific designs for specific buildings. In other words, the potential is there for the designer to regain a level of control over the industrialized building process previously thought possible only with craft building techniques.

The potential is there, but it is far from clear that the architectural profession, and just as important, the architectural schools, are currently in any position to take advantage of the tremendous opportunities ahead. For all their efforts, Gropius and his followers had failed to deliver the promised 'new kind of collaborator for industry and the crafts'.[6] Even when architects have sought to harness conventional industrial power to the production of system building, with rare exception, they failed to grasp the essentials of manufacturing.[7] More generally, architects have since come to accept an increasingly circumscribed role as form makers, to the point where the selection of components from a catalogue is all that is left of most architects' contact with the building industry. Where they do get involved at all in the making of new components, it is usually in the writing of performance specifications.

DESIGN DEVELOPMENT

A notable exception is the work of Foster Associates. In their early projects, the Foster team mostly confined themselves to making the most out of ready-made components, though put together with imaginative understanding of the industrialized materials at their disposal, and rare attention to detail. However, in the Hongkong and Shanghai Bank headquarters, Foster has produced a very different kind of building, requiring an entirely new approach to the design and construction process. Almost all the components used in the project were designed by the Foster team itself in close collaboration with manfacturers' own

4.2.
IBM Advance Head Office, Cosham, 1971.
Architect and photo: Foster Associates.

4.3.
Hongkong & Shanghai Bank, 1986. Architect and photo: Foster Associates.

4.4a.

4.4b.

4.4a.
Hongkong & Shanghai Bank. Test rig for prefabricated aluminium cladding. Architect and photo: Foster Associates.

4.4b.
Hongkong & Shanghai Bank. Batch production of varied cladding pieces. Architect and photo: Foster Associates. Courtesy of Cupples Building Products.

design and shop-floor people, an exhaustive process which included the making and testing of full prototypes.[8]

But it was in the design and making of the special aluminium cladding for the steel structure that the Foster team achieved what is their most important breakthrough in industrialized building technology. The masts, trusses, suspension rods and cross-bracing of the bank's unique suspension structure required layers of corrosion protection and fire-proofing materials, which in turn required some kind of maintenance-free cover. In order that the structure underneath should be still expressed as directly as possible, it was necessary that the finished aluminium cladding should closely follow the complex geometry of the structural members. Reductions in the size of the structure as the vertical loading diminished skywards magnified the problem, necessitating the design and production of thousands of separate pieces of cladding with almost as many variations in shape and size. The complexity of the geometry in some cases was difficult enough even to visualize, let alone manufacture.

SMART TOOLS

Problems such as these called for a major retooling by Cupples, the US firm selected for the job, which included the acquisition of computerized, variable presses, as well as a number of robot welders. The benefits accrued from this massive investment in new technology

4.5.
Unimate robot welders fabricating aluminium mullion trusses for the Hongkong & Shanghai Bank. Architect: Foster Associates. Courtesy of Cupples Building Products.

included months of labour saved in drawing board work and the rejigging that conventional presses would have required, as well as distortion-free welds in assembly. More than that, given the nature of the task and the constraints of the 'fast track' programme into which the whole operation fitted, it is doubtful that this unique job could have been completed satisfactorily at all without the help of these 'smart' tools.

The project involved the largest application to date of computerized production machinery to a single building. But it is in the special relation between the method of design used by Foster and his team and these special tools of production that the real significance of this case study lies. For here we have one of the first true examples of the unification of craft and industry which Gropius alluded to, but which is only now made possible by the new technology at our disposal. Note again all that this case study involves: architects working in close collaboration with industry to design, test, produce and assemble an enormously varied range of building components, for one building project only, using fully automated but flexible tools of production. What all this adds up to is craftsmanship on a grand scale, and it completely reverses those industrial developments which underpinned Modern Movement dogma, and which have led to architects' alienation from the tools and products of the building industry upon which they rely.

Given the very high cost of the bank, it is right and proper to ask if technology of this sophistication does not carry a cost penalty. Leaving aside the issue of the very high standards stipulated for the project by the client, the general answer is no, despite the initial high capital cost of the special production machinery. It is here that popular beliefs concerning the nature and cost of automated production lines break down. The high cost of conventional, fixed-purpose automated machinery of the sort still used to make engine blocks, for example, can only be justified by producing tens or even hundreds of thousands of identical engine blocks. The computerized machinery Cupples acquired also involved a sizeable capital investment, but, because of its inherent flexibility, it has almost unlimited capacity for use on other jobs requiring similar manufacturing operations. Initial purchase costs do not therefore have to be recouped by producing the maximum number of the same component, but can be amortized over a very wide range of different products.[9]

CAD + CAM = CRAFTSMANSHIP

Aside from questions of cost, the other question that arises is, given the amount of time and care that the Foster team were willing and able to give to these projects, is the design development process replicable by less committed architects, working for less committed clients and with less adventurous manufacturers? The answer here is less certain, and we may have to wait for further advances in computer-aided design, as well as in manufacturing technologies, before we see the model accepted as normal practice. Some portion, and possibly a large portion at that, of the unique expertise which the Foster team as well as the manufacturers brought to bear on the project, may have to be taken up by automated expert systems and other advances in artificial intelligence (AI),[10] if the approach is to become more widely available.

It may be asked if this further degree of computerization represents a loss of human control, and thus a regression from the craft-orientated model of design and production just described, but this need not be so. It may be more useful to think of such aids in the same way that cyberneticians and AI researchers do, as intelligence amplification.[11] Just as we recognize true craftsmanship when we see it, as the result of a combination of artistic intelligence and technical dexterity, then so is it also possible to represent both developments in computer-aided design (CAD) and computer-aided manufacture (CAM), as extensions of the same human faculties of control over the quality of the end product.

To these innovations we can now add the more recent encroachment of computerized automation onto the building site itself.[12] Already,

4.6.
Hongkong & Shanghai Bank. CAD technology was used for design of complex cladding. Architect and photo: Foster Associates.

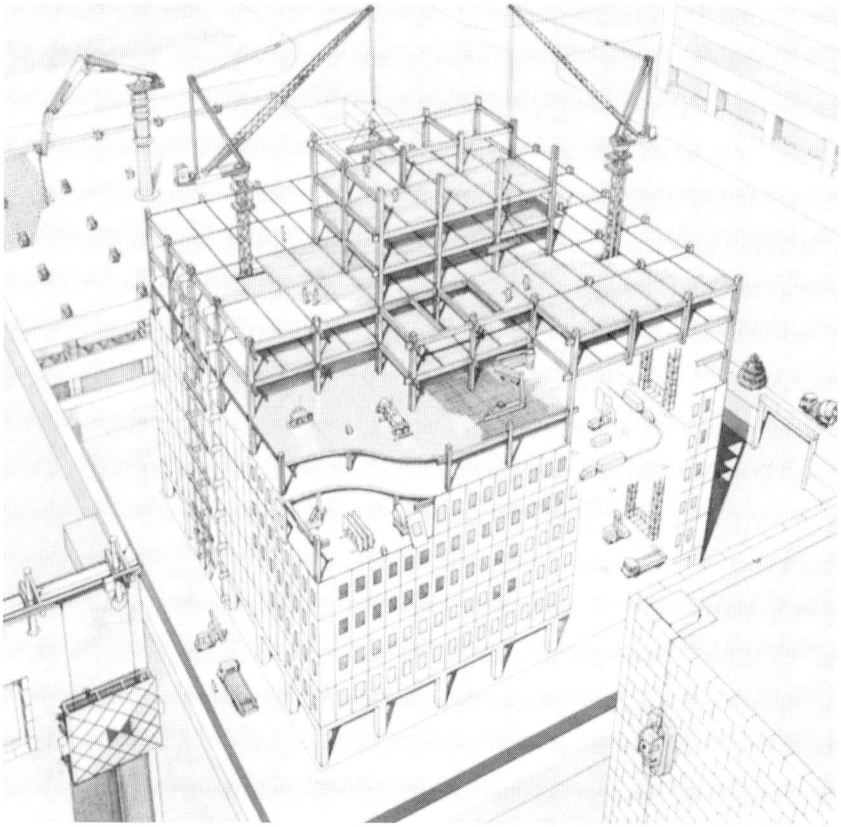

4.7.
The Japanese construction firm Takenaka have developed a variety of robots for use at all stages of the construction process. Applications shown include: concrete distributing crane (top left); automated cranes (top); automated material transportation systems (centre); concrete floor screeding robots (centre); automated coating delamination robot (bottom left); and self-climbing wall inspector (bottom right). Courtesy of Takenaka.

4.8.
Takenaka's concrete floor surface finishing robot, 'Surf Robo'. Courtesy of Takenaka.

several types of robots have been developed to deal with different construction tasks. They range from assembly robots which help to put building structures together, reinforcement and concrete laying robots, interior finishing robots, including robots for concrete slab finishing and spraying fire-proofing materials, and exterior finishing robots, as well as drilling and cutting robots used for heavy excavation and engineering works.

The movement of robots from the relatively safe and predictable environment of the factory shop floor to the more rigorous and constantly changing environment of a construction site represents a considerable increase in demands on robot technology, especially on sensory capacity and durability, over that needed by their industrial cousins. The reasons cited to justify their use in these more strenuous conditions include savings in human accidents and improvements in working conditions, increases in productivity and improvements in the quality of the work carried out. Shortages of skilled manual labour in Japan and other parts of the industrialized world are also a main incentive in those affected regions. Preliminary studies suggest that widespread use of construction robots in most areas of the construction sequence is not only technically feasible, but economically desirable.[13]

There is little question that the prospect of a fully integrated, computerized design, manufacturing and construction process summons up a challenging vision, in which, at its ultimate, on-site robots complete the reinforcement of human intelligence and craft skills described earlier. At the same time, the use of robots throughout the manufacturing and construction process raises the same vexing questions regarding the redistribution of labour as have been raised in other industries which have already been fully automated.[14] We should be careful to distinguish, for example, between cases where there is a genuine shortage of skilled labour, or the work involves levels of danger or some other conditions which are humanly unacceptable, from those where the social costs of automation outweigh the economic gains. Clearly, this is a Pandora's Box, but better it should be opened now, while there is still time to contemplate what we find there, than later, when it might be too late to influence events.

RESPONSIVE ARCHITECTURE

All of this points towards a very different kind of Modern architecture from that which we normally associate with factory production methods. As a so-called 'High-Tech' architect, Foster is widely assumed to be still clinging to those Modernist preferences for universal solutions that Postmodernists now eschew. But the observation is only true of his early work, and it would be a mistake to view the Hongkong and Shanghai Bank and his later work in the same terms. The bank's Second Machine Age technology may be global, but the structural expressionism and spatial qualities are distinctly Pacific, if not precisely local: lightweight floating floors and delicate transparent screens against a massive, aggressive supporting structure: Madam Butterfly meets Godzilla.[15]

Works of this quality suggest a convincing resolution of what are usually considered to be opposing architectural tendencies, and are the outcome of a more general shift from the use of ready-made components towards a craft-orientated approach more suited to a responsive architecture. Like that other master of the modern tools of industry,

4.9.
Banking Hall Interior, Hongkong & Shanghai Bank. Architect and photo: Foster Associates.

Renzo Piano, Foster repeatedly emphasizes the importance of process in the art and craft of making architecture, as much as any end product. This shift can in turn be interpreted, at a higher level, as part of a new, more balanced Modernist philosophy, which allows the architect to pay due respect to what is particular to a place and regional environment, as well as making the most of the technological culture all industrialized countries now share. And while variable production technology does not in itself guarantee high quality design or even respect for cultural and place identities, it will certainly facilitate those architects capable of responding to those issues.

BATTLE FOR THE REAL MODERN MOVEMENT

These then, briefly, are some of the more significant implications and opportunities which the current technological revolution presents us with. The changes involved cannot be overestimated. It is going to take an equivalent revolution in architectural and educational practices for architects to come to grips with the post-industrial age these technological advances represent. Should it happen, we may have to re-evaluate that earlier revolution trumpeted by the Heroes of the Modern Movement for the very misleading event it was. For all the rational and scientific trimmings that went with it, the ideal of mechanization at the heart of orthodox Modernism has turned out to be defunct, at best a staging post on the way to a very different Machine Age. The crucial battle for the *real* Modern Movement – the one in which architects and humankind in general finally master their machines and bend them to humane use – has only just begun.

5 VISIBLE AND INVISIBLE COMPLEXITIES

Published in *The Architectural Review*, February 1996, as an extract from this book.

A distinguishing feature of much architecture in the 1990s has been a preoccupation with complexity for its own sake, most of all with its formal expressions. Rejecting both the reductionism of early Modernists and the eclecticism of Postmodernists – healthy reactions in themselves – many architects and students instead favour irregular and hard-to-fathom compositions based on mixed geometries, fragmented or folding surfaces and other abstract devices.[1] Project drawings, which are treated as having a purpose and value of their own, often seem intentionally obscure and offer few clues to the uninitiated.[2] Usually, but not always convincingly, such exercises are rationalized by reference to the complexities of the programme, the context, or even modern life in general. At a more consciously elevated level, they have been justified by other criteria borrowed from literary theory and criticism[3] or, most recently, from scientific theories concerning the general nature of complexity itself.[4] Occasionally, perhaps more honestly, the architect concerned is content to rest on the aesthetic merits of his or her designs in the time honoured fashion of the profession.

Coincidental with the surface complexities of this movement, other more profound forces for complexity have been at work shaping the environment. These are the invisible systems of electronic communication and production which are revolutionizing the way architecture is conceived and made. Though not as tangible as the built or paper products of the former movement, it is arguable that these invisible human creations provide the more significant evidence of an emergent architecture appropriate to the twenty-first century. Not least, they challenge the role of architects themselves in directing the future course of building.

AGE OF COMPLEXITY

Organic machines

The origins of this revolution lie in a series of related developments in science, technology and architectural theory mostly concentrated between the late 1940s and mid 1970s. The star of all these developments is the computer, a machine made like none other before it. Previously, all machines were built for a specific and limited purpose,

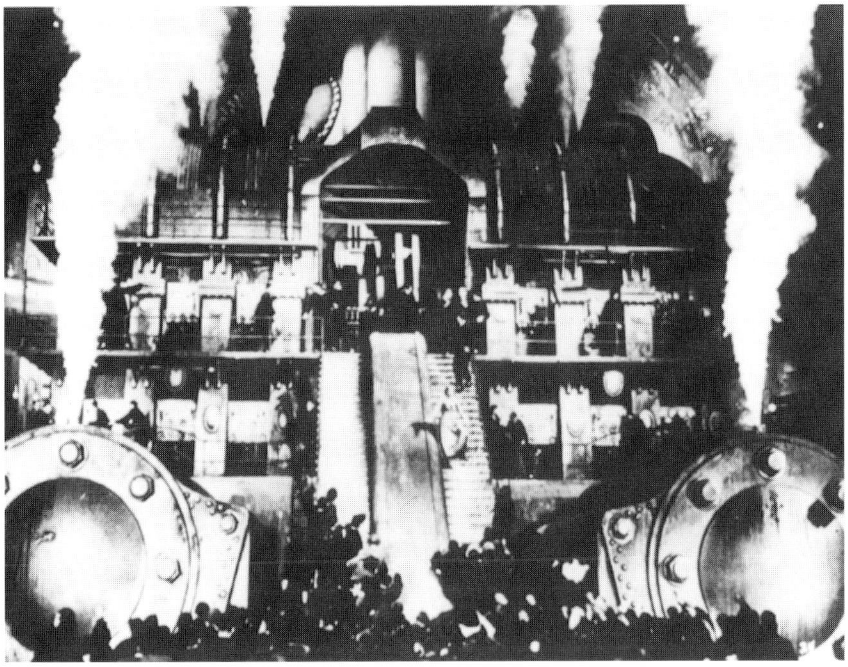

5.1.
Still from Fritz Lang's 1925 sci-fi film, 'Metropolis', depicts slavery of man to machine. Courtesy of the British Film Institute.

conceived and designed to handle a predetermined and never varying sequence of operations, each following the other as effect follows cause until the designated task was complete. The very description 'machine-like' conjures up threatening images of something unbending and essentially inhuman and unnatural. Inserted as they were into human and natural environments with which they had little or no exchange, the products of the First Machine Age have created as many if not more problems as they have solved.

The first fully working electronic computer in 1949 marked the arrival of the general-purpose machine, designed and built for no particular task other than to make whatever decisions it was called upon by its human users.[5] Significantly, the binary principles on which it was designed were essentially the same as those which governed the switch-like neurons and neural nets of the human brain. Around the same time, a whole new computer-based science, cybernetics, was evolving whose special focus was decision-making and control systems, especially the sorts of self-regulating or self-organizing systems which characterize organic life.[6] The combined epoch-making result of these scientific and technological innovations was machines with feedback; adaptive machines capable of responding to changing tasks and situations and even, through self-learning, improving on their own performance.

The basic meaning of a machine and its relation to the human and natural environment was therefore completely reversed. Instead of bending nature and human behaviour to the dictates of inflexible, fixed-purpose machines – an attitude which included picturing the entire universe as a kind of predictable clockwork[7] – machines are now modelled on the known principles of nature's own organic processes.

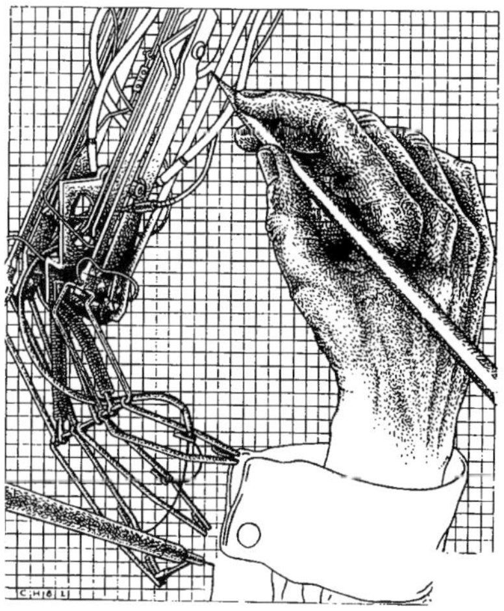

5.2.
Machines are now modelled on organic life forms. Drawing by Cliff Harper. From 'A Council for Science and Technology Report' *New Technology*, 1981.

Indeterminant forms

By the early 1960s, the new era was already beckoning architects and surfaced in a number of experimental projects by a small avant-garde in Britain, France and the US. Beginning with the 'Fun Palace' and 'Potteries Thinkbelt', Cedric Price explored the impact of information technologies on indeterminate forms of architecture whose invisible attributes were as important, if not more important, than any physical or formal aspects.[8] Partly influenced by Price's work, students at the Architectural Association (AA) School of Architecture in London proposed 'computer communities' and dispersed urban educational networks, all intended to widen community access to the new resources.[9] Detailed design studies included computerized 'mobile learning stations' which could be fitted into both old or new buildings with equal ease and be programmed to respond to different spatial functions as required. Based on biological and cybernetic concepts, the work stations-cum-space modules were designed to resemble living cells, combining together and splitting off just like the organisms which inspired them.[10]

In 1975 Yona Friedman in Paris presented another liberating vision of the flexibility information technology proffered.[11] For Friedman, it was not so much the form of a dwelling that counted as who was responsible for it. He suggested that ordinary people could use the new technology to design their own homes as part of a larger, open-ended structural and services framework. Unlike other megastructure designers, however, Friedman was more interested in the software than the hardware. In place of conventional design and build procedures he posited a new process which does away with the architects' intermediary role, incorporating instead direct feedback from the user to the builder via a host of information technologies, computer-aided design techniques and adaptable building structures. As part of a more comprehensive feedback system he also envisaged city-wide computer infrastructures which would monitor changes in the urban fabric and oversee transportation systems.

Man–machine dialogue

Whilst all these visions were purely speculative, a group of young architects and computer experts at Massachusetts Institute of Technology were pursuing a more rigorous, experimental approach toward similar goals. Led by Nicholas Negroponte, the Architecture Machine Group, as it was known, was formed with the specific purpose of harnessing computer power to create a new man–machine dialogue.[12]

The group's research was concentrated on three parallel developments: technical improvements to the man–machine interface, especially graphics, which enhanced a professional designer's skills; user-friendly techniques and aids which helped non-professionals to become their own architects; and personalized, 'intelligent' environments or 'soft architecture machines', which would respond to occupants' individual whims and environmental needs.[13] All three investigations built on parallel cutting-edge research at MIT and other universities into artificial intelligence or

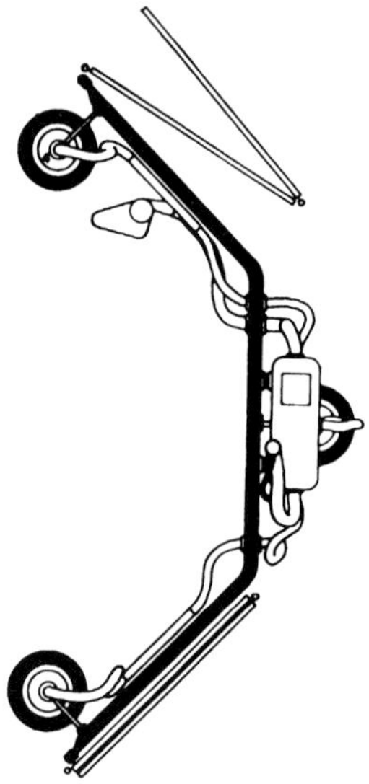

5.3a.
Mobile Learning Station. Architectural Association student project by Chris Abel, 1967.

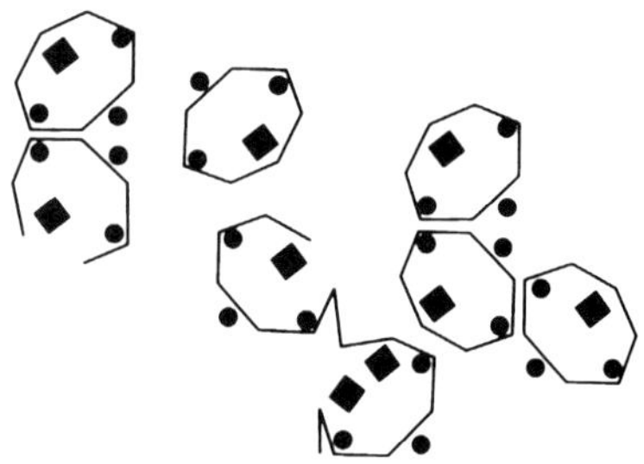

5.3b.
Mobile Learning Station. Plan. Chris Abel.

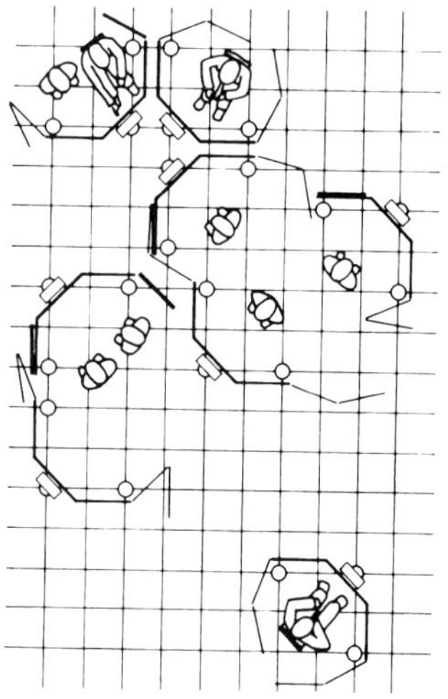

5.3c.
Cluster of Mobile Learning Stations. Stations are programmed to form variable spaces over electronic grid in floor which controls automatic movement. Plan. Chris Abel.

machine cognition, which was itself based on research into human cognition.[14] With the guidance of Gordon Pask, the British cybernetician and cognitive scientist, the idea was developed that human being and machine-environment might together form a reciprocal learning system, each building his/her/its knowledge from what he/she/it learns about the other.[15]

Uncertainty and change

Over the same period, architectural theory was also undergoing a sea-change, from a claustrophobic field inhabited solely by critics with an art-historical inclination, to a vibrant interdisciplinary forum in which science, once again, played the lead role. Unlike the deterministic sciences once favoured by orthodox Modernists, however, the sciences that now aroused such intense excitement and speculation were the postwar new sciences of complex systems: cybernetics and its cousins, information theory, general systems theory and the theory of self-organizing systems.[16]

From the late 1960s on, occasional articles on related environmental topics began showing up in the less conservative architectural journals. They included discursions on the self-organizing features and future directions of dispersed cities,[17] at that time a much scorned model of urban form:

> *Instead of looking for formulas to impose on urban growth we should be learning to manipulate that growth through its own intrinsic adaptive properties. The kind of problems that Los Angeles exemplifies will be met, not by the introduction of any planned centre for the conurbation, but by the development of the planned urban 'nervous system'... If we are going to work with these adaptive processes we need to think in a very different way about just what does constitute the underlying structure of an urban social system. In coming to such an understanding we shall probably enlist the aid of cross-disciplinary sciences that up till now have been thought of as alien to planning and design. The analytic cross-referencing implicit in these sciences is liable to wreak havoc with our (system of) intellectual categorizing.*[18]

These individual forays were substantially reinforced in late 1969 and 1972 with the appearance of two special issues of *Architectural Design* on the subject of complexity, edited by Royston Landau,[19] a teacher at the AA School. Together, the two journals presented a heady mix of philosophical analysis, abstract concepts and speculation on the relevance of the new sciences to architecture, planning and computer-aided design. The overriding message which emerged from this double-barrelled blast at architectural and urban conventions was that uncertainty, change and conflict were inseparable features of both natural and human evolution. This was the 'age of complexity',[20] and architects and planners were going to have to grasp its nettle if they were to continue making any serious contribution.

NETWORKS WITHIN NETWORKS

Customized architecture

After a period of incubation, the pace of innovation quickened again in the 1980s, which also saw the application to architectural practice of many earlier ideas and inventions. A small group of mostly British architects working in collaboration with a few adventurous engineers and manufacturers began using increasingly sophisticated methods of customized building production, in which information technology and flexible manufacturing systems played a vital role. Smart tools of a kind already widely used in other industries were used in the production of the unique steel structure for Norman Foster's Renault Centre,[21] as well as in the tailor-made cladding for the same architect's Hongkong and Shanghai Bank.[22] Like Richard Rogers' Lloyd's HQ in London, the bank was one of the first office buildings to be designed specifically for the information era and incorporates raised floors of the type first developed for computer centres. Both buildings were also among the first to introduce fully computerized building management systems monitoring energy use, performance and maintenance schedules 24 hours a day. In addition to these less visible systems, the Hongkong Bank features a computer-controlled, tracking 'sunscoop' directing its rays to illuminate the interior 'atrium' in spectacular fashion.

5.4.
Computer controlled plasma arc cutters were used in the fabrication of steel trusses for the Renault Centre. Architect: Foster Associates. Courtesy of Ove Arup & Partners.

5.5.
Parts Distribution Centre for Renault UK, Swindon, 1983. Architect: Foster Associates. Photo: Dennis Gilbert.

Since these early breakthroughs the idea of the self-regulating, 'intelligent building' has gained widespread currency and even entered popular culture. In his sci-fi novel, *Gridiron*, Philip Kerr[23] depicts an intelligent building gone haywire which turns on and kills its own architect. Entertaining as the thought is, it remains a remote prospect. For the most part, aside from building management systems the description applies to such relatively benign features as responsive skins which absorb, distribute and generate energy,[24] or automated lift systems which use fuzzy logic to build their own models of changing use patterns. Looking ahead, Mike Davies of Richard Rogers Partnership foresees a more encouraging prospect than *Gridiron*'s author: 'I propose that the average building should know how it feels. Such a building is an intelligent building; basically a building which is aware of itself; aware of the energy falling on its façade; aware of the energy coming through the façade; aware of the people inside the building and what their needs are.'[25]

These innovations have been supplemented by an even greater explosion in the nature, distribution and availability of computer-aided design and production methods. The most advanced multi-user systems, like Reading University's knowledge-based engineering (KBE) system,[26] reach into the entire process of design and manufacture, enabling designer, fabricator and user to explore alternative designs in real time. Virtual reality has also literally added another whole new dimension to the design, manufacture and build process, enabling future users as well as designers to 'walk through' and visually test a design concept before it goes into production. Related advances in virtual prototyping promise

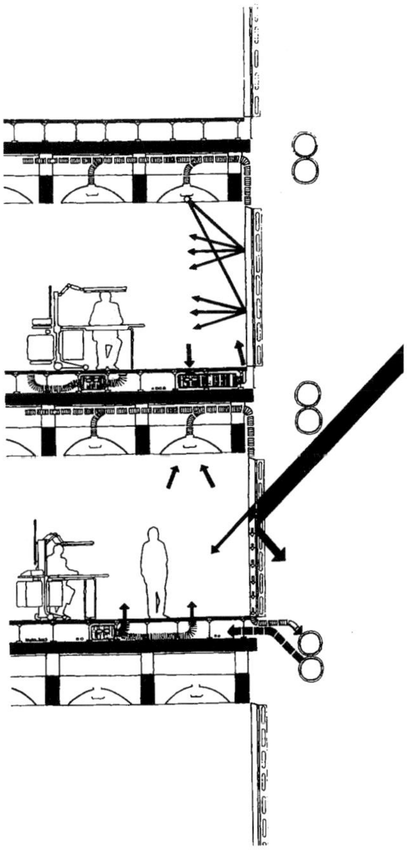

5.6.
Lloyd's HQ, 1986. Detail of wall and floor systems. Architect: Richard Rogers Partnership.

5.7.
Hongkong & Shanghai Bank. Tracking 'sunscoop' directs sunlight into interior atrium. Architect: Foster Associates. Photo: Chris Abel.

5.8.
The Singapore Arts Centre features a two-layer skin whose scales are computer optimized to cut out direct sunlight. Architect: Michael Wilford and Partners with Ateliers One and Ten (London) and DP Architects (Singapore). Courtesy Ateliers One and Ten.

5.9a.
Virtual reality simulation of store design by Intelligent Systems Solutions Ltd allows retail staff to view features interactively and to participate in design decisions. Courtesy of Intelligent Systems Solutions Ltd.

5.9b.
Virtual reality simulation of external store design. Courtesy of Intelligent Systems Solutions Ltd.

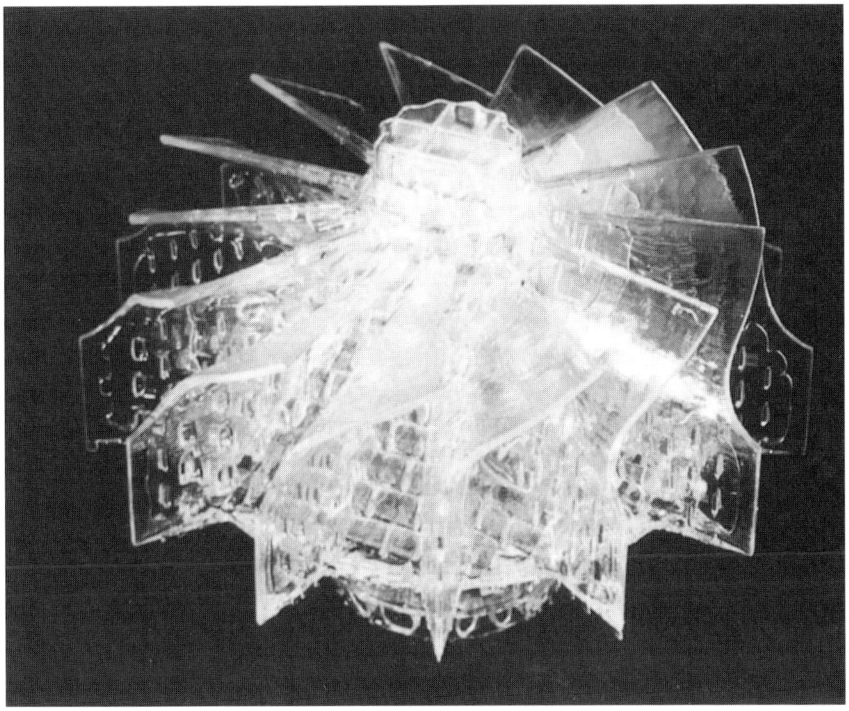

5.10.
Rapid prototyping: laser technology enables designers to produce complex shapes such as this turbocharger fan directly from CAD data in a matter of hours. Courtesy of the University of Nottingham.

not only to speed up design and production but also – crucially – to open up the whole process to wider inspection and participation. Combined with other innovations such as rapid prototyping and Japanese-style Just-In-Time production methods, which have already narrowed previous gaps between demand and production in other industries, virtual reality technology marks a major step in the direction of a user-orientated architecture.[27] At the extreme cutting edge of building research, the development of customized smart materials able to respond to changing structural and environmental conditions[28] heralds the further prospect of a completely tailor-made building, from the molecular level to the rooftop.

Cybercity

The future shape and impact of this electronic architecture may already be detected in the explosive growth of the Internet and other shared computer networks. Described by Negroponte, now head of MIT's Media Lab and a familiar cyberspace guru, as a 'network of networks',[29] the Internet has transformed communication between computer users, knitting together smaller networks and connecting people in different parts of the world who would otherwise have no contact. In the process, new forms of both professional and non-professional collaboration have been created which are reverberating throughout all levels of society. Even more radical in its implications is the argument advanced by Kevin Kelly[30] and others, that the Internet as a whole exhibits self-organizing characteristics similar in kind to those of a living organism, or to be more precise, clusters of organisms. Kelly likens the phenomenon to the behaviour of a swarm of bees searching for a new location for the hive.

Scouts will check out a number of alternative locations and compete for attention from the rest of the swarm for their choice. Somehow a collective decision on the new site by the whole swarm eventually emerges even though it is impossible to trace it to any single prior event or signal. In the same way, the Internet may already be reshaping the nature of human intercourse in ways that cannot be predicted from any particular use or application of the system, but which nevertheless has a direction of its own.[31] The ongoing development of semi-autonomous, intelligent software agents or 'alter-egos' which would roam cyberspace, digging out information for their owners,[32] is only likely to boost claims that such networks are nothing less than an evolution of human intelligence, albeit in a distributed form.

The extension of self-organizing networks and software agents into all aspects of urban life along the lines predicted earlier is probably only a matter of time, and not much time at that. Singapore already boasts a fully integrated traffic control system which monitors traffic loads online and changes signals in different parts of the city to help ease the flow. Satellite navigation systems which present drivers with information on traffic flow and alternative routes on purpose-made receivers are also now commonplace. Other more diverse forms of community-based networks are proliferating. In the US, the common language used to describe the habitation of cyberspace is that of the New Frontier. Typical of the new 'settlements' is the Blacksburg Electronic Village in Virginia, a collaboration between the town of Blacksburg, Bell Atlantic and Virginia Tech University, which ties the university town's businesses, citizens and students together and also gives them access to the wider world of the Internet.[33] Just like the original settlers in the New World, the new settlers often borrow their place names from more familiar terrain. In Europe, Amsterdam's Digital City offers a whole urban world in cyberspace, complete with a 'Digital Town Hall', a 'social centre', 'neighbourhoods' and other 'sites' where citizens can pursue their representatives on local issues, socialize, just wander or 'surf'. Created as an experiment in civic networking and citizen participation, in addition to its regular inhabitants the Digital City supports thousands of passing

5.11.
Logo for Nottingham Cyberpub. Courtesy of Cyberpub.

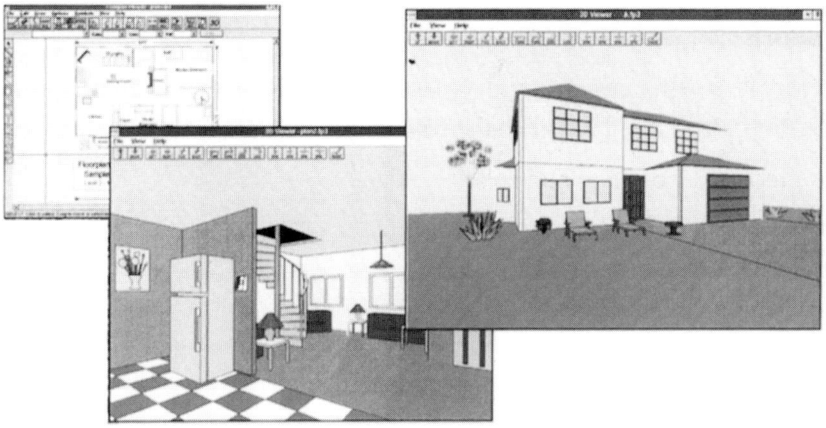

5.12.
Advertisement offering computer-based self-build services. Courtesy of FastCad.

tourists seeking information on the city and its services.[34] What began earlier this century with the impact of the automobile and telecommunications on changing urban patterns is now rapidly reaching take-off speed with the nascent cybercities of today, producing new configurations of urban life and form.[35]

The implications of shared networks for architectural practice are no less profound. The UK's Construction Industry 'Superhighway Initiative', a joint venture between BT, Hewlett Packard, and On-Demand Construction Information, now provides a comprehensive information service to all members of the industry. High-powered modelling and test facilities, such as Cham Ltd's PHOENICS Computerized Fluid Dynamics (CFD) program, which uses simulation techniques to model environmental performance, are also now available as a service to architects who could otherwise afford neither the hardware nor software to test their own designs. Coupled with other KBE systems and CAD packages, such remote information services empower even the smallest practice with the potential to design, test and deliver large-scale and complex projects. Given that over half of the architectural practices in the UK consist of one or two person enterprises, the model of the small, virtual practice, linking up on-line as necessary with other specialized firms and services, could become the norm. By the same token, similar user-friendly services designed for non-professionals may shift the balance of power toward the self-builder, at least for dwellings and simple building types, bringing Friedman's visions of a self-building community closer to reality.

PSEUDO-COMPLEXITIES

Superimpositions

The essence of all these innovations and developments, as of the organizational and social complexities which arise from them, is that they involve multiple human and technological agents combining together with unpredictable consequences. No single designer or team of designers could possibly substitute the same order of complexity which is the natural and unplanned result of so many freely interacting agents. Yet

5.13.
Gröninger Museum, Holland, 1995. Architect: Co-op Himmelblau. Photo: Alistair Gardner.

that is precisely what many of the most fashionable architects appear to be attempting, by ever more devious and contrived means. Ostensibly responding to the problems of the age, they only confirm architects' continuing obsession with formal abstractions.

Co-op Himmelblau exemplify the worst traits of the movement. Their early angst-ridden projects in Vienna – a city identified with the troubled subconcious – most clearly betrayed the violent undercurrents shaping what they revealingly declared as the 'architecture of the spiked chest'.[36] Rejecting more rational design methods, the architects employed such 'spontaneous' techniques as sketching blindfold. The design for the Gröninger Museum in Northern Holland springs from the same random methods and indifference to conventional restraints, since 'we didn't care too much about the functions of the space'.[37] The original drawing, a frenetic blur of abstract lines (it isn't clear if it was produced blindfold but it could have been), was overlaid three times and transformed into a block model, over which the same drawing was laid again. The combined drawing and model was then scanned straight into a computer and converted into plans by a process of further abstract transformations. All the resulting practical errors of the generative process are purposefully retained in the final construction, including an inaccessible courtyard.

Sometimes, as with Bernard Tschumi's Parc de la Villette in Paris, a deliberately complicated design method has had an unexpectedly (and presumably unwanted) simple outcome. For his masterplan, Tschumi employed the then novel method of superimposition, or superposition as it is also called, whereby three independently composed plans based on different ordering systems and features were overlaid to produce a composite design. Promoted by Tschumi as an alternative to the logocentric architecture of Western traditions, the method is intentionally disruptive of any preconceived order.[38] Marginally more structured than Co-op Himmelblau's overlays, the

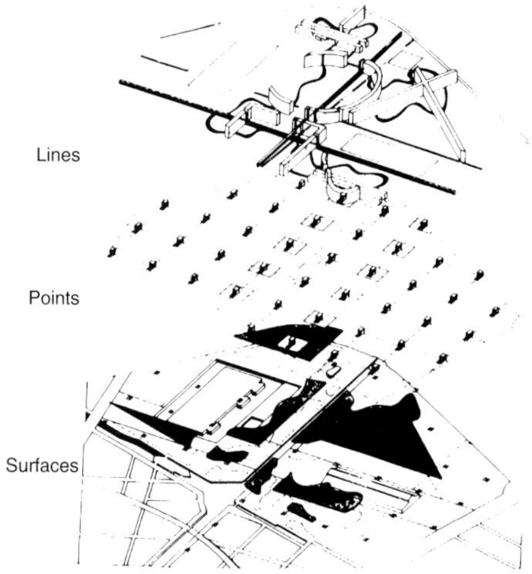

5.14.
Parc de la Villette, Paris, 1982–85. Superimposition of concept plans. Architect: Bernard Tschumi. After architect's drawing, from Johnson and Wigley, 1988

5.15a.
Parc de la Villette. Typical 'functionless' Folly. Architect: Bernard Tschumi. Photo: Chris Abel.

5.15b.
Parc de la Villette. Some Follies, such as this gatehouse to a submarine tour, can be easily distinguished from the rest as a functional building. Architect: Bernard Tschumi. Photo: Chris Abel.

resulting disjunctions between the different schemes, like the latter firm's 'errors', were carefully preserved in the final plan, the aim being that the resultant voids and ambiguities of purpose and meaning would be resolved by observers in their own fashion. However, far from producing the intended tensions between order and disorder, the final result turns out to be a remarkably well-ordered and predictable composition in the grand French manner, with few ambiguities. Part of the reason is the dominating presence of the three main buildings in the park, the Museum of Science and Industry, Grande Halle (the former market) and Zenith Concert Hall, all vast structures. Other easily distinguished landmarks, like the arrow straight canal through the centre of the park and the regular grid of crimson red 'Folies', establish a clear system of coordinates and baroque vistas by which a person may grasp the whole, as easily as at Versailles. The Folies themselves, which were intended to refute conventional links between form and function, can also be readily separated by their configuration and bulk into those that are habitable and serve a purpose, and those that do not. Contrary to the architect's declared aims, la Villette demonstrates all too clearly that random methods are no guarantor of either complexity or ambiguity.

Like Tschumi, Peter Eisenman bases his approach on Derridan literary theory and other non-architectural sources, on the assumption that they will offer critical insights into and a way out of outdated conventions.[39] These do little, however, to disguise the ultimately wilful nature of this cerebral architect's highly abstract compositions and forms, which invariably negate whatever worthy cross-disciplinary exercise might otherwise be involved. Promoted as an exercise in self-similar patterns inspired by complexity theory, the Social Housing at Kochstrasse for the Berlin IBA is as vapid an exercise in façadism as any Postmodern architect's. In the Rebstockpark residential scheme near Frankfurt more elaborate methods are employed with similar arbitrary results. An orthogonal web laid over the site is contorted in several dimensions, and the resulting warped lines allowed to slice through and distort an otherwise conventional medium-rise development. The effect on the individual blocks is akin to that of an earthquake, rending asunder whatever original order guided their design. It is no coincidence that most of Eisenman's schemes, models or drawings are best illustrated from an elevated viewpoint. Like the Rebstockpark scheme, the eccentric folds of the Columbus Convention Centre in Ohio can only be fully appreciated from above, where they resemble the produce of a giant shredding machine. Worst of all, Eisenman's 'collapsed' design for the Nunotani Headquarters in Tokyo – where real earthquakes are an ever present threat – shows just how far removed from human sensibilities architecture has travelled in some quarters.

The prevailing anthropocentric attitude towards nature – at best treated, as at la Villette, as just another compositional element, or at worst, as with Saha Hadid's Peak Club project for Hong Kong, denied altogether – is equally revealing of the movement's underlying priorities and contradictions. For the Peak Club, Hadid proposed clearing and remoulding the sloping, vegetation-shrouded site on the crest of The

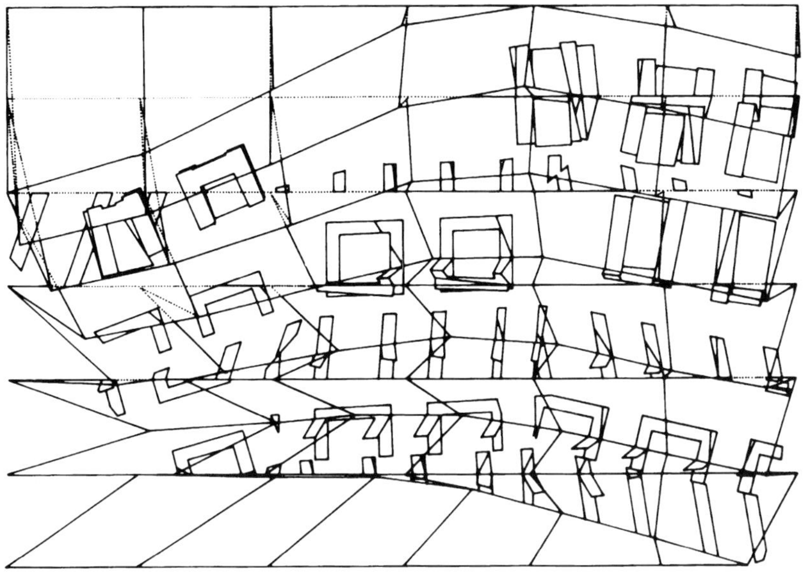

5.16.
Rebstockpark residential scheme, near Frankfurt, 1992 'Folded' concept plan. Architect: Peter Eisenman. After architect's drawing from Maggie Toy (ed.), *Folding Architecture*, 1993.

5.17.
Colombus Convention Centre, Ohio, 1990–93. Roof and site plan. Architect: Peter Eisenman. After architect's drawing from Maggie Toy (ed.), *Folding Architecture*, 1993.

5.18.
Peak Club project, Hong Kong, 1982. Site plan. Architect: Saha Hadid. After architect's drawing from Johnson and Wigley, 1988.

Peak mountain to better suit her abstract, horizontal composition. The main area was to be dug out down to the rock and the excavated granite rebuilt as artificial cliffs and finally polished to form a more sculptural setting.[40] Mercifully unbuilt, the competition-winning project would have left a permanent open wound on Hong Kong's famous landmark to record the architect's passing.

Sham images

One way or another, whether by suspending conscious design control, applying complicated transformational techniques or simply ignoring conventions of scale or purpose, all these architects attempt to replicate larger real-world complexities by spurious means. Though the methods employed are purposefully arbitrary they are assumed by their users to impart a legitimacy to their designs that more rational methods would not. Yet the resultant architecture has little to do with the complexities of the real world, especially those of real cities, which arise out of more mundane but genuinely complex processes of decision making. Sim City, the popular computer simulation game, provides a good illustration of these processes. Using computer techniques originally developed by AI researchers, Sim City accurately reproduces the complexities of urban growth.[41] Cellular automata simulate myriad conflicting agents, each one of which may involve basically simple decisions but when multiplied and combined with numerous other agents produces complex outcomes. Bill Erickson explains: '[The game] highlights the fact that designing cities is as much to do with tempting and coercing as it is with planning and that the form of cities derives as much from localized independent actions as it does from grand plans.'[42]

In Sim City, as in the real world, complexity originates in simple events. What is missing in the projects described above are the multiple independent decisions, conflicts and dialogues between different individuals and interest groups which underlie real-life growth and development. The use of techniques like superimposition, also favoured by Rem Koolhaas, Jeffrey Kipnis and many others, does nothing to hide the essentially exclusive nature of their designers' approach, which is as much determined by professional ideology and aesthetic prejudice as any logocentric practice's. Hailed by Charles Jencks as 'a kind of ultimate democratic method',[43] superimposition is nothing of the sort, and opens up the design process not one iota to any circle or value outside the architects' own. Nor do the method or the designs originate in any self-generated pattern of human activity. Rather, they point to a deep malaise in architecture. Unable to give up their elite status and prima donna ways, or to accept the loss of whatever influences their profession once exercised over urban form, these architects disguise their narrowing concerns by contriving sham images of complexity. Instead of genuine human development or dialogue, what we get is a poor substitute, usually dressed up in obscure language to resist detection. In place of the more open design process which has been claimed for the movement, we get increasing mystification and self-obsession.

TOWARD AN ARCHITECTURE OF DIALOGUE

Open approach

It is questionable how long the architectural profession can sustain the deceits and delusions of these architectural dinosaurs in the wide open, participatory world of the Internet. At one extreme, Freidman and Negroponte's radical vision of a computer-based, democratized architecture of non-architects offers a drastic alternative. It would be tragic,

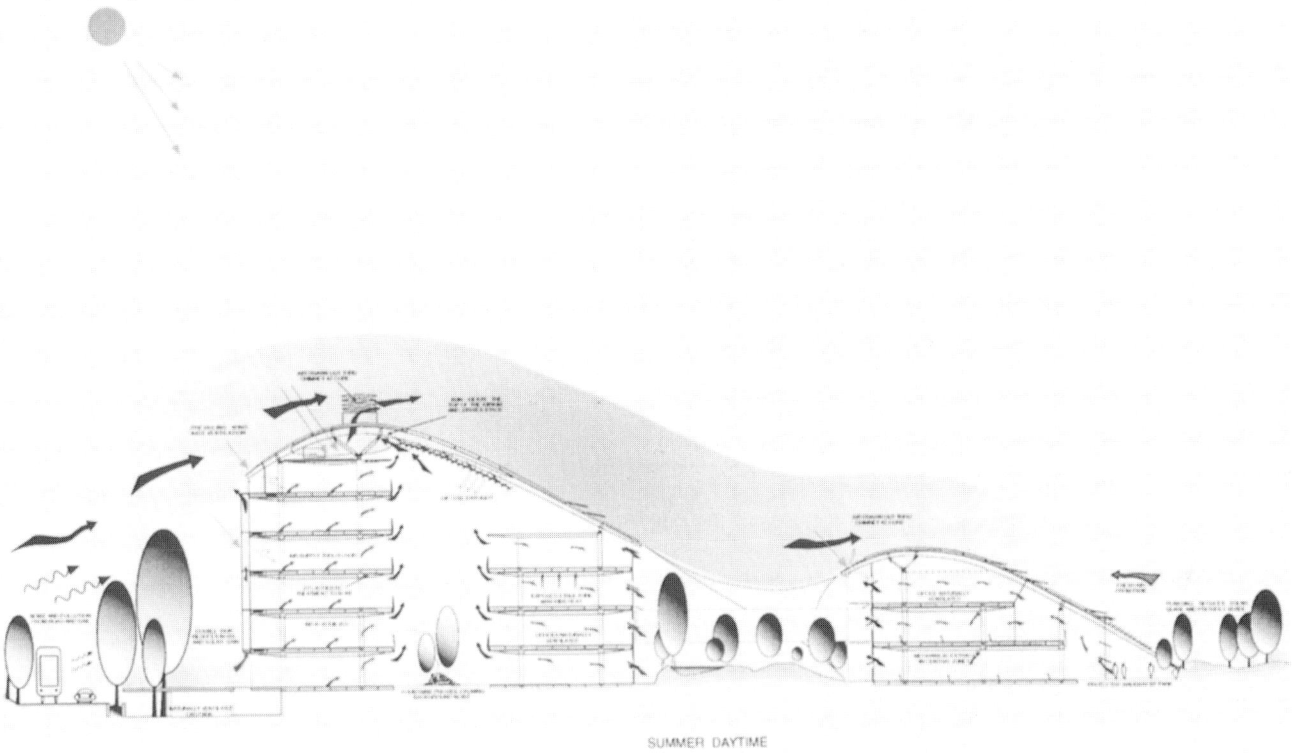

5.19a.
Bio-Tech architecture. Inland Revenue HQ, Nottingham, 1992. Competition drawing. Cross section showing climate control systems. Architect: Richard Rogers Partnership.

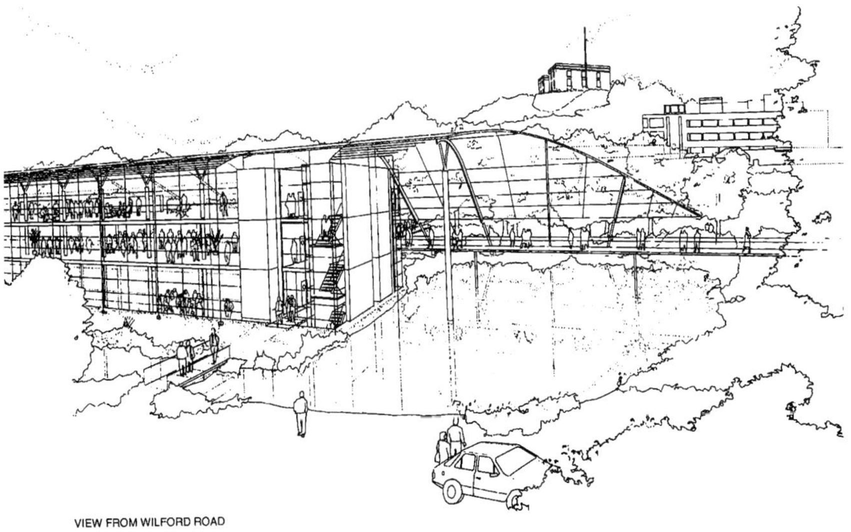

5.19b.
Inland Revenue HQ. Competition drawing. Architect: Richard Rogers Partnership.

however, if the creative talents of architects were to be lost altogether because of an inability to drop ingrained habits of their class. Other architects like Giancarlo de Carlo,[44] Ralph Erskine,[45] Lucien Kroll[46] and even Charles Moore in his early Californian projects,[47] have chosen a genuinely more open and inclusive approach, and encouraged a creative dialogue with the users of their residential schemes and other buildings. De Carlo is especially clear about the true source of complexity in architecture: 'One can renew architecture and make it a significant activity in contemporary life only if it is fully exposed to the complexities of human affairs.'[48]

In the same spirit, the diverse forms of Ivo Waldhor's housing development in Malmö reflect the genuine complexity of full tenant participation in the design process.[49] For single authored designs, Alvar Aalto's heterotropic planning technique[50] offers an enduring model of how architects can respond to the conflicting demands of complex programmes without resort to random gimmickry. Significantly, most of the foregoing designers include a sensitivity to regional difference as an essential part of their approach. The so-called High-Tech school of architects (most designers so tagged never accepted that limited description) have also opened up the profession in their own way by crossing class-ridden professional boundaries to create a collaborative, craft-based architecture rooted in the industries and skills which produce their buildings.[51] The intelligent building concept, which the same architects helped develop, has also contributed substantially to a revitalized architecture, responsive both to nature and to its human users. Lately, as with Richard Rogers[52] and Future Systems' work,[53] or Ken Yeang's office towers in the Far East,[54] these advanced buildings have taken on the character as well as the operational capacities of the green machines they are. More Bio-Tech than Hi-Tech, they suggest their designers are well tuned to the real complexities of the age.

Local space, global mind

Japanese space concepts,[55] which are fundamentally different from the logocentric Western concepts Tschumi et al. seek to escape, provide other valuable lessons. In the Western baroque and neo-classical traditions of geometrically defined space, the designer assumes a more or less passive observer, able to grasp the entire space concept from a single static viewpoint. The designer's vision is total and complete in itself; the observer merely partakes of what has been wholly predetermined by someone else. By contrast, the Japanese tradition of movement space assumes a mobile observer and constantly changing

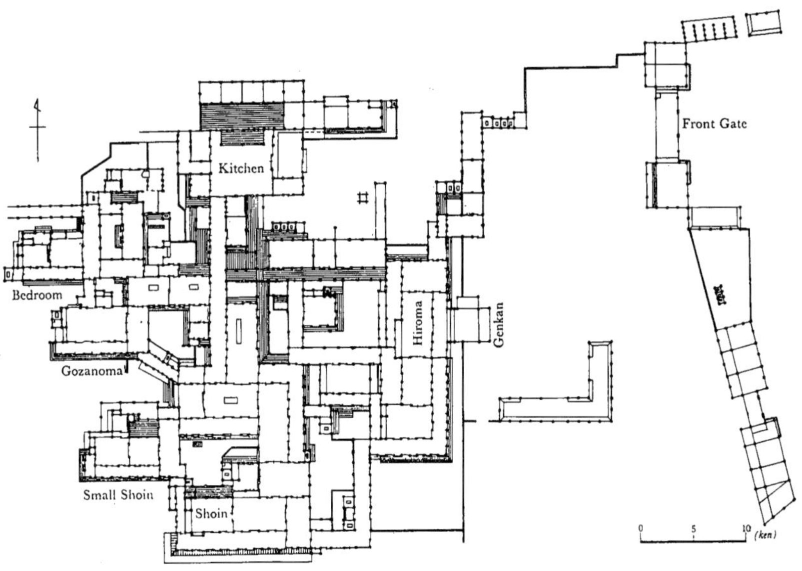

5.20.
Shoin Style Datè residence, Edo, 1658. Ground plan. From Kiyoshi Hirai, *Feudal Architecture of Japan*, 1973.

5.21.
University Library, Eichstatt, Germany, 1986. Interior of main circulation space. Architect and photo: Gunter Behnisch.

viewpoint. In place of a single, unitary concept and view, Sukiya and Shoin Style houses and gardens offer a series of sequential experiences whose spatial relations are invariably obscured by discontinuous or intervening events. The observer knows where he has been, but not where he is going. Japanese architecture offers up an incomplete world inviting participation. It exists as much in the observer's mind as it does in the designer's, whose work is meaningless without the other's involvement. All this, it may be noted, is achieved in building terms by the use of a basically simple rectangular module, the *tatami*, used in a loose and irregular fashion. Neither does Japanese architecture pretend to be all

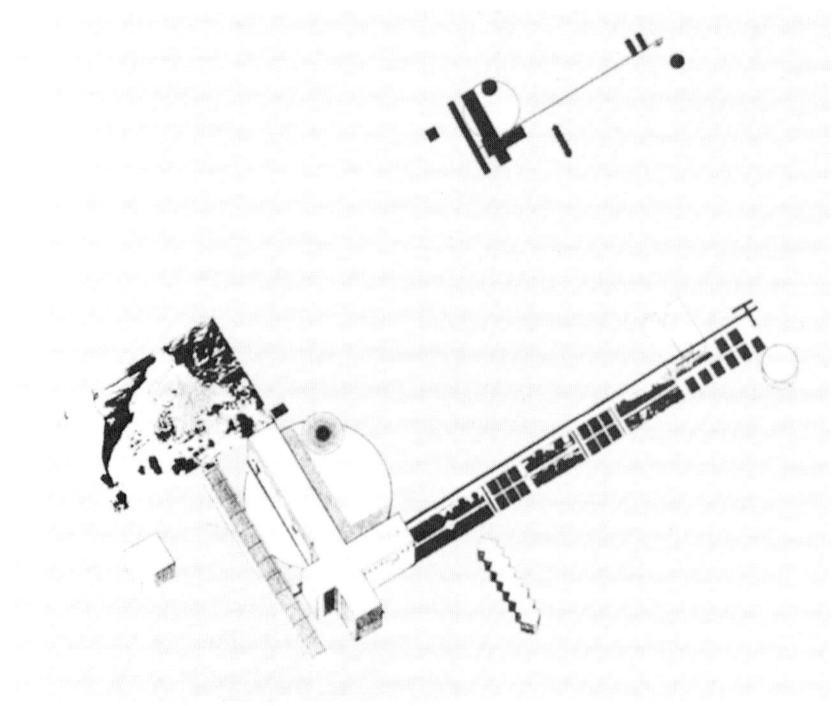

5.22.
Project for Sovkino Film Studios, 1927. Architect: Leonidove. From Catherine Cooke, 'The lessons of the Russian avant-garde' in *Deconstruction in Architecture*, 1988.

things to all men, nor succumb under the weight of its own intricate cosmology. Each building or garden offers a highly localized experience, so that the universal and particular coexist in subtle and complementary relations appropriate to the scale of the design.

Though Western Modernists were influenced by Japanese architecture, the decentred quality of Japanese space was lost on most of them, including Frank Lloyd Wright, who imposed his own hierarchical compositions and values, negating whatever qualities of openness he strove for. Hans Scharoun recaptured the idea of movement space for postwar Modernism, producing a series of complex sequential spaces which can only be appreciated by passing through them. Preferring non-orthogonal geometries, he also showed they required just as much, if not more, discipline and restraint as conventional forms. At the Berlin Philharmonie and later performance halls, Scharoun achieved in three dimensions what the Japanese had only achieved in a horizontal plane, creating stunning circulation spaces best experienced when full with perambulating concert goers.[56] More recently, Gunter Behnich has explored a similar approach,[57] exploiting a different and lighter technology to infuse his own equally vibrant and complex spaces with a transparent and layered quality even closer to the Japanese model.

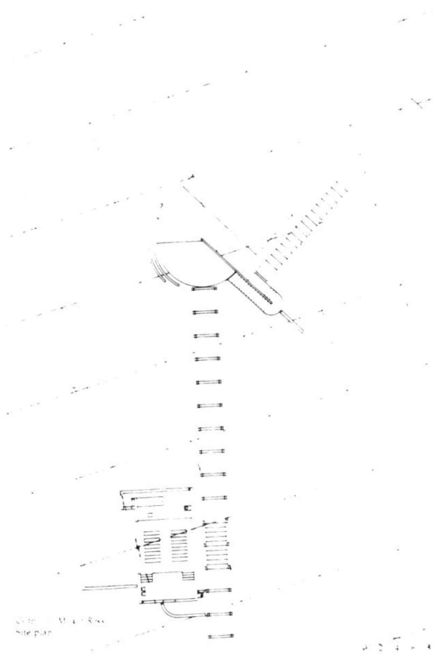

5.23.
Chapel on Mount Rokko, Kobe, 1986. Site layout. Architect: Tadao Ando. From *Tadao Ando*, 1990.

Where Scharoun's and Behniche's spaces represent a conceptual shift from West to East, Tadao Ando's work[58] represents an equivalent shift from East to West. While Ando's handling of movement space and his sensitivity to nature derive from Japanese traditions, his recent compositions bear a strong likeness to those produced by Russian Constructivists and Suprematists between the wars. Like Chernikhov, Leonidove or Malevich, Ando favours simple shapes arranged in a free fashion. The resultant complexity and dynamic quality in his work arises from the tension between the purity and simplicity of the rectangular and circular forms of the different elements, and their free juxtaposition and intersections, which often disrupt the simpler order. However, unlike those Deconstructionists or Deconstructivists who cite similar sources, Ando controls the fragmentation of elements in accord with the scale of his programme, and not least with the landscape, to which finally everything in his architecture answers.

Like the best work of other modern regionalists, Ando's architecture simultaneously reflects both the local space of nature and the global mind of human culture, of which the Internet and cyberspace are now a fast growing part. We have yet to see what kind of architectural dialogue might be produced out of a conjunction of all the technological, social and cultural developments described here (it is significant that Japanese movement space and cyberspace are topologically identical[59]). For the time being, however, Ando's simple shapes arranged in complex relations provide an appropriate metaphor for the changing world we now inhabit, and for the evolutionary processes which have made it the way it is.

6 THE BIO-TECH ARCHITECTURE WORKSHOP

First published under the title 'Networking the studio: architectural education and the virtual practice' in *Environments by Design*, Winter 1997/98.

Historical exceptions apart, architectural education continues to be mostly shaped by an elitist model of the architect as sole artistic creator of the work, isolated from the process of production and those involved in it.[1] For all the influence of the Bauhaus on Modernist ideology, Walter Gropius's call for the integration of architecture with industry had little actual impact on either teaching methods or the relation of architecture schools with the world beyond. Rather, it was another Bauhaus teacher, Johannes Itten, with his introspective methods and highly abstract foundation exercises, that eventually had the greater influence on design education, resulting in carbon copies of his renowned Basic Course throughout the world, irrespective of location or culture.[2]

As the sole postwar exception, the Hochschule für Gestaltung at Ulm made a brave but short-lived attempt to revive Gropius's original programme, teaching design students from all fields to master modern production methods and interdisciplinary skills before it, too, prematurely expired.[3] It was left to the American pioneers of industrial design, Walter Dorin Teague, Raymond Loewy, Henry Drefus, and Charles and Ray Eames, to forge the direct working links with industry the architectural and academic establishment failed to accomplish.[4] Significantly though, it was the Eames's own prefabricated house and studio in Santa Monica, rather than their mass-produced furniture designs, that most influenced architects' subsequent attitudes to industrialized technology. Made entirely from off-the-shelf components, practitioners and teachers alike saw in it a convenient rationale for leaving the hard business of component design and manufacture to others.

VALUABLE KNOWLEDGE LOST

The form and conduct of the typical design studio today encapsulates the architecture schools' still entrenched isolation. Once considered an exemplar of project teaching,[5] the studio is increasingly distanced from the real world it is intended to simulate. Teamwork of any kind, even amongst architecture students, let alone between students from different disciplines or professions, is rare. Technical knowledge is generally restricted to separate lectures on construction and materials and occasional advice on the same subjects in the studio. Understanding of contemporary production methods, either of materials or components, is practically zero. 'Architectural production' as such is confined instead to a final set of large-format drawings, usually hand-drawn and rendered or supplemented by CAD drawings, displayed on a wall at the final review together with physical models on neighbouring tables. Explanation of the design process and the reasons for the work are likewise limited to students' verbal presentations at interim or final reviews, infrequently supported by technical evidence. Often, the emphasis will be on the graphical quality of the drawings as art forms in themselves, at the expense of clarity of students' designs or intentions. The review process, or so-called 'jury', with its panel of familiar critics and sympathizers, will also be generally couched in a language that would be incomprehensible to other building professions, let alone to any client or lay person. All too often, visiting practitioners treat the event uncritically as a nostalgic return to their own student days, applying the same methods and criteria they were taught by. Quite aside from any other failings, the format severely restricts communication of the design to insiders only and is difficult to record or transport, with the result that valuable design knowledge and experience are lost each year.

NEW MODEL OF DESIGN EDUCATION

The antiquated format and closeted nature of architectural education contrasts with the necessarily open and collaborative nature of advanced architectural practice, now increasingly driven by computer-based technologies of production.[6] Many firms – not necessarily the largest – now work as a matter of course in close harmony with the engineers and fabricators who make the parts of the buildings they design, researching and developing each component to bring it up to the required performance.[7] Modes of architectural production are likewise increasingly designed to ensure continuous and effective co-operation amongst all the parties involved as the project develops and changes.[8]

The Design Research Studio (DRS) at the University of Nottingham School of Architecture was the first in a series of experimental design studios aimed at creating a new model of design education in keeping with advanced practice, and was purposefully invented to simulate such working and communicative features. Beginning in the spring of 1993 with an optional graduate programme in tropical architecture,[9] it differed from the conventional studio format in a number of ways. As with the Bauhaus and Ulm schools, process was emphasized as much as product. However, where the former schools equated process with rigid mass-production technologies and 'scientific methods',[10] the DRS equated process instead with open communication and flexible modes of production. From a fixed process and a universal architecture, the process–product equation was thus reversed in favour of an open-ended process and a specific architecture, adapted to place and purpose.

The main form of communication at this stage, which was also the main 'product', was likewise modelled, partly on contemporary practice, after the consultative document widely used by architectural firms like Sir Norman Foster and Partners and engineers Battle McCarthy. Photographically reduced drawings and explanatory text were combined in one convenient A4 (landscape) sized document, covering every stage of the design process, from brief and precedent studies, through concept sketches, trial models and technical studies, to the final design and component details.

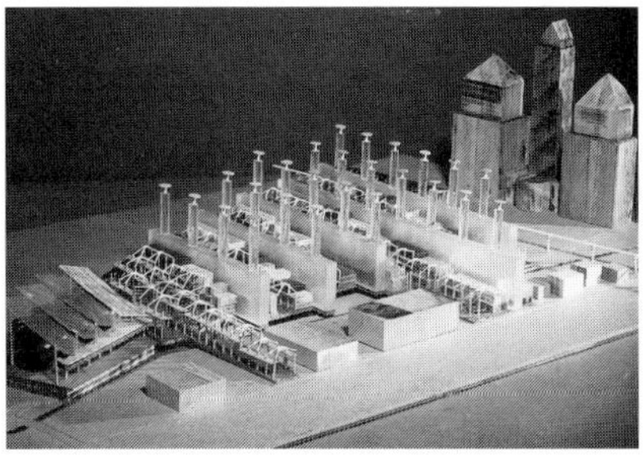

6.1.
Design Research Studio, Spring 1995. Project for Tropical Retail and Commercial Centre in Petaling Jaya, near Kuala Lumpur. Model showing ventilation towers over linear circulation cores. B. Arch students S. Forgan, M. Lucas, A. Wraight.

As with the professional version, the emphasis throughout is on clarity of communication, the aim being to present the research and thinking behind the solutions and to open participation in the design and production process to everyone involved. To this end, desktop publishing techniques were used wherever possible to achieve an attractive and professional quality result that could be readily comprehended by a wide and multidisciplinary group. The complexity of the projects and the heavy workload of research, design, and professional standard presentations, necessitated that all students work in small teams, thereby also simulating real-world practice.

In this way, a growing body of research and design expertise was accumulated and passed on to later students working on related projects, providing a valuable springboard for the next programme and so advancing the subject.[11] The graphical methods employed, which included simple explanatory diagrams for energy strategies and other aspects, also lend themselves readily to publication in both printed and electronic media, opening possibilities for the further distribution of knowledge. Above all, students acquired special experience in communications skills which have already proven their worth in their professional lives since.

The projects themselves were likewise purposefully designed to simulate actual conditions in the tropics and were all based on briefs supplied by leading local practitioners such as Hamzah and Yeang[12] in Kuala Lumpur, or by government agencies in Singapore.[13] As the programme developed, so the approach became more rigorous. Visiting staff included Ken Yeang, Chris McCarthy of Battle McCarthy and Brian Ford of Short, Ford Associates,[14] all low energy design experts with tropical experience. Research and energy strategies were refined for each building type and wind-tunnel tests were employed where possible to simulate the effect of natural air movements on scaled working models. Reports also became increasingly detailed and offered clearly recorded exemplars and working procedures for later students to learn from and to improve upon, similar to the way research papers function in other areas of knowledge (significantly, when shown to prospective students, these professional-looking reports, offering clear evidence of previous achievements, were often cited as a major reason for enrolling in the programme). The same reports also

6.2.
Design Research Studio, Spring 1996. Project for Secondary School in Singapore. Working model of adjustable sunscreen over classroom window bay. E. Babington, H. Weng.

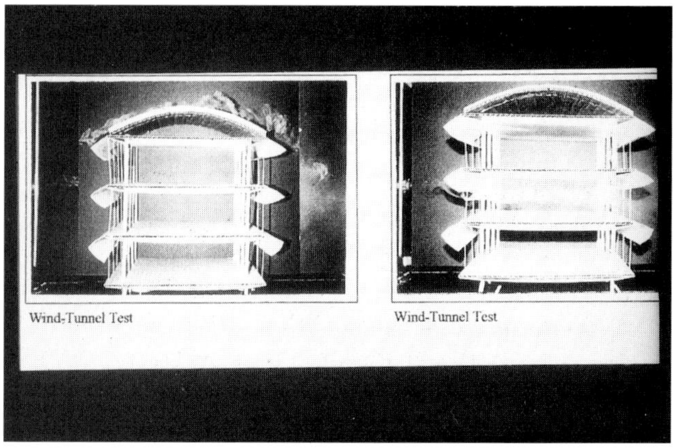

6.3.
Design Research Studio, Spring 1996. Wind-tunnel test simulating natural air movement through sectional model of classroom. E. Babington, H. Weng.

provided the material for project reviews, which consisted of slide presentations extracted from selected pages in the manner of professional presentations to clients and consultants, backed up by the full reports. The ultimate aim, as in practice, was that the report should be self-explanatory, and could be taken away and consulted by anyone after the live presentation without serious loss of information.

BIOLOGICAL PRINCIPLES

While a body of valuable design experience and communicative techniques was accumulated, the DRS still fell short of a realistic model of architectural production. In particular, prototype development and manufacture was limited to conventional models built to scale in simulated materials, usually wood and metal, which severely restricted testing. The reliability of wind-tunnel tests for low velocity air movements was also questionable and was unsuitable for simulating vertical 'stack effects', an essential technique for passive cooling in the tropics and elsewhere. The complexity of the projects itself also turned out to be a constraining factor, making it difficult to advance any further along the production process in the time available. CAD development was also restricted at this stage, as it generally is, to various techniques for visualizing solutions; in effect, limited to little more than a sophisticated drawing tool. It was realized that, in order to take the next step, an additional studio course was required where further development of design solutions and prototypes could be made, and more advanced computer-based techniques of production could be employed.

At the same time, underlying theoretical concepts were also being refined in concurrent lectures and seminars exploring new architectural paradigms and related disciplines.[15] A concept of 'Bio-Tech' architecture was defined which went beyond established concepts of a climatically responsive architecture to model the entire spectrum of a building's lifecycle – from initial conception through the use of flexible production systems to the recycling of building materials – on biological principles of adaptation to purpose and environment. In accordance with the same principles, design and production for the new 'living architecture' was to be based on advanced information technologies, using feedback from test simulations to achieve desired structural and environmental performance levels. Adaptable, computer-aided manufacturing systems were likewise to be employed wherever possible for machine fabrication of components, tailor-made to need.[16]

KEY FEATURES

The outcome of these deliberations was the 'Bio-Tech Architecture Workshop'©, which ran in the Winter term, 1996–97. Key features of the Workshop, which like the DRS on tropical architecture, was offered as an optional course in the graduate programme, included:

- Design solutions customized for place, purpose and climate.
- Full integration of design and production processes.
- Advanced information technologies at all stages of the project.
- Interdisciplinary teamwork involving close collaboration with other professions and practices both on and off campus.

- Virtual prototypes as well as working models which can be tested prior to final production.
- A transparent design and production process.

These basic features were continually elaborated in the course of the programme in the form of a succinct 'manifesto' (Appendices I and II), setting out what Bio-Tech architecture and the Workshop stood for, and, just as important, what they stood against.

In order to shorten project time and to reach the desired stage of advanced production, students were invited to take an existing or outline design project as their starting point, and to select some aspect or component of that design for further development. This, too, simulated current practice, where architectural firms now frequently subcontract out parts of a large or complex design project – be it a cladding system or some other part or subsystem – to another design firm with a proven expertise in the required area. Outline designs could be taken from either: a) a previous design studio, including, but not necessarily, the DRS on tropical architecture; or b) a design from an 'outside' source, i.e. a project already under development by an architectural office willing to collaborate.

As in the DRS, the students – many of whom had taken the previous course – grouped themselves into small teams according to mutual interests and project choice. After consultation, four projects were eventually chosen, three from London-based practices and one from a participating student's earlier project, each of which had a quite different character and research and development thrust. The three from practice consisted of: design development and structural frame for a mobile folding kiosk by Koski, Solomon and Ruthven; a multi-anchored structural node for a tensioned fabric roof by Ateliers One and Ten in collaboration with Eva Jiricna Architects; and environmental modelling for an atrium office building (then under construction) by EPR Architects. The student project selected was for an automated external sunscreen system, including an electronically operated model.

6.4.
Bio-Tech Architecture Workshop, Winter 1996–97. Design and prototype development of structural node for tensioned fabric roof. CAD model showing roof connections. S. Chew, P. Lee, W. Tsang.

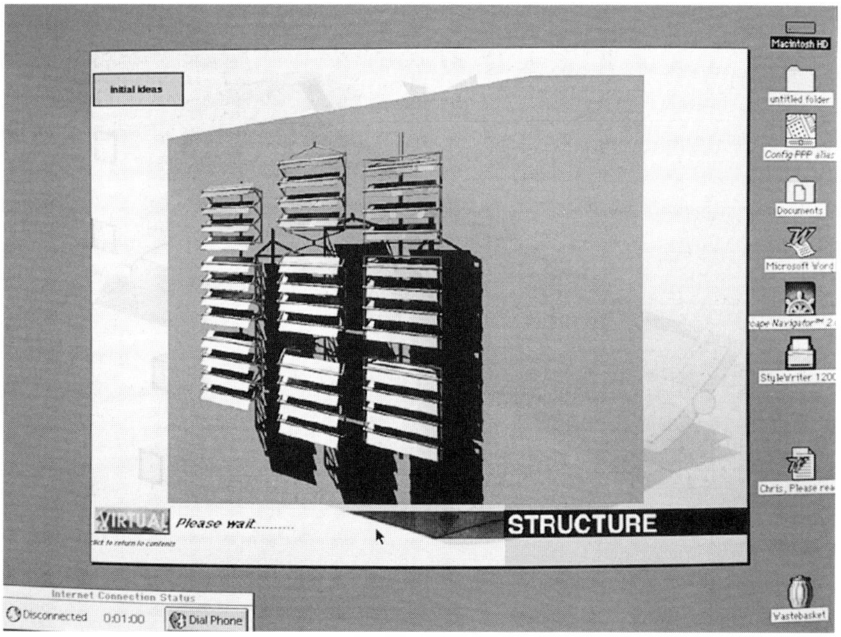

6.5.
Bio-Tech Architecture Workshop, Winter 1996–97. Automated external sunscreen system. Movement of 'heliotropic' louvres is controlled by light-sensitive resistors. Virtual reality sequence showing changing shadow effects behind. S. Bhavra, L. Ching, S. Hart.

Working links were also established with other departments at Nottingham University for prototype development. Under the guidance of staff at the Mechanical and Production Engineering and Civil Engineering Departments, advanced computer-based production and testing facilities were made available, including rapid prototyping (for all projects) and technologies for fabricating structures from composite materials (for the mobile kiosk).[17] Civil Engineering staff also lent the use of 'Fluent', their computational fluid dynamics (CFD) program, for environmental performance analysis of the atrium design. Specially developed to simulate both full range air velocities and temperature variations, the program provided dynamic and readily comprehensible visual evidence of changing conditions within the atrium space (a separate CFD programme was also used for stress analysis of the structural node). In addition, the Workshop was closely observed by a multidisciplinary team of researchers from the School of Social Studies examining collaborative practices. Other external links were forged as the Workshop progressed, notably with Andrew Hall of Ove Arup Partnership, who had previously lectured at Nottingham on advanced cladding systems, and who now lent guidance on the same subject.[18] Paul Craddock and Simon Cardwell, also of Ove Arup, advised students on structural node design and fabrication, while Martin Gunton of W.S. Atkins Engineering Software, shared his firm's experience with their own 'CFD 2000' program.

Development of computer skills and communication techniques, supported by linked teaching programmes,[19] progressed hand-in-hand with research and project development. A network-based, collaborative work pattern was established, with all the ingredients of the emergent 'virtual practice'.[20] Central to this evolution was the idea of the 'virtual prototype',[21] which was both the changing focus of design development, and also the main communications medium, shuttled between students and participating departments and architects, either directly on-line or on disk. A highlight of the Workshop was the changing shape on screen of a structural node, as students responded to the results of simulated

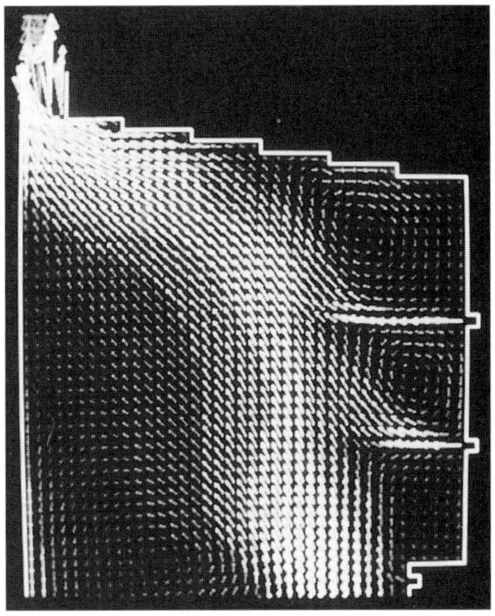

6.6.
Bio-Tech Architecture Workshop, Winter 1996–97. Computational Fluid Dynamics (CFD) modelling of atrium space simulates environmental performance. Different tones show temperature differences in upper air space under vented roof. Similar techniques are used to plot air velocities and other parameters. G. Barker, S. Taylor, A. Thornton.

6.7.
Bio-Tech Architecture Workshop, Winter 1996–97. Evolution of CAD models of node for tensioned roof, from early (top left) to final designs (bottom right). S. Chew, P. Lee, W. Tsang.

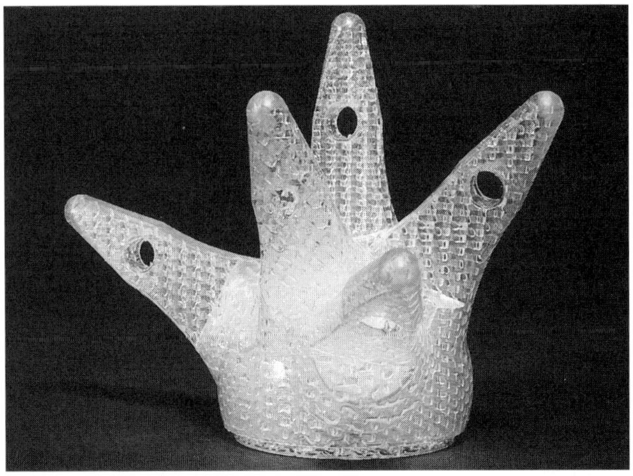

6.8.
Bio-Tech Architecture Workshop, Winter 1996–97. Part solid model of node made with rapid prototyping techniques direct from CAD model shown in Figure 6.7. S. Chew, P. Lee, W. Tsang.

stress analysis tests and advice from other departments and external consultants. Equally absorbing was the sight of a solid prototype emerging from a vat of liquid resin, built layer by layer by laser beam driven directly from students' CAD models. A continuous feedback cycle of design development and testing approximating to advanced practice was quickly achieved. Ideas would take shape on screen and would be tested in simulated real-world conditions, the results of which would then guide students in their next steps. Process and product effectively became indistinguishable. Most important was the tangible sense of engagement with the actual process of *making* architecture, which all students acclaimed, in a way which lent new meaning to the idea of a design 'studio'.

ANOTHER DIMENSION

The same criteria regarding clarity of presentation and full explanation of the design and production process as applied with the DRS also applied with the Workshop. However, in place of hard copy reports, projects were composed and recorded entirely on disk as the work progressed. One team worked from the outset directly onto the Architecture School's website, experimenting with multimedia techniques, including virtual reality, and sharing their experience with anyone with access to the Internet as they went along. Others later recorded their projects on additional web pages or else created their own compact disks. 'Point and click' was widely used to enable browsers to control the presentation and to steer their own path through alternative sequences, just as they would searching through any website. The aim in all cases was the creation of a convenient and accessible record of the work, which, if so desired, could fit into a pocket.

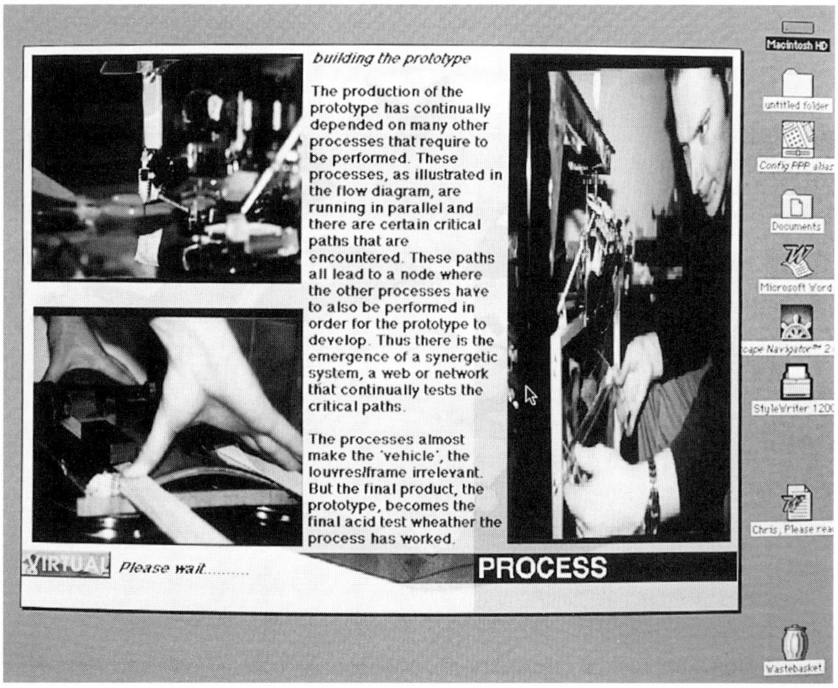

6.9.
Bio-Tech Architecture Workshop, Winter 1996–97. Page from multimedia presentation on project for automated sunscreen (see Figure 6.5) explaining production technologies used in working model. S. Bhavra, L. Ching, S. Hart.

Towards the end of the Workshop, all these developments received a boost following a demonstration by Nottingham University's Centre for Industrial and Medical Informatics (CIMI) of their 'Reality Centre', and its state-of-the-art virtual reality facilities.[22] Assisted by CIMI research staff and Director Farhang Daemi, students expanded their projects to include virtual reality sequences where they were not already included, or else elaborated existing sequences, adding another dimension to the Workshop.[23] CIMI also agreed to stage students' final presentations in the Reality Centre, using its triple projector wide screen. The effect of these professional standard, wholly computer-based and dynamic presentations, left a deep impression on the multidisciplinary review panel of University staff and participating architects.

FUTURE DEVELOPMENTS

Whilst all the production facilities used were situated on or close to the Nottingham campus, experience with the Bio-Tech Architecture Workshop suggests that physical proximity was not a primary factor in its success, no more than was the location of the architectural practices involved. As with advanced practice elsewhere, communications and software technologies effectively displaced the conventional idea of the design studio as the spatial focus of activity, replacing it with the virtual workplace and the virtual prototype. In some respects, as in the combined use of rapid prototyping and virtual reality technologies, students forged ahead of leading architectural firms. Limited as the projects were, the Workshop heralds the day when architecture students will be able to put their ideas through the full range of architectural production, simulating visual, functional, structural, environmental, and even economic properties – a much neglected aspect – as the design evolves, modifying them until such point as the required result is achieved.

Familiar distinctions between education and practice died a similar death in the course of the Workshop. Aside from rare examples of architecture schools running their own in-house practices, students' professional experience is normally separated from teaching and confined to the 'year out', or else brief periods snatched during vacations. By contrast, the role description that might be best applied to the Workshop students' relations with their London-based firms is 'on-line design consultants', albeit unpaid ones.

Both aspects, the use of research and production facilities and active engagement with practising architects on current projects, place special strains on normal university programmes and timetables, as well as on the various participating departments and firms. Flexibility – of both working habits and attitudes – is the key to success in these areas, no less than it is with the new modes of production themselves. Linking different courses together can also help, as happened between the DRS, the Workshop, and concurrent computer courses. Though the actual Workshop programmes were limited in focus, there is no reason why a full and complex building project could not be handled in its entirety with similar linkages between courses, backed up by co-ordinated student and staff teamwork. The availability of student-friendly software programs for computational fluid dynamics and similar applications would also facilitate similar exercises.

RADICAL SOLUTIONS REQUIRED

These are, however, only partial answers. Ultimately, more radical educational and administrative solutions will be required to bring architecture schools into line with cutting-edge practice. Most important, co-operative links with industry and practice need to be recognized, not as a restriction on creative freedom, as they often tend to be, but as a means of helping students and staff alike to master the skills which make such freedom possible. Most likely these will involve long-term research programmes requiring the sharing of both physical and human resources between campus and industry in joint research ventures, such as are typical in other fields. University-based research institutions have a special role to play in supporting such measures, with mutually beneficial results, as the Bio-Tech Architecture Workshop has already proven. Two students from the Workshop have since worked with CIMI, one of whom, now graduated, coordinates architectural applications as Development Manager.[24] Contacts already forged during the Workshop between CIMI and Ove Arup and other firms have also been pursued further, with concrete results.[25] A graduate programme in informatics is also planned, including optional programmes in the architecture and construction fields, to be run by CIMI in conjunction with its research and industrial activities. Developments such as these may eventually help to ensure that architecture graduates will be properly equipped throughout the whole gamut of interdisciplinary skills required of the Bio-Tech architecture of tomorrow.

Appendix I

WHAT IS BIO-TECH ARCHITECTURE?

Bio-Tech architecture is not a ***style****. It is a computer-centred* ***process*** *of architectural design, production and use.*

Bio-Tech architecture combines ***global technologies*** *with* ***local responses*** *to site and social conditions.*

Bio-Tech architecture is ***information****-based, not* ***form****-based. It does not prescribe what a building should look like, but how it should* ***behave****.*
Bio-Tech architecture uses ***smart technologies*** *to achieve a dynamic,* ***interactive relationship*** *between a building, its users and its environment. In the near future,* ***smart materials*** *will be used to help achieve the same result.*

Bio-Tech architecture aims for ***customized design*** *from the molecular level to the rooftop!*

Bio-Tech architecture is ***self-organizing****. It is not a fixed or final product, but is more like a* ***biological organism*** *which continuously learns about itself and its surroundings, adapting to changing conditions and improving its own performance.*

Diversity *is as important to Bio-Tech architecture as* ***bio-diversity*** *is to nature.*

Bio-Tech architectural design is a ***total design approach*** *with continuous feedback from the production process to the design process and vice versa.*

Bio-Tech architectural design is ***multidisciplinary*** *and* ***network-based****. It involves co-ordinating a number of* ***simultaneous dialogues*** *with different people in different locations using complementary skills, covering all aspects of design, production and use, including clients and future users wherever possible.*

The heart of the Bio-Tech design process is the ***virtual prototype****, which is both a design and communications medium. Used together with* ***rapid prototyping*** *and associated* ***virtual reality*** *technologies, Bio-Tech architecture actively encourages full and open* ***participation*** *in design.*

Bio-Tech architecture demands ***radical changes*** *in education and practice!*

Appendix II

THE BIO-TECH ARCHITECTURE WORKSHOP

The Bio-Tech Architecture Workshop was created in response to the ***isolation, complacency****,* ***and lack of vision*** *which governs architectectural education everywhere today.*

The Bio-Tech Architecture Workshop ***rejects*** *the architecture schools' continuing preoccupation with form and appearance, and the consequent* ***separation*** *of design from production and use.*

The Bio-Tech Architecture Workshop takes over where the Modern Movement left off! It ***accepts*** *the original Bauhaus programme of* ***integrating architecture, industry and product design****, but* ***rejects*** *the ideology of standardization and the rigid mass-production technologies which went with it.*

The Bio-Tech Architecture Workshop values and respects ***individual, social and cultural identities****. It teaches students in the use of* ***responsive technologies and flexible manufacturing systems*** *which can be used to customize buildings for place, purpose and climate.*

The Bio-Tech Architecture Workshop ***abhors*** *architectural elitism and the closed forms of communication and representation which have shaped architectural education this century. It favours* ***accessible design processes and forms of representation****. Workshop projects are developed as* ***multimedia presentations*** *on websites and CDs which are available to anyone who may be interested, architect or not.*

The Bio-Tech Architecture Workshop has no room for professional or academic divisions. It networks architecture students together with other professionals as well as practising designers in multidisciplinary ***virtual workplaces*** *which simulate* ***real-life working relationships****.*

PART TWO

CRITICAL THEORY

'. . . as human beings, we must inevitably see the universe from a centre lying within ourselves and speak about it in terms of a human language shaped by the exigencies of human intercourse. Any attempt rigorously to eliminate our human perspective from our picture of the world must lead to absurdity.'

Michael Polanyi, 1962

7 ARCHITECTURAL LANGUAGE GAMES

First published under the title 'The language analogy in architectural theory and criticism: some remarks in the light of Wittgenstein's linguistic relativism'. In *Architectural Association Quarterly*, December 1979.

In his book, *Morality and Architecture*, David Watkin[1] offers scathing criticism of early Modernists and their historians for failing to give proper due to the artistic traditions of architecture as a form of human creativity in its own right. Instead, he claims, they invariably interpreted architecture in terms of 'something else'; usually science and technology or political ideology.

To critics like Watkin, the fashionable language analogy no doubt seems like much the same kind of exercise. Given the naive scientism of early Modernists, it is easy to sympathize with Watkin's point of view. Nevertheless, science itself has moved on apace since Modernists first gave form to their ideas, and provides little comfort now to the sorts of architectural determinists targeted by Watkin.[2] It can also be argued that there is a right and proper place for interpreting architecture in 'other' terms, most especially in the terms of a language. The reason is that the language analogy, like the other forms of analogy Watkin condemns outright, serves a quite definite purpose in the critical discourse of architecture, and in the development of architectural knowledge. If that sounds like trying to have architecture both ways, 'as architecture', and as 'something else', then in a sense it is. The resolution of this apparent contradiction lies in understanding the epistemological function of analogy in generating new ideas and helping us to understand things we do not yet understand.

ANALOGICAL THINKING

Functions of analogy

First, it should be noted that when the language analogy is used in architectural discourse, a claim is generally being made, not that architecture *is* a language, but that in some important respects it is *like* a language. 'The language of architecture' is no more than a metaphor, or the name given to a specific relation by analogy between otherwise different ideas.[3] Architecture and language are therefore assumed to have at least some attributes in common, but by no means all.

Secondly, not all forms of analogy serve the same purpose. A poet such as T. S. Eliot, for example, is mostly concerned with the emotive potential of his metaphors, as the following evocative passage from *The Waste Land* shows:

Here is no water but only rock
Rock and no water and the sandy road
The road winding above among the mountains
Which are mountains of rock without water
If there were water we could stop and drink
Amongst the rock one cannot stop or think
Sweat is dry and feet are in the sand
If there were only water amongst the rock
Dead mountain mouth of carious teeth that cannot spit
Here one can neither stand nor lie nor sit
There is not even silence in the mountains
But dry sterile thunder without rain[4]

In a cogent analysis of the same passage Marcus Hester[5] draws attention to the line, 'Dead mountain mouth of carious teeth that cannot spit', in which Eliot's use of metaphor brilliantly suggests all the dryness and desolation of the preceding lines:

*The mouth cannot spit because, of course, the mouth of a skeleton, the 'dead mouth' with 'carious teeth' cannot spit. Not only does the metaphor suggest the dry mouth of a skeleton but the mouth of a man so thirsty that he is unable to spit...*to read these metaphors is to have the illusion that one is experiencing life[6] [my emphasis].

The scientist, by contrast, makes use of analogy in order to extend his or her knowledge of the world and is accordingly more interested in its innovative and explanatory powers. In his wide-ranging studies of creativity, Arthur Koestler[7] offers the discoveries of Johannes Kepler and Charles Darwin among other examples of the innovative function of analogy. Before Kepler, astronomy had been a purely descriptive geometry. But since the movement of the planets was observed to be both non-uniform and non-circular, Kepler had realized that other concepts were necessary in order to account for these irregularities. Kepler found his answer in an analogy which had haunted him already for twenty-five years and which he was to pursue till the end of his life:

The sun in the middle of the moving *stars, himself at rest and yet the source of motion carries the image of God the Father and Creator. He distributes his motive force through a medium which contains the moving bodies, even as the Father creates the Holy Ghost.*[8]

For all Kepler's skilful use of poetic expression, the idea of a 'motive force' – the force of gravity – functions in the passage mainly to explain hitherto mysterious events in nature, so introducing an entirely new way of thinking into an established science.

Something similar occurred in Darwin's mind when he sought to explain the apparent diversity of living species, and their peculiar fitness to their specific habitats. Like many Englishmen of his class, Darwin was familiar with domestic breeding practices. It came to him that there might be a parallel between the improvement of domestic breeds by selective mating and the evolution of species in the wild. The difficulty was that in the former case, humankind was the obvious agent of selection. But what was the natural agent? The breakthrough came with his second bold analogy, inspired by Thomas Malthus's theory of population control. If hardship could lead to the 'survival of the fittest' in the human population, then the same principle could also apply to nature at large: '...any being, if it vary ever so slightly in a manner profitable to itself...will have a better chance of survival, *and thus be naturally selected*'.[9]

In the two examples just quoted, both scientists extended their understanding of nature by the simple expedient of explaining some unexplained phenomena in the terms of an already familiar but previously unrelated idea or process. In both cases also, despite the odd sources of inspiration, the explanation was later found to be supported by empirical evidence.

Given the popular image of science, it might be thought that such examples as these are no more than colourful exceptions to an otherwise rational logic of induction, deduction and verification. On the contrary, like Koestler, a number of writers have suggested that the use of analogy in scientific discovery, as in other forms of innovation, is not so much the exception as the general rule.[10] Some have even gone so far as to suggest that argument by analogy, and not mathematical or logical ability, is the *sine qua non* of scientific success.[11]

Analogy in architecture

Much the same use is being made of the language analogy in architecture. Its primary purpose is to extend our knowledge of architecture as a form of culture. It may be argued, therefore, that far from being just a fad, the language analogy constitutes a perfectly legitimate and even rigorous method of enquiry into the nature of architecture.

Given the exploratory function of analogy, what kind of new knowledge of architecture can we expect the language analogy to provide us with? The choice of analogy itself gives us a good part of the answer. We select a particular analogy because we already have in mind a particular 'something' which needs explaining. Darwin needed to explain what it was that caused species to change and sometimes to disappear. His realization of the relevance of selective breeding techniques, was, therefore, no arbitrary act of cognition, but was prompted by those aspects of nature he sought to explain. Similarly, we have identified something in architecture in need of explanation, namely its function as a system of social communication. Having recently rediscovered the semantic dimension in architecture, we have also come to realize how little we understand of it. The realm of signification and meaning in architecture constitutes the unknown toward which the language analogy is addressed. In referring to architecture as a language, we embark upon a voyage of discovery into the unfamiliar territory of architectural meaning. Our familiarity with the known features of human language provides us with the chart with which to plot our course. Because language is familiar to us, because we have a rapidly growing body of knowledge expressly dealing with language as a communication system, with the way we attach certain meanings to certain signs, and with the rule systems governing the use of signs, we look to language as a model for those communicative processes in architecture we do not yet understand.[12]

A note of caution is advisable at this juncture. While it may be legitimate and even desirable to promote the use of creative analogical reasoning, it is also necessary to be aware of its limitations. Analogies have a way, as it were, of 'taking over' our perceptions, to the point where we begin to forget, if we are not careful, the differences between the two halves of the analogy and begin saying that architecture really *is* a language. It is just this kind of over-extension of analogical thinking that lies behind Watkin's complaint that the autonomy of architecture has been overridden. Nevertheless, if we do not wish to rest content with present knowledge, then such risks are unavoidable. Despite the hazards, there is simply no way of advancing knowledge other than by something like the process of analogy. The crucial question therefore centres, not on whether or not we should use analogies, but on the problem of the balance of analogical reasoning and criticism; how we use it, and how it relates to other forms of reasoning and criticism.

LINGUISTIC THEORY

Relativism

A primary issue in the use of the language analogy concerns the choice of architectural attributes involved. Which attributes are involved in turn depends very much on the theory of language being assumed. The selection of a suitable theory will be governed by matters relating both to the explanatory power of the theory and to our special interests in the subject of architecture. For our purposes, which centre, as we began, on the nature of architecture, we shall be less concerned, say, with the minutiae of semantic analysis favoured by semioticians, than with what linguistic theory can contribute to our understanding of the role of architecture as a culture-form[13] in its own right. More specifically, we shall be asking how linguistic relativism might help us to understand the role of architecture in the creation of social and cultural identities.

The introduction of relativism[14] into the study of language is mostly due to the work of two linguists writing in the first half of this century, Edward Sapir[15] and Benjamin Whorf.[16] The 'Sapir Whorf Hypothesis' stresses the link between thought and language and the unique way each distinct language thus shapes the language user's perception of events:

Human beings do not live in the objective world alone, nor alone in the world of social activity as ordinarily understood, but are very much at the mercy of the particular language which has become the medium of expression for their society. It is quite an illusion to imagine that one adjusts to reality essentially without the use of language and that language is merely an incidental means of solving specific problems of communication or reflection. The fact of the matter is that the real world *is to a large extent unconsciously built upon the language habits of the group [my emphasis]...We see and hear and otherwise experience very largely as we do because the language habits of our community predispose certain choices of interpretation.*[17]

Whorf provided much empirical evidence for the relativistic thesis with his studies of different language cultures. Principally, his work was concerned with the differences in world view between what he called the Standard Average European (SAE) languages, which all share a common cultural heritage, and the more esoteric North American Indian languages, notably the Hopi and the Navajo. Whorf's studies include fascinating material on differences in perception of even such basic measures of reality as time itself, as well as an endless variety of subtler shades of experience.[18]

Language games

It has been Ludwig Wittgenstein,[19] however, who, in his later work, has had the greatest influence in propagating the relativistic thesis of language. Wittgenstein argues that the links between words and meanings derive neither from any finite correspondence with objects (realism), nor from any shadowy 'inner meanings' (dualism), but always from their *use* in a particular social situation. For Wittgenstein, human language is purposeful: there are as many languages as there are customary forms of behaviour. Further, meaning varies according to the behavioural context in which words are used. The word 'fix', for example, may mean one thing to a handyman and quite another to a drug addict. This may seem obvious in relation to a single word, but seen in the context of a whole pattern of speech, such variations of meaning reflect distinctive subcultures, with their own internal dynamics.

Wittgenstein's theory of meaning gave a new twist to the notion of a linguistic rule. In linguistics, a rule of language conventionally refers to a grammatical rule. But in Wittgenstein's theory, 'rule' refers to the behavioural rules governing the use of language. Since meaning, according to Wittgenstein, is something which is always shared, the behavioural rules of language are also social in origin.

The key features of Wittgenstein's theory come together in his concept of a 'language game'.[20] To use a favourite example of his, the meaning of a chess piece is not given in any simple one-to-one relation between the name and the chess piece, nor even in its specific use. It is given by its relationship to the entire range of possible moves of all the chess pieces as governed by the social rules of the game of chess. Such meaning only makes sense so long as the players agree to abide by the rules of the game. To enter into any language game, therefore, is to enter into a tacit form of social contract governing the use of words in a particular context of human action. Unlike a sentence, a language game cannot therefore be analysed in terms of the rules of grammar alone, but must be analysed by reference to both kinds of rules, behavioural as well as grammatical.

Wittgenstein's theory stresses the relation of language use to the functions, codes of behaviour and modes of expression of specific forms of social interaction and culture. Pushed to its logical conclusion, the implication is that the 'language of religion', for example, expresses a practical 'form of life' in itself, and can be understood only from within, by reference to the rules and criteria of religion:

Assessment can occur within a linguistic frame, but the latter cannot itself be assessed. In adopting a religious form of life one's standards are transformed, what was once called failure may now be called success. Believer and unbeliever don't play the same game or appeal to the same criteria.[21]

Similar arguments may be made for other principal forms of culture and knowledge. History, myth, science, art and architecture are all given expression in one form or another by different forms of language. The commonsensical view would be that a primary language culture treats each of these pursuits in the same basic language. But, according to Wittgenstein's theory, each of these culture-forms constitutes a complex language game in itself, separate and distinct from other uses of the 'same' language.[22]

I shall call the view represented by this kind of argument the *strong thesis* of relativism. In summary, the strong thesis stresses the unique aspects of any language game. The validity of observations, the rightness or wrongness of a given statement; such matters are regarded as entirely relative to the standards and criteria of belief established by the specific rules of the game. Each language game therefore has its own integrity, its own style, and its own logic. Understanding of an individual's use of a particular game is achieved by a process similar to empathy. The observer adopts the criteria and outlook of the language user as his or her own and looks out at the world, so to speak, through the same linguistic spectacles.

Applied to architecture, the strong thesis of relativism results in conclusions much like those drawn by Watkin. Architecture is conceived as a language game all of its own, with its own independent language, traditions and aims. From this point of view, any attempt to present architecture as 'something else' is to deny the integrity of architecture and is in any case doomed to failure. Architecture can only be understood from within, according to the terms of its own criteria as established by the history of architecture.

Critical relativism

The strong thesis of relativism suffers, however, from a number of serious defects which need addressing. For one thing, if it were so that there were no shared criteria at all between language games, and that each game could only be understood within its own terms, then there would be no possibility of comparison or interaction between different language games. But Whorf was indeed able to make the world of the Hopi intelligible to English language users, even though their world is a very different one from that to which a member of the English-speaking community is accustomed. Significantly, Karl Popper[23] was drawn to make the same observation on the Hopi language when discussing problems of comparison between different scientific theories. The very possibility of comparison and explanation, states Popper, which Whorf himself never attempted to deny, suggests the existence of some shared criteria; sufficient at least to effect an understanding of the special qualities of the Hopi world.

Furthermore, if theology was also supposed to be a wholly autonomous language game, then Kepler would not have conceived of his new theory of planetary motion in the fashion that he did. The fact that both theology and astronomy belong to two very different realms of human discourse, each with its own modes of expression and criteria, did not prevent a meeting of ideas between the two. Moreover, the general role of analogy in innovation suggests that exchanges of ideas between quite different frames of reference or universes of discourse (what Koestler calls 'matrices of association') are not only common but are an integral feature of the creative process.

Finally, it can also be argued that it is logically impossible to talk of the uniqueness of one thing without reference to another, different thing. The very idea of relativism is itself dependent upon the possibility of making comparisons between different forms of culture. Such arguments lead us to a more tenable position which I shall call *critical relativism*. According to this position, while each language game may have its own rules and criteria, this does not prevent us from comparing one set of observations with the kind of observations that a very different language game allows us to make. We can acknowledge the existence of alternative worlds of reality, therefore, without necessarily falling into the objectivist trap of insisting on universal standards of measurement, with the consequence that one of those worlds or perhaps both might be 'false'. Each language game can be regarded as serving its own intrinsic purposes and has to be understood in those terms. But we can understand – indeed, *only* understand – what those criteria signify if we have a basis for comparison; that is, another language game with a different set of criteria.

Relative autonomy

I suggested at the outset that it might be possible to have architecture both ways: as 'architecture' and as 'something else'. It may seem peculiar that an analogy with something else, a language, should provide the occasion for focusing on the unique qualities and attributes of architecture. But the generality and explanatory power of Wittgenstein's theory of language is such that it allows us to extend the concept of a language game to the manifold ways in which we use language to give form and meaning to life. The relations between language and behaviour suggest that even within the same broad language-speaking community, differences in language use reflect significant differences in subcultures.

In sum, architecture is properly interpreted as a semi-autonomous language game, subject to its own rules and criteria, but also to influence from external sources. I stress the qualifier because, as we have noted, creativity in architecture, as in other realms of human activity, depends upon open interaction with other culture-forms. It does not necessarily follow, therefore, that architecture ought *only* to be assessed within its own terms as a form of artistic creativity (indeed, the very notion that architecture is mainly an art form is questionable). On the contrary, the only proper way of understanding architecture is to contrast it with a different form of life.

We can therefore consider three types of evaluation when dealing with different culture-forms or aspects of them. We can either evaluate a culture-form according to those rules and criteria established internally, in which case the subject in question, whether it be a behaviour, theory or artefact, is deemed successful or unsuccessful only according to internal criteria. Or we can question the rules and criteria which led to the behaviour, theory or product, in which case the only valid method of criticism is by reference to the external standards provided by one or more alternative world views, which may or may not coincide. These two methods may be distinguished from the third method of criticism by analogy described above, whereby a specific culture-form which is normally interpreted in the context of one set of rules and criteria is now interpreted in the context of another equally specific culture-form (the main difference between the second and third methods is that the second may involve partial analogies with a number of quite different sources of criteria, whereas the third method involves a complete substitution of one set of criteria by another). The function of the former two methods is purely critical, while the function of the third method by analogy is both critical and innovatory. The latter two methods – criticism by comparison of alternative world views and criticism by analogy – describe the two valid processes of interaction between culture-forms.

All three methods of evaluation together describe the major directions in which culture-forms evolve. However, there is a significant difference between the first method and the other two. The first method simply allows knowledge to increase within the terms of the existing rules and criteria of the culture-form. The other two, by initiating criticism of the rules and criteria of the culture-form itself, have a more radical effect on the evolution of knowledge. Changes in the rules and criteria of a culture-form brought about by critical comparison or analogy with other forms may eventually alter the internal logic of the form so much that it is no longer valid to regard it as the 'same game'.

As Watkin presents his position, the effect of restricting evaluation and criticism to the internal criteria of architecture, as defined by its own history (and its own historians), would be to exclude those more radical forms of criticism upon which the evolution of architectural knowledge, like that of any culture-form, normally depends. Put another way, if the criticism of architecture were confined to the terms and criteria of architecture as already established then we would effectively bring architecture to a grinding halt. Watkin's error therefore lies not in emphasizing the autonomy of architecture, which deserves respecting, but in narrowing the range of legitimate forms of critical discourse.

SYSTEMS OF BELIEF

Comparison of architectural languages

Up till this point I have dealt with architecture as though it were some kind of homogeneous form of culture, with no internal divisions. In so far as it can be regarded along with other major culture-forms as a distinct realm of human activity, then this is a reasonable assumption to make. Looked at more closely, however, the homogeneity of any culture-form rapidly breaks down. It is no more correct to regard architecture as a homogeneous form, than it is to regard religion in the same way. Just as religion takes many forms, so does architecture.

To return to the original analogy with language, what we find then, is a hierarchy of language games, with at least three levels. At the broadest level, we have what linguists usually refer to as language cultures. Such cultures are often, but not always, synonymous with specific geographical regions and national boundaries. They may also contain more than one recognizable language, where all the languages in the group share a common cultural background: Whorf's SAE languages, for example.[24] At this level, the differences between the way a Frenchman or a German looks at the world are less significant than the similarities in their outlooks due to their common European cultural heritage.

At the next level, we have those distinct language games which mark different culture-forms.[25] At this level, history, literature, science, religion, myth, art and architecture all have their own distinct cultural purposes, inner logic and criteria of evaluation. Though a scientist and an architect may both speak the English language, for all practical purposes, the way they use the language in their respective professional roles is very different. In most respects, despite acknowledged similarities in processes of innovation, the universe of discourse of the scientist is quite unlike that of the architect. It is, therefore, more accurate to think of each as 'speaking a different language'.[26]

At the third level, we meet those divisions within a culture-form which betoken yet another layer of differences. Such differences are most apparent in religion, where differences in the world views of a catholic or a protestant or different muslim sects can lead to open and violent conflict. Less obvious, but no less real, are the divisions between theoretical positions in science, most marked in the human sciences, where there is less consensus about fundamentals than in, say, physics.[27]

Internal divisions within architecture also arise out of differences in values and modes of expression. My contention is that different forms of architecture are properly evaluated in the same manner in which we would evaluate any language game with its own aims and internal logic. The three types of valid criticism of language games we have identified, therefore, also apply to the criticism of works of architecture. First, we can criticize a building according to those criteria of evaluation established internally to the form of architecture adopted. Secondly, we can criticize the approach itself by applying external rules and criteria drawn from various other sources. Or thirdly, we can adopt the method of criticism by analogy, applying the specific rules and criteria belonging to another, equally distinctive, form.

Partisan criticism

Given these three methods of valid criticism, we can also more properly evaluate particular criticisms made of different works and approaches or even theoretical movements. Though the following discussion is focused on two specific approaches, the method of criticism and evaluation employed is equally applicable to other forms of architecture.

A number of writers have contrasted the classical tradition with the organic tradition as two of the most enduring forms of architecture, with the classical tradition usually coming off second best. Both Bruno Zevi[28] and Peter Blundell Jones,[29] for example, make no attempt to disguise their personal preference for an organic architecture. For them, classical architecture represents an obsession with ideal form at the expense of function, universal standards at the expense of the particular characteristics of site and client, rationality at the expense of human intuition and emotion. Organic architecture, on the other hand, represents a more responsive architecture: responsive to function, to the identity of client, place and region, to climate, and to the non-rational side of human nature.

I believe that this kind of partisan criticism, though perfectly normal to the theoretical discourse of opposing theories, misrepresents the essential character of both traditions.[30] Classical and organic architecture each embody quite different, though complementary systems of values, both of which represent equally valid and important aspects of the human condition. While it may be desirable to support architecture with an ecological, regional, or populist emphasis, there has always been a place in architecture for reverence of the ideal, both as a measure of

7.1.
National Gallery, Berlin, 1968. Architect: Mies van der Rohe. Photo: Reinhard Friedrich.

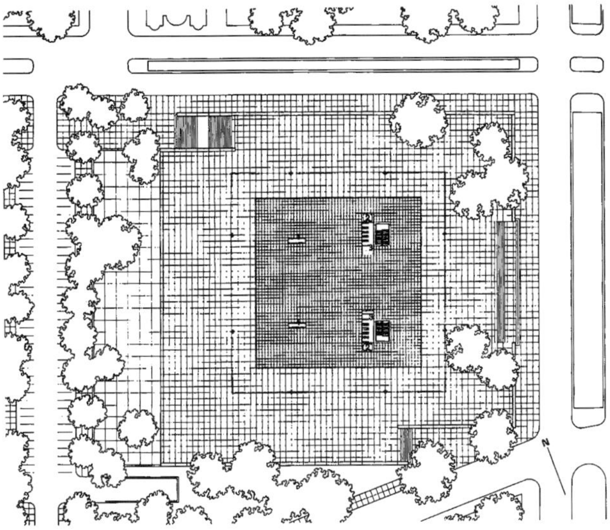

7.2a.
National Gallery, Berlin. Plan at podium level. Architect: Mies van der Rohe. From Kuhne, 1969.

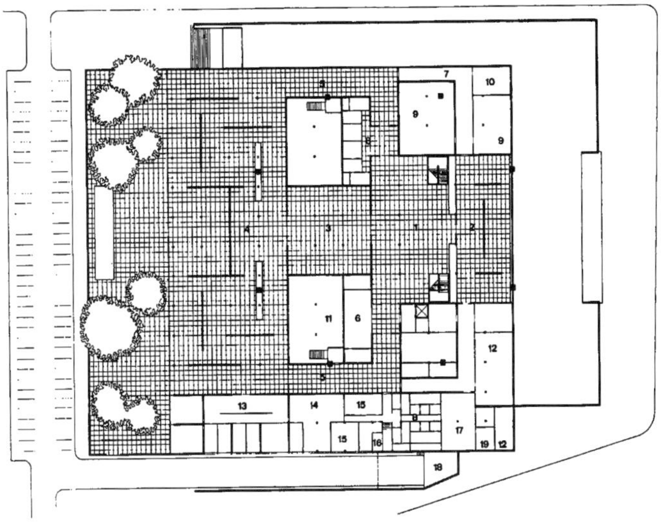

7.2b.
National Gallery, Berlin. Lower ground floor plan. Architect: Mies van der Rohe. From Kuhne, 1969.

7.3.
National Gallery, Berlin. General view with Hans Scharoun's Berlin Philharmonie in the background. Architect: Mies van der Rohe. Photo: Reinhard Friedrich.

present conditions and as something to aspire to.[31] It can, therefore, be argued that the classical ideal is no less a legitimate source of architectural inspiration than that which is particular to a place and a people.

Classical architecture, like organic architecture, obeys its own logic and meets its own criteria. As such it needs to be evaluated in its own terms as well as by reference to any external criteria. However, this has not generally been the case. Mies van der Rohe's New National Gallery in Berlin has suffered more than most works of architecture in this respect, and offers a good example of the application of criteria of evaluation which have nothing to do with the intrinsic purposes of the work itself. Jones[32] condemned Mies's National Gallery on several grounds. First, according to Jones, the building does not function very well. This criticism appears to be largely based on the fact that the fully glazed upstairs gallery, which receives abundant natural light, provides only for temporary exhibitions. The permanent collection of paintings is actually housed in the 'basement', or lower podium, and has to be artificially lit. Secondly, Jones argues that the building does not express its function. As is well known, the design was first conceived for the Bacardi Corporation Headquarters in Cuba in the 1950s. Mies lost this first project to the Cuban Revolution and had to wait another ten years before he found an opportunity to use his design again. The same design has therefore been used for totally different building functions and has evidently been conceived irrespective of any particular purpose. Thirdly, for all Mies's touting of the different uses to which his 'universal' spaces may be put, flexibility is limited. In particular, Mies made no provision for future expansion.

7.4.
National Gallery, Berlin. Detail of column, compared with Ionic column. Architect: Mies van der Rohe. From David Spaeth, *Mies van der Rohe*, 1985

Given Jones's confessed predilection for organic architecture, such criticisms are hardly surprising. In effect, what Jones has done is to evaluate the National Gallery solely according to those criteria which are special to the organic tradition of architecture. Inevitably, a classical or neo-classical building measured exclusively in the terms of an organic architecture is going to come out as a 'failed' building. True, Jones does concede, rather grudgingly, that Mies's building 'does exert a strong fascination for most of us'.[33] But in his estimation, the price we pay for this aesthetic pleasure is too high to justify the building's failings.

However, if we look at the National Gallery from another point of view, namely as a work of architecture within the classical tradition – albeit a very modern interpretation – then we arrive at a quite different conclusion. For one thing, Jones's criticism that the building does not express its function is completely irrelevant to that tradition. We enjoy a classical or neo-classical building for its purity of form, not for its faithful expression of whatever goes on inside of it. The expressive function of a classical building is of an altogether different order to that of an organic building, and needs to be evaluated by completely different criteria. Furthermore, in criticizing the building for not providing sufficient natural light to illuminate the permanent collection, Jones ignores the fact that many art galleries are purposefully designed on the principle that artificial light is preferable to natural light. The argument is that artificial light affords greater control over internal conditions and also protection from the more harmful effects of the sun's rays on fragile works of art. Jones's preference for natural light cannot, therefore, be justified solely as a functional criticism, but derives from a tacit rule of organic design which states that a building should make the most of the available natural resources, which include natural light.

Jones's other major functional criticism, that the building cannot be expanded, is perhaps the most serious criticism that might be levelled at the building as an art gallery. But before condemning the building on these grounds, we need to ask why Mies actually chose a finite form. The answer again derives from those criteria which are special to the classical tradition of architecture. An ideal building cannot be seen to be incomplete, but must on the contrary express completeness and perfection. As a classical design – in the city of Shinkel, moreover – Mies's choice of form was absolutely correct. There could be no more complete

7.5.
Berlin Philharmonie, 1964. Auditorium. Architect: Hans Scharoun. Photo: Dennis Gilbert.

form than the square steel structure Mies created. Standing solidly on its podium, the building is the ultimate statement of finality. While this sense of completeness has undoubtedly been bought at the price of future expansion (it is not clear if expansion was ever part of the original brief), we have to ask ourselves what is most important to the building in this case? If we apply classical criteria rather than the 'borrowed' criteria of organic architecture, then we must conclude that the building's evident success as an expression of ideal form far outweighs any functional criticisms that can be brought to bear against it.

Different worlds of reality

Where Watkin errs in excluding criticism by analogy as a legitimate form of critical discourse, Jones errs in the other direction by limiting such discourse to criticism by analogy only. In both cases the quality of the criticism suffers from the resulting imbalance. By criticizing Mies's National Gallery in terms more appropriate to a different form of architecture, Jones overplays his hand to the point where he is unable to appreciate the merits of the building for what it is, a splendid 'latter day temple',[34] inexpressive of any specific function but virtually timeless in its aesthetic appeal as a monumental work of architecture.

The 'language of classical architecture' therefore differs in fundamental respects from the 'language of organic architecture'.[35] When we make use of one language we 'play a different game' than when we use the other. No better demonstration of the contrast between these two languages can be found than by the experience involved in walking the few yards from the National Gallery to Hans Scharoun's Berlin Philharmonie, just down the road. To enter Scharoun's concert hall after being in Mies's building is quite literally to cross between different worlds of reality. All the criteria which were applicable to the National

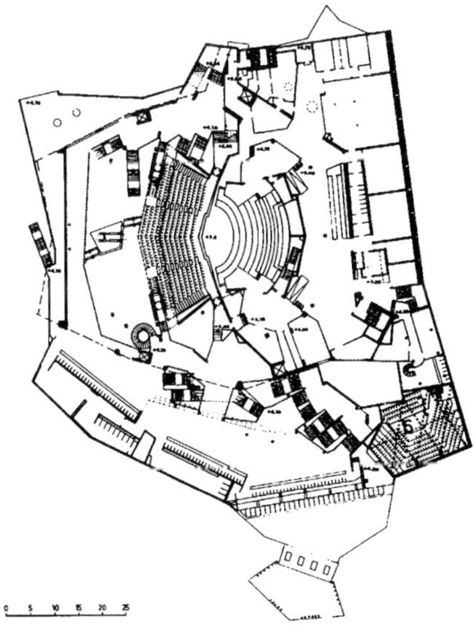

7.6.
Berlin Philharmonie. Plan at main foyer level. Architect: Hans Scharoun. From Jones, 1978.

7.7.
Berlin Philharmonie. Exterior view towards entrance. Architect: Hans Scharoun. Photo: Dennis Gilbert.

7.8.
Berlin Philharmonie. Main foyer space. Architect: Hans Scharoun. Photo: Reinhard Friedrich.

Gallery are now stood on their head. Where Mies's architecture is best appreciated from outside, in the round, Scharoun's has little appeal as an object, and is appreciated mainly from the interior. Where the vast space enclosed by Mies's steel superstructure is undifferentiated and bears no relation to function, Scharoun's spaces are extremely complex, each saying something unique about the nature of the enclosed activity. Where one interior can be appreciated from a static viewpoint, the other must be fully experienced in movement. And so it goes on.

Each building is a masterpiece of its kind. But, whereas Jones offers the buildings of Scharoun[36] and other architects of the organic school as demonstrations of how buildings *ought to be* in the typically prescriptive manner of architectural theorists and critics, the comparison of the two buildings is offered here as a paradigmatic lesson in the comparison of architectural traditions – different language games. As masterpieces of each tradition, each building offers a measure of the other, not in the same terms or criteria of evaluation, but in the terms of a comparison of *different systems of belief.* When we compare one building with the other, we compare distinct languages, each with its own rules and internal logic, each offering a quite different interpretation of reality. We do not just compare building with building, therefore, but ideas with ideas, and values with values.

ADDENDUM

Since the above chapter was originally written, a number of writers have criticized the usefulness of metaphor and analogy as a way of understanding architecture. Though these criticisms are usually directed against the uses of linguistic analogy in architecture, they imply a more general confusion regarding the nature and functions of analogy, particularly in the generation of new ideas.

Much of the confusion arises from an apparent lack of understanding or acknowledgement of the tripartite character of analogies. As Ian Barbour[37] explains, all analogies are composed of three parts. The *positive* analogy refers to those attributes which are clearly shared in common between the two separate ideas referred to in the analogy. The *negative* analogy refers to those attributes which are clearly not shared in common and so describes the differences between the two ideas. The *neutral* analogy refers to those as yet unspecified attributes of each separate idea which belong as yet to neither the positive nor negative analogies, but might at some time in the future be identified one way or the other. It is the neutral analogy that provides the source for the discovery of both new similarities and new differences and so fuels the extension of analogies.

Critics of the language analogy in architecture invariably assume a literal interpretation; that is, they assume that what is meant by the analogy amounts to the statement that architecture *is* a language.[38] In so far as some theorists may use the analogy in a literal fashion, such critics may be right in pointing out that a literal interpretation is untenable. Clearly, there are significant differences between architecture as a form of communication and symbolic system and the form of spoken language. Other critics take a different position and treat the analogy between architecture and language as a 'heuristic device',[39] or as a temporary aid to theory building; what Barbour calls a 'useful fiction', helpful in the initial stages of enquiry but something to be dispensed with as soon as a 'proper' representation of the subject of investigation is arrived at.

Neither of these common criticisms is able to account for key uses of analogy. The treatment of analogies as literal statements of reality ignores their creative role in the innovation of ideas as described in the above essay. The treatment of analogies as useful fictions cannot account for their persistent function in the extension of existing theories and denies the key role of the neutral analogy as a source for the discovery of new similarities and differences.[40] While not all analogies are guaranteed to be useful, many seem to thrive on longevity and continue to generate new ideas and new discoveries.

This is so even in the most rigorous proving grounds for new ideas, such as the basic sciences. In physical science the concept of a force[41] and the mechanical analogy[42] have long histories. The 'billiard ball model' of a gas[43] and the concept of the virus as a micro-organism in pathology[44] are two more examples of the staying power of analogies in science. In architecture, the biological analogy[45] dates back to the middle of the eighteenth century, as does the linguistic analogy,[46] both of which are still thriving and, if anything, enjoying increasing influence. In all these cases, the use of the analogy involves a process of discovery in which the unfamiliar subject under investigation is at least partially explained in terms of the known attributes of the familiar idea.

The temptation to take analogies either literally or else as useful fictions is of course always with us. But it is not necessary to do so, and interpreting the use of any form of analogy in either fashion obscures its real creative function both in the process of discovery and in the extension of theory. We might therefore well heed Barbour's advice and take analogies *seriously*, but not *literally*.

8 ROLE OF METAPHOR IN CHANGING ARCHITECTURAL CONCEPTS

First published in B. Evans, J. Powell and R. Talbot (eds). *Changing Design*, John Wiley & Sons, 1982.

When we speak of changes in the relations between people and their environment, we refer implicitly to changes in our conception of those relations. This view is, of course, premised on something like a Kantian notion of the active role of humankind in the mental construction of events.[1] But if we accept the intermediary function of concepts or mental categories in human action, then all forms of human change boil down to changes of ideas, which are in turn mediated by the form of the language in which ideas are expressed. Metaphor plays a central role in this process, with architectural concepts no less than with other kinds of ideas. Understanding the role of metaphor in changing concepts can therefore help us to better appreciate the nature of architectural creativity, and perhaps also teach us how to generate more positive forms of change than we have been accustomed to seeing in recent times.

DEFINITIONS OF METAPHOR

There are many uses and definitions of metaphor, but the most common derive from Aristotle, who stresses the cognitive transfer involved between concepts related by analogy:

Metaphor consists in giving a thing a name that belongs to something else; the transference being either from genus to species, or from species to genus, or from species to species, or on grounds of analogy...That from analogy is possible whenever there are four terms so related that the second (B) is to the first (A) as the fourth (D) is to the third (C), for one may then metaphorically put D in lieu of B and B in lieu of D.[2]

But there is another side to Aristotle's thought. Aristotle also says: 'Metaphor, moreover gives style, clearness, charm and distinction as nothing else can: and it is not a thing whose use can be taught by one man to another.'[3] Writing on poetic metaphor, Marcus Hester[4] argues that this view of metaphor differs radically from the view of metaphor as analogy and amounts to something of an inconsistency in Aristotle's thought. It suggests instead that metaphor is essentially a decoration or ornament to enliven style. This so-called *ornamental* view therefore emphasizes, in contradiction to the analogical or *rational* view, the non-cognitive function of metaphor.

Other definitions mostly fall within one or the other of these main viewpoints, or else lie somewhere in between the poles established by the two extreme cases. We have then a dimension of meanings attached to the various uses of metaphor, ranging from the ornamental view at one end to the rational view at the other. For example, D. Berggren[5] analyses several types of metaphor, each of which lies at a different point along a similar spectrum. First, the 'structural' metaphor involves an abstract relation of structures by analogy and therefore lies towards the rational end of the spectrum. Secondly, there is the 'textural' metaphor, based on an emotional intuition of similarity or disparity between concepts, usually involving an indirect association of images conveyed through words. This use of metaphor gravitates towards the ornamental definition. Thirdly, the 'isolated pictorial' metaphor involves, as the name suggests, a direct association between different visual images and falls somewhere between the two poles, since it comprises both objective and emotional components. The three types in turn appeal to intellectual, poetic and visual sensitivities.

METAPHOR IN ARCHITECTURAL CRITICISM

We can identify similar distinct uses of metaphor in architectural criticism, which is often heavily reliant on metaphor both as a form of expression and a tool of analysis. The textural metaphor, for example, is put to similar uses as in other forms of writing, particularly poetry, where the intent is to make full use of the emotional responses that words can arouse, so as to enrich the description of a building.

The writings of Vincent Scully provide many good examples of this type of metaphor. Describing Frank Lloyd Wright's Unitarian Church, Scully writes:

So his Unitarian Church at Madison, Wisconsin, of 1947, is both plow and ship, hitting into the prairie like something moving forward. Its choir is raised up behind the glass and under the 'praying hands' of the roof, like the suspended pulpit, reached by a rope ladder drawn up behind, in which Melville's New Bedford parson preached of whales.[6]

The reference to Herman Melville's book, *Moby Dick*, underscores the literary, i.e. non-literal and non-scientific use to which Scully puts language so effectively in arousing such powerful images in the mind of the reader. Does it help us to understand Wright's creation better though? Possibly. It certainly helps us to enjoy it all the more, even if Wright never read Melville. The same lyrical use of metaphor characterizes Scully's eloquent but biased comparison of Antoni Gaudi's Casa Milá with Erich Mendelsohn's Einstein Tower:

The Casa Milla, both in plan and elevation, is like a sea hollowed cliff, its rock-cut façade water-smoothed and eroded, hung with metal seaweed, and dug with windows like eyes. The whole 'roles around' like Wordsworth's early 19th century image or a late painting by Van Gogh. It seems to embody a total human participation in the rhythms that infuse the natural world. That is why the strange gods that crowd

8.1.
Unitarian Church, Madison, Wisconsin, 1947. Architect: Frank Lloyd Wright. Photo: Ezra Stoller ©.

8.2.
Casa Milá, Barcelona, 1906–10. Architect: Antoni Gaudi. Photo: Glyn Halls.

8.3.
Einstein Tower, Potsdam, 1917–21. Architect's sketch. Architect: Erich Mendelsohn. From Whittick, 1940.

the roof of Gaudi's sea formed acropolis enjoy such an eerie life. They come, as icons and guardsmen, from somewhere underneath – hollow, plated and helmeted – and take their places above and beside broken stairs. This is also why Gaudi's is a convincingly Expressionist architecture, in its own way a forerunner of Surrealist sculpture and painting (like that of Picasso, another Catalan) and why later 'Expressionist' buildings, like Mendelsohn's Einstein Tower, tend to be less convincing. The latter is mechanically streamlined, but is not moving and therefore, means nothing, but Gaudi's forms, like the best of Art Nouveau as a whole, are infused with the action of nature and are therefore somehow real.[7]

In this case, such is Scully's enthusiasm for Gaudi's power of expression that he allows it to affect his judgement of Mendelsohn's work. Simply because the Einstein Tower is not actually moving does not necessarily imply that the streamlined design is without meaning – Wright's Unitarian Church is also stationary but that did not prevent Scully from likening it to a ship. For other writers, the Einstein Tower succeeds very well in conveying a powerful image of the Mechanical Age.[8] But in Scully's view Mendelsohn's work fails to capture the imagination or engage our feelings in the way that Gaudi's work does and he makes skilful use of metaphor in persuading us of that view.

Other critics have made equally skilled use of structural metaphors in arguing their case. The stimulus here has often been the use of communication models derived from the more general field of semiotics. While such models have generated much theoretical discussion and many elaborations of the models themselves, there is a notable lack of application of the concepts to the analysis of real buildings. Charles Jencks's critique of James Stirling's New Training Centre for Olivetti in Hampshire, England, is one of the few exceptions.[9]

Stirling's design consists of a new building connected directly to a former country house. The new building consists essentially of four distinct units: two wings constructed of plastic panels, one plastic box-like element with cruciform clerestories, and a flared glass and steel link with the old building. The contrast between the old and new buildings emphasizes Stirling's unconventional use of form and materials and it is the plastic wings, as the most unusual elements, on which Jencks focuses his analysis.

Jencks detects a number of metaphors in the varied responses to the design, each metaphor conjuring up a distinct image in the mind, reflecting either positive or negative reactions. If the reaction is positive, Jencks suggests, the metaphor might imply a semantic chain along the following lines: 'The wings look like a train or a bus made from curved plastic or metal, the definition of which (a vehicle to move people fast) is appropriate to the building by association with the 1930s notions of "futurism" and the "machine aesthetic".'[10] Another positive metaphor might run as follows: 'The wings look like an Olivetti machine made from curved plastic with clipped joints, the definition of which (an operative, miniaturized instrument) is appropriate to the building because it is for training Olivetti salesmen and technicians and because these machines connote "contemporaneity", "modernity", etc.'[11] Not

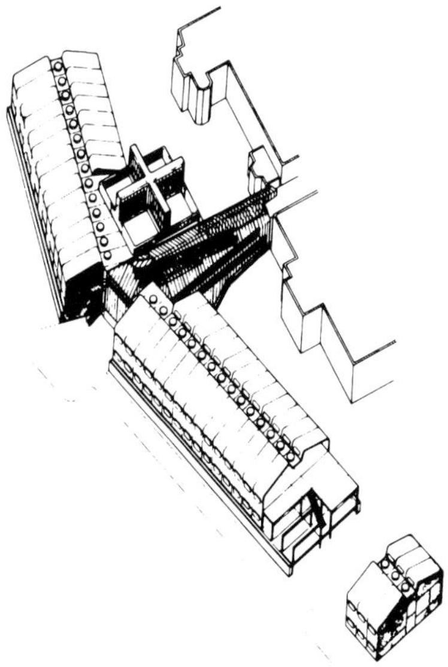

8.4.
New Training Centre for Olivetti, Hampshire, 1969–72. Axonometric. Architect: James Stirling. From Arnell and Bickford (eds), *James Stirling*, The Architectural Press, 1984.

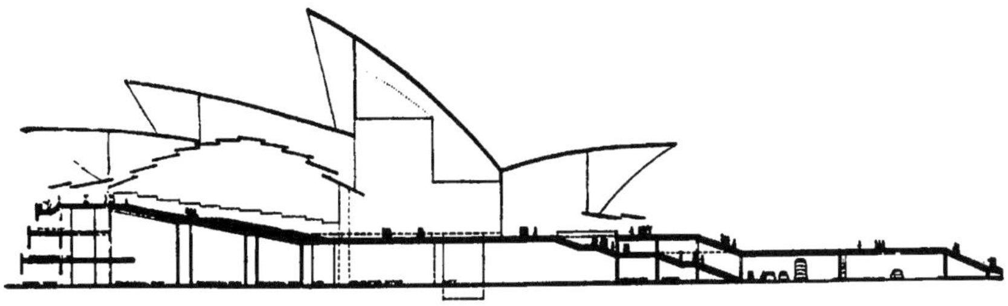

8.5.

8.6.

surprisingly, Jencks observes, it is the last metaphor which the architect intended people to see.

Other, more negative interpretations were recorded by Jencks in several lectures and interviews. The most negative of all involved seeing the classroom wing as a series of stacked, plastic trash-cans. This reading is guided not only by the context and sub-signs (the windows pivot like lids for refuse) but also by what Jencks calls the 'sub-code' of the viewer, arising from personal experience. For example, one person interviewed, who lived in a traditional Regency house and disliked the idea of a plastic building attached to an Edwardian mansion, immediately saw the wing this way as a caravan, even before Jencks had asked what it looked like. Other people, perhaps politically motivated or just sceptical of Olivetti's cultural salesmanship, also saw it in similar terms. The implicit value guiding these interpretations was that the wing (or metaphor) was banal and grubby or *petit bourgeois* and sprawling like a park for mobile homes.

Jencks's aim is to demonstrate that architectural metaphors work in coherent ways and that architects might profit from taking responsibility for how people see their buildings. A laudible recommendation, if hard to achieve. However, we might also note in passing that Jencks did not comment on what seems to be the most significant element in accounting for the differences between positive and negative metaphors. From the knowing words and phrases used, it is apparent that the positive metaphors are all generated by a special knowledge of the history and theory of architectural design, while the negative metaphors are equally evidenced by a lack of knowledge of such. Jencks does not mention the occupation of his interviewees and other commentators, but it would be interesting to know.[12]

The third type of metaphor, the isolated pictorial, is also common to architectural description and criticism and may be the easiest for architects and others to comprehend, since it is reliant on direct visual communication. Buildings like Eero Saarinen's TWA airport terminal (a bird in flight) and Jorn Utzon's Sydney Opera House[13] (a sailboat) readily spring to mind, both of which quickly found their way into public consciousness as well as critical approval via the readily comprehensible images they communicate. Elsewhere Jencks[14] also offers a number of pictorial metaphors which students have attached to the Sydney Opera House and other familiar Modern works. These witty illustrations speak for themselves.

8.5.
Sydney Opera House, 1957. Section through original design. Architect: Jorn Utzon. From *The Builder*, March 1957.

8.6.
Sketch of a Japanese house by Jorn Utzon. From Giedion, 1967.

DYNAMIC AND CREATIVE ROLE OF METAPHOR

It is evident from the above that the role of metaphor in conveying meaning in architecture has been acknowledged, either implicitly, as in the architectural criticism of the past, or explicitly, as in more recent semiotic theories of architecture. What, then, might be missing from the interpretations discussed so far? Namely its most important aspect: the creative role of metaphor in changing and bringing about new ideas. Stressing the dynamic character of metaphor, Donald Schon[15] argues that by causing us to see one thing in terms of another, metaphors help us to see things in some manner that is new to us. Schon describes such shifts in our way of looking at a thing as 'the displacement of concepts', and it is metaphor that is the principal cognitive mechanism involved. Essentially, it is the process by which all new ideas come into being.

Schon differentiates his dynamic conception of metaphor from what he describes as the essentially static interpretation underlying the analogical or rational view, represented by Schon with a quote from S. J. Brown:

The metaphor in a word lives when the word brings to mind more than a single reference and the several references are seen to have something in common. Sometime in the past someone or other noticed that the foot of a man bears the same relation to the body as does the base of a mountain to the whole mountain. He thought of extending the foot *to the mountain's base. The word* foot *then referred to two categories. These categories share a relational attribute which makes them one category. Within this superordinate category, which we might name the foundations or lower parts of things, are two subordinate categories – the man's foot and the mountain's base. These two remain distinct within the larger category because members of each subordinate category share attributes that are not shared with the members of the other subordinate category...Metaphor differs from other superordinate–subordinate relations in that the superordinate is not given a name of its own. Instead the name of one subordinate is extended to the other and this...has the effect of calling both references to mind with their differences as well as similarities.*[16]

For Brown, as for others adopting the analogical view, including Jencks, a metaphor calls to mind two categories of reference and points to an attribute they share – in this case 'the foundation or lower parts of things'. Brown sees metaphor as nothing more than a way of identifying two categories as a subspecies of a common genus. The only difference is that in metaphor, the genus, or superordinate, is not given a name of its own. But, as Schon points out, Brown does not see in metaphor the emergence of a new concept nor does he see that the concept or the superordinate may come into being only through the metaphor.

By contrast, Schon interprets the role of analogy and metaphor as a process of thought *by means of which* a new conception of the concepts and events involved is introduced. While he accepts the meaning of analogy in the conventional sense as a similarity of relations between concepts, Schon stresses that such a similarity does not exist, as the analogical school generally treats it, in some already given sense, but comes into being only *through* the finding of the analogy. The displacement of concepts, therefore, does not consist of the observation of such a similarity, since at the time of the displacement these shared relations have not been conceived. But the displacement begins with the intimation of such a similarity and may be justified after the fact by pointing out the similarity in terms which are *themselves* the results of displacement:

New concepts do not spring from nothing or from mysterious external sources. They come from old ones...new concepts emerge out of the interaction of old concepts and new situations, where the old concept is not simply re-applied unchanged to a new instance but is that in terms *of which the new instance is seen. This is what is described as the displacement of concepts – a process in which old concepts, in order to function as projective models for new situations, come themselves to be seen in new ways.*[17]

There are, therefore, intimate relations between new and old ways of looking at a thing. Invoking an evolutionary metaphor, Schon suggests that human language is full of the traces left by the displacement of concepts. Concept formation and innovation, in Schon's terms, are inseparable from human language and must bear its imprint in the form of metaphors:

The metaphorical character of language (whether merely 'ubiquitous' or universal) is due to the fact that our language, at any given time, gives us a cross-section of our processes of concept formation or discovery. The metaphors in language are to be explained as signs of concepts at various stages of displacement, just as fossils are to be explained as signs of living things in various stages of evolution.[18]

NEW ARCHITECTURAL CONCEPTS

Schon's approach casts a new perspective on the nature and uses of architectural metaphor. As a visual image, Hans Hollein's 1960s collage, 'Aircraft Carrier City', might be simply interpreted as a pictorial metaphor along the lines of the previous examples. Seen in the light of Schon's dynamic view of metaphor, however, Hollein's powerful image acquires a different dimension. We see at once two images, not one. We see an aircraft carrier, certainly. But it might be readily agreed that it looks a little out of place. Or does it? It could also be some kind of futuristic city – a dense and compact habitat built for many thousands of occupants, created out of the most advanced technologies (which is indeed what aircraft carriers are), buried part underground in the manner of Paola Soleri's fantasies in the Arizona desert. More sinister, it could equally well represent some future division of humanity into masters and slaves, with the slaves living in a perpetual underground world as they do in Fritz Lang's science fiction movie, *Metropolis*.

8.7.
Interpretation by Hillel Schocken of Le Corbusier's Chapel at Ronchamp. From Jencks, 1977.

By placing a familiar concept, an aircraft carrier, so far out of normal context, but somehow still managing to make it plausible, Hollein deliberately evokes such shifts of imagery and meaning in the mind of the viewer. The aircraft carrier becomes a metaphor for the city and causes us to envisage the city in a new form. At the same time we see the concept of the aircraft carrier also in a new light; we see it now as a special form of floating city with many of the recreational facilities, cinemas, theatres, restaurants, gymnasia, etc., that we would expect to find in a small city.

Perhaps the same processes of thought occurred in the mind of Hollein when he originally conceived his image. Something of the kind most certainly occurred. But what is most important is that the process is generated again in the mind of the observer. The power of the image causes in each viewer's thoughts a shift in meaning in the course of which the metaphor, 'The City as an Aircraft Carrier', comes into being and a new concept of the city is born.

Another suggestive example from the 1960s – then a fertile period for new ideas – is Archigram's 'Plug-in City'. The words 'plug-in' conjure up a strong image in themselves, as indeed they were intended to. In fact, the Archigram group always made as much effective use of the images words can summon up as they have of their graphical productions. In Warren Chalk's design for one component of the city, a Plug-in apartment

8.8a.

8.8b.

8.8a and b.
'Aircraft Carrier City', 1964. Collage.
Architect: Hans Hollein.

tower, Archigram are encouraging us to drop our old concepts of the city or the home as something of permanent value, built of solid and enduring materials, and to adopt instead their own vision of the city as an ever changing construction site built from mass-production methods and lightweight materials. Permanence has no place in Plug-in City. Such a city would not only be responsive to change, but would positively encourage it by building in obsolescence into the dwelling units in order that there would always be a demand for new models.

As there were no readily available images for such a city, Archigram sought to project a plausible vision of it by using those existing images which already encapsulated the attributes of mass production and built-in obsolescence. All those attributes and qualities, in fact, which the ordinary person identified, not with homes and cities, but with the familiar products of manufactured consumerism. Their drawings of Plug-in City are therefore heavily laden with images of automobiles, caravans, and plastic products of all kinds. In addition, the image of the moveable crane and the Meccano kit is everywhere to reinforce the general impression of impermanence.

Like Hollein's work, Archigram's drawings create a new vision of the city by appealing to existing concepts but placing them in an entirely new context. Plug-in City was new for its time, but it provided sufficient semantic clues for it to be easily understood. As Reyner Banham wrote, this was precisely Archigram's intention:

A Plug-in City must look like a Plug-in City. If people are to enjoy manipulating this kind of adaptable environment (and if they don't enjoy it, we have gained nothing over our previous environments), then they will have to be able to recognise its parts and functions so that they can understand what it is doing to them, and what they are doing to it.[19]

It is not necessary to approve of the consumerist values implicit in Plug-in City in order to appreciate Archigram's use of metaphor in generating new ideas, nor the skill with which they controlled such use. There are many other, more positive examples we might refer to – Buckminster Fuller's 'Space-Ship Earth', for example – which have caused us to re-evaluate our present concepts and attitudes in relation to the environment in which we live.

But the lesson should by now be clear. New architectural concepts do not emerge independent of past associations, as the founders of the Modern Movement believed, or liked to pretend, as some form of direct expression of the *Zeitgeist*. Nor are they independent of the language through which our experience as individuals and members of a shared culture is mediated. On the contrary, new ideas come into being by virtue of seeing the new in terms of the old, and it is our unique human language which makes the generation of such ideas possible at all, and which carries the history of ideas in its forms.

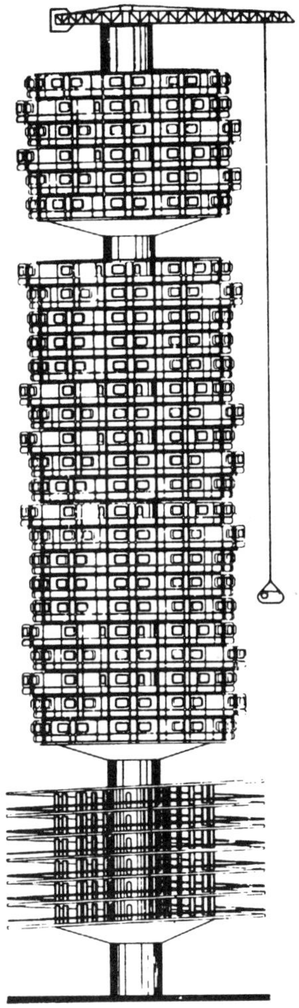

8.9.
Capsule Homes Tower, 1964. Architect: Warren Chalk. From the Folkestone exhibition catalogue 1966.

9 FUNCTION OF TACIT KNOWING IN LEARNING DESIGN

First published in *Design Studies*, October 1981.

In an influential study, Christopher Alexander[1] identified unself-conscious design with traditional cultures (hence good) and self-conscious design with modern cultures (hence bad). Alexander's thesis was that traditional cultures were more likely to evolve stable equilibria with their environments by virtue of their unself-consciouness than modern cultures, which by their nature were inherently unstable. He argued that the conceptual structures or mental pictures that distinguish the self-conscious culture were deeply corrupting and only serve to get in the way of such equilibria, preventing the more direct relationships that more primitive cultures obtain with their environments. Consequently, the only way to restore architecture to its former traditional values and qualities was to circumvent modern (self-conscious) design procedures, cutting out the architectural middle man and substituting more objective and logical procedures.

Aside from the questionable rationality and objectivity of Alexander's preferred design methods – an approach he later retracted[2] – the assumption that modern designers are any more self-conscious than their counterparts in traditional societies is open to serious doubt.[3] Moreover, any general assumption that a clear-cut distinction can be made between unself-conscious and self-conscious thought processes is itself questionable.

TACIT KNOWING

A quite different and more ambiguous picture of the relation between conscious and unconscious thought is presented by Michael Polanyi[4] in his theory of 'tacit knowing'. Asked to specify from memory, for example, all those unique features which make up a familiar human face, most of us would be hard put to describe such features in any degree of convincing detail. Faced with similar problems in getting witnesses to describe the faces of suspected criminals, police experts devised the now familiar technique of facial reconstruction. Assisted by an experienced officer, witnesses build up a composite picture of the suspect from an 'identikit' of various types of noses, foreheads, jaws, etc., changing whatever features do not fit the remembered whole until an accurate portrait is constructed.

The example, Polanyi suggests, demonstrates a fundamental principle of human knowledge: 'we can know more than we can tell'.[5] The statement seems obvious, but its explanation is less so. Taking another example, Polanyi describes an experiment in which patients who were subjected to a mild shock whenever they uttered certain syllables in conversation, soon learnt to avoid the use of the shock-producing syllables, even though when questioned afterwards they were unable to identify those syllables. As with the problem of facial recognition or the recognition of any complex physiognomy, the recognition of the syllables involves a constructive mental process whereby the 'knower' establishes a cognitive relation between what Polanyi calls the two terms of tacit knowing. Taking the electric shock as the second or 'distal' term and the specific shock-producing syllables as the first or 'proximal' term, Polanyi explains that while the patient is able to specify the second term of tacit knowing because full attention is focused in anticipation upon the shocks, he or she becomes aware of the particular shock-producing syllables only indirectly, as they direct his or her attention to the shocks. As Polanyi puts it, the patient attends *from* the shock-producing particulars *to* the shock itself, and is aware of the syllables to be avoided only by virtue of his or her awareness of the shock. Hence the patient's knowledge of those particular syllables remains tacit:

This is how we come to know these particulars, without being able to identify them. Such is the functional relation *between the two terms of tacit knowing:* we know the first term only by relying on our awareness of it for attending to the second.[6]

In the case of the recognition of a face or facial expression, we attend *from* the particulars of the face *to* the face which we recognize, by virtue of attending from those particulars of which we are otherwise unaware except in the act of recognition. In a similar fashion, Polanyi argues that the manner in which we acquire most knowledge, and also most skills, is not by having things always precisely specified for us, but by tacit immersion in the subject in question.

INDWELLING

Polanyi calls this essential process of immersion in a form of knowledge 'indwelling'.[7] The concept has to do with the pivotal role played by bodily experience in all forms of cognition:

Our body is the ultimate instrument of all our external knowledge, whether intellectual or practical. In all our waking moments we are relying on our awareness of contacts of our body with things outside for attending to these things. Our own body is the only thing which we never normally experience as an object, but experience always in terms of the world to which we are attending from our body.[8]

Thus when we make use of a probe or a stick to feel our way, we rely upon our awareness of our own body and the sensations the stick transmits to our hand (the first term) for attending to the point of the stick as it touches the ground (the second term). Hence the name 'proximal', meaning near to the body, and 'distal', meaning far from, for the two terms of tacit knowing. But the example of the stick, Polanyi says, suggests a much wider and quite fundamental generalization about the nature of knowledge and its relation to the experience we have of our own bodies:

Whenever we use certain things for attending from them to other things, in the way in which we always use our own body, these things change their appearance. They appear to us now in terms of the entities to which we are attending from them, just as we feel our own body in terms of the things outside to which we are attending from our body. In this sense we can say that when we make a thing function as the proximal term of tacit knowing, we incorporate it in our body – or extend our body to include it – so that we can come to dwell in it[9] [my emphasis].

The role of indwelling in learning different disciplines is most clearly evidenced in human science itself. According to Thomas Kuhn[10] it is historical exemplars of crucial experiments – key models of how science is actually done – that form the backbone of science education, rather than explicit rules or principles. They suggest both directions for future research and provide students with a coherent tradition or paradigm of scientific theory, method or technique, within which they can work. The process of initiation into science is therefore largely by virtue of an uncritical assimilation of traditional methods and concepts. The careers of most scientists are dedicated thereafter to the continuance and further elaboration of the normative science in which they were trained. Only very rarely do scientists break free of this set pattern to usher in or else change their allegiance over to a new form of enquiry.

Kuhn's picture of scientific development has gone a long way to revise the popular image of the scientist as a wholly detached figure, concerned only with the objective facts and free of all prejudice. It is now more commonly accepted that no scientist can be free of the essential traditionality of science as both Kuhn and Polanyi describe it. What is still not generally understood is the process of cognition whereby students learn to assimilate the enormously complex wealth of theory, method and technique made available to them, mostly by reference to a relatively small number of exemplars and with minimal benefit of any critical or explicit description of all the principles and rules of scientific discovery involved.

From Polanyi's theory of tacit knowing we may deduce two essential points of concern to understanding the process whereby students acquire their knowledge of science, and, by implication, also architecture and any other complex discipline. First, contrary to the frequent criticisms levelled against Kuhn, Polanyi's theory shows us that the process of assimilation is rational, even though parts of the cognition may not be explicit. In Polanyi's terms, when a student of science is shown a model of a scientific experiment, he or she attends to the exemplar – which is specifiable in terms which are publicly accessible – from the particulars of the scientific tradition into which he or she is being initiated, which are not specified and hence remain tacit. The student becomes aware of these particulars, which include underlying central purposes, principal concepts, modes of reasoning and expression, methodology and criteria, only by relying upon them for attending to the experiment itself.

As Polanyi explains, whenever we rely upon the proximal term of tacit knowing for attending to the distal term, we allow the proximal term to function in much the same way in which we use our own body for attending to external events. Interpreted in the light of Polanyi's theory, the familiar phrase, 'body of knowledge', acquires a new dimension. The student *enters into* a tradition of science in effect by metaphoric extension of his or her own body into that body of scientific knowledge from which he or she attends to the specific experiment. Thus the second term of tacit knowing constitutes the public aspect of knowledge. But the first term, which remains tacit, is also 'rational' by virtue of the critical awareness (which, as the shock experiments demonstrate so well, can be used to control a behaviour) the person has of the particulars by attending from them to the second term.

LEARNING TO DESIGN

I suggest that the same argument also holds for the manner in which students and young architects learn to design. The principles and rules of architectural design are very seldom made explicit, yet somehow students usually emerge with sufficient knowledge and skills to be able to enter into practice and to contribute to the tradition of architecture in which they have been trained. Occasionally, they might even be able to modify the tradition itself or else invent a new one.

There is something in this phenomenon which says a great deal for the seeming ability of students to deal with uncertainty and ambiguity in the course of learning. How is it, it may be asked, that in situations where the problem or task is always incompletely specified and about which full information is always lacking, students actually manage to learn anything at all? Most likely, the larger part of the credit must go to some possibly innate creative ability to make sense of the chaos and fragmented knowledge with which students are usually presented. Polanyi's theory of tacit knowing confirms this sombre evaluation. At the same time, his theory also suggests that it could hardly be much otherwise and that instead of bemoaning this state of affairs we should perhaps simply learn how best to live with it in a more positive fashion. By way of example I should like to describe an exercise in architectural education in which students' tacit knowing manifests itself quite clearly.

Some years ago I conducted a series of studio design projects in which individual students were first required to research a specific and identifiable architectural style of their choice, and then design a family dwelling in the same style. As the project was first conceived, the selection of styles was restricted to those identified with a well-known individual architect.[11] Later, it was recast to include anonymous approaches and given the title 'Architectural Paradigms', after the manner of Kuhn.

In the first research phase, each student was asked to elicit the relevant underlying principles and rules of his or her chosen paradigm, whether anonymous or not, and to present their findings to the staff and other students in a formal review. While some of these presentations were very thorough, in no case were the principles and rules of design made explicit or clear enough such that, say, another student who was previously unfamiliar with the paradigm, might have been able to make use of them to produce a convincing design 'in the manner of' that specific form of architecture. So much, at least, could be deduced from the evaluations of the review panel.

Clearly, there exist more rigorous approaches to an exercise such as this. But let us assume for the sake of argument that the review panel's evaluations were correct, and that what all the students had actually told us of the principles of design involved was *not* a sufficient basis from which anyone else unfamiliar with the paradigms in question could derive a working knowledge. How then do we account for the fact that in nearly all cases each student involved in the project was able to produce very convincing designs in his or her chosen manner?

Allowing for the obvious gaps, the exercise tentatively confirms Polanyi's dictum: 'we know more than we can tell'. Expressed in the terms of tacit knowing, selected exemplars of a paradigm constitute the second term, or point of 'focal awareness' as Polanyi also describes it. The principles and rules of design underlying each paradigm (which could only be described in a partial fashion), constitute the particulars of the first term of tacit knowing, also described by Polanyi as the constituents of 'subsidiary awareness'. Both in the research and in the design phases of the project, we can say that students were attending from their knowledge of the particulars to the specific exemplar. In both cases, however, students' knowledge of the particulars remains tacit. For the most part students are aware of the particulars only by relying upon them for attending to the exemplar, i.e. the point of focal awareness.

During the course of the project we frequently encouraged students to approach their respective tasks by taking the role of their chosen individual architect, or else that of the kind of architect or builder they imagined worked in the anonymous paradigm.[12] This approach, which we noted appeared to help students achieve their goals, now appears in retrospect to acquire special significance in the light of Polanyi's theory of knowledge. As it has been explained, to acquire knowledge of something is by its very nature to 'enter into' the 'body of knowledge' from which the object of focal awareness emerges and of which it is a product or exemplar. In the case of the selection of an individual architect as the source or model, the process of indwelling entails taking the role of a specific individual – in effect of entering into the mind and body of the architect by metaphoric extension of the student's own mind and body. In the case of the anonymous paradigm being selected the student enters into that 'body of architectural knowledge' which produced the examples upon which the student's attention is focused and which he or she is attempting to replicate. In either case something like a process of indwelling takes place by which students become aware of the particular principles and rules involved in the production of a given paradigm, only by relying upon them for attending to the business of reproducing that approach.

EDUCATIONAL IMPLICATIONS

It becomes apparent from such exercises that much of the direction of current theory and research in architectural education is based upon a basic misunderstanding of the nature of human cognition and its function in learning architectural design or any other form of knowledge. It is generally assumed that the natural progression of theory and research lies in the direction of eventually making explicit (preferably in quantifiable terms) all that which at present remains inexplicit. But Polanyi's theory of tacit knowing throws into doubt most of those premises upon which this linear and progressive image of the role of theory is based. Far from being opposing forms of cognition, Polanyi shows that both unself-conscious and self-conscious forms of cognition are intimately related, each complementing the other. Moreover, the inherent complexity of the processes by which all knowledge emerges and evolves means that the transference and development of design knowledge between individuals will always be at least partly – and possibly mostly – by tacit means. Instead of directing research and theory in architectural education on the assumption that all will eventually be made clear and unambiguous we might well recognize learning for the ambiguous process it is; meaning that it is normal for us to rely upon 'only' a subsidiary awareness of those particular principles governing the forms of knowledge which we enter into when we learn any new discipline.

In architectural design, knowledge of the relations between all the particulars involved, that is, between technology, method of planning, relation to site, etc., is mostly gained indirectly, by attending from those particulars to the point of focal awareness provided by selected exemplars. The implication is that the form of knowledge we call architecture is therefore most effectively taught, not as an additive collection of assorted fragments of knowledge, as it generally is, but by allowing students to enter into as many different exemplars of architecture as possible.

To an extent, the traditional design studio meets many of the educational requirements appropriate to tacit skills of knowing. The very fact that students receive the greater part of their architectural knowledge in this fashion probably explains why they actually manage to make sense of all the rest of their education, fragmentary though it is. The studio project acts as the main catalyst by which students are able to integrate whatever they learn in the classroom, lecture hall and seminar. This unique function of the live project has been recognized as relevant not only to the problems of architectural education but to the integration of knowledge in other areas of higher education.[13]

However, there are good reasons why the continued use of the studio project in its present form does not of itself ensure the architectural education most needed. In the first place, the experience students gain in the studio of different approaches to design has traditionally been quite limited, according to the specific philosophy propagated by a school and its teachers. The still prevailing dogma that students must strive to be as original as they can, even in their first year of design, mitigates against any really thorough grounding in the use of exemplars as models from which students can learn how to design. Only recently has this dogma been seriously questioned, and it is interesting to note that the recognition of the role of precedent and analogical thinking in architectural creativity has followed closely upon the recognition of the traditionality of science and the role of analogy in scientific discovery.[14] Creativity, it can now be safely acknowledged, does not proceed from a blank mind.

The other factor to be taken into account in not taking the studio project for granted is the increasing tendency for schools of architecture to devote more and more study time to the classroom and lecture hall (this, despite all the research on educational methodology which suggests that the classroom large group format is an inefficient mode of teaching and learning[15]). That is to say, explicit knowledge as taught in the classroom is increasingly valued over the tacit knowledge gained in the studio.

CONCLUSIONS

Much of the confusion which characterizes architectural education today therefore arises from basic misconceptions concerning what is presumed to be 'rational' in the process of design and what is not. As we learn from Polanyi, just because a large part of our knowledge remains tacit, it does not mean that such knowledge has no worth. On the contrary, we know that it does because it shows up in purposeful behaviour. The type of behaviour may range from the skilful avoidance of electric shocks by subjects who cannot otherwise identify their cause, through to the assimilation of the major disciplines, within any one of which a person can spend a lifetime of productive work and yet still not be able to specify in any explicit and unambiguous fashion the guiding principles he or she is following from day to day.

It may be useful, therefore, to take a good look at architecture and architectural education and try to understand what it is that architects and students actually *do* in the real-life process of design, rather than try to make what they do conform to some idealized flowchart. In conclusion, assuming that architectural educators were to duly recognize and appreciate the function of tacit knowing in design, the following points should be considered:

- *The traditionality and unity of architectural knowledge*, upon which architects and building users depend in order to be able to interpret and create architecture, should be accorded full recognition.
- *Curricula* should be designed in order to present students with experience of architecture as an integrated form of knowledge, in contrast to the present practice of planning additive collections of courses which provide different and uncoordinated fragments of knowledge.
- *Architectural exemplars* should be used as the main educational vehicle by means of which students enter into and assimilate the various kinds of knowledge and guiding principles that are already integrated within architecture as an independent discipline.
- *Critical awareness* should be actively encouraged through comparative studies of alternative historical and contemporary paradigms, including exercises of the kind described above.

- *Architectural creativity* is facilitated, not hindered, by a thorough knowledge of architectural exemplars, both present and past.
- *The number of hours* spent in classroom teaching and in lectures should be reduced, in favour of more efficient methods of project teaching, both in the studio and in 'live' projects organized in conjunction with the local community within which a school is located.
- *Methods of teaching* should be encouraged which give students opportunity to enter into the 'thought worlds' of other people, especially non-architects. In addition to live community architecture projects, attention should be focused on the use of various architectural games which simulate interaction between architects and other parties in the building and planning process, and which present students with rich opportunities for the development of tacit skills of knowing and interpersonal communication.
- *New research* should be focused on the function of tacit knowing in architecture, both in the process of design and in the role of architecture as a place-making activity.

The last point holds out promise of some of the most exciting insights yet to come in understanding architecture and its role in human individuation and in the formation of cultural identities. Relevant problems include: How is it that some architects can comprehend the regional attributes of both a people and a local architecture without explicit training? What is the role of tacit knowing and indwelling in the processes of orientation and identification with a place? It may be surmised that place identity itself is a function of tacit knowing, by which individuals come to dwell in a place not only physically but also by metaphoric extension of their own bodies. By implication, people communicate and interact with other people also in large part by making use of their architecture, much in the same way they make use of their own bodies, as the proximal term of tacit knowing.

The picture presented here of complementary forms of cognition therefore sharply contradicts any polarized picture of self-conscious versus unself-conscious design. The reality is both more ambiguous and challenging. Yet coming to terms with the complex relations between tacit and explicit design processes may yet provide us with knowledge of far greater scientific and educational worth than former methods of design education ever did.

10 THE ESSENTIAL TENSION

Presented as an illustrated lecture to the Faculty of Architecture, Middle East Technical University, Ankara, 29 May 1989. First published in *Architecture and Urbanism*, July 1991.

Consciously or not, the words tradition and modernity generally conjure up images of fierce tugs-of-war between opposite and irreconcilable forces. For many architects in the West, they have come to mean a bitter disillusionment with forward looking orientations and a frantic scramble to make up for recent neglects by plundering the history books. In the developing world, the two words suggest a desperate battle to offload backward economic and political systems and catch up with the advanced industrialized nations, usually at the expense of traditional values and lifestyles, including regional forms of architecture.

What is always apparent in these schizophrenic debates is how narrowly differing schools interpret either concept, and how outdated underlying assumptions are, especially those concerning the nature of modern science and even tradition itself. If any real progress is to be made in reconciling the two orientations then we should be asking what kind of thinking it is that leads people to see modernity and tradition as opposing concepts in the first place.

WAYS OF THINKING

Limitations of stylistic categories

A major obstacle to any fresh outlook is the way architects generally think about what is modern and traditional exclusively in formal terms. Accordingly, the first implies rejection of historical models, standardization, an abstract purity of form, open frame structures and flexible spaces, while the second implies historical and vernacular forms, variety, rich lines, solid wall structures, fixed spaces and so forth. None of this stands up in the face of familiar exceptions like the Japanese Sukiya Style, but for most architects they provide a ready-made way of dividing up the built world into separate and easily identifiable categories.

Postmodern architects and critics in particular cling onto and propagate this cartoon image of Modernism as a way of validating their own preferred architecture. As Postmodernism's original and leading theorist, Robert Venturi[1] lambasts the 'puritanically moral language of orthodox Modern architecture'.[2] He advocates instead an architecture of complexity and contradiction, meaning 'elements which are hybrid rather than "pure", compromising rather than "clean", distorted rather than "straightforward", ambiguous rather than "articulated"',[3] etc.

10.1.
Extension to the National Gallery, Sainsbury Wing, London, 1986. Architect: Venturi and Scott Brown. Photo: Chris Abel.

For Venturi, Modernism means no more than a restrictive formal style characteristic of design in the twentieth century. He allows that some of the works of Le Corbusier, Alvar Aalto and Louis Kahn are interesting enough to merit praise, but they are treated as exceptions that prove the rule. He pointedly eschews the sorts of analogical thinking whereby Modern architects – including the three just mentioned – tried to 'improve the connections between science and technology on the one hand, and the humanities on the other...and make of architecture a more social art'.[4] Instead, he supports the 'autonomy' of architecture and its traditions and suggests that the architect can best solve his problems by 'narrowing his concerns and concentrating on his own job'.[5]

Just what Venturi thinks the architect's job is, is apparent from the way he chooses and discusses his preferred examples. Like his concept of Modernism, the language of Venturi's favoured architecture, whether he is referring to contemporary or historical works – usually mannerist, baroque or rococo – is the language of form and style. Only briefly does he concede that 'architecture is necessarily complex and contradictory in its very inclusion of the traditional Vitruvian elements of commodity, firmness and delight'.[6] Thereafter, 'commodity' (use) is barely mentioned and 'firmness' (technology) not at all. Only 'delight' continues to hold the stage.

Flirtation with form

Venturi is not alone in limiting the scope of architecture in this fashion and encouraging the current popular flirtation with form. Aldo Rossi's theory of urban types[7] virtually excludes function as a serious consideration and completely ignores technology. Leon and Rob Krier[8] propagate their own versions of an evergreen urban architecture abstracted out of European formal traditions. Both Charles Jencks[9] and Roger Scruton,[10] for all their differences in approach, are absorbed with external appearances. David Watkin,[11] like Venturi, accuses Modernists of moralizing and always thinking about architecture in terms of something else. All urge architects to pay more attention to their own aesthetic traditions. Not one is a bit concerned with how buildings are made, how they stand up to the forces of gravity, how they deal with the climate, or how they are used.

I concur with Venturi's rejection of purity, and gladly embrace, as I shall show, impure or hybrid architecture as a valid expression of cultural exchange and heterogeneity. I also think that architects should take their traditions seriously. But I protest the current narrow definition of what those traditions are supposed to include. I also question the illogical conclusions these critics draw, that better architecture, especially hybrid architecture, can be produced when architects turn in on themselves. The irony is that while all these criticisms were aimed at liberating architecture, in many respects the actual result has been the reverse. The past has been opened up, but only at the cost of closing down the future. And while aesthetic barriers may have been demolished, others have taken their place, leaving architects with an increasingly circumscribed role as exterior decorators.

Emphasis on process

Stylistic debates alone do little justice to the many-sided character of the Modern Movement, which was as much about processes as it was about products. For Reyner Banham,[12] who understood better than most critics the more profound meaning of both tradition and modernity, tradition implies, 'not monumental Queen Anne, but the stock of general knowledge (including scientific knowledge) which specialists assume as the ground of present practice and future progress'.[13] Even modern architects therefore have their own 'operational lore', amounting to a 'Modern tradition' in architecture. Technology, on the other hand, represents not just new products, but 'the method of exploring, by means of the instrument of science, a *potential* which may at any moment make nonsense of all existing knowledge, and so of the very ideas founded on it, even "basic" ideas like *house, city, building*'.[14]

What Banham presents is more like an opposition between different ways of thinking, rather than anything to do with architectural forms *per se*. The questioning, exploratory role of science has much to do with the heart of modernity. In short, 'to be modern' is to have a distinctive attitude of mind, rather than a style. However, like most architects, modernists or otherwise, Banham has a simplistic idea about the way scientists go about their work which obscures the more complex reality. Not all scientists live up to popular mythology as intrepid explorers on the frontiers of knowledge. On the contrary, scientists have their own preferred traditions of knowledge and practice based on precedent, much like anyone else. Most scientific work is carried out within these paradigms, and only 'extraordinary science' actually fulfils the sort of radical role Banham assumes for science in general.[15] If anything, what the history of science teaches us is that there are 'trads' as well as 'mods' in science, just as there are in architecture, or, for that matter, any other walk of life.

Banham therefore takes us some of the way toward a new understanding of modernity and tradition, but not far enough. We have progressed from contrasting forms to contrasting processes, but Banham's interpretation is still set out in terms of oppositions and boundaries which do not accord with reality. To go the next step, we have to dispense altogether with those fundamental habits of thought which lead us to see all of our world in terms of separate and opposing categories, and not just this particular troublesome pair.

OPPOSITES ARE COMPLEMENTARY

Eastern world view

As Fritjof Capra[16] writes in the *Tao of Physics*, those habits of thought are deeply ingrained in Western culture, though not in other cultures. Capra traces their origins in Western thought to the atomists of ancient Greece, a group of philosophers who identified the atom as 'the smallest indivisible unit of matter'.[17] The atomists held that the endless variety of forms in nature and the changes observed in these forms were the result of the mixture and separation of these ultimate particles. The atoms themselves, however, were believed to be fixed and invariable. There arose therefore a conception of a dual universe composed on the one hand of these finite basic building blocks, and on the other of the ephemeral forces which shaped them, and which were associated with mysterious or spiritual phenomena and were entirely different from matter. Centuries later, this same divided universe was to find its most extreme expressions in the mind–body dualism of Rene Descartes and in the mechanical universe of Isaac Newton, wherein all that could not be explained in terms of the strict laws of motion was consigned to the irrational and inexplicable world of the spirit.

Although twentieth-century physics has outdated the atomists and subsequent mechanistic philosophies, their way of thinking about nature and matter still survives in our everyday habit of seeing and dealing with the world in terms of separate and opposing categories, with increasingly negative consequences. Most serious, Western humankind has developed a view of itself as separate from and in opposition to nature, an arrogant and selfish position that has brought the planet to the brink of ecological catastrophe.

This reductionist outlook is contrasted by Capra with the Eastern world view, as embodied in the major Eastern philosophical and religious systems, Hinduism, Buddhism, Taoism and Zen:

The most important characteristic of the Eastern world view – one could almost say the essence of it – is the awareness of the unity and mutual interrelation of all things and events, the experience of all phenomena in the world as manifestations of a basic oneness. All things are seen as interdependent and inseparable parts of this cosmic whole; as different manifestations of the same ultimate reality. The Eastern traditions constantly refer to this ultimate, indivisible reality which manifests itself in all things, and of which all things are parts. It is called Brahman in Hinduism, Dharmakaya in Buddhism, Tao in Taoism. Because it transcends all concepts and categories, Buddhists also call it Tathata, or Suchness...In ordinary life, we are not aware of this unity of all things, but divide the world into separate objects and events. This division is, of course, useful and necessary to cope with our everyday environment, but it is not a fundamental feature of reality. It is an abstraction devised by our discriminating and categorizing intellect. To believe that our abstract concepts of separate things and events are realities of nature is an illusion'[18] [my emphasis].

While good and bad, beautiful and ugly, winning and losing and so on, appear to the Western mind as separate and opposing categories, the Eastern mind interprets these ideas as polar aspects of the same reality. Without a concept of what is beautiful there can be no concept of what is ugly. Without losing, there can be no winning. The meaning of each idea is defined relative to its polar opposite and is complementary to it.

Where the Westerner sees nothing but hard and fast choices between good and bad, beauty and ugliness, the Easterner recognizes that he or she can never have one without the other and therefore strives for a dynamic balance between the two. This notion of a dynamic unity of complementary opposites is clearly expressed in the Chinese symbol of *t'ai-chi*. The symbol comprises the archetypal female and male poles, *yin* and *yang*, as interlocking mirror images circling each other in the appearance of movement and also making up a complete circle, or unity. As the symbol shows, neither *yin* nor *yang*, female or male, exists independently of the other. They are simply two sides of the same coin.[19]

10.2.
When knighted in 1947 the Danish physicist Niels Bohr chose to include the Chinese symbol of *t'ai-chi* in his coat-of-arms. The Latin inscription reads 'Opposites are complementary'.

West meets East

Capra's purpose in outlining the Eastern world view is to draw attention to the numerous parallels he finds between it and the fundamental concepts of contemporary physics and quantum theory. He suggests that physicists have arrived at similar relativistic concepts of an underlying and dynamic unity in nature and of the complementary function of opposites. However, they lack an adequate philosophical basis for their new outlook since Western philosophy is still constrained by the reductionist influence of classical physics. He proposes, therefore, that physicists should look East for a compatible unitary philosophy.

However, while Capra's assessment of Western thought is true in the main, there are a number of significant exceptions. Aside from the likenesses that Capra draws between the findings of modern physics and the Eastern world view, similar parallels can be found in other advanced fields of knowledge in the West. For example, Ludwig von Bertalanffy[20] created his general systems theory specifically to bridge conventionally separate disciplines and concepts and to provide a unitary framework of great generality. It, too, focuses on the interdependence of phenomena, whether they belong to human or natural systems, or to both. Ecologists such as James Lovelock[21] with his Ghaia theory of planetary ecology, have also adopted similar holistic ways of thinking, with special implications for the relations between man, machine and nature. In psychology, George Kelly's personal construct theory[22] also stresses the bi-polar nature of psychological constructs, defining a construct as a continuous dimension of differentiation between linked opposites. Relativistic schools of Western philosophy are also now having a significant impact on the interpretation of science, as well as on language and other fields[23], and may eventually help fill the philosophical void pointed out by Capra. While these and other emergent approaches have yet to overcome the entrenched ways that created our divided world, they suggest a potentially significant shift in Western thought toward Eastern modes.

Related constructs

Building on these new ideas in Western thought and following Capra's example, it is possible to reconstruct an alternative interpretation of modernity and tradition which emphasizes their complementary and ambiguous nature.

I shall approach the problem by first defining both ideas in terms of related ways of thinking – as distinct from forms or styles – each of which is described by a specific pair of bi-polar concepts, or 'constructs' as I shall henceforth call them, in keeping with Kelly's definition.[24] Most commonly, differences between modernity and tradition are associated with 'new' and 'old' ideas. In similar fashion we can extend our list to include 'empirical' and 'intuitive', 'rational' and 'romantic', 'objective' and 'relative', 'self-conscious' and 'unself-conscious', 'universal' and 'particular', and 'mechanistic' and 'organic'. Altogether they suggest different but related aspects of our main construct, the first polar concept of each pair being synonymous with modernity and the second with tradition.

As with our main subject, each pair of polar concepts is also usually conceived as separate and opposite categories, i.e. 'new' *versus* 'old'. However, if we care to look beyond conventional distinctions we can seek out the dynamic unity which binds each pair together; hence I use 'new' *and* 'old'. As all the constructs are related to modernity and tradition there is inevitably a large degree of overlap in their interpretation. In particular, much emphasis is given to the common equation of modernity with modern science and technology, concepts of which have been updated here to conform more closely with recent developments and interpretations.

New and old: We are often taught that in order to create something new we must first clear our minds entirely of existing ideas and start afresh. However, the creative act involves not so much a rejection of old ideas as a process of analogical thinking in which familiar ideas come to be used in new combinations or situations, and in so doing undergo some kind of transformation. New concepts in architecture emerge in similar fashion.[25] Machines were already a familiar part of twentieth-century life when Le Corbusier conceived of his 'house as a machine for living in'. What was new was his combination of two familiar but previously unrelated concepts in such a manner as to compel a shocked public to reinterpret their idea of 'house' in the changing context of the First Machine Age. At the same time, his parallel reinterpretations of Palladian themes complicate the same designs with more traditional models and defy simple mechanistic interpretations.[26]

Empirical and intuitive: Popular belief distinguishes science from art according to differences in methodology and creative approaches. The scientist, it is assumed, discovers new knowledge about the world we live in by patiently searching out and accumulating new facts, whereas the artist creates his works out of unconstrained and intuitive flashes of insight. In actuality, both scientist and artist are heavily reliant on precedent and analogical thinking. The role of tradition in science has already been acknowledged above. Scientific theories may also originate out of what seem like bizarre analogies between previously unrelated ideas;[27] empirical tests are usually only applied after the theory is sufficiently well formulated that it can be 'falsified'.[28] Art, like science, also has its own dynamics.[29] However, this does not prevent the more creative artists, especially Modern artists, stepping outside their own traditions and borrowing ideas and techniques from any source they like.[30]

Rational and romantic: Rationality is usually equated with a strictly deductive approach which, when applied to architecture, takes the designer from supposedly irrefutable truths to inevitable conclusions in the manner of a syllogism. Since reasoning this way from the same premises produces the same outcomes, rational architecture tends to produce like forms irrespective of geographical or cultural context. The romantic designer, by contrast, shuns the abstract and universal forms of pure reason and prefers to design for the real world as he or she finds it, with all of its regional variations and quirks. Rationality may also, and more usefully, be equated with critical awareness. In this case, rational design is defined as a process of dialogue involving 'the critical adjustment of design decisions according to the search for social communication'.[31] According to this definition, architecture which makes good social and cultural sense, including regional variations, is more truly rational than architecture which does not.

Objective and relative: As a philosophy, objectivism is based on the belief in absolute or universal standards of judgement. By contrast, relativists argue that there is no such thing as pure objectivity, even in science. Theories usually precede the search for empirical evidence, rather than the other way around, and inevitably colour scientist's methods and interpretation of that evidence. Any assertion of the truth of a statement is therefore always relative to a given frame of reference; 'bare facts' do not exist. However, while absolute truth may be a mirage, competing theories provide a workable form of objectivity in so far as each theory provides external criteria for the criticism of others.[32] A similar approach, which I call 'critical relativism', may be applied to architectural criticism.[33]

Self-conscious and unself-conscious: The architecture of modern societies is commonly distinguished from the architecture of traditional ones according to sharply differentiated cognitive patterns. However, even for modern societies and disciplines, a large part of learning how to do one's job involves learning by example, in which unself-conscious or tacit processes of cognition work together with self-conscious processes. In science, it is the use of key exemplars of how science is actually done rather than any reference to explicit rules or principles which serves to initiate students into the discipline. Architects also learn best by example. The complex forms of knowledge and skills involved in architectural design cannot be acquired by explicit means alone but must be supplemented by 'learning by doing' and immersion in the works of acknowledged masters. At the same time, critical awareness of alternative approaches provides further insights into exemplary work, as well as opening up potential choices.[34]

Universal and particular: Regional architecture is commonly upheld as a purely local cultural product in contrast to the imported and universal forms of Modern architecture. However, close inspection shows that most regional architecture in history comprises a hybrid mixture of indigenous traditions and other forms which were imported from abroad by cultural exchange of one kind or another, and then adapted to local conditions.[35] It can also be argued that an efficient response to climate is one of several common characteristics of regional architecture all over the world and is therefore in some sense a universal feature. On the other side, the nature of machine production – still usually identified with standardization – is undergoing profound changes. The First Machine Age was typified by fixed-purpose or specialized machines built for universal markets which first had to be forcibly created and then controlled by producers. By contrast, the Second Machine Age is typified by highly flexible computerized production lines: universal machines for specialized markets. The effect is to significantly reduce differences in the meaning of craft and industrialized building production as well as to greatly increase the potential for variety and users' choice.[36]

Mechanistic and organic: As Capra[37] suggests, there has been a consistent mechanistic strain in Western thought which interprets the natural universe exclusively according to deterministic principles of cause and effect. Such a view often went well beyond analogical thinking. To Isaac Newton the universe did not simply work as though it were like a gigantic machine; it *was* such a machine.[38] Judeo-Christian beliefs in the uniqueness of humankind and in their rights of domination over nature worked together with this mechanical philosophy to encourage an instrumental and exploitative attitude toward nature.[39] If man was created in God's image then nature was also created in the image of man and his machines. However, recent developments in ecology and also in computer science and technology promise to upset and reverse many of these assumptions. Ecologists have not only helped make us understand how nature works to keep her countless life forms in dynamic equilibrium, but they have also made clear the heavy price we pay for upsetting that equilibrium.[40] Equally important, new kinds of adaptive machines, including industrial robots and 'intelligent' buildings, are now designed according to cybernetic principles derived from studies of living systems.[41] Rather than treating nature as though it were a machine built for the exclusive use of humankind, we now create machines in the more responsive and responsible image of nature herself.

In sum, there is no important facet of modernity which does not imply its complement in tradition and vice versa. However contradictory the above pairs of concepts at first appear, the closer we look the more difficult it becomes to separate them out from each other. What is equally important, though we tend to identify modernity with our own century, most of the attitudes of mind exhibited in these examples can be identified at any point in history for at least the previous four hundred years.

TIMELESS MODERNITY

Innovative spirit

The work of Sinan ibn Abdulmennan,[42] the prolific Turkish architect of the sixteenth century, provides a good example of what I mean by timeless modernity. Because Sinan is a historical figure, architects tend automatically to regard his work as belonging to the past – the Ottoman past, to be precise – and therefore as belonging to a specific tradition of Turkish architecture. But this is a contemporary viewpoint, and if we care to look at Sinan's work from the point of view of his own time as well as our own, then I suggest that we might find a very modern spirit at work.

Sinan was, first and foremost, an innovator of the highest order. The great domed mosques that are now most frequently described as representing the peak of Ottoman classical architecture were at the time of their conception quite original.[43] They were original not because they sprang from nothing, but because like all great innovators Sinan created something new out of existing but previously unrelated ideas. From the West, Sinan took the post-Roman idea of the domed space. From the East, he took both the dome-on-squinch and the rectilinear planning which were typical of the Islamic mosque tradition. The result was totally different from anything then coming out of East or West, but which had both regional and universal meaning. The domed Hagia Sophia, which Sinan took as the model to beat – as he did so with his Suleymaniye Mosque – could have been roofed in some other way. Like all centralized Christian churches, the Hagia Sophia was conceived from the plan up, and therefore starts out from a formal concept. The basilica plan with nave and side aisles retains much of its horizontal directionality and competes with the vertical direction beneath the central dome. By contrast, the Suleymaniye, like all Sinan's mosques, was conceived from the top down, with the dome and baldachin and surrounding semi-domes dictating the form and quality of both interior space and exterior aspects. The main and uncontested axis is the vertical one and the centralized space presents a unified whole, symbolizing both religious and political aspects of the Ottoman culture: 'heaven-dome, and sultan-dome'.[44]

Designing a building top down in this way implies a structural rather than a formal approach and consequently Sinan's architecture is as much about process as it is about style. The size of the central dome and the geometry of the baldachin determine both the form and the size of the semi-domes and enclosure. Together with the balancing ambulatory spaces and buttresses, roof and enclosure form part of an integrated structural system. It is no coincidence that Sinan was renowned as

10.3.
Suleymaniye Mosque and adjacent complex, Istanbul, 1551–57. Architect: Sinan ibn Abdulmennan. Photo: Ara Guler.

much for his engineering skills as for his architecture: 'the greatest engineer and the Euclid of his time',[45] as his contemporaries described him.

Throughout his working life Sinan searched for new structural and spatial solutions, always pushing at the boundaries of existing engineering knowledge and technology and always master of the means of production of his time. He learnt from the examples of history and tradition but his work was characterized by constant research and experimentation 'as if he was living in a laboratory'.[46] Even more explicit parallels can be drawn between Sinan's work and the architecture of more recent times: the skeletal character of Sinan's interconnecting arches and supports suggests modern ferroconcrete construction while his efforts to 'design the structural system itself as an aesthetic composition' also anticipate the same 'purist architecture concept' of the early twentieth century.[47]

If we were describing the work of a nineteenth- or twentieth-century architect in this fashion we would probably call it structural rationalism. I see no significant differences between the spirit of Sinan's early work and that of some of the pioneers of the Modern Movement, who believed that 'architecture can only equip itself with new forms if it seeks them in the rigorous application of a new structure'.[48] What is more to the point, there is in Sinan's approach to all his work precisely that exploratory attitude of mind typified by modern science and technology. Moreover, though Sinan started out as something of a

10.4.
Suleymaniye Mosque. Cutaway isometric. Architect: Sinan ibn Abdulmennan. From Arik, 1985.

purist, the description only applies to his early buildings. In his later or 'anti-classical' phase, Sinan frequently modified his unitary approach, raising up his domical structures above tall prismatic enclosures which no longer directly express the internal structural or spatial configuration from all sides, but which fit comfortably into their cramped urban surroundings.[49] Yet Sinan's experiments never degenerated into mere formalism and combined the same external changes with new spatial and structural developments. What these later buildings show is that Sinan could treat his own previous work in the same manner as he treated historical precedent generally, not as a dead vocabulary of forms to be merely reshuffled, but as the natural springboard for further innovation.

Balancing contrary themes

In our own period the work of Sir Norman Foster and his team provides a parallel example of how tradition and modernity can be harmonized in the same architecture. Notably Foster insists that his use of new technology is no different in spirit from what innovating architects have always done throughout history. His explicit and oft repeated – but generally ignored – references to historical exemplars also show that Foster is as ready to learn from past models as he is to build for the future.[50]

10.5.
Willis Faber and Dumas Head Office, Ipswich, 1975. Architect: Foster Associates. Photo: Ken Kirkwood.

Foster's special talent for balancing contrary themes was already apparent in his early work. The Willis Faber and Dumas building in Ipswich achieves, as Banham describes it, an extraordinary fusion between '...two completely different (some would insist, utterly opposed) sets of architectural approaches, expectations and customary usages.'[51] On the one hand, there is the immaculate exercise in glass architecture standing 'for the illumination of the dark places of vernacular superstition by the light of pure rationality'.[52] On the other, there is the curved perimeter bending in picturesque deference to the existing pattern of the town and reflecting its varied images.

10.6.
Willis Faber and Dumas Head Office. Central atrium and circulation space. Architect: Foster Associates. Photo: Ken Kirkwood.

Glass architecture and contextualism may not go together in the townscape gospel according to Gordon Cullen et al., but here they do. The same complementary approach is apparent in the handling of space and structure in the WFD building. There are the characteristic Miesian horizontal spaces defined by floating roof and floor planes, unrestricted by even so much as a glazing bar. Against this powerful, outward sweeping centrifugal tendency, Foster throws in the centripetal space of his luminous atrium, creating an equal and opposite effect.

What is more important than these specific formal and spatial attributes, however, is the experimental attitude of mind which not only reconciles opposing aesthetic conventions, but also shapes the Foster team's approach to both programme and technology. The WFD is only one in a long line of Foster's programmatic experiments in improving the social as well as physical quality of the workplace. In class-ridden Britain that means getting management and workers out of their usual separate boxes to share both workspace and social amenities. Wherever possible Foster also manipulates programmatic boundaries between normally private and public realms to offer substantial amenities to the places in which his buildings stand.[53]

Green machines

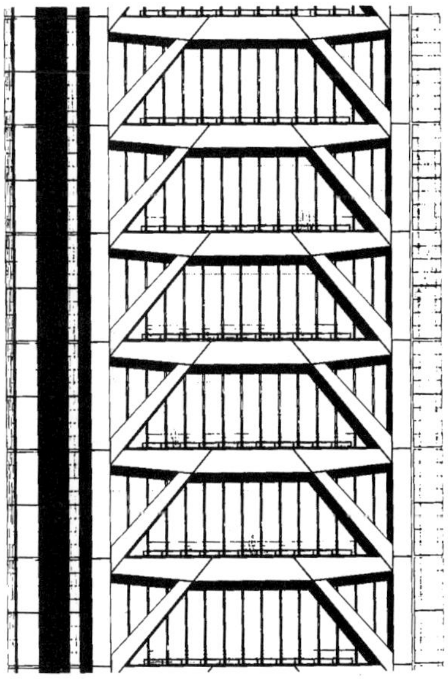

10.7.
Century Tower, Tokyo, 1987. Detail of earthquake resistant structure. Architect: Foster Associates.

Foster's later works demonstrate the same mastery over complementary themes. Like the Hongkong Bank, the Century Tower in Tokyo provides a fitting architecture for the 'Pacific Century'. With it, Foster produced what Japanese architects themselves have so far failed to produce: a convincing translation of Japanese aesthetic traditions to a modern tall building. By contrast, the Stansted Airport terminal marks a return to a cooler, more economic approach. Function nor economics alone, however, can explain the building's impact. The design intentionally captures the poetry and drama of air travel, in the same way Victorian engineers captured the spirit of rail travel. There are suggestions, too, of an older architectural order in the regular grid of 'trees' and lightweight domes, all mounted on a discrete 'podium' of services. In sum, the Stansted terminal is a super-efficient machine, but a 'green' machine in keeping with the New Age, designed in accordance with nature's own energy-efficient principles; and also a national symbol with a hint of a Roman past, set neatly into the landscape like some vast temple of flight.[54]

To Foster's own buildings we can also now add a growing repertoire of sensitive works of advanced technology by other architects, some of

10.8.
Third London Airport, Stansted, 1985–91. Architect: Foster Associates. Photo: Richard Davies.

10.9a.
Cutlery Factory for David Mellor, Hathersage, Derbyshire, 1989. Architect: Michael Hopkins. Photo: Martin Charles.

10.9b.
Cutlery Factory for David Mellor. Interior roof structure. Architect: Michael Hopkins. Photo: Martin Charles.

whom, like Michael Hopkins and Jan Kaplicky, have worked with Foster at earlier stages in their careers, and who represent an English school of experimental Modernists. In his best known work, the grandstand at Lord's cricket ground, Hopkins integrates a graceful, lightweight superstructure of steel and cable-tensioned fabric, with an existing heavyweight Victorian substructure of brick and iron, in such a fashion that each architectural form and technology complements the other. A similar integration of old and new materials and technologies is achieved at the circular Cutlery Factory in Derbyshire, where a tension-trussed steel roof structure clad in lead sits happily on top of a stone-walled enclosure, all carefully designed to fit into its rural, farmyard-like setting.

Other works show further evidence of new attitudes towards integrating modern architecture with the natural environment. Kaplicky's and Future Systems' project for a semi-underground museum beneath the Acropolis in Athens makes effective use of proven energy-saving techniques, tucking the g!ass-roofed structure neatly into the base of the hill. The work of the most prominent continental representative of the movement, Renzo Piano, also demonstrates comparable skills, both in the manner in which Piano integrates advanced technology into historical settings in his urban renovation projects, and in his increasingly

10.10.
The Menil Collection Museum, Houston, 1981–86. Partial section through exhibition room and roof. Architect: Piano Workshop. From Massimo Dini, *Renzo Piano*, 1984.

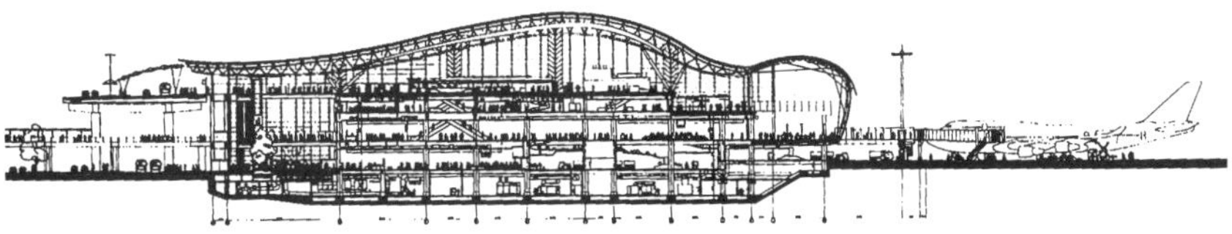

10.11a.

10.11a.
Kansai International Airport Terminal, Osaka, 1988–94. Section through centre of Terminal. Architect: Piano Workshop.

10.11b.
Kansai International Airport Terminal. Main roof configuration was shaped to direct natural airflows. Architect: Piano Workshop.

10.11c.
Kansai International Airport Terminal. Main roof structure. Architect: Piano Workshop.

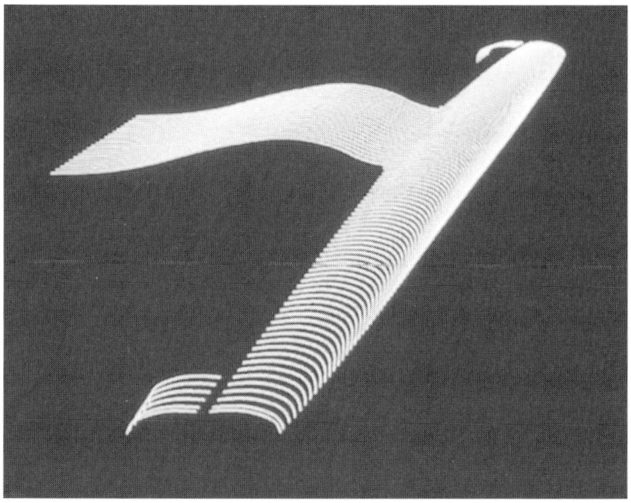

10.11b.

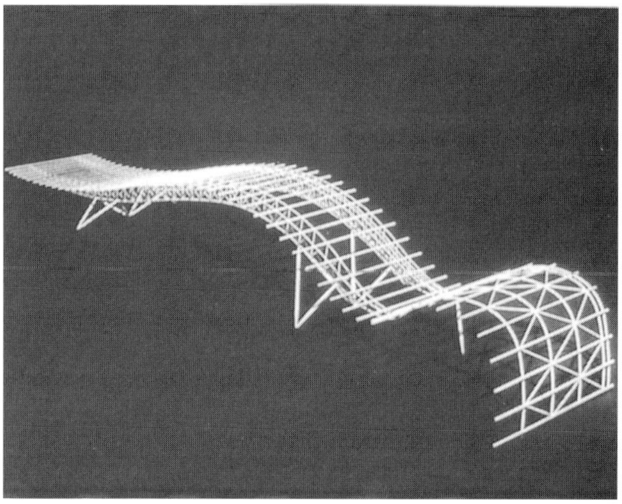

10.11c.

10.12.
Kansai International Airport Terminal. Main roof structure. Architect: Piano Workshop. Photo: Dennis Gilbert.

sensitive responses to natural elements. The aesthetic and functional success of the interior spaces at his Menil Museum at Houston, for example, is entirely the result of Piano's skilful handling of the natural top light filtered gently down through the sculpted shapes of the roof deflectors.[55] At Kansai International Airport, Piano's winning competition design successfully challenged Foster's entry, showing that the most modern of building types can be made to harmonize with nature in a way generally thought contradictory to Modernist principles and technologies. The aerodynamic cross-section of the terminal structure was literally shaped by natural forces as it follows the dynamic of the ventilation air blowing from the land side to the air side of the building. An interior garden running the length of the terminal underscores the dominant theme. Writing of the Kansai project, the Piano team claim with justified self-confidence that their building achieves 'the best that is possible at the end of this century, a mature and totally new balance between technology and nature, machine and man, the future and tradition'.[56]

Another kind of ambiguity

Venturi, too, professes an inclination for complementary elements: 'I prefer "both-and" to "either-or", black and white, and sometimes grey, to black or white.'[57] He also admires a related quality of 'tension' in architecture, meaning the tension that arises from controlled and purposeful ambiguity. But despite passing references to other factors it is always clear that what Venturi actually means are the visual ambiguities created by his favourite mannerist, baroque and rococo architects.

There exists another kind of ambiguity, however; not the surface tension that arises out of a narrow concern with form but the essential tension that has always existed and will continue to exist between tradition and modernity in all its complementary facets. The social, cultural and environmental issues that arise out of this endless give and take between the past, present and future are unlikely to be resolved by the kind of siege mentality which dictates most Postmodern architecture. For all its faults, Modern architecture was created out of an open-minded belief in both the necessity and virtue of experimentation and making the most out of the available knowledge of the day, from whatever source. At its best it was a profoundly liberating movement. Where orthodox modernists went wrong was not just in their Platonic choice of standard forms but in the limited interpretations of modern science and technology which they used to justify what were all along mostly aesthetic prejudices. Real modern science and technology, as opposed to the simple myths that still govern most architects' conceptions, is both more responsive to the complex human condition and a great deal more interesting than either orthodox Modernists or Postmodernists ever dreamt it to be. It is out of exposure to such knowledge and other cultural exchanges of substance that the more valuable hybrid architecture of the future will emerge, not from any introverted exercises in style.

Which brings us in conclusion to an interesting question. In his *Concept of Mind*, Gilbert Ryle[58] argues that the mind–body dualism which held sway over Western culture for so long was a 'category mistake'; change your way of looking at the problem and the dualism fades away to reveal a unity between thought and behaviour. The meaning of Postmodernism largely rests on a description of Modernism as being related to a fixed period in time – that's just what 'post' means – 'coming after'. What happens to the Postmodern idea, however, if tradition and modernity are treated as two sides of the same never ending cultural process? Does the idea make any sense at all or is it just another category mistake, soon to fade away in the face of timeless modernity?

11 TRADITION, INNOVATION AND LINKED SOLUTIONS

Presented to the Fourth Conference of the International Association for the Study of Traditional Environments, Tunis, 17–20 December 1994.

One of the more fruitful developments in architectural thought to emerge in the last quarter century is the changed perception of tradition and innovation and the growing realization of their interdependence. Making connections between existing but previously unrelated concepts is now understood to be as much a part of the creative process as having a free and lively imagination.[1] Nothing comes from nothing, it could be said, and tradition is both a potential launchpad for new ideas as well as a potential hindrance. The present task therefore is to better understand the reciprocal relations between the two, the way one complements, feeds into, stimulates or hinders the other.

Much of the change in approach has been due to the influence of intellectuals outside architecture, such as Arthur Koestler[2] and Donald Schon,[3] writing in the early 1960s. Other non-architectural writers from the same period who have influenced the way we think about tradition and innovation in design, if only indirectly, include Thomas Kuhn[4] and George Kubler,[5] whose most important single works were both published in 1962. The first will be familiar for his widely read book, *The Structure of Scientific Revolutions*, while the second has yet to attract the attention from architects that his own highly original work, *The Shape of Time*, merits. Though each writer addresses different fields of human endeavour, both are deeply concerned with the more profound aspects of tradition, innovation and change, and with their interrelations.

MEANING OF A PARADIGM

While Kuhn's work may be relatively well known, neither his key concept of a paradigm nor its implications for understanding tradition and innovation are generally understood as well as they might be. It is therefore worth restating what it is that Kuhn actually means by the term, and what it is that he is drawing our attention to by his use of it.

Kuhn himself is actually extremely vague about what he means. In her definitive paper, 'The nature of a paradigm', Margaret Masterman[6] finds twenty-one different uses of the term in his book. She boils these down to three basic themes or facets of the same idea, each of which is related to the other in a hierarchy of meaning, from the most abstract to the most concrete level. Thus, at the highest level, Kuhn equates a paradigm with 'a set of beliefs', 'a myth', 'a metaphysical speculation', 'a new way of seeing' or 'an organizing principle governing perception itself'. At the next level, a paradigm is defined as 'a universally recognized scientific achievement', 'a set of political institutions', or 'an accepted judicial decision'. Lastly, at the most concrete level, Kuhn uses the term to refer to an actual 'work' in itself, an 'analogy' or 'gestalt-image', or even a 'set of tools'.

Masterman names each of these forms of use in turn as metaphysical paradigms, sociological paradigms, and artefact or construct paradigms. She goes on to argue that, in focusing on metaphysical paradigms, philosophers of science have generally failed to understand the key role of sociological and artefact paradigms, and especially the latter, in situations where well-formed theories do not yet exist.

Before Kuhn, all philosophers, no matter what school of thought they subscribed to, had concerned themselves exclusively with the scientific criteria affecting the use and viability of fully developed theories. Thus Karl Popper[7] was concerned with the objective conditions under which a well-formed theory might be falsified, while Paul Feyerabend[8] was more concerned with the problems of relativity involved in evaluating competing theories, each of which laid special claims to reality. Both objectivists and relativists, however, assume scientists to operate with clearly defined objectives, which are themselves firmly rooted in widely accepted and testable theory.

Kuhn's special contribution to the understanding of science, by contrast, is that he is the first historian and philosopher to focus on the conditions in which scientists operate *prior* to the emergence of an acceptable, well-formed theory. The practice of normal science, according to Kuhn, as opposed to revolutionary science, depends not so much upon theory but upon widely accepted, concrete scientific achievements, usually in the form of key experiments, which provide a continuing source of inspiration as well as problem-solving tools and other work habits. The same models provide sufficient room for individual interpretation to encourage creative deviation from standard practice. For Kuhn, therefore, a paradigm is not so much a way of maintaining the scientific status quo, in the way that a tradition might normally be interpreted, as a kind of holding operation in lieu of an acceptable theory:

...by assigning the central place, in real science, to a concrete achievement rather than to an abstract theory, Kuhn, alone among philosophers of science, puts himself in a position to dispel the worry which so besets the working scientist confronted for the first time with professional philosophy-of-science, 'How can I be using a theory which isn't there?'[9]

DISCIPLINARY MATRIX

In a later work, Kuhn[10] adopts the term 'disciplinary matrix' to cover many of those elements previously described under artefact or construct paradigms. Models and exemplars, he argues, are especially important to understanding the pragmatic nature of scientific development. Setting out the problems involved in matching symbolic generalizations to particular situations, Kuhn wonders '...whether there is not some alternate way in which scientists correlate their symbolic expressions with nature'.[11] The answer, he concludes, lies not with any explicit correspondence rules, which scientists usually have great trouble in nailing down anyway and which rarely feature in any text books, but in modelling one problem solution onto another:

I suggest that an acquired ability to see resemblances between apparently disparate problems plays in the sciences a significant part of the role usually ascribed to correspondence rules. Once a new problem is seen to be analogous to a problem previously solved, both an appropriate formalism and a new way of attaching its symbolic consequences to nature follow.[12]

Models, explains Kuhn further, '...are what provide the group with preferred analogies, or, when deeply held, with an ontology'.[13] As such, they fulfil an essential heuristic function in providing insights into little known phenomena; seeing the behaviour of a gas, for example, as a collection of microscopic billiard balls in random motion. Exemplars in turn 'are concrete problem solutions, accepted by the group as, in a quite usual sense, paradigmatic'.[14] The student scientist, argues Kuhn, is initiated into his field through the acquisition of key exemplars which define the range of problems and solutions specific to the subject. 'Acquiring an arsenal of exemplars', Kuhn explains, is essential not only to gaining access to existing concepts and practices, which may not otherwise be accessible, but also in solving new problems by analogy. Confronted with a new problem, the student or mature scientist will attempt, just as a child does when confronted with an unknown figure, to map the unsolved problem onto a familiar idea, searching around until an appropriate match is found.

Conversion to a new theory, when it does eventually emerge, hardly lessens the reliance upon exemplars. The transition from one way of thinking and doing science to another may be stimulated as much by a progressive loss of faith in the dominant paradigm brought about by an accumulation of unresolved anomalies, as by any external theoretical innovation. Allegiance is transferred, almost reluctantly from the old to the new paradigm, which appears, though vaguely at first, to offer more promising results.[15] Neither is the final paradigm shift, when it comes, necessarily total. Often, the new paradigm retains much of what was useful in the old one, but sets it within a broader and more inclusive framework. Moreover, acceptance of a new theory, always inherently limited in scope, can never provide all the answers. Every new theory generates a whole new range of questions, opening up new gaps in present knowledge to be partially filled, as always, by reference to known exemplars. Theories may come and go, therefore, but the basic makeshift method by which science proceeds remains much the same.

DYNAMIC MODEL

For Kubler,[16] as for Kuhn, concrete artefacts may function as exemplars and so carry in themselves both the seeds of tradition and of innovation. Kubler argues that conventional art history approaches based upon stylistic systems of classification are essentially static descriptions and fail to account for changes in art forms. Biological models are found equally wanting, since though they posit an evolutionary process of mutation, they fail to account for the occasional radical innovations which characterize human, as opposed to natural evolution. Biographical approaches, on the other hand, present radical innovation as an autonomous product of individual genius, separate from and in reaction to prevailing conventions, and therefore fail to give due account to social and cultural factors.

In their place, Kubler posits a dynamic model which locates all art objects as members of a series of similar artefacts – 'linked form solutions' – produced in response to similar problems which arise out of prevailing cultural and social conditions. Taking his cue from anthropology, among other disciplines, Kubler's schema stresses the species over the individual. Thus every art object has its precedent and its progeny. All artefacts, therefore, are replications or variations of earlier artefacts; individual significance lies only in the position of an artefact in the time-governed sequence of related art objects. Anticipating D'Arcy Thompson's topological studies of species variations,[17] Kubler describes a topology of changing forms, each variation producing in turn further variations away from the original form. Furthermore, any sequence of forms exceeds the capacity of an individual artist to exhaust its possibilities: 'An occasional person, born by chance into a favourable time, may contribute beyond the usual measure of a single life span, but he cannot alone stimulate in his life the corporate entity of a whole artistic tradition'.[18]

Change, according to Kubler, can occur in different ways. Most often it involves a simple modification of what went before. Other times it may involve creative innovation, resulting in a more drastic departure from precedent. Borrowing from information and communication theory, Kubler employs ideas like 'drift', 'noise' or 'interference' to explain how various factors may combine to prevent exact replication of previous models. Purposeful change, or invention, also takes different forms:

The more common category of inventions embraces all discoveries arising from the intersection or confrontation of previously unrelated bodies of knowledge...Whether extensions of a principle, or new explanatory principles be the results of such intersections, they all arise from confrontations among elements already given to the observer[19] [my emphasis].

By contrast, Kubler explains, the more rare, radical innovations involve a near total rejection of precedent and a disruptive confrontation between the new and the old. Among other examples, Kubler cites the displacement of indigenous building traditions in Mexico by new methods introduced by Spanish colonists in the sixteenth century, who trained Indian labourers in the tools and techniques needed to recreate the colonists' preferred forms of building. The result was that, 'Any Indian sense of need or problem surviving from pre-Conquest life was driven underground or out of existence.'[20]

Kubler characterizes different art objects in a series according to the manner of their introduction into the sequence. Thus 'prime objects' are the product of radical invention, and assume, as their name implies, primary significance in the consequent development of a series. The more common 'replicas', on the other hand, vary from their archetypes by relatively small degrees, and are the product of either 'noise', or modest innovations resulting from exchanges between existing solutions. Kubler observes that, as a series ages, the number of prime objects decreases, in favour of ever more numerous replicas.

CONTINUITY AND DISCONTINUITY

Since its publication, Kubler's theory has itself met with considerable resistance, as well as much support and constructive criticism. Of the latter, Joyce Brodsky[21] offers an important modification to Kubler's schema, while retaining its essential spirit and key ideas.

According to Brodsky, Kubler's stress on disruptive invention over variation and on the radical nature of prime objects, undermines the sense of basic continuity in the idea of linked form solutions. Most seriously, it threatens to push the whole schema back toward the conventional biographical emphasis on the individual genius as someone outside of and in confrontation with the general current of history. Innovation, she argues, just does not work like that: '...an innovator is one who comes closest to *revealing the pattern* [my emphasis] and rarely one who creates a new pattern'.[22] Accordingly, in place of Kubler's oppositional pairing of 'convention and innovation', Brodsky substitutes the construct, 'continuity and discontinuity'.

The difference in emphasis can produce quite different interpretations of the same events. Kubler's own earlier studies of the religious architecture of New Mexico[23] contradict the draconian, one-sided picture of colonial influence portrayed in *The Shape of Time*. As the earlier work shows, though the Spanish friars based the designs of their missions on European styles, they were compelled to adapt these to the new environment and available materials. Moreover, far from acquiescing

11.1.
Church of Cristo Rey, Santa Fe, New Mexico, c. 1600. Photo: Chris Abel.

with the situation, as Kuhn suggests in the later book, Indian workmen are described in his former study as actually *resisting* European ideas, and had no use, till this day, for either arches or domes. The adobe brick architecture that emerged out of this process of adaptation is a unique product, in Kubler's own earlier words, of 'the interaction of local and alien traditions seen in building activity under minimal economic conditions'.[24] He even goes on to argue that the balance of cultural exchange was toward the 'indianization' of church architecture, rather than the strict imposition of colonial forms suggested in the later work.[25]

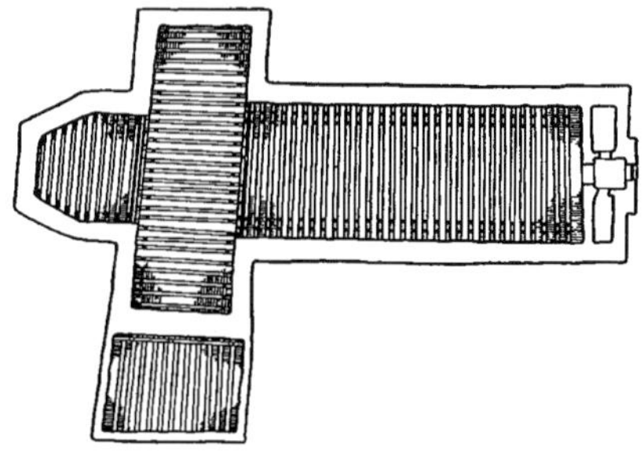

11.2a.
Ranchos de Taos, c. 1600. Reflected plan showing timber roof structure. From Kubler, 1940.

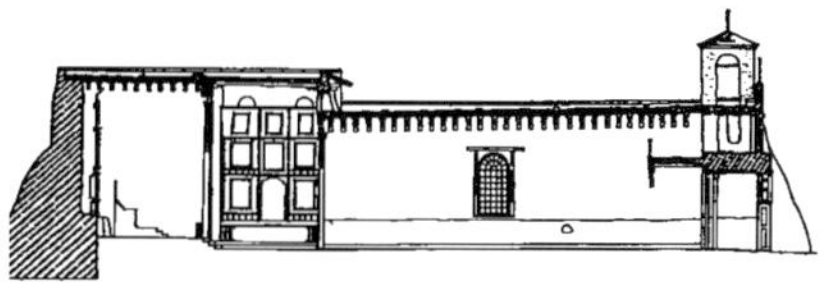

11.2b.
Ranchos de Taos. Longitudinal section. From Kubler, 1940.

Kubler's treatment of the classical tradition in the twentieth century is no less contentious. For Kubler, writing in 1962, the tradition was as dead as a dodo; a 'closed sequence', never to be reopened. He sees instead in the sudden transformation of Western art and architecture in the early part of the century a rejection of prevailing conventions from which there was no return:

The fabric of society manifested no rupture, and the texture of useful inventions continued step by step in closely linked order, but the system of artistic invention was abruptly transformed, as if large numbers of men had suddenly become aware that the inherited repertory of forms no longer corresponded to the actual meaning of existence. The new outer expression with which we are familiar today in all the figurative and structural arts is an expression corresponding to new interpretations of the psyche, to a new attitude of society, and to new perceptions of nature.[26]

However, a focus on continuities and discontinuities rather than on newness produces another perspective. While in its early phase, the Modern Movement did introduce new, dynamic and irregular compositional forms in direct opposition to prevailing classical preferences for static compositions, unitary forms and regularity, this condition did not persist beyond the Second World War, at least, not as a dominant force

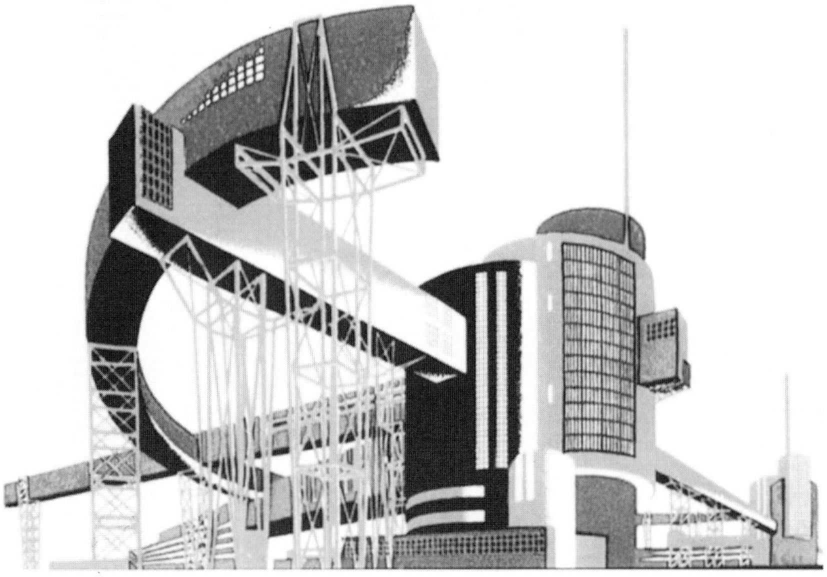

11.3.
Architectural composition, 1933. Architect: Chernikhov. From Catherine Cooke, *Chernikhov: Fantasy and Construction*, 1984.

for change. Already, as early as the 1920s, Le Corbusier was drawing up his plans for suburban villas based largely, as Colin Rowe[27] later revealed to shocked postwar Modernists, on Palladian precedents. By the 1950s he was designing all his buildings based on his 'Modulor', a system of related ideal proportions derived from the Golden Section of antiquity. In similar fashion, Mies van der Rohe underwent his own postwar conversion, rejecting his earlier dynamic, centrifugal compositions in favour of Palladian centrism and other neo-classical expressions of static order, culminating in his National Gallery in Berlin.[28] Later neo-classical works by Philip Johnson, Eero Saarinan and others added further exemplars to those of the two masters, firmly establishing the now familiar International Style.[29]

It was these deeply ambiguous works, rooted as much in the past as in the present, rather than the far more radical prewar experiments, that eventually set the pattern for postwar Modern architecture. A compelling case might therefore be made for seeing the Modern Movement less as a disruption and more as an opportunity – duly taken up – for the dominant cultural order to readjust to changed circumstances, and in so doing to reassert its authority.

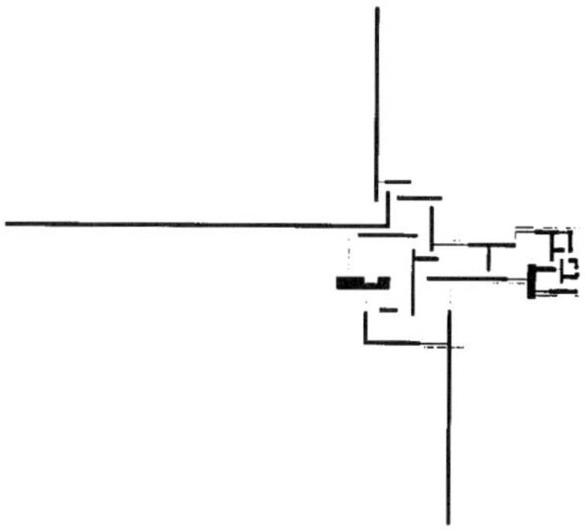

11.4.
Brick Country House project, 1923–4. Plan. Architect: Mies van der Rohe. From Franz Schulz, *Mies van der Rohe*, 1985.

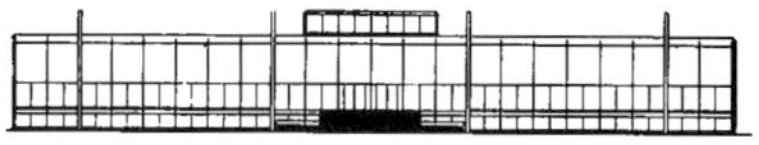

11.5a.

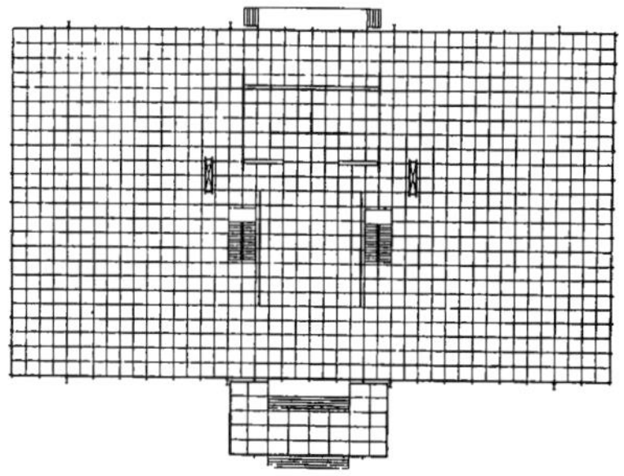

11.5b.

11.5a and b.
Crown Hall, Chicago, 1956. Elevation and plan. Architect: Mies van der Rohe. From L. Hilberseimer, *Mies van der Rohe*, 1956.

INTEGRATIVE PROCESS

What else may be gleaned from these alternative approaches and insights into the nature of tradition and innovation? First, both Kuhn and Kubler place the weight of responsibility for cultural cognition and transfer on the knowledge embodied in and acquired from concrete artefacts or exemplars. In essence, learning by example, rather than relying on explicit rules or theoretical formulations, is presented as the principal mechanism of cultural development.[30]

Secondly, both writers also subscribe to a metaphorical theory of creativity, and, like other writers of the same mind, place analogical thinking at the centre of innovation: making connections between existing but previously unrelated 'matrices of thought', as Arthur Koestler[31] describes it (note the similarity with Kuhn's later terminology), or seeing the new *in terms of* the old, as Donald Schon[32] puts it.

Thirdly, both writers treat radical innovations as rare exceptions to the general rule. Change is normally characterized by a slow accretion of small variations on existing models, which, in Brodsky's account, never quite get lost, but, should circumstances warrant, have the potential to re-emerge in a new and sometimes even stronger guise.

In conclusion, significant innovation may be further characterized, after Brodsky, as an essentially integrative process. Far from creating a break with the past, what an innovator does is to reveal an emergent new order, which is at least partially rooted in prevailing traditions. In the same fashion, the most successful works in contemporary architecture are likely to be those that abstract from the past what is still relevant today, and at the same time, by process of analogy, project a vision of the future out of the present.

PART THREE

REGIONALISM AND GLOBALIZATION

'Ecology raises the issue that the very notion of man's domination of nature stems from man's domination of man.'

Murray Bookchin, 1980

12 ARCHITECTURE AS IDENTITY

Presented to the 5th Annual Meeting of the Semiotic Society of America, Lubbock, 16–19 October, 1980. First published in M. Herzfeld and M. Lenhart (eds). *Semiotics 1980.* Plenum Press, New York, 1981.

Various analogies have been drawn between the symbolic function of architecture and the formation of personal and social identities. Their accumulation has reached the point where the idea of 'architecture as identity' now rivals that of 'architecture as space'[1] and 'architecture as a language'[2] as one of the principal metaphors and themes in architectural discourse.

Though they all revolve around a basic psycho-social analogy, numerous theoretical approaches have been taken to the subject. Kevin Lynch[3] is usually credited with generating interest in the relation between the formal characteristics of cities and problems of orientation. Lynch's pioneering studies of the mental images people had of the cities in which they lived spawned a whole new field of research called cognitive mapping, focused on the mental processes involved in the formation of such images.[4] The significance now attached to the concept of place identity as the interrelation of cognitive processes, social activity and formal attributes is one of the more important results of this research.[5]

Other writers have emphasized the importance of being able to interact in a personal way with architecture, most of all in the area of the dwelling, in order to give proper expression to the personalities and social status of the occupants. Here, the focus upon relations of identity between home and occupant provides a common theme. Anatol Rapaport,[6] for example, argues for 'open-ended' design in housing to permit occupiers to take an effective part in the design of their homes. In a similar fashion, John Turner[7] suggests that self-built housing not only meets a pressing need for low-cost shelter for the poor, but equally important, provides opportunities for those expressions of personal and social identity which come from having control over one's own home and neighbourhood. In a different vein, David Appleyard[8] appeals to Erik Erikson's theories of personal identity formation[9] in support of architectural opportunities for self-expression, while Clare Cooper[10] digs even deeper for support into Karl Jung's concepts of the collective unconscious, the archetype and the symbol, in order to explain why it is that people apparently attach such importance to personal expression in the home. Yi-Fu Tuan[11] in turn adopts an 'experiential' perspective, and finds evidence in developmental psychology to explain the reciprocal nature of man's relation to his physical environment.

For Christian Norberg-Schulz,[12] the works of Martin Heidegger[13] have been the main source of inspiration, leading the writer eventually

12.1a.
Gharghur village, Malta, presents a traditional image of architectural and cultural continuity, dominated by the outline of the 17th century Parish Church. Photo: Chris Abel.

12.1b.
Gharghur village. View towards Parish Church and main square. Photo: Chris Abel.

towards a 'phenomenology of architecture'. According to Norberg-Schulz, the relation of man to place is more than simply a matter of being able to orientate oneself to one's surroundings, as Lynch implies, but has to do with a much deeper process of identification, by which he means 'to become "friends" with a particular environment'.[14] In turn, human identification with a place presupposes that places have 'character', that is, attributes which distinguish one place from another and which lend to a place its unique presence or *genius loci*. The essential purpose of architecture is defined accordingly:

The basic act of architecture is therefore to understand the 'vocation' of the place. In this way we protect the earth and become ourselves part of a comprehensive totality. What is advocated here is not some kind of environmental determinism. We only recognize that man is an integral part of the environment, and that it can only lead to human alienation and environmental disruption if he forgets that. To belong to a place means to have an existential foothold, in a concrete everyday sense.[15]

THE PROBLEM OF ESSENCE

It could be argued that an obsession with overriding themes of one kind or another characterizes much of the history of architectural ideas, from the Vitruvian triad of firmness, commodity, and delight, through to the recurring idea that creating architecture has to do, first and foremost, with qualities of space. The emergent interest in architectural identities is likewise premised on the assumption that architecture has a specific essence, the understanding of which is essential both to the discourse and practice of the field.

Norberg-Schulz's own motivation in describing this essence clearly derives from the phenomenological method he adopts from Heidegger and his followers: 'Phenomenology is the study of essences, and according to it, all problems amount to the finding of essences.'[16] The main problem for the phenomenologist therefore is to somehow surmount or put aside preconceptions, especially scientific abstractions, and to try to understand the nature of 'the things in themselves'.

Many critics, however, view architecture very differently, and argue instead that there is no such thing as the 'essence of architecture', that architecture is instead a changing composite of many different factors and considerations. Thus Charles Jencks[17] claims that '...architecture is irreducibly *plural*...an unstable hybrid based partly on codes external to itself',[18] making use of other practices such as engineering and sociology, etc., in unique combinations. Thus the content and 'signifieds' of architecture '...can be just about any idea or set of ideas as long as they aren't too long or complex (one can't represent Einstein's equations with buildings, whereas language, in its way, can form an adequate if not perfect representation of these things...)'.[19]

Umberto Eco,[20] who also compares architecture as a communication system to a linguistic model, takes a similar approach to Jencks in stressing the unlimited flexibility of language. At the same time he acknowledges the possibility of an alternative viewpoint:

A verbal language serves the formulation of messages of all kinds, messages connoting the most diverse ideologies (and is inherently neither a class instrument nor the superstructure of a particular economic base). Indeed the diversity of messages produced under the codes of a verbal language makes it all but impossible to identify any overall ideological connotations in considering broad samplings of them. Of course this characterization may be challenged, for there is some evidence to support the theory that the very way in which language is articulated obliges one speaking it to see the world in a particular way (there might be, then, ideological bias and connotation of some kind inherent in language). But even given that, on the most profound, ultimate level, one could take a verbal language as a field of (nearly absolute) freedom, *in which the speaker is free to improvise novel messages to suit unexpected situations.*[21]

The validity of Norberg-Schulz's interpretation of architecture as a purposeful, place-making activity, is therefore bound up with the more basic question as to whether or not it is valid to speak at all of *the* essence of architecture. How we choose between these two viewpoints – either to accept the notion that architecture has some kind of overriding, central purpose, or to reject that position and to treat architecture instead simply as an aggregate of many and varied contents – affects not only any definition, description and explanation of architecture, but also our attitudes toward those factors that help to shape architectural form in all its manifestations. Essentially, the argument revolves around the question of the relative autonomy of architecture as a form of human culture in its own right, with its own central purposes, inner logic, and forms of expression.

In turn, Jencks's interpretation of architecture, like Eco's, clearly derives from a specific language model. But an interpretation of architecture based on linguistic analogy depends itself on the theory of language assumed.[22] The choice between viewpoints therefore largely comes down to a choice between theories of language. Put another way, Jencks's use of the language analogy in architecture, which leads him to reject the idea of an essence in architecture, and by implication the relative autonomy and identity of architecture itself as a culture-form, may be set against an alternative use of the analogy – which Eco grudgingly acknowledges – which supports that idea. Further, it may be argued that the same alternative linguistic analogy supports the contention that the essence of architecture as a culture-form has especially to do with the formation of personal, social and cultural identities.

UNIVERSALISTS VERSUS RELATIVISTS

When we compare architecture with a language, therefore, we implicitly compare a specific theory of architecture with a specific theory of language. Here we may observe that in so far as the study of architecture is concerned, that choice, as in the cases of both Jencks and Eco quoted above, has been invariably restricted to what George Steiner[23] calls the universalist philosophy of language. To accept Jencks's own interpretation of architecture and his rejection of an essence of architecture is therefore also to accept the universalist philosophy.

The universalist position, however, may be set against a quite different view of language, called the monadist view, or relativity principle. As Steiner explains, the two philosophies represent radically different viewpoints on the question whether or not accurate translation from one language to another is possible. The difference in viewpoints has also important implications for what we might learn about architecture from the use of the language analogy.

The universalist view is founded on the premise that 'the underlying structure of language is universal and common to all men'.[24] Differences between languages are of lesser significance, belonging only to the surface structure of language, and simply arise from arbitrary accidents of the historical development of different cultures. All languages are therefore 'cut to the same pattern' and all grammars derive from essentially the same deep-seated genetic universals. Translation between languages is possible precisely because it depends upon the operation of such universals, which can be identified as operating beneath the surface form of every language, no matter how bizarre the apparent form.

Almost all linguists today subscribe to the 'working vision' of a universal grammar, with its concomitant claims to psychological and philosophic authority. But, says Steiner, the task of actually identifying the sought-for linguistic universals is plagued by anomalies at every level of investigation. Noam Chomsky's theories of grammatic universals,[25] for example, have enjoyed wide currency among linguists and have even been taken up and converted for various analogical purposes in other fields, including architecture (both Jencks's and Eco's approaches bear the Chomskian stamp, in addition to other writers[26]). For Chomsky, no theory of language learning as a simple matter of stimuli and memetic response could account for the incredible rapidity with which children are able to acquire the complex skills of human language. He therefore sought an alternative explanation in the form of an innate knowledge or 'deep structure' of grammar from which not only an individual child's own language is generated, but from which the 'surface' form of *all* languages is generated. But, Steiner queries, 'what are these "universal deep structures" like? In actuality it is exceedingly difficult to say anything about them.'[27] Chomskian deep structures appear to be located well out of reach of actual or even potential consciousness. At best, they may be likened to relational patterns of an abstract order far greater than the simplest of grammatical rules. But even this is too concrete a representation. The innate qualities of deep structures, suggests Steiner, quoting from Chomsky, puts them on a par with: '...the category of essential arbitrariness inherent in the fact that the world exists. Thus, "there is no reason to expect that reliable criteria for the deeper and more important theoretical notions of linguistics...will ever be forthcoming".'[28]

Whatever evidence has been put forward in support of Chomsky's theories is confounded by anomalies. For example, 'one would have expected all languages with a distinction of gender in the second-person singular to show this distinction in the third person as well. In nearly every known instance, this holds. But not in a very small cluster of tongues in central Nigeria.'[29] The exceptions may be few, but, Steiner contends, the existence of just one exception refutes the whole concept of a grammatic universal.

In summarizing the universalist view Steiner suggests that linguists may in truth have been equating what could be valid general features within their own language or language group with the situation in all languages. Chomsky's own equivocations regarding the possibility of complete and accurate translation between languages are symptomatic of the contradictions and confusions which undermine the universalist position. If there really were such a thing as linguistic universals, argues Steiner, then there would be no need for Chomsky to hedge this vital question.

By contrast, monadists, or relativists, as they are more generally known, hold that the search for universals is mostly a pointless effort, resulting in abstractions of such an order as to be hardly conceivable. Relativists focus their attention instead on the actual forms of human speech in everyday use. The diversity of ordinary language, so they claim, is so complex as to deny any attempts to reduce the workings of language to any universal model. The extreme relativist position as expounded by Benjamin Whorf and others[30] leads logically to the belief that 'real' translation between languages is virtually impossible, and that we only ever achieve approximate correspondences between statements in one language and statements in another:

The fact of the matter is that the 'real world' is to a large extent unconsciously built up on the language habits of the group. No two languages are ever sufficiently similar to be considered as representing the same social reality. The worlds in which societies live are distinct worlds, not merely the same world with different labels attached.[31]

Steiner draws our attention to the emphasis on the word 'group' in the passage. The semantic field of a culture – a notion to which all relativists subscribe to in one form or another – is a 'dynamic, socially motivated construct';[32] the 'language and reality game' played by different language communities depends on the historically evolved and agreed-to customs of the particular society involved.

Compelling as it is, the relativists' doctrine of linguistically determined thought patterns suffers in turn from its own weaknesses, the chief of which is its circularity. To assume that the use of a specific language determines a specific thought pattern, and then to say that differences in cognition reflect differences in the pattern of languages, is tautologous. Moreover, says Steiner. 'Any operational model of the linguistic process, e.g. Wittgenstein's proposal that "the meaning of a word is in its use in the language", will refute Whorf's deterministic parallelism of thought and speech.'[33]

A relativistic stress on the differentiation of language forms and their relation to variations of culture is not therefore necessarily dependent upon any deterministic notion of the relation between language and thought. Rather, as in Wittgenstein's operational theory of language, it may be interpreted more fluidly as an expression of the forms of social interaction. Taking a position close to Wittgenstein's, Steiner concludes:

What we find here is a dynamic mentalism: language organizes experience, but that organization is constantly acted upon by the collective behaviour of the particular group of speakers. Thus there occurs a cumulative dialectic of differentiation: languages generate different social modes, different social modes further divide languages.[34]

In summary, Steiner argues that no simple theory of language as communication could account for the incredible diversity among human languages; such diversity serves to guard the privacy of individuals and cultures. In the same way, language is used to achieve *separation* as well as communication. Secreted within the idea of identity, therefore, is the idea of *difference*:

To the extent that every individual speaker uses an idiolect, the problem of Babel is quite simply, that of human individuation [my emphasis]. *But different tongues give to the mechanism of 'alternity' a dynamic, transferable enactment. They realize needs of privacy and territoriality vital to our identity. To a greater or lesser degree, every language offers its own reading of life.*[35]

MEANING IS USE

As already stated, the overwhelming bias in the use of the language analogy in architecture has been in favour of the universalist view of language, at the expense of the specificity of language and culture. The

12.2.
Postmodernism. Public Services Building, Portland, Oregon, 1980–82. View from Fifth Avenue. Architect: Michael Graves. From Wheeler, *Michael Graves*, 1983.

relativist thesis has either been generally ignored or, as with Eco, quickly dismissed. Instead, a pervasive impression – much encouraged by Jencks's work on Postmodernism[36] – runs throughout the discourse on architecture as a language, that the manipulation of architectural symbolism is an arbitrary affair. This attitude, which smacks of the universalists' downgrading of the so-called surface variations between different languages, is most apparent in Postmodern architecture. Typically, numbers of singular elements borrowed from different styles of architecture are randomly assembled together on the assumption that each element brings with it some meaning carried over directly from its original historical context. At its worst, the result can only be called extreme permissiveness, even promiscuity (Philip Johnson once cynically described architects as 'whores') toward issues of meaning in architecture.

It goes without saying that architecture is inclusive of many different forms of knowledge derived from many and varied sources. For this reason architecture is commonly taught as an *ad hoc* collection of assorted disciplines and skills. However, no enumeration of the contents of architecture, no matter how long or inclusive the list or taxonomy might be, can describe, let alone explain, what architecture *is*. In this sense, the primary function of architecture in the formation of place-identities is catalytic, acting upon and giving form to the infinite variety of ideas, modes of expression, methodology and technological means, to which every architect, professional or otherwise, has access, and through which every work of architecture is interpreted.

If we take the analogy between architecture and language 'seriously but not literally', the purposeful nature of architecture becomes manifest in the identity between the specific forms of 'the language of architecture' and the life of the people who use that language. This is not, however, meant to imply a new kind of architectural determinism, any more than Norberg-Shulz's approach is. Rather, we may simply follow Wittgenstein's dictum, 'meaning is use',[37] which is to say that meaning in architecture is governed by the dynamics of social custom and practice.

STYLE AND FORM

Wittgenstein had his own way of expressing the true being of languages, and described them as 'forms of life', by which he meant to emphasize the reciprocity between language and human action.[38] Returning to the analogy with architecture, it can be argued that within the primary form of life we call architecture, there are an infinite number of other potential forms of life, depending upon the social uses of the language of architecture. Some of these, but not all, we recognize as styles, movements or simply forms.

Any use of the word 'style' in architecture invites caution. Styles of architecture tend to be conceived as either the result of cultural and social 'forces', or else as something which is *applied* to architecture. Alternatively, architectural style may be looked at as a *distinctive structuring of human action*. Clearly, there are many different ways in which the specific identity of individuals and cultures manifests itself. As Steiner suggests, human language itself serves just that purpose. But among all the major culture-forms, architecture alone offers what Norberg-Schulz describes as a tangible, 'existential foothold' in the landscape.[39] To the extent that both architecture and language give expression to the differences as well as the similarities among peoples, then the metaphor 'architecture as identity' has an affinity with Steiner's interpretation of language as a process of human individuation. Since at the present time we have more knowledge of the workings of language in the structuring and differentiation of human experience, the language analogy offers a useful way of clarifying similar functions of architecture.

Some of the most dramatic evidence of the complex relations between architecture and human identity may be found in processes of cultural exchange. Colonial architecture, for example, is the outcome of a process whereby a people quite literally recreate familiar environments in alien locations, thus retaining that part of their identity which is their architecture. The transformations specific styles of architecture undergo in the process of *dis*location and *re*location reveal to us the inner core of stability and logic which enables us still to recognize a 'family resemblance' between the original style and the colonial style. The differences between the original and the colonial style reveal to us the processes of adaptation to the new environment which the original style has undergone.[40]

12.3.
Spanish colonial architecture at Santa Barbara Mission, Santa Barbara, 1820.
Photo: Chris Abel.

WAYS OF BEING

In all of this, what we are seeing is not so much what Steiner calls 'mentalism', but *transformations of mind.* There is some support for this in cybernetic theory. In his 'theory of conversations', Gordon Pask[41] argues that a 'psychological individual' ('P' individual) is not necessarily concordant with a physical or 'motor individual' ('M' individual), and may even be usually not so. What we call 'thought' is a process of interaction between at least two psychological individuals who may or may not be identified with the same physical individual. Parallels may also be drawn between Pask's theory and George Herbert Mead's concept of mind as a dialogic process of exchange.[42] According to Mead, thinking, or the emergence of mind, takes the form of an internal 'conversation of gestures', the completion of which implies the expression of that which one says to an audience, what Mead describes as 'taking the role of the other'. The implication is that what we call 'mind' may be distributed among a number of physical individuals. The cybernetic emphasis on the purposefulness and dynamic stability of human mentation is also in keeping with Wittgenstein's claim that different ways of using language serve different purposes and that such usage rests upon tacit social agreements of some kind. In sum, Pask's psychological individuals are Wittgenstein's forms of life.

Herbert Blumer,[43] a disciple of Mead, claims that in so far as objects have meanings, then they must enter into the human group consciousness much as the meanings we attach to our own behaviour and the behaviour of other persons do. A theory of mind which disperses the processes of human mentation among the group must also take into account the role of the physical environment in the evolution of mind. Such claims support the related claim made by Pask, that there is no such thing as an inanimate object.[44] That is to say, there are no artefacts – including buildings – in the human realm of being without meaning, and thus no artefacts that do not somehow become animate within the processes of human interaction and individuation.

We do not *have* architecture, therefore, but rather, a part of us *is* architecture. Architecture is a way of being, just as science, art, and the other major culture-forms are ways of being. So when we come to define the true and deeper functions of architecture, we will not be simply describing the production of a certain type of artefact, but explaining one of the original ways in which we know ourselves.

13 LIVING IN A HYBRID WORLD

First published in R. Langdon and N. Cross (eds), *Design Policy*, Vol. 1, Proceedings of the 1982 Design Research Society Conference, London, 20–23 July. Design Council, 1984.

The indigenous Malay house form provides a good example of one-to-one relations between social and built forms typical of traditional cultures. The house is well adapted to the larger social and economic unit of the *kampong* or village, to the single family unit, and to the local climate and ecology. Malay houses stand in small clusters dispersed among tall palm trees in what seems like a random, informal arrangement. The houses, which are framed and clad with local timber, are raised up off the ground on the legs of their main frame supports. The random spatial distribution serves to encourage cooling breezes to flow without interruption between the dwellings, which have no fences. Likewise, the palm trees,

13.1.
Malay house-on-stilts, Penang. Photo: Chris Abel.

which have no lower foliation, provide shade from above but present no obstacle to the movement of air at ground level. In addition, their foliage provides the traditional *atap* roofing material for Malay houses. The lack of surrounding barriers and raised form of the dwellings further maximize the effect of the slightest breeze, which is carried into and through the interior via generous floor to roof window openings, vents underneath roof overhangs, and gaps over internal partitions.[1]

While all of the above features might be construed to be the product of a response to the tropical climate and ecology of the region, they are also much more than that. The detached form of the houses, the lack of barriers between them and the external and internal openness of the dwelling form all say much about the specific social and economic forms involved.[2] The detached form reflects the importance of the nuclear family and individual house ownership in Malaysian peasant society, while the open settlement pattern of the *kampong* reflects past traditions of shared land use between the dwellings themselves. The other reason for the lack of fences or other subdivisions is the low premium Malays traditionally place upon individual privacy, at least by Western standards, in favour of intimacy at the level of community. The same factor makes it possible for Malays to live happily with their dwellings, open to both breezes and neighbours alike, where similar attributes would cause serious problems for a Western family, accustomed to maximum privacy, even among members of the same household.

TRANSFORMATIONS

But though it may seem perfectly valid, for all practical purposes, to speak of one-to-one relations between the Malay house form and *kampong* life, such relations do not pertain to other, more complex architectural languages. By 'complex' I mean to refer to an architectural language which takes on all the defining characteristics of a particular culture-form or 'form of life', with its own internal consistency, modes of practice and expression, and criteria of evaluation.[3] As a relatively autonomous form of life, such architecture is distinct from, but still interacts with, those other forms of life which go to make up complex cultures. With such languages it becomes more sensible, when we speak of their relations with social and economic forms, to refer instead to *relations of degree*.[4]

A number of buildings in Malaysia will clarify what I mean by relations of degree between built and social forms. The buildings selected all draw upon two of the major architectural languages of the world, classical architecture and Islamic architecture. None, however, might even remotely be called a pure example of either form, each owing its special character and quality to a multiplicity of sources. It is central to my thesis that these hybrid forms of architecture tell us more about the general nature of the relations between built and social form, than do the relatively purer architectural forms we commonly refer to as typical of a given architectural language or style.

My first example is that of a large house in the suburbs of Georgetown, on the island of Penang, off the north-west coast of Malaysia. Georgetown was founded by the British in 1786, and the

13.2a.
Colonial villa, Georgetown, Penang, c. 1900. Photo: Chris Abel.

13.2b.
Villa Cornaro, Piombino Dese, near Padua, 1560–70. Architect: Andrea Palladio. Photo: Chris Abel.

house is typical of many similar dwellings built by British colonists during the late nineteenth and early twentieth centuries.

The basic form, architects will easily recognize, is that of Palladio's *villa suburbana*. It is, at one level, a most successful illustration of the manner in which classical architecture travels over time and space. In this case, from Venitia in northern Italy, where Palladio built almost all his villas during the middle of the sixteenth century,[5] to England by courtesy of Inigo Jones and the English Palladians of the eighteenth century, to this very different locale but still very English suburb on Penang Island in Southeast Asia. Surely, there is no more convincing evidence of the attachment of individuals and societies to familiar ways of building than this epic architectural journey halfway around the world, and this recreation of the European idyll on an exotic tropical island.

Like many others of his day, Palladio believed that the form of Greek temples derived from earlier forms of dwellings. So he justified his joining of the pedimented temple front to his villas on the grounds that he was returning the form to its original source.[6] Its use here traces back to the two-storey portico on the Villa Cornaro in Piombino Dese. However, while the basic form may be easily recognizable, the villas of Georgetown are clearly very different from the purer model. The open colonnades of both storeys in the Villa Cornaro have been replaced on the upper storey by a habitable room, and in keeping with the creation

13.3.
Chiswick House, begun 1725. Architect: Lord Burlington. Photo: Chris Abel.

of a space for living, the full columns have become pilasters, joined to the enclosure.

The result is therefore something rather different from those faithful exercises in architectural scholarship by which the English Palladians brought the Villa Almerico (La Rotunda) at Vicenza to Mereworth Castle and to Chiswick House, with few concessions to the change in climate.[7] Instead, we have what is still most certainly an alien import, a building type and architectural style favoured by Europeans, but hitherto quite unfamiliar to Southeast Asians. But in the process of relocation from a temperate to a tropical climate the suburban villa has undergone a significant transformation. The building is clearly no longer *of* Italy and England alone or even together, but also now belongs *to* tropical Malaysia.

While it may seem appropriate to describe this transformation in terms of a straightforward adaptation to a change in climate, it is not unreasonable to suggest that in settling themselves in, the colonists learnt something from what they saw of indigenous building. In this case, it is more accurate to describe the transformation involved as a result of an interaction between different culture forms, or 'forms of life', one imported, the other of local origins.

As we saw, the Malay house works on the principle of exposing as many as possible of its external surfaces to the movement of air, bottom as well as top, usually three wall surfaces to each enclosed space, and then opening up those surfaces as far as possible with floor to roof window apertures. We see precisely the same principle at work in the design of these villas, especially in their porticoed front portions. In addition to encouraging the circulation of air around the room over the porch, the sheltered space below offers welcome protection to visitors from both the tropical sun and torrential rains, which would otherwise easily drench a visitor crossing just the few feet from carriage (now automobile) to front door. At the same time, something of that lighter-than-air look of the Malay house gets transferred in the process.

STREET ARCHITECTURE

My next example, a group of Chinese-built shophouses, also in Georgetown, shows the classical language of architecture being used for a non-Western building type and social form.

The occupants of these dual-use terraces are typically Chinese extended family units common to pre-industrial urban and rural societies, where family life and economic life go hand in hand, both functionally and territorially.[8] As the name suggests, the shophouse provides for both home and economic activity in the same building, with business taking up the ground floor, where it is open to customers from the street, and living accommodation provided upstairs. It is a thoroughly urban piece of architecture, suited to both climate and social purpose. The upper storey projects over the street pavement to form a sheltered arcade, or 'five-foot way' (after the standard width stipulated by colonial ordinance) for pedestrians and customers, while internally, ventilation is provided within the deep plan form by one or more atria.[9]

The classical orders work with the supporting arcade, and regulate the whole as an integrated group of buildings. Aside from the rhythmic use of the orders on both lower and upper storeys, the outstanding element here is the so-called 'Venetian window' – one of numerous Renaissance inventions based on the Roman triumphal arch – comprising a 'triple

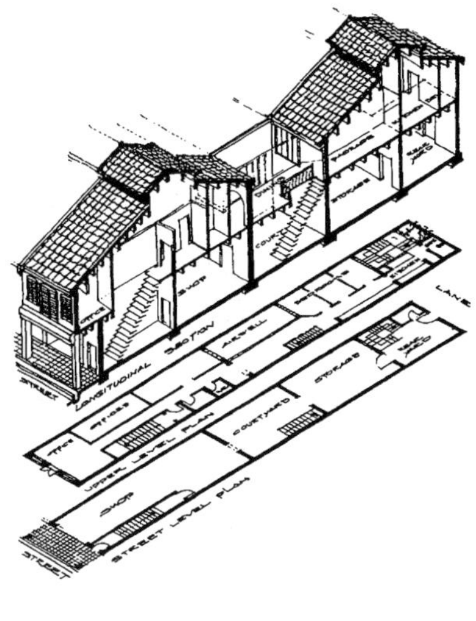

13.4.
Typical Chinese shophouse of Malaysia. Cross-sectional isometric. From Gurstein, 1984.

13.5.
Block of terraced shophouses, Georgetown, Penang, c. 1900. Note the 'Palladian motif' at first floor level. Photo: Chris Abel.

13.6.
Chiswick House. Detail of 'Palladian motif' on southwest façade. Architect: Lord Burlington. Photo: Chris Abel.

13.6.

opening in which the wider central opening is closed by an arch, while the side openings have lintels'.[10] Invented by Bramante, the arch–lintel combination was used so effectively by Palladio that it became known as the 'Palladian motif'. But here in Georgetown the Venetian window appears, not as a part of some grand Renaissance design for a European élite, but as a modest and effective element of Southeast Asian street architecture, sheltering modest but industrious entrepreneurs.

How is it that this extraordinary range of applications of the classical language came about? As John Summerson's lucid account[11] explains, the story of the classical language as it has evolved since its origins in Greece and Rome is that of an architecture which has travelled not only across regional boundaries and the boundaries of time, but also across the boundaries of social form and function. The builders of the temples of ancient Greece could hardly have anticipated Rome's use of the orders on the multi-storey Colosseum. But as Summerson claims, the transformation was to provide one of the most potent sources for Renaissance classical form. The displacement of the orders from temple to arena thus signalled the arrival of a major architectural language, which, with appropriate invention and sensibility, might be drawn upon for virtually any social function.

The relations of degree between built form and social form indicated here therefore suggest not so much the arbitrariness of built form – such as is supposed to follow upon the disintegration of traditional cultures – as an*other* integrity, such as is demonstrated by those consistencies of form which enable the classical language to be still instantly recognizable anywhere in the world, despite subsequent changes in development. That integrity of form which survives, for example, the journey across time and space from Venitia to Penang, and then survives those transformations brought about when the English builders of Georgetown's villas recognized in the Malay house something of value they could use in making colonial suburban dreams come true, with neither sacrifice to bodily comfort, nor to aesthetic taste.

WORLD ARCHITECTURES

Classical architecture is, however, not the only extant form of architecture which exhibits the complex properties of a distinct form of life, and it is only that peculiar blinkered vision due to Western cultural hegemony which encourages us to ignore the lessons of parallel developments in non-Western cultures. It is, for example, no coincidence that, when scholars of Islamic architecture remark upon the lack of any obvious, direct relations between form and function,[12] they are referring to a well-travelled architecture that, like the classical style, has evolved out of much the same process of global exportation by conquest and cultural dominance, whereby the immense variety of Islamic forms developed out of a repeated crossing of both regional and functional boundaries.

My next series of buildings demonstrates the kind of hybrid architecture that results from an interaction between what I shall call world architectures, meaning languages of architecture that have arisen out of the kind of global developmental processes just described.

13.7.
Former Selangor State Secretariat, Kuala Lumpur, 1894–97. View across Padang. Architect: A. C. Norman. Photo: Chris Abel.

The former Selangor State Secretariat was constructed to house all the government departments of the British colonial administration of what was then Selangor State, soon to become part of the Federated States of Malaya. It was the first of a group of buildings of similar design, all built around the turn of the century by the newly formed Public Works Department (PWD),[13] that were to become major landmarks of the future capital, Kuala Lumpur. They remain so today.

The architect for the new building, A. C. Norman, had originally conceived of a design in the classical style. But E. C. Spooner, Norman's superior as State Engineer, had worked for a time as an engineer in the Ceylon PWD and had come to know and admire the Saracenic architecture of India. He was of the opinion that the style was 'more in keeping with a tropical environment'[14] and on his urging, a building of this design was approved by the Colonial Secretary. Construction began in 1894 and was completed in 1897.

In every way, this is a true hybrid: an *alien* building type rises in Malaya, to house the imported apparatus of a *colonial administration*. Built by another imported institution, the Public Works Department, it was designed by an English architect in the Saracenic style, under the supervision of an *English engineer* who had borrowed the style from *northern India*.

Fusion of Islamic and classical forms

We could easily dwell at length on this building, or any of the others in the group built by the PWD around the same period. It must suffice to draw attention to one or two points concerning the use of Islamic forms in this example, and what that use says for both the flexible qualities of the architecture, and the ingenuity of the designers.

First, it should be noted that Islamic forms have been used here for a building type and social form, neither of which belongs to historic Islamic culture. Nevertheless, the adaptation works very well, as perhaps we might expect it to from the aforementioned comments on the non-relations between form and function typical of Islamic architecture. Less obviously, aside from the interaction between Islamic architectural style, colonial building type and social form, the style itself is a hybrid product of a creative interaction between diverse architectural forms. Once again we find ourselves confronted with an example of that internal dynamic and discipline of form, which makes possible and controls the outcome of a crossing of architectural styles.

Another important facet of Islamic architecture is its tendency to look inwards. It is an architecture of courtyards and enclosed spaces, of 'the inside as opposed to the outside, the façade or the general exterior articulation of a building'.[15] In this respect it is apparent that the building we see here presents a very atypical work of Islamic architecture. Above all, what we do see is a very outward looking building, facing onto and responding to the *Pedang*, a major public open space in the centre of the city. The building is clearly meant to be seen and admired from the outside, especially from across that vast open expanse of green, which still provides a splendid view of the entire length of the building (approximately 470 feet), as well as of three neighbouring buildings of the same period and style. Consequently, the building makes special demands, in addition to those already imposed by a new building type and social form, on the Islamic style of architecture itself. In this case, those demands were also happily met, but not without further exchange between culture-forms.

13.8.
Courtyard house in Sousse, Tunisia. Photo: Chris Abel.

Now, the placement of the building in this fashion, to be seen in the round from a public open space, creates a situation which, though relatively unfamiliar to Muslim architects at that time, was very familiar indeed to a British architect who knew his Renaissance architecture. Among the most likely models we may find Palladio's design for the Basilica at Vicenza. Palladio was commissioned to construct a two-storey loggia around the existing Pallazzo della Regione, the great meeting hall of Vicenza's Council of the Five Hundred.[16] The outstanding feature of the design is its quality as an architectural response to Vicenza's major square. It is therefore precisely as a response to the external demands made upon the design by its position facing a major public open space that Palladio's elaborate and expensive two-storeyed loggia is completely justified. And precisely the same argument may be levelled in justification of Norman and Spooner's design for their administrative building in Kuala Lumpur.

Islamic and Renaissance forms have therefore been fused together here to produce what are now instantly recognizable as the characteristic features of the historic governmental buildings of Kuala Lumpur. The architectural device of the multi-storey loggia, a Renaissance invention, but designed here in Islamic style, is repeated on all of the buildings produced by the PWD around the turn of the century. We see it again on the General Post Office, and next door on what was the original building for the Federated Malay States (FMS) Railway Headquarters (later moved opposite the main railway station), and on the High Court Building. All of

13.9.
Basilica, Vicenza, 1549–50. Detail of façade. Architect: Andrea Palladio. Photo: Chris Abel.

13.10.
High Court Building, Kuala Lumpur, 1909. View across Gombak River. Architect: A. C. Norman. Photo: Chris Abel.

these buildings were designed by Norman[17] and lie alongside each other facing, if not directly then diagonally, the same vast open space. The loggia screen also reappears as the main element of architectural expression, not forgetting the practical advantages the loggia device affords in the way of protection against the tropical sun and rain, as well as providing sheltered circulation around the building. In each case, like the former building, it is once again the use of Islamic forms in a unique combination with an imported building type and architectural device which is responsible for the striking effect these works have upon the observer.

Cultural innovation

It is quite impossible to stand in front of any of these buildings and not feel that you are in a very particular place. For all its diverse origins, the architecture communicates itself to us as a unique response to a particular location. As such it will, I suspect, outlive the specific historical circumstances of its construction – which, to put it bluntly, arose out of a typical colonial exercise in the exploitation of local raw materials – to lend to Kuala Lumpur an important part of that city's identity.

Most importantly, there is also something of that process whereby different architectural styles interact to produce the hybrid architecture of Malaysia, which points to the very essence of the creative process. That is, something new was produced out of a fusion between concepts drawn from previously unrelated cultural contexts, often representing different worlds of reality.[18] Further, that creative fusion appears to be made possible, at least in part, by the significant looseness of fit between built and social form which I have described here in terms of relations of degree.[19] The colonial villas and street architecture of Malaysia embody, I submit, original forms of architecture, born out of that same fusion of interacting culture-forms which demonstrates the results of a genuine creative act. The Palladian villas of Georgetown are patently *not* the Palladian villas of Venitia, nor of anywhere in England,

13.11.
'Rifle Range' housing estate, Georgetown, Penang, 1965. Built over a former British Army firing range, the estate overlooks a Chinese graveyard, something which traditional *feng shui* practice does not permit. Photo: Chris Abel.

nor even of the hot-humid regions of the southern United States, with its own variations on the same theme. They are recognizably different from any and all of these other variants; they are the *Palladian villas of Malaysia*. These buildings may therefore be called Malaysian, if one is so inclined to accept them as such, because of what it is they contribute to Malaysian culture that cannot be found anywhere else.

To my mind, the proper and most useful definition of cultural identity will arise out of a fuller understanding and appreciation of the creative processes of cultural interaction, not out of some kind of pre-selection of the supposedly more pure elements of regional or national culture. It is extremely doubtful that any culture still exists which has not, at one time or another, been exposed to alien genes and culture-forms. But what has emerged, when we look at the historical development of specific regions like Malaysia, is not some mere substitution of local culture-forms for imported forms, but a new and original product, which is not exactly like any of the previously existing elements, but presents to us a cultural innovation.

Modern architecture and neo-colonialism

But if the importation of alien cultures has led until recently to creative interactions of this kind between imported and local culture forms, why is it that we now see a very different kind of result emerging from the influx into developing countries of Western Modern architecture, for example in the high-rise apartments at the 'Rifle Range' estate (so named after the former use of the site by the British colonial forces) on the outskirts of Georgetown. Though a familiar sight not only in northern countries, but also now in the developing regions of the South, these apartments are significant for demonstrating the results of Malaysia's first experiments with the highly mechanized, mass-produced building methods of industrialized countries.[20] And here we might well pause for thought and question the wisdom of designating these buildings 'Malaysian'. For these apartment blocks demonstrate the very worst effects of orthodox Modernism, in particular that set of dogmas which insists upon the use of a standardized architecture the world over. I call this kind of architecture 'neo-colonial' for what it says of a continued cultural dependency of developing countries upon the industrialized countries of the North, which not infrequently offload their unwanted products – including these now unpopular mass-produced building systems – on the less experienced populations of the South.[21]

There is therefore a vitally important qualitative difference between the Rifle Range apartments and those other cultural imports discussed earlier, which raises important questions concerning the underlying processes of cultural dominance of one part of the world by another. For all its imperial motivations, historical colonialism functioned for the most part as a parallel culture to those local cultures which it needed to dominate, up to a point, for the express purpose of economic exploitation. It is also the general case that, though colonists held their own culture to be superior to local cultures and taught local peoples that such was the case, those local cultures continued for the most part to thrive, relatively untouched.[22] However, when historical colonialism, along with the heterogeneous culture of the industrial era which it supported, falls away to be replaced by modern neo-colonialism, we see a quite different global picture emerging. For postwar, neo-colonial systems of economic exploitation not only require that the newly 'independent' nations of the former colonies continue to export their natural resources to the old centres of empire, but their ravenous growth also necessitates that the peoples of those same countries now also become consumers. In this case, the former colonial system of parallel and heterogeneous cultures no longer suffices for purposes of exploitation. It now becomes necessary to take the next step and obliterate local cultures entirely, replacing them with a Western-style consumer culture aimed at creating the social and psychological attitudes required for mass consumption of Western goods and products.[23]

Given the economic imperatives of neo-colonialism, which make necessary the continuation and expansion of Western cultural hegemony, it is inevitable that we should have, in addition to every other Western culture-form, Western forms of architecture dominating local forms to the point of their virtual extinction. It is all a part of that cultural and commercial penetration of local cultures which the former colonial powers now require to maintain their own economic dominance and well-being.

Herein lies the present and future danger, not only to Malaysian identity, but to the identity of most developing countries. It is that neo-colonial *covert* forms of cultural domination and exploitation present a far greater challenge to militarily and economically weaker nations than the now outmoded and inefficient *overt* forms of historical colonialism.

13.12.
Komtar Tower, Georgetown, Penang, 1980–84. Shown here under construction. Architect: Team 3 International. Photo: Chris Abel.

The neo-colonial architecture of the global consumer society therefore represents, to the extent by which modern culture is unified by the values of commerce, and by the manner in which all other values are made subordinate to those values, a homogenizing force on a hitherto unprecedented scale.

Alternative experiments

But if the global picture is none too encouraging, there are signs of emergent alternative forms of culture which might yet permit a rediscovery of the historically evolved purpose of architecture in the formation of cultural and locational identities. They may be observed in the countless small-scale experiments in cultural innovation around the world, all of which are aimed in some fashion at breaking current political, economic and cultural monopolies.[24] Sometimes called the green movement, or in the developing world context, ecodevelopment,[25] these experiments have their architectural counterparts in a renewed interest in regional architecture and history, which usefully serves to focus attention upon previously neglected concepts of cultural and place identities.

Nonetheless, current discourse falls short of providing either explanatory or prescriptive theories of social and built forms which encompass those problems of mixed and ambiguous culture-forms such as are likely to feature within any future global context of interacting cultures. Invariably, arguments for alternative futures polarize around familiar Western-dominated cultural models, or else those comforting ideals of cultural purity and self-sufficiency which models of traditional cultures seem to afford. Plausible models of hybrid culture-forms offering greater political and economic autonomy while eschewing fantasies of a purified identity are lacking.

The hybrid architecture shown here is therefore offered, not only as an example of what individual architects have achieved in the past, but also as a more general metaphor for other possible future hybrid culture-forms. It is possible, therefore, to look upon such architecture as representing the product of a creative process of cultural interaction, which, while being associated in these cases with colonialism, might also be produced out of other sorts of global interactions, and other, less destructive cultural balances of power; in short, wherever two or more vital cultures meet and produce their hybrid offspring.

14 REGIONAL TRANSFORMATIONS

First published in *The Architectural Review*, November 1986.

Regionalism attempts to put back into architecture what orthodox Modernism conspicuously took out, namely, continuity in a given place between past and present forms of building. As a movement, its gathering appeal is as strong in the West as it is in the rest of the world, to which Modernism was exported. But it is in the countries of the Third World, where the effects of Modernism's break with the past have been compounded by a drastically speeded-up rate of development, that regionalism has a special meaning. For the inhabitants of these countries, the business of deciding what does or does not belong in their region acquires political and emotional dimensions that smack of a basic struggle for cultural survival, frequently couched in the plaintive terms of a 'search for identity'.

Yet the requirements of a viable architectural continuity are anything but clear cut. Even the most favoured architectural images of local culture are suspect. These are the non-monumental forms usually lumped together as the products of 'non-architects',[1] or 'unselfconscious' developmental processes.[2] They are selected in the belief that such architecture alone represents the ideal, seamless harmony between built form, culture, place and climate that was lost to international Modernism, and must be regained. However, sufficient anomalies abound to confuse this romantic picture and to discredit any simplistic notions of a folk architecture unaffected by extraneous influences.

CROSS-CULTURAL EFFECTS

Contrary to these images, such architecture is not always local in origin and may derive, wholly or in part, from other sources. Where truly indigenous examples are found, as in the mud-brick architecture of the central Nejd area of the Arabian Peninsula, they are the outcome of relatively isolated situations. More often, as in the dwellings on either coast of the same Peninsula, contact with other cultures, whether by trade, conquest or pilgrimage, has left an indelible mark.[3] For example, the 'hanging' balconies, or *rowshans*, that embellish the dwellings of Jeddah and other cities of the Hijaz, are exclusive to that area only in detail, and were introduced by Ottoman Turks. As well as being found in Istanbul, similar features turn up in cities across the Mediterranean region, including Cairo, Tunis, and Valletta, on the island of Malta.

14.1.
Indigenous mud-brick dwellings of the Nejd region, central Saudi Arabia. Photo: Chris Abel.

14.2a.
'Hanging balconies' and bay windows, or *rowshan* of Jeddah, Saudi Arabia, are based on Turkish models. Photo: Chris Abel.

14.2b.
'Hanging balconies' of Istanbul, Turkey. Photo: Chris Abel.

14.3.
Traditional 'hybrid' houses in Malacca State, Malaysia, typically feature Chinese style tiled stairways, introduced by immigrants. Photo: Chris Abel.

The typical house-on-stilts of Malaysia provides another instance of 'indigenous' architecture that has actually travelled from somewhere else. More accurately described as a family of related dwelling types, the form originates in various islands of the Malay Archipelago, now Indonesia, and the major types found in Malacca, Perak, and the east coast states of Malaysia, each reflect something of the respective cultural groups which came to settle in different parts of the mainland.[4] To these basic types were then added other features, also sometimes imported. The distinctive tiled stairways of the Malacca houses, for example, derive from the architecture of Chinese immigrants who also settled in the Malacca Straits.

Even more perplexing are the anomalies to be found between culture and built form, such as occur where major forms of religion have been imported from other regions, and adopted by the local population as their own. The peoples of Southeast Asia, who embraced first Hinduism, then Islam, resolved the different building requirements of the two religions by largely ignoring those differences. By the time Islam was introduced by traders into the Malay Archipelago in the fifteenth century, the defining attributes of the mosque had already been established elsewhere for several hundred years. Yet the building type that was actually adopted for the purpose, first in the islands, then in the Malay Peninsula, already existed in the region. It is traced to both a quasi-religious component of the well to do Javanese house, and more importantly to the typical Hindu–Javanese temple structure, also familiar in Bali, and has its antecedents in even earlier animistic beliefs and practices. A characteristic of the form is its centripetal plan and *meru* roof type, a pyrimidal form of several layers supported by four central pillars, all features expressive of Hindu–Javanese cosmology.[5] By adapting Islamic practices to a local building type, rather than importing more orthodox but 'alien' building forms, potential conflicts between new and old ways of life

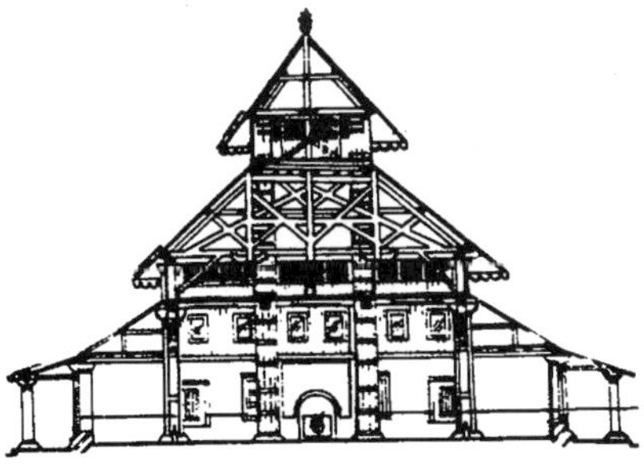

14.4.
Great Mosque, Demak, Java, Indonesia, c. 1750. Cross section showing layered roofs and supporting pillars. From Nasir, 1984.

were reduced, but with the odd and probably unanticipated result that any interpretation still yields ambiguous results.

The aims and methods of regionalists are further complicated if it is acknowledged that even the strongest of monumental architecture may be adapted to different conditions of place and culture. In the West, the extreme example is the Pantheon in Rome, with its countless progeny and their regional variations.[6] Roman precedents are also traced in Islamic architecture. Since the Islamic Empire covered much the same ground as the earlier Roman Empire, the builders of Islam in these areas assimilated many of the forms and techniques of antiquity. Consequently, the typical hypostyle mosque owes much to Roman building types,[7] notably the basilica-forum complex, as well as to the Prophet's own courtyard house, which was the original source of inspiration. Though the model never took hold in Southeast Asia, later variants throughout the remaining Islamic world show further evidence of the simultaneous expression of both local and imported influences.

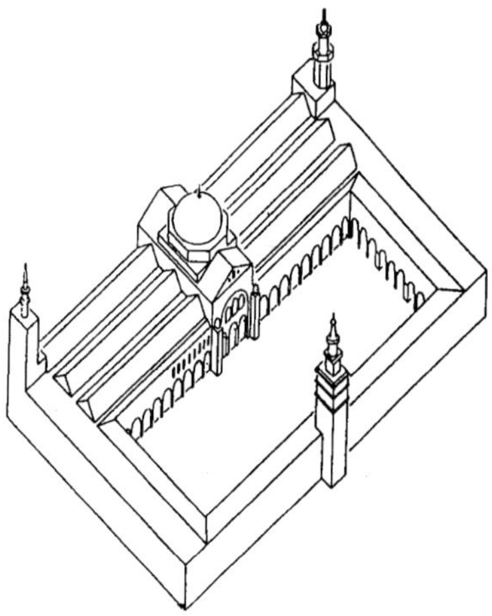

14.5.
Great Mosque, Damascus, AD 706–714/5. The configuration was based on Roman archetypes and in turn became a model for later hypostyle mosques throughout the Islamic world. From Kuban, 1974.

MIXED LESSONS FROM COLONIAL ARCHITECTURE

Colonial architecture offers further examples of the mixed fruits of cultural exchange. In order to function effectively, colonialism required that the representatives of the metropolitan centre should be settled in reasonable comfort, even in the most peripheral reaches of the empire. Since to 'function effectively' also meant impressing local inhabitants with the power and 'superior' culture and lifestyle of their exploiters, those comforts might include anything from full-blown replicas of the Colosseum, to more recent Tudor-style cricket clubs and inns. Once again, Southeast Asia, which has assimilated so many different cultures[8] as to be the world's premier multi-cultural laboratory, yields plentiful examples. The hill stations of Malaysia, which were themselves modelled on hill stations in British India, notably at Simla,[9] offered not merely the chance to shake off the latest bout of malaria at a cooler altitude; they recreated the complete ambiance of the Sussex country retreat. From the cosy furniture right down to the reassuring rose bushes and mown lawns in the garden, and even the strawberries on the dining-room table (which, like the roses, flourish in the cooler climate of the hills), the whole environment is a homage to the colonists' place of origin.

Such exacting duplication of the familiar environment was, however, by no means the whole story. In the process of settling in, some of the colonists' architectural baggage underwent major transformations, not least to accommodate the tropical climate at normal elevations. And while, as with the colonial villas of Malaysia and Singapore, such adaptation might be safely described as a straightforward response to the natural elements, it might also be argued that the colonists did not work it all out for themselves from scratch, but were taking their cues from the traditional Malay house. The result is an authentic series of residences,[10] a marriage of East and West, brokered by practical builders who also knew their Palladio, and bearing clear traces, not only of ancient Rome – what better source of imperial inspiration – but also of the wide open and breezy forms of the Malay house type.

14.6.
Colosseum, El Jem, near Sousse, Tunisia, AD 230, was built by the Emperor Gordian for Roman colonists. Photo: Chris Abel.

14.7.
Tudor-style inn, Cameron Highlands, near Kuala Lumpur, was built early this century as part of the colonial hill station. Photo: Chris Abel.

14.8.
Colonial villa built for former British army officers, Penang, 1936. Photo: Chris Abel.

14.9.
Former Malayan Railway Administration Headquarters, 1917, and Kuala Lumpur Railway Station and Hotel (left), 1911. Architect: A. B. Hubbock. Photo: Chris Abel.

It might be said that the typical European villa and the Malay house are both detached, family dwellings, ideally standing in natural surroundings, and that a practical exchange between the two culture-forms was in the offing. But British colonists also imported new building types, for which there was no conceivable local parallel, and which were also localized.[11] The solution in Malaysia, as well as in India, was to make free use of monumental Islamic architecture (imported, in the case of Malaysia, on the assumption that the style was in keeping with the local religion), by which the British governors of New Delhi and Kuala Lumpur transformed their administrative and public buildings, all the better to sweeten the imperial pill.[12] Again, it may be noted that the significant result was not any single building, but the production of a consistent series. That there have been recent local changes of heart and a new willingness to regard these buildings, for all their quirks, as belonging to the national heritage, is owed to a growing sense of regional self-confidence, as well as the capacity of building forms to take on new meanings. While Asians may not yet embrace their colonial past with the same equanimity with which the British regard their Norman architecture, there is an increasing awareness that more recently imported models of buildings make the earlier colonial forms look, by comparison, like the genuine home-grown thing.[13]

RELATIONS OF ANALOGY

The problem in trying to deal with such anomalies is that the social psychology commonly used to describe cultural identities is often mixed up with logical concepts that are unsuited to the ambivalent nature of the continuities involved. Any logical question of identity demands an unequivocal answer. Either one thing is identical to another in some respects, at the same point in time or at any other point, or it is not. Used in the context of defining continuities of human behaviour, the requirement for logical symmetry poses questions that are impossible to answer, even for continuities of individual behaviour,[14] let alone culture-forms. Things become more realistic, and manageable, if it is allowed that the sought-for continuities are not the all-or-nothing relations of identity, but more tolerant connections of some sort between different states of existence, most usefully described in terms of relations of analogy. Looked at this way, how the archetypal mosque, the Malay house and the colonial villa originate in diverse precedents and come to function in their own respective roles as models of architectural form, is more relevant to understanding the nature of architectural continuities than any romantic ideal of pure culture.

For both monumental and non-monumental architecture generally, the crucial measure of historical import is not the individual work taken separately, but the whole linked series of precedents and later variants, with all their transformations over time, each of which in turn becomes an actual or potential model which can beget still more transformations.[15] Replications of the model provide those essential elements of continuity through change by which cultures measure their lineage. Transformations of building form are the imprint made on these enduring models by the more particular circumstances of place, programme and history, as interpreted by the builders of the day. Nor, as used to be thought, does the influence of existing models hinder creativity. On the contrary, the creation of new models in architecture most often arises out of a cross-pollination between existing but previously unrelated ideas and forms, a process also best described as analogical,[16] and which is often stimulated by exchanges between different cultures. In these confusing times of the global village, some comfort may therefore be taken from observing that the true grist of regional architecture lies in a creative process of cultural cross-fertilization and localization of imported models, rather than in the purified identities[17] associated with the usual references.

BAUHAUS BRAINWASH

If normality, as well as due importance, were to be ascribed to the sorts of journeys made across the boundaries of time, place and culture, by persistent but adaptable models of building form, the range of possible references for contemporary regionalists might be broadened. Nevertheless, given a more liberal interpretation of what is regional, it must still be wondered why contemporary architects generally achieve less satisfactory results than their acquisitive predecessors.

Unfortunately, the tendency to import Western forms of architecture brought with it the worst aspects of Bauhaus educational ideology and method. According to this legacy, the ideal state of mental preparedness for beginning students of architecture is assumed, in line with the clean sheet theory of creativity, to be that early state of childhood innocence as yet uncorrupted by historical awareness or any other cultural or educational persuasion.[18] Though this all-too efficient system of brainwashing has now exhausted its most destructive effects in the West, its influence is still strong among teachers in the developing world (who usually picked up their methods while completing their own occidental education), with negative consequences for the encouragement of any sensitivity toward regional culture. While constructive experiments occasionally surface, the educational knowledge base required for any widespread and creative reinterpretation of regional history simply does not yet exist.

14.10.
Walian House, Kuala Lumpur, 1984. Cross-section through central open space. Architect: Jimmy Lim.

RECENT INITIATIVES

Fortunately there are a few exceptions to prove the rule, mostly the work of self-taught architects who instructed themselves in their own regional traditions to compensate for what formal education left out. Nevertheless, even these successes, especially in the tropics, tend to be limited to those building types such as dwellings, resort hotels and educational buildings, where the function, limited scale and natural surroundings permit a relatively uncomplicated adaptation of local forms and materials.

Into this category falls most of the work of Geoffrey Bawa in Sri Lanka, who is also much influenced by local colonial models.[19] Less well-known but accomplished architects include Jimmy Lim in Malaysia, who takes Bawa as his role model, the Kampulan Akitek Group in Singapore, and Francisco Manosa in The Philippines, all of whom have produced interesting houses and hotels inspired by local precedents. Otherwise the pastiche, or traditional 'hat' placed atop standard International Style forms, is the common answer to the problem of expressing regional character and identity. Even some traditional building types, such as the shophouse of Chinese origin,[20] which would seem to be easily adapted for contemporary urban purposes, have, with rare exception, been ignored by local architects in favour of the usual international solutions.

14.11.
Dynasty Hotel, Singapore. Photo: Chris Abel.

It is tempting to think that the main problems in those regions where timber is the traditional building material are the structural and formal limitations of the technology. Yet the example set by contemporary Japanese architects in producing a convincing body of regional architecture analogous with their own traditions, but using different materials and technologies, belies such defeatism.[21] The Japanese success needs to be better understood, but it may well be due to the uninterrupted respect contemporary architects have retained for past ways of building. As well as benefiting from the 'Modern' qualities of traditional Japanese architecture, with its flexible modular spaces and open, timber-frame structures, the historical tendency towards structural expressionism evident in the larger-scale palaces and temples also presents Japanese architects with a powerful aesthetic tradition capable of translation into modern ferro-concrete or steel structures. The Hongkong and Shanghai Bank headquarters by Norman Foster is one recent, if indirect, beneficiary of Japanese experiments; the 'oriental' look of this otherwise ultra-modern building having not a little to do with traditional Japanese transparency as well as the exaggerated display of exposed structural elements that characterizes Buddhist temples and pagodas.[22]

Some individual initiatives elsewhere in the developing world are also receiving much deserved attention. Charles Correa's highly eclectic regionalism draws freely upon the works of Le Corbusier, Louis Kahn, Luis Barragan and Charles Moore, as well as more local sources, to solve modern building programmes in India.[23] More on the fringe of the developing world but still relevant, Richard England has addressed himself to the special problems of tourism in Malta.[24] His hotels seem to grow straight out of the limestone rock from which the island fortress is made, and offer lessons for those developing countries wishing to exploit the character of their region, without destroying that character in the process.

14.12.
Sky House, Bunkyo-ku, Tokyo, 1957–58. Architect: Kiyonori Kikutake. Photo: Y. Futagawa.

RENAISSANCE OF ISLAMIC ARCHITECTURE

But it is the rediscovery of Islamic building traditions that currently offers the greatest potential, where they are relevant, for the development of a viable contemporary regionalism of consistent high quality, capable of providing for many building types, both old and new. The potential derives from the sheer richness of the heritage, which, as an adaptable language of form, diversified over 1200-odd years of continuous development across several continents, rivals the classical language of the West in its range of application.[25]

Despite its many roots in antiquity, a Renaissance of Islamic architecture could not have been easily foreseen in the West. It seems astonishing now, that though Western students of architecture are still taught

14.13.
Festaval Tourist Village, Mellieha Bay, Malta, 1980. Architect: Richard England. Photo: Chris Abel.

14.14a.

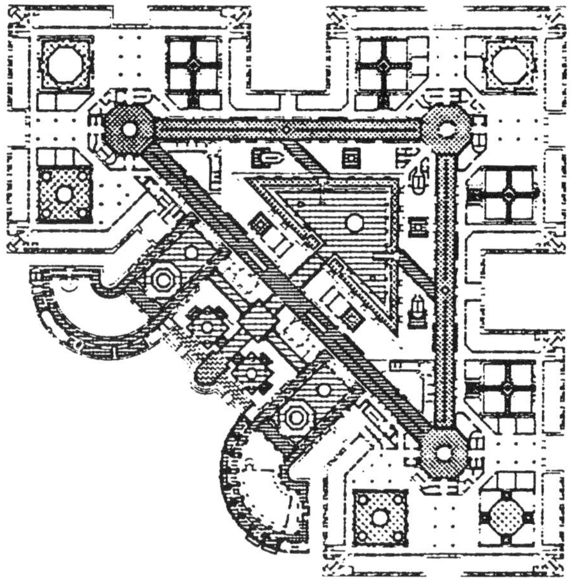

14.14b.

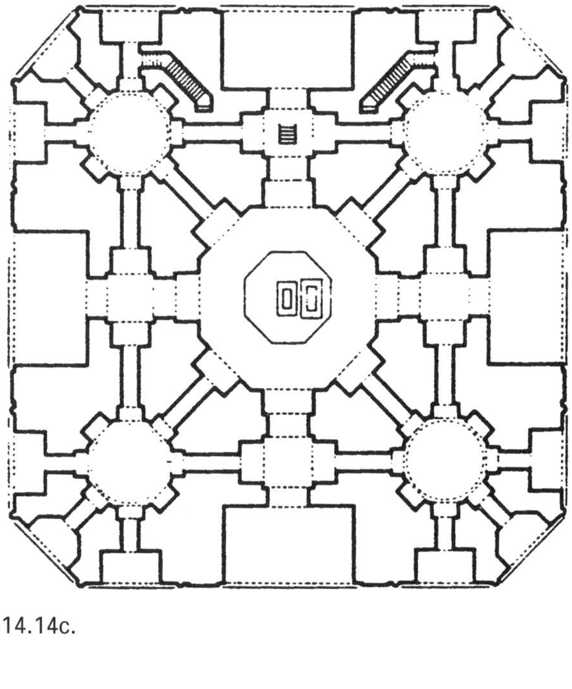

14.14c.

14.14a.
Ministry of Foreign Affairs. Interior view of 'street' or *souk*. Architect: Henning Larsen. Photo: Chris Abel.

14.14b.
Ministry of Foreign Affairs. Plan at upper ground floor level. Architect: Henning Larsen.

14.14c.
Taj Mahal, Agra, India, 1632–54. Plan. From H. Stierlin, *Encyclopedia of World Architecture*, 1979.

the beginnings of civilization in Mesopotamia, and are familiarized with the monuments of ancient Egypt, history lessons should thereafter abruptly change location, to be redirected to the northern coasts of the Mediterranean, never to return further south. If we consider also that it was the diligent efforts of Arab scholars in resuscitating early Greek science that eventually helped fuel the European Renaissance,[26] the sudden irreversible leap across the Mediterranean looks mightily suspicious. Add to this that the European 'Dark Ages' coincided more or less with the 'Golden Age' of the Islamic Empire, and the Eurocentric pattern becomes lamentably clear. In turn, the same educational lobotomies as

14.15.
Haj Terminal, King Abdul Aziz International Airport, Jeddah, 1982. Architect: Skidmore Owings and Merrill. Courtesy of the Aga Khan Award for Architecture.

14.16a.
Figure-ground study of Ad-Dira district, in the historic core of Riyadh, showing dense pattern of courtyard houses and narrow streets. From Al-Hathloul, Al-Hussayen and Shuaibi, 1975.

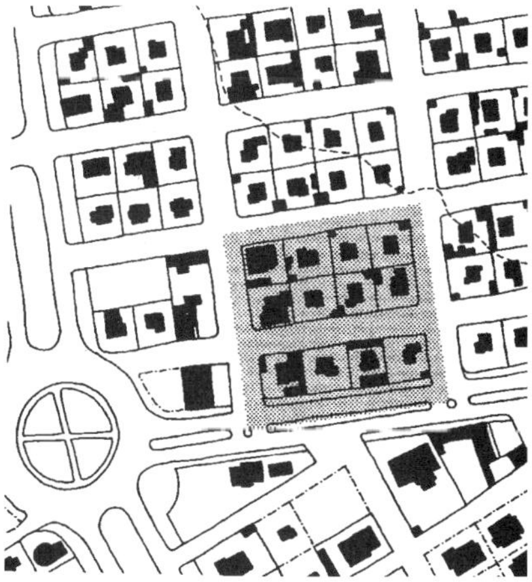

14.16b.
Figure-ground study showing modern residential pattern in Malazz district, Riyadh. From Al-Hathloul, Al-Hussayen and Shuaibi, 1975.

were performed elsewhere, were also carried out on Muslim architects, with like devastating effects on any historical consciousness. Thus we have the ironic situation where some of the best regional architecture in the Islamic world is designed by Western architects, the pick of whom have been recruited by wealthy patrons in Saudi Arabia and elsewhere to try to create an alternative to the prevailing international models.

As one notable example of this trend, Henning Larsen's building for the Ministry of Foreign Affairs in Riyadh represents an extraordinary feat of empathetic imagination. Though Larsen's appreciation of Islamic architecture has its blind spots (mainly with regard to the use of ornament), it may be asked whether more reverential attitudes would have allowed the architect to do what he did, which was to take the plan of the most famous tomb in the world, the Taj Mahal in India, to house a modern bureaucracy in Saudi Arabia, producing some memorable spaces in the process.[27]

Larsen's bold reference to a familiar Islamic monument contrasts with the more orthodox approach of Skidmore Owings and Merrill. Though SOM shun any too explicit use of traditional models, both their tented Haj Terminal[28] at Jeddah Airport and their introverted office tower for the National Commercial Bank,[29] also in Jeddah, offer dramatic metaphors for regional forms of shelter, as well as rational responses to the harsh local climate. Like Foster's Hongkong Bank, SOM's buildings give Modernism a subtle but telling shove in the direction of regionalism.

RESPONSES TO CHANGING URBAN CONTEXT

The introduction of new urban building types and their related social and commercial institutions, as well as modern transport systems, has been paralleled by a restructuring of major urban centres along the lines of the dispersed Western city. The historic cores, where they have been allowed to remain at all, now stand as only mute reminders of a recent but already remote past and way of life. The result is a complete reversal of the spatial pattern of the traditional Arab city with its courtyard dwellings, from a compact mass of building-with-holes-in, to the familiar international pattern of detached buildings strung along new highways.[30]

A handful of committed local architects who survived their orthodox Modernist education, have made attempts to recreate the original dense structure of housing and *souks*, or markets, of the historic core. The rebuilding of the El Hafsia quarter in the Medina, or old city of Tunis, by

14.17.
El Hafsia Quarter, Medina, Tunis. Architect: Wassim Ben Mahoud. Photo: Chris Abel.

14.18.
Modern suburban villas, Riyadh. Photo: Chris Abel.

Wassim Ben Mahoud, is one of the more successful projects of this kind.[31] On a larger scale, the Justice Palace District in Riyadh, by the Beehah Group and Rasem Badran, provides modern commercial facilities and apartment buildings in like form. The last team also produced a similarly inspired dense linear core of public buildings and housing for the new Diplomatic Quarter situated in the suburbs of Riyadh.

But such attempts to recreate or update historic urban patterns are few and far between. More typical is the sort of standard international exercise, represented at its dubious best by Kenzo Tange's Alkhairia Centre, also in Riyadh, which makes no concessions at all to either climate or tradition. The courtyard house type that went along with the older pattern has likewise been displaced by the free-standing villa. Despite its unsuitability for the climate and the lack of privacy and related inconveniences following on from the loss of the traditional internal open space, the villa is now the preferred status symbol for old and new generations alike.

SPECTRUM OF APPROACHES

It is against this changing urban context that the work of two architectural practices in particular merits special attention. Of the two, the Egyptian architect, Abdelwahed El-Wakil, takes the more strictly traditionalist approach, following on from the example set by his mentor, Hassan Fathy.[32] The courtyard dwellings and mosques which dominate El-Wakil's practice have enabled the architect to exploit a well-established vocabulary of form, mostly drawn from the historic buildings of his native Cairo. However, El-Wakil's carefully researched designs do more than bring back to life a neglected body of traditional knowledge and technique. They also present would-be creative regionalists with timely reminders of the old adage that, 'in order to break a rule, first know the rule'.

El-Wakil's own transformations, especially on the theme of mosque architecture, are not immediately apparent to those who see nothing but the familiar courtyards, arcades, domes and minarets. They have more to do with a subtle response to the new, low density, exposed urban context of nearly all his sites. Contrary to his historic models, which are hemmed in by surrounding buildings and present deadpan faces to the outside world, El-Wakil's buildings mostly stand apart and alone. In the case of his mosques on the Jeddah Corniche, they are spectacularly isolated; delicately sculptured forms designed to be appreciated in the round. Still following tradition, the intimate spaces of the courtyards and prayer rooms beckon with no less appeal. Increasingly, as El-Wakil plays more and more freely with the sculptural qualities of his buildings, they exhibit both a contemporary as well as a distinctively northern Mediterranean flavour, perhaps pointing towards another cross-cultural merger.[33]

14.19.
Rewais Mosque, Jeddah Corniche, 1986–87. Architect: Abdul El-Wakil.

The Aga Khan University and Hospital complex in Karachi, by Payette Associates, affords lessons of a different kind, both in the complex nature of the modern functional programme involved, and in the way the architects approached the problem of interpreting Islamic traditions. In this last respect it is noteworthy that, though Payette Associates is an American firm, the design of the hospital benefited from the participation of Moshan Khadem, an Iranian born consultant respected for his knowledge of Islamic architecture. In addition, as part of their preparation, the architects undertook an extensive tour of Islamic monuments in Pakistan, the Middle East, North Africa and Spain.[34]

The resulting architecture reflects more of a liberal interpretation of Islamic design principles than any direct transposition of specific forms, though there is evidence of that, too, at a more detailed level. If anything, the principal language of form used is confidently Modern, Corbusian *brise-soleil* and Ronchamp-inspired entrance ways (much enlarged versions of the window openings inside the chapel, with their deep, asymmetrical reveals) being much in evidence. Beyond specific features, the whole complex has something of an 'industrial' look about it, which can throw the careless observer off the track of the building's other origins.

14.20.
The Aga Khan University and Hospital, Karachi, Pakistan, 1985. Much of the complex is naturally ventilated and incorporates a number of technical features based on regional practice, such as roof level 'wind catchers' (which look like northlights), open timber and terracotta screens, and a special textured render which casts countless tiny shadows on the surface and reduces heat gain and glare. Architect: Payette Associates. Photo: Chris Abel.

The regional qualities come across in the introverted spatial pattern of connected courtyard buildings and carefully managed sequence of oblique transitions from one discrete space to the next, as well as in the very un-Modern attention to the surface treatment and ornamentation. The lavish use of water, both as ornament and humidifier, and open timber *jali* screens also add traditional touches, and help to modify the climate. Even the low key, industrial look can be ascribed to the architects' desire to tone down the external features of the design, in favour of focusing on the internal spaces. Despite this, the geometry of the outward-facing wards and other sections asserts itself to the point where, as in El-Wakil's mosques, a judicious balance is achieved between internal and external aspects, in keeping with the building's open site in the Karachi suburbs.

Aside from the individual merits of these buildings, the two practices between them define a broad spectrum ranging from direct to indirect approaches to regional architecture. The first leans toward a creative interpretation of specific regional building forms, while the second leans more toward designing from general principles extracted from the same traditions. Neither approach can ever be mutually exclusive, each relying to some extent on the other, but the differences are significant enough to suggest a wide range of alternative strategies for future regionalists.

A similar spectrum might have been drawn between Larsen's MOFA building in Riyadh and SOM's buildings in Jeddah. But it is less clear at this time whether or not either of these unique buildings constitutes the making of a viable series. The chief strength of El-Wakil's dwellings and mosques, and of Payette's building, is that they offer a clear promise of reproducible models, capable of adaptation to the specific contingencies of place and programme. El-Wakil's mosques already constitute a series in themselves, each new building developing further the model established by the last one. In the case of the university and hospital in Karachi, it is possible to see the emergence of a more general model of building, based upon what might be called the concept of an urban oasis, which responds to the realities of new functional programmes and urban frameworks. At the same time, the urban oasis offers the security and privacy of enclosed spaces and other familiar elements of traditional Islamic architecture.

CHALLENGE TO WESTERN HEGEMONY

Beyond these specific architectural achievements, a broader pattern is emerging, pointing to a cultural shift of global dimensions. Given the power still wielded by the industrialized nations of the North, not least in the fascination American popular culture exerts throughout the developing world, it may be premature to talk of the end of Western cultural domination in architecture. But what is new and striking is that increasing numbers of architects and their clients in developing regions, as well as Western designers operating in the same countries, are now turning to local and other alternative culture-forms for appropriate models. After being brainwashed for so long into thinking that what is West is best, the change in attitude is significant. At the very least it may be hoped that the divergence of cultural models may help to counteract, if not yet reverse, the convergent global patterns till now taken so much for granted.

15 PRIME OBJECTS

Aside from the automobile, the high-rise office building, whether tower, slab or block, is probably the most easily recognizable symbol of modernity the world over. Like the former, it is also just as much a focus of popular abuse as of admiration. Yet while architects might be blamed for the specific failings of their own designs, they can hardly be blamed for the type itself. Much as they may like to claim the credit for such things, modern building types are generally the product of economic, social and technological forces beyond architects' responsibility or power of control. By the same criteria, whereas the first tall buildings in Chicago would have grown just as tall without the aid of Louis Sullivan's embellishments, they could not have done so without the invention of the steel frame or the mechanical elevator.

But if Chicago's upwardly mobile skyline was shaped more by a combination of central city land prices, corporate needs, and engineering and mechanical ingenuity rather than aesthetic considerations, individual designers have since made significant modifications to the basic office form, often going well beyond the skin-deep attentions to which we have become accustomed. The result has been a number of innovative deviations from the standard 'kebab' of stacked floors around a service core, each of which in turn has spawned replicas of its own. As such these exceptional buildings merit the special designation of 'prime objects'[1] in the development of twentieth-century architecture.

15.1.
New York Life Building, Chicago, 1894–5. Architect: Jennie and Mundie. From Ada Louise Huxtable, *The Tall Building Artistically Considered*, 1992.

BREAKING THE MOULD

The first to break the original mould was George H. Wyman, with his Bradbury Building in Los Angeles, completed in 1893.[2] Instead of a solid core, Wyman created a top-lit, atrium-cum-circulation space considerably enhanced by the iron lacework of the exposed lifts and stairways. Aside from this major innovation, however, the surrounding cellular offices maintained the same spatial and visual separation between office workers characteristic of the standard tower. It was left to Frank Lloyd Wright, with his Larkin Company Office Building (1904) in Buffalo, to go the next step. Wright literally turned the standard form inside out, replacing the solid central core with a full height atrium, and moving the vertical circulation systems and services into hollow towers and ducts placed around the perimeter of the building.[3] He also left each floor completely

15.2.
Bradbury Building, Los Angeles, 1889–93. Interior of atrium. Architect: George H. Wyman. Photo: Chris Abel.

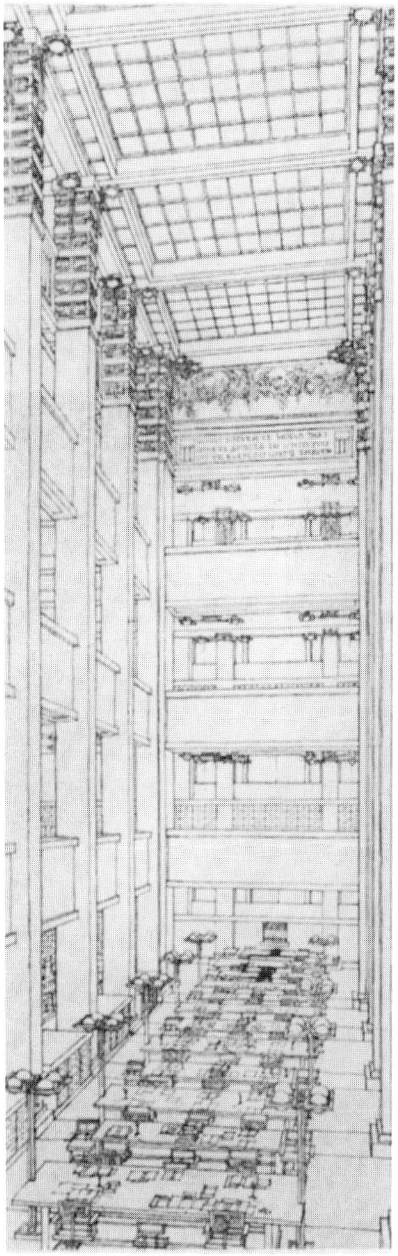

15.3.
Larkin Building, Buffalo, 1903. Interior of atrium. Architect: Frank Lloyd Wright. From Scully, 1960.

open to the atrium, creating a vast unitary space from any point of which it was possible to see into most other parts of the building.

Wright's primary aim was undoubtedly the creation of a new kind of continuous space – a vertical version of his horizontal experiments – but the open interior also had the result of introducing a new sense of corporate unity to the office environment. Previously, all employees were spatially, visually and socially separated into vertical strata and connected between floors only indirectly by lifts and stairways. Specifically designed for one corporate owner, the Larkin Building changed all that, making each and every employee dramatically aware that they belonged to a larger – and no doubt in executive eyes – more significant whole.

The second major deviation to impact on office design was Mies van der Rohe's sharply angled Glass Skyscraper project (1919) in Berlin, which was followed soon after by a second similar project based on a curvilinear plan.[4] Though both projects shared irregular plan geometries Mies adhered to the standard arrangement of identical floors radiating out from a central core (split into twin cores for the second project). The originality of the two projects lay more in the use of an all-glass skin, displacing the conventional stone cladding with a daring new transparency. As both the drawings and models demonstrate, Mies also clearly understood the potentially expressive qualities and reflective properties of glass, capable of mirroring both surrounding buildings and an ever-changing sky.

It was Gordon Bunshaft, however, who, as chief designer for Skidmore Owings and Merrill, gave the Glass Skyscraper its definitive form thirty years later in the curtain-walled Lever House (1952) in New York. Air-conditioned to be habitable in all weathers, the all-glass Lever House was swiftly adopted as the standard corporate home and is the primary source of all those thousands of crystalline replicas dotted

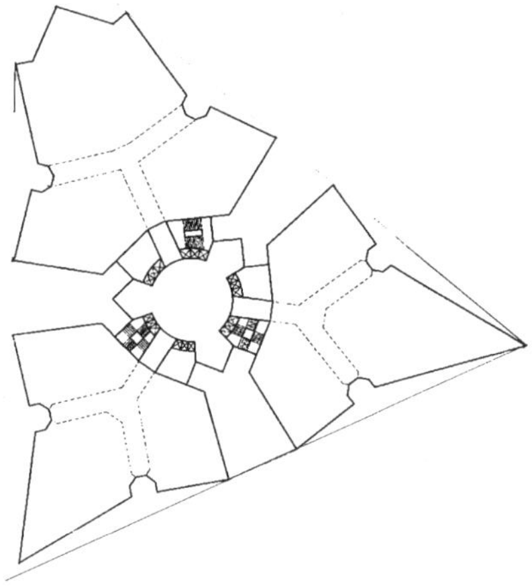

15.4a.
Glass Skyscraper project, Berlin, 1919. Architect: Mies van der Rohe. From Spaeth, 1985.

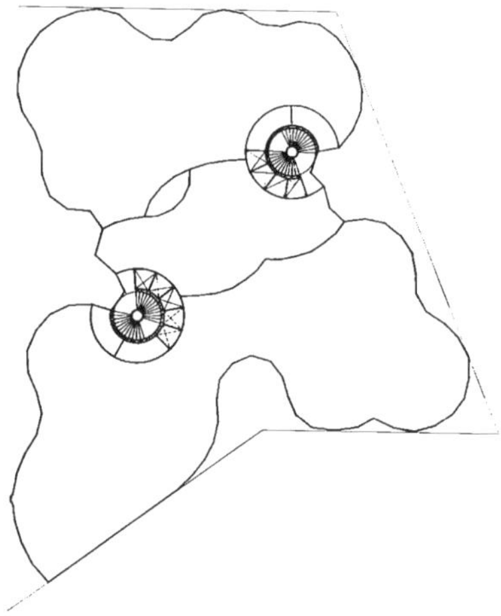

15.4b.
Glass Tower project, Germany, 1921. Architect: Mies van der Rohe. From Spaeth, 1985.

15.5.
Lever House, New York, 1952. Architect: Gordon Bunshaft for Skidmore Owings and Merrill. Photo: Ezra Stoller ©.

15.6.
National Commercial Bank, Jeddah, 1982. Architect: Gordon Bunshaft for Skidmore Owings and Merrill.

around the world, which have done so much to negate climatic and cultural differences. Yet at the time it was built, the design was quite unique. Not only was it the first to realize Mies's earlier visions of a glass architecture, but the dynamic composition of a thin vertical slab mounted over a floating horizontal podium was also directly in the revolutionary, anti-classical spirit of early Modernism, though a great deal more subdued than any Constructivist exercise.

The National Commercial Bank,[5] Jeddah, also designed another thirty years later by Bunshaft for SOM, presents the third major deviation from the standard form. The design represents not only a complete turnabout in its architect's philosophy, but also a radical shift in Modern architecture, away from universality, towards a regionalized Modernism. While the triangular building shares the same purity of form as its Modern predecessors, it also introduces a number of innovations specific to its location, including several features designed to modify the impact of the intense sun on the surface of the building. Thus all glazed surfaces are recessed and face into three shaded 'skycourts' or 'hanging gardens', making deep incisions into the otherwise monolithic block, two on one side, one on the other, alternating vertically in a spiral arrangement. All other external surfaces are covered with a well-insulated stone cladding. A vertical shaft in the centre of the structure formed by the overlapping 'V'-shaped floor plans facilitates the upward movement of air through the courtyards, further cooling the glazed walls.

The idea of the skycourts was partly inspired by regional courtyard building typologies, and if the change in scale makes the visual connection seem somewhat remote, there is no doubting the effectiveness of the solution as a form of climate control, as well as a sheltered recreational space, which is also just what traditional courtyards provide. For all its obvious modernity, therefore, SOM's tower represents a significant step in the development of a localized, high-rise architecture.

VARIATIONS

While the Larkin Building, the Lever House, and the NCB Building are all the first of their kind and may therefore be properly described as prime objects in their respective series, later architects have also introduced innovations of their own which have led in turn to significant variations, without breaking the essential continuity of the series. They may also, by introducing variations of this kind, have helped to sustain the line in a changing cultural and technological environment. Thus Mies van der Rohe and Philip Johnson's Seagram Building, with all its neo-classical refinements and subtleties, helped to make the glass and steel tower series more acceptable to a prestige-conscious clientele. Built on New York's Park Avenue across from the Lever House, Mies's much modified version of his own earlier visionary projects presents a markedly different impression to SOM's building. In place of the former's horizontally and vertically opposed slim-line slabs, Mies offers a single, dominant tower of stouter proportions, set well back from the street line so as to offer the best possible view of the free-standing structure. If not as obvious a neo-classical design as some of Mies's

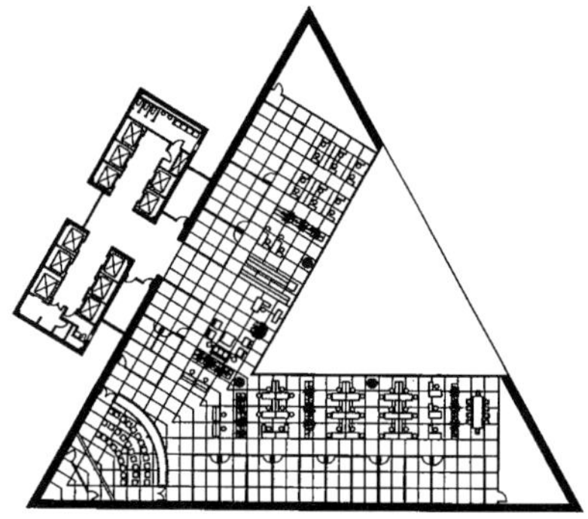

15.7a.

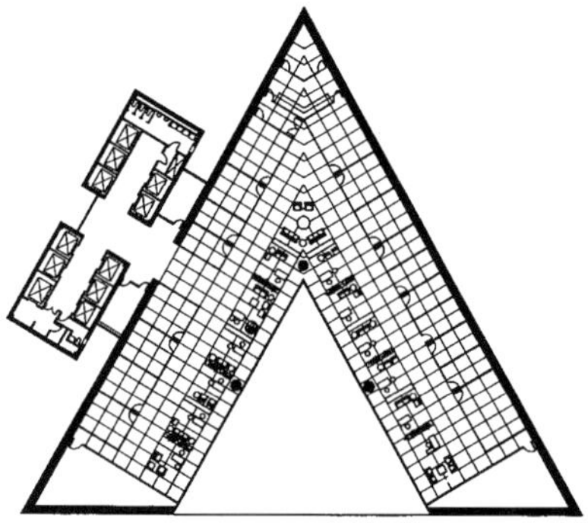

15.7b.

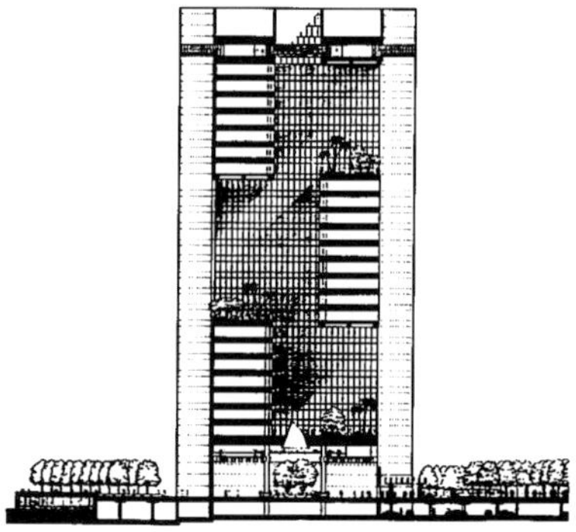

15.7c.

15.7a and b.
National Commercial Bank. Plans showing alternating triangular configuration. Architect: Gordon Bunshaft for Skidmore Owings and Merrill.

15.7c.
National Commercial Bank. Section. Architect: Gordon Bunshaft for Skidmore Owings and Merrill.

15.8.
Seagram Building, New York, 1954–8. Architect: Mies van der Rohe with Philip Johnson. Photo: Ezra Stoller ©.

other works, the Seagram Building's simplified form, solid composition and proportions, all fronted by an open 'piazza', represents a parallel development and updating of the classical ideal of pure form and geometry, now in the service of corporate America, lending a much-valued image of timeless authority.

More recently, both Sir Norman Foster and Sir Richard Rogers revived a previously moribund atrium series with their radical designs for the Hongkong and Shanghai Bank and Lloyd's HQ.[6] Like the Larkin Building, both focus an open floor layout on spectacular internal atria, supplemented by a host of technological innovations which helped to breathe new life into the form. These include an exposed megastructure and a dual vertical circulation system comprising high-speed lifts for long journeys and moving escalators for short journeys. Aside from the convenience, the highly visible localized movement system was purposefully designed to increase social

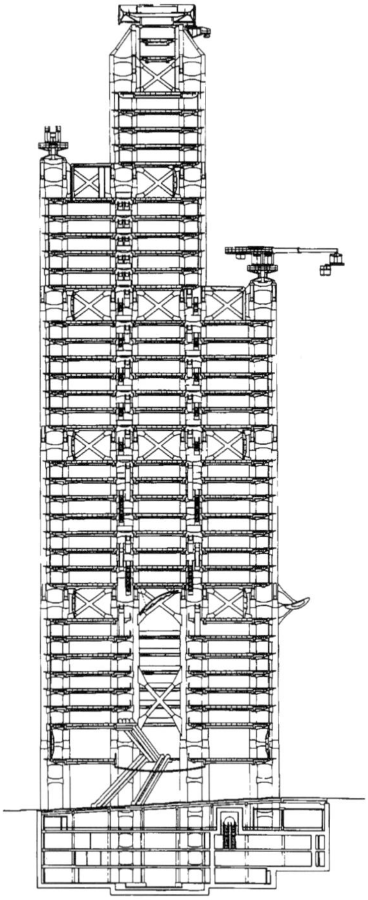

15.9.
Hongkong & Shanghai Bank, 1986. Section. Architect: Foster Associates.

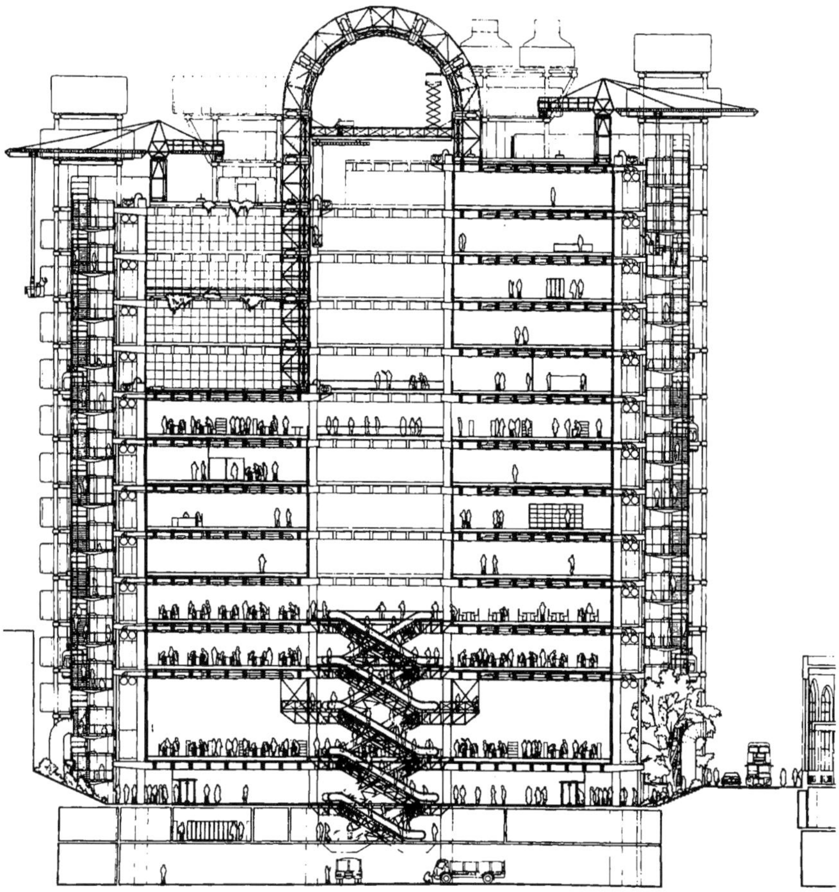

15.10.
Lloyd's Building, 1986. Section. Architect: Richard Rogers Partnership.

contact between the building's occupants, thus consolidating one of the major features of the series associated with the Larkin Building. Though belonging to the same series, they also differ in significant ways from each other. Where the Lloyd's HQ replicates the Larkin Building's internal orientation with its mostly opaque skin covered in service ducts, the Hongkong Bank achieves an external as well as internal transparency which owes as much to Mies's early projects as to Frank Lloyd Wright's and takes full advantage of the splendid views of Hong Kong. Where also the spatial and corporate unity of the Lloyd's HQ is confirmed by the full height atrium, the unity of the bank is substantially modified by the structural division into batches of suspended floors separated by double height floor spaces, which also serves to accommodate the organizational divisions within the bank.

Ralph Erskine's 'Ark' in London marks the latest development in the same series, towards greater spatial and social complexity.[7] Whereas the Larkin Building, the Hongkong and Shanghai Bank and Lloyd's HQ were designed primarily for their single owners' use, the 'Ark' was conceived as a speculative office development for multiple occupancy. While only the top floors were closed off from the atrium at the official

15.11.
'Ark', London, 1991. Interior of atrium. Architect: Ralph Erskine. Photo: Chris Abel.

opening for purposes of smoke control, similar modifications can be made to any of the other floors, should any client so desire it. The changing floor plan up through the building has also been designed to accommodate a large variety of functional configurations, from open 'landscape' and cellular offices to exhibition spaces, in keeping with the flexible and informal needs of offices in the information age. The key to Erskine's social conception of the office as a 'village' lies in the central free-standing structure rising up through the atrium space, which is intended as a kind of community centre, and indeed looks much like a combined village pub and church tower. Serving all users, the centre provides both a visual and social focal point for an increasingly itinerant working population.

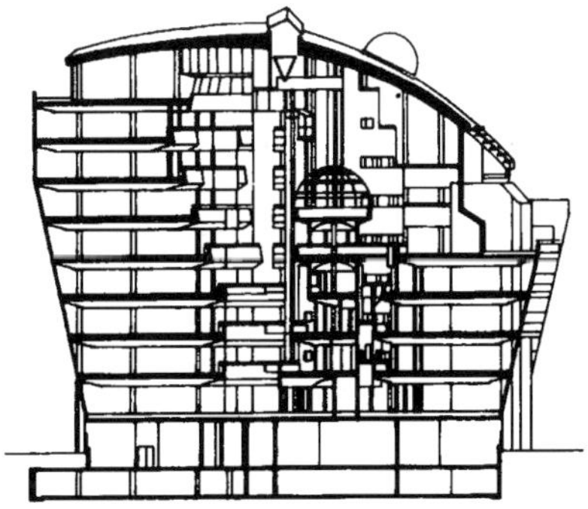

15.12.
'Ark'. Section. Architect: Ralph Erskine. From *Architects' Journal*, June 1992.

15.13.
Menara Mesiniaga Building, Kuala Lumpur, 1992. Architect: Hamzah and Yeang.

15.14a.
Capita Centre, Sydney, 1989. Architect and photo: Harry Seidler.

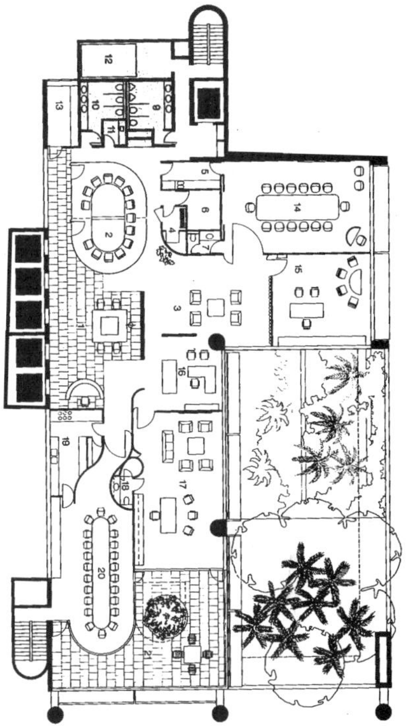

15.14b.
Capita Centre. Plan. Architect: Harry Seidler.

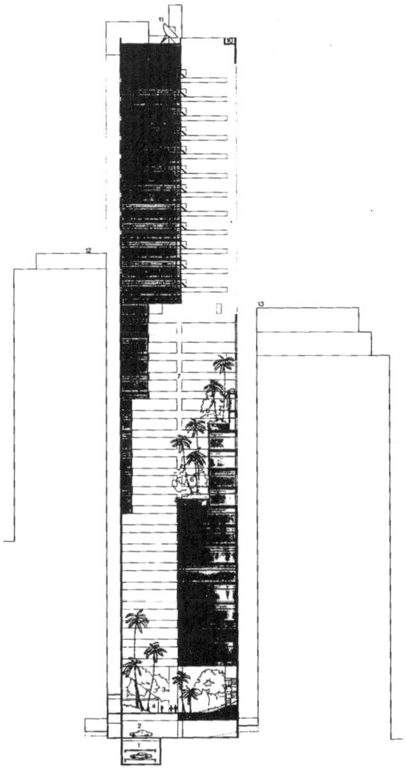

15.14c.
Capita Centre. Section. Architect: Harry Seidler.

The NCB building also now has its own innovative followers, confirming its potency as a prime object in the series capable of begetting healthy and independent offspring. Foremost among these is Hamzah and Yeang's tropicalized office tower built in 1989 near Kuala Lumpur for Menara Mesiniaga,[8] an affiliate of IBM. The main features of the NCB building, it was noted, were the large-scale external incisions made into an otherwise monolithic block. Yeang's tower takes the process of fragmentation a step or two further, starting this time with a basic cylinder. This simple form is drastically corrupted by the irregular stepped incisions made by the skycourts, their spiral arrangement perfectly matched to the geometry of the cylinder. The surface texture is further complicated with numerous forms of climate control devices covering the outer skin, which vary in direct relation to orientation. An exposed megastructure similar to Lloyd's serves to contain the fragmentation and surface variation. Many if not all of these features are the outcome, like SOM's tower, of a conscious attempt to adapt a universal building type to a specific and difficult climate and were inspired by local building forms as well as by other models in the series.[9]

Harry Seidler's glass and steel Capita Centre[10] in Sydney continues the series, based this time on a rectilinear geometry. The broken outline creates a striking impression and appears at first sight quite different from the previous works. However, the design of the Capita Centre was created in much the same fashion as the Jeddah and Kuala Lumpur towers out of a simple basic geometry, which has then been carved into by its designer, so to speak, to create a spiralling series of articulated blocks of offices fronting onto landscaped skycourts. As with Yeang's building, an exposed megastructure frame helps tie the fragmented form together.

Foster's Commerzbank[11] in Frankfurt confirms the durability of this series, and returns many 'foreign' innovations to the West. The basic form, once again, is the equilateral triangle, and we also see what is by now the characteristic feature of the series: a spiralling 'staircase' of deep incisions in the block, creating numerous, generously landscaped skycourts. As with the former towers, the design is shaped as much by energy-saving considerations as by other factors. The skycourts and central airshaft will help to maximize natural ventilation in all seasons, while a glazed windbreak will allow occupants to open external windows even in adverse conditions.

Ken Yeang's most recent project for the Hitechniaga Corporation[12] (so named for its data communications business) in Kuala Lumpur, heralds what may be a still further and even more radical stage in the evolution of the office tower. While all the above designs are based on a regular geometrical figure which has then been modified, albeit sometimes drastically, the Hitechniaga Tower[12] abandons any pretence to geometrical regularity. Instead, what we see is an odd assortment of irregular blocks of floors, terraces, stairways, ramps, metallic 'visors' and other projections loosely hung upon an exposed structural frame. The whole assembly looks as though the frame has been magnetized and then waved over the corner of some giant metal workshop. Despite appearances, however, the same rigorous design principles govern these innovations as shaped Yeang's earlier designs, showing that a rational response to climate need not necessarily lead to either dull or uniform architecture.

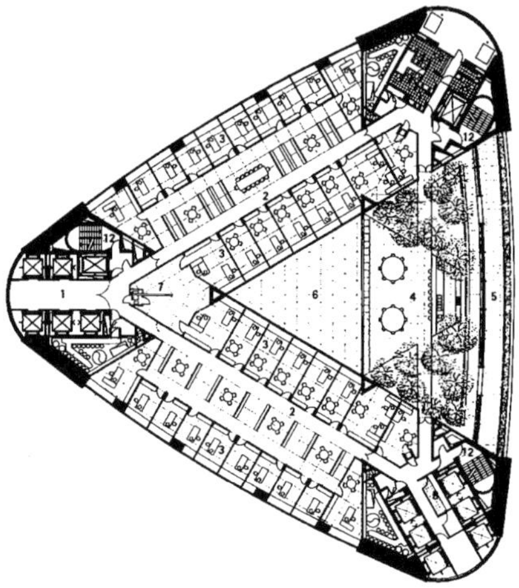

15.15a.
Commerzbank, Frankfurt, 1996. Plan. Architect: Foster Associates.

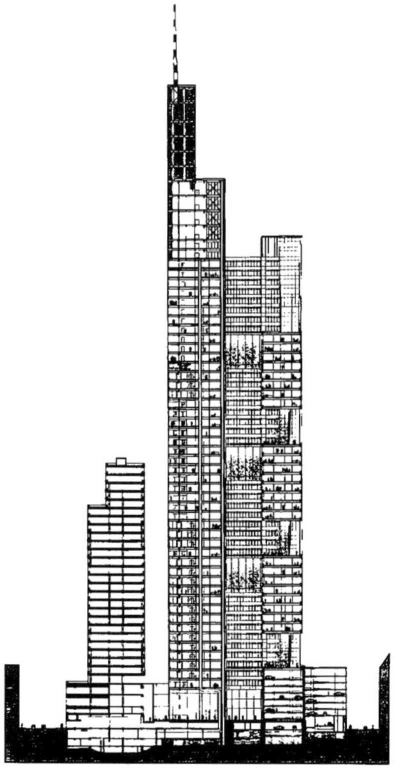

15.15b.
Commerzbank. Section. Architect: Foster Associates.

INCREASING SPECIFICITY

Looking through these linked solutions, we can see ample evidence of the sorts of continuities and discontinuities which characterize the birth and life of a new series, and the interactive nature of precedent and innovation. For every specific feature there is always a model, whether it derives from earlier buildings in the same series, as with the use of a glazed skin in the Lever House, or from a confrontation or analogy with a different series, as with the sudden emergence of skycourts in the Jeddah tower. Over and above any specific changes of form, however, a general pattern may be detected in the direction of increasing specificity, possibly reflecting an emergent new order of cultural complexity at a deeper level. It is most apparent in the new series introduced by SOM with their NCB tower and its hanging gardens. No matter how daring the internal spatial and social changes wrought by Frank Lloyd Wright and later architects, the relation of the atrium tower form to its surroundings and its urban status as a detached object remain relatively unaffected. For all its reflective or 'invisible' properties, the same might also be said of the Glass Skyscraper. The NCB tower could be counted as the most radical departure from precedent this century in that for the first time a secondary ground level was created in the form of a large external incision in the building. More than any other previous development this single innovation changed the relation of internal to external space for tall office buildings. No longer were occupants condemned to look down onto a distant and vertigo-inducing ground. Instead, they could enjoy the relative security of a well-planted terra firma at close proximity. That the same incisions and unusual geometry were the product of a direct response to the local harsh climate is also no coincidence, but signifies a new level of exchange between a tall building and the local environment it occupies.

How much these new problem solutions reflect the pressures for energy conservation, changes in cultural and environmental values, or changes in the nature of the business institutions which occupy all of these buildings, remains an open question. Most likely it is a combination of all of these factors. What is beyond question is that what started out as a standard solution to be applied indiscriminately around the globe has been lately skilfully adapted to many different situations and climates.

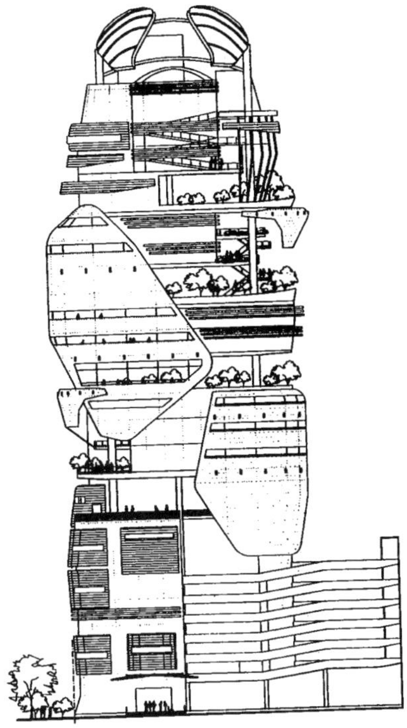

15.16.
Hitechniaga Corporation Building, Kuala Lumpur, designed 1994. Elevation. Architect: Hamzah & Yeang.

16 LOCALIZATION VERSUS GLOBALIZATION

First published in *The Architectural Review*, September 1994.

Looking at Kuala Lumpur or Singapore today, it is easy to conclude that the forces of a globalized consumer culture have all but won. Both cities, but especially Singapore – the city Western critics love to hate – exhibit all the visual attributes of familiar Western models: the Central Business Districts; the air-conditioned office towers; the kitsch condos; the McDonald's franchises; the shopping centres selling the same consumer products; the jam-packed highways spreading out into the suburbs, and the suburbs themselves, with their 'Dallas'-inspired mixture of neo-classical and Spanish-style villas. What is left of the original urban fabric of Chinese-built shophouses with their arcaded 'five-foot ways' has been cut back to ever smaller enclaves of usually dilapidated streets or expensively tarted-up but lifeless conservation areas. Otherwise the odd urban

16.1.
General view of Singapore, looking towards the central business district (CBD). Construction site in foreground is on reclaimed land. Photo: Chris Abel.

fragment, temple or mosque serves as an occasional reminder of an earlier, other world, hanging on by the skin of its teeth. For many Western visitors, it all adds up to a disappointing and disturbing spectacle of cultural abdication.

IMPORTED CULTURES

Yet all is not quite what it seems to the Eurocentric eye and critical comparisons of a globalized and apparently uniform present with a more pure Asian past misrepresent the essentially complex nature of Southeast Asian culture. Even prior to colonization, the region had been exposed to layer upon layer of imported cultures which had been localized over time, and adapted to regional conditions.[1] Hybridization was not so much the exception as the norm. When it did arrive, colonization brought with it a whole new set of cultural imports to be absorbed, both Western and non-Western. Singapore, for example, was never a Chinese city in the sense that a city on mainland China could be so described, but developed in the typical dualistic pattern of a colonial city, with a European half and a 'native' half;[2] the latter – already virtually a separate Chinatown – populated by overseas Chinese who migrated to

16.2.
Singapore. Conservation area between the Singapore River and the CBD. Photo: Chris Abel.

16.3.
Kuala Lumpur. Physical evidence of a mixed cultural history. Photo: Chris Abel.

the Malay Peninsula to seek fortune in Stamford Raffles' new trading post.

The history of Kuala Lumpur is even more complicated, since British colonists not only founded a city where, as with Singapore, no urban culture had existed before,[3] but Chinese and Indian immigrants – encouraged by the British to help service the colony – soon dominated the indigenous rural Malay population. The legacy of this history includes both the typical but misnamed 'native' urban fabric of shophouses and temples, and an awkward cultural and political situation for Malaysians to cope with ever since. The apparent indifference to urban conservation and the eagerness with which many Malaysian planners and architects have embraced more recent imported models of building is therefore at least in part due to a lack of identification with much of the local heritage. Something of the sort also applies to postcolonial Singapore, which is viewed by proud Singaporeans as an Asian city, not so much because it *looks* like one, but because it was *created* by Asians, as opposed to the historic rumps which were originally built, or otherwise controlled, by their erstwhile colonial rulers.

STRUCTURE OF ASIAN CITIES

Aside from these historical complications, it is questionable whether cultural difference can be assessed solely by reference to the forms of buildings. This is not to say that architecture is not important, but that it is not the *only* measure of difference. Experienced analysts warn against the habit of Western architects and planners to impose preconceived, i.e. Western urban models, onto Asian cities, which may look superficially similar to modern Western cities, but do in fact function very differently. The economic cultures of Western cities, for example, are distinguished primarily by the impersonal nature of the principal economic unit, the firm, which selects and treats its employees strictly according to their specialized economic value. Work and family life are totally separate. By contrast, the economic cultures of Asian cities are based upon not one but two economic systems: a modern, firm-based and a pre-industrial urban economy, comprised of complex networks between diverse, usually small operators and activities, all functioning within extended systems of kinship. In the latter, community, family life and work are all intimately interconnected, and employment opportunities are generally spread as widely as possible within the kinship system, even where underemployment is the result[4] (in effect, the system safeguards against *un*employment).

One does not have to look far to see this dual economic structure at work, even in Singapore, which boasts vigorous cottage industries[5] along with its more obvious high-tech corporate enterprises. Not unexpectedly, it visibly operates in the multitude of small family businesses which still characterize the older sections of the city. Yet anyone taking a walk through the middle of any public housing estate or suburban shopping centre will readily find the same diverse services, open-air food stalls and cottage industries. Likewise, anyone looking underneath almost any high-rise housing block will find the ground floor – specially reserved for the purpose – alive with a row of tiny shops and

16.4.
Shops and cheap open-air eating places crowd the ground floor spaces beneath most high-rise apartment blocks in Singapore. Photo: Chris Abel.

eating places, peopled by individual entrepreneurs and their family helpers, all bustling with activity, in stark contrast to the graveyard atmosphere associated with Western housing estates. Out of sight, operating from within some of the flats themselves, yet more industrious family enterprises may be found. The same dual economic culture is visibly active in Kuala Lumpur and other Malaysian cities, especially so in the older city of Georgetown, on Penang Island, where cottage industries and five-foot-way traders still dominate the city and let their untidy presence be felt in an infectious street life.

16.5.
Street scene in Georgetown, Penang. Photo: Chris Abel.

PACIFIC SHIFT

Many would argue that these are no more than signs of a temporary truce between opposing and irreconcilable forces, the last gasps of a more complex Asian urban culture, soon to be swept away by those same global economic pressures which have already brought not only depersonalized firms into Asian culture, but also all the other uniform elements of the Western city. Globalization in this view is a one-way street, an irredeemable, centralizing phenomenon, concentrating economic and cultural power into fewer and fewer centres composed of ever larger economic units, most of them based in Western industrialized countries. As such, the process continues what was already begun with colonization. The recent explosion in information technology, so the argument runs, has lent a new impetus, facilitating the global circulation and unhindered distribution of capital and resources to suit Western interests, raising the economic stakes as never before.

Much of this picture is in turn based on the assumption that Western developed countries will go on dominating the world economy as they have done for centuries. That assumption is now seriously undermined by the economic dynamism of the Asian-Pacific countries, of which Malaysia and Singapore are prime exemplars, and the related change

16.6.
Malaysian Institute for Microelectronic Systems (MIMOS), Kuala Lumpur, 1996. Model. Architect: Ruslan Khalid.

from an Atlantic based world economy toward a Pacific-based one, dominated by Japan and the US.[6] How long it will be before the entry of China into the picture finally tips the balance in favour of the Asian coast remains to be seen, but only the most die-hard Western observer could claim that continued Western domination is a foregone conclusion.

GLOBAL PARADOX

Even were this not the case, other convincing arguments have arisen for not taking the pattern of increasing, Western-orientated centralization and standardization for granted. Challenging the model of a homogenized world future, Stuart Hall[7] argues that globalization has its own unanticipated imperatives, and that the very processes which typify global economic and cultural activity carry within themselves their own tensions and contradictions. In order to extend their markets into new areas, multinational corporations are increasingly finding it necessary to adapt themselves to the particular demands of local consumers, which means bending their activities and production lines to suit local cultures as well as other regional factors. In meeting these new demands, the shape of the multinational corporation itself is rapidly changing from a centralized institution with corporate headquarters in the North, to a more flexible confederation of smaller and semi-autonomous units, better able to respond to local conditions. It may all be just another game of subterfuge designed to disguise the same old corporate ambitions, but, as Hall suggests, it just might possibly lead to a more diverse and unpredictable result than that envisaged in the usual scenarios.

In similar vein John Naisbitt[8] argues that the demand for increased flexibility and quickness of response is compelling large firms to fragment and diversify in order to compete effectively in a diversified global market. Small firms, by contrast, are finding that affordable information technologies and computerized, flexible tools of production are greatly increasing their range of operation, creating hitherto undreamed of access to new world markets and in the process also creating unexpected competition for the established multinationals. As Naisbitt puts it: 'The bigger the world economy, the more powerful its smallest players.'[9] The conclusion is that small is not only beautiful, it is also efficient; the virtues of pre-industrial economies are rapidly becoming also the virtues of post-industrial economies.

Such arguments tie in with the more abstract but equally compelling theories of self-organizing systems which first emerged in the 1960s[10] and which are now enjoying renewed attention under the general rubric of complexity theory.[11] Viewed in these terms, which are rooted in biological analogies, the same organic processes which are leading towards centralization and integration on a global plane are having equal and opposite decentring effects on a sub-regional plane.[12] The result may look like chaos and fragmentation at a local level, but is more accurately described as a spontaneous adjustment of human activity to cope with exposure to a larger and less predictable world environment. The whole reciprocating process is boosted by an environmental crisis which demands at one and the same time a global awareness of the interconnectedness of all things, and local actions which raise levels of self-sufficiency in such vital areas as food and energy consumption. If there is such a thing as an emergent global culture, it may well arise out of these contradictory processes.

PACIFIC AGE VISION

The architecture in Malaysia and Singapore that is now surfacing out of this cauldron is, true to Southeast Asian traditions, a hybrid mix of imported and local elements.[13] Many of the leading architects in the new movement received their professional education abroad in the UK or Australia, and were thus exposed early on to an international architectural culture. For those belonging to the first and second generations of postwar Modernists to return to their origins, the benefits of the exposure were often offset by the later realization that they were ill-equipped to understand their own regional culture or know how to respond to it. What followed has been a slow and difficult process of re-education, with few clearly defined goals, other than a shared conviction that Southeast Asian architects must somehow strive to belong to both architectural cultures, the local *and* the global.

The approaches to these apparently conflicting demands are many and varied, but overriding all is a growing consensus that the new architecture, if it is to meet the challenge of the environmental crisis, aside from more parochial issues, must be firmly grounded in ecological principles. At the very least, it should be a *tropical* architecture, responsive to and expressive of its geographical and climatic situation. The technological means for achieving this end range from the employment of timber-framed structures updated from traditional models, to high-tech materials and techniques of production. But the works that define the movement share a common pragmatic concern with energy conservation combined with a celebration of a lush tropical nature and a climate that invites open-necked shirts and year-round open-air living. The emerging result is a loose-limbed, permeable, generally lightweight

16.7a.
Institute of Education, Bishan, Singapore, 1993. Open-air assembly area. Architect: Tenggara II.

16.7b.
Institute of Education. View down garden 'street' between curved teaching blocks. Architect: Tenggara II. Photo: Chris Abel.

architecture that is recognizably Modern in the best experimental sense of that ambiguous description, but is also true both to its specific locations and to a Pacific-wide tradition of framed building.

What is most significant is that the search for a tropical architecture appropriate to its time and place should also now be taking in the wider urban environment represented – conceptually and empirically – by the Southeast Asian city. The idea of the tropical city or, as it is more ambitiously called, the 'intelligent tropical city' is now the focus of increasing attention from both theorists and official planners,[14] driven by the growing realization that idealized urban models based on different climates and cultures do not apply in this part of the world, and that what is needed instead is a home-grown model. What was a vague but attractive notion is now rapidly taking shape in the form of a number of yet-to-be-realized but far-sighted plans and projects in both Malaysia and Singapore. They portray a twenty-first-century vision of sustainable urban development, based in the main on energy-efficient, decentralized and pedestrian-orientated, dense urban subcentres connected up to the main city centres by Mass Rapid Transit systems – already in operation in Singapore and under construction in Kuala Lumpur. For 'intelligent', read a city with a self-regulating infrastructure and a population plugged into a global culture's resources via the information superhighway. For 'tropical', read a city and architecture tailor-made to its natural and cultural ecology. It is a fitting vision for the Pacific Age, in which the local informs the global and vice versa.

16.8.
Peter Eu House, Kuala Lumpur, 1988. Detail of open-air living deck. Architect: Jimmy Lim. Photo: Chris Abel.

17 TOWARDS A GLOBAL ECO-CULTURE

First published under the title 'Ecodevelopment: toward a development paradigm for regional architecture', *Traditional Dwellings and Settlements Working Papers Series*, Vol. 44, Proceedings of the 1992 Conference of the International Association for the Study of Traditional Environments, 8–11 October, Paris, University of California, Berkeley, 1993.

In so far as they help to shape the environment, all development plans involve an element of global design. In the same way, the general form and quality of a region's architecture is also largely shaped by favoured development strategies, having direct and lasting effects on the choice of settlement patterns, building types, technologies and modes of production. The personal and social alienation associated with the introduction of unsuitable building forms and methods in developing countries is accordingly symptomatic of a wider loss of local control over the economic and cultural forces that presently affect all aspects of the environment in those regions. It would be unrealistic, therefore, to expect any general improvement in the quality of building without prior changes in these influential factors.

CENTRE AND PERIPHERY

In their critical comparison of contemporary Western imperialism with former Western empires, Johan Galtung et al. argue[1] that present patterns of development are essentially an extension of well-established colonial patterns of domination and exploitation. According to this scenario, the underdeveloped nations of the periphery, which are mostly situated in the southern hemisphere, are controlled by the developed nations of the centre, which are situated in the northern hemisphere.[2] Far from bringing civilization and prosperity to the subdued regions, as Northern myths have it, colonialism actually meant a diversion of local energies away from those pursuits which were necessary for self-sufficiency, such as the growing of food supplies for local consumption, toward the mining and cultivation of resources for export to service the metropolitan economy.

17.1.
Kuala Lumpur. General view of central area. Courtesy of Hijjas Kasturi.

When it came, territorial independence did little to relieve the imbalance, and subsequent attempts at modernization along Western lines have only created new problems, actually increasing dependency upon the developed nations. Essentially, orthodox policy concentrates development resources on building up an advanced industrial base in the urban centres. The assumption behind the strategy is that the new growth centres will eventually have a 'spin-off' effect, drawing in and creating new resources, the benefits of which will eventually spread out to the country as a whole. Critics claim, however, that the basic strategy itself is fundamentally flawed.[3] The new imported industries are by nature capital intensive and highly mechanized, and therefore make little use of local human labour. Consequently, they provide little work or opportunity to improve people's living standards for all but a small minority. While local, mostly urban élites, have undoubtedly prospered, the predominantly rural populations of the South have not, and in many cases have suffered an actual decrease in real terms of material prosperity. Much of the new wealth created does not even stay in the local region, but adheres to the Western multinational corporations who usually build and control the industrial base, and who effectively substitute for the departed colonial powers. Last but not least, the new industries frequently have a detrimental, even devastating, effect on local ecologies, with which they are rarely compatible.[4]

In short, given that the system works in favour of the centre at the expense of the periphery, the underdeveloped nations cannot become like the developed nations without upsetting the whole system.

ALTERNATIVE PARADIGM

Entrenched though Northern economic interests are in the present system, the ecological damage done by uncontrolled, Western-style development – exemplified by the greenhouse effect[5] – alone presents incontestable arguments against existing development patterns. There is now also a widespread recognition among development agencies, planners and political leaders in the developing nations themselves that orthodox development strategies are simply not yielding the regional benefits they were expected to, and even exacerbate an already desperate situation.

Alternative development paradigms have therefore emerged in recent years which challenge orthodox theory and practice. The most promising of these is 'ecodevelopment', named by Maurice F. Strong,[6] the first Executive Director of the United Nations Development Programme and coordinator of the 1992 Earth Summit in Rio. The new paradigm adumbrates related concepts of 'sustainable' development[7] and has the added merit of being more firmly rooted in a coherent system of values based on ecological principles.

In the balanced human and natural ecosystem, cultural diversity is as vital to evolution as biological diversity. Ecodevelopment policy therefore explicitly rejects the assumption that development should always be modelled on Western industrial patterns, or that such development should be concentrated in the urban centres, or even that unfettered urbanization is a natural or desirable consequence of development. Instead, ecodevelopment focuses on rural development and is based upon the idea that:

...development at regional and local levels should be consistent with the potential of the area involved, with attention given to the adequate and rational use of the natural resources, and to appreciation of technological styles (innovation and assimilation) and organizational forms that respect the natural ecosystems and local socio-cultural patterns.[8]

The approach affords fruitful comparisons between current development patterns and nature's own ecosystems. Whereas young, natural (non-human) ecosystems usually reach stable equilibrium states after early periods of growth and change, development patterns focused on maximizing productivity and growth invariably have destabilizing effects, leading to a subsequent, often irreversible, loss of natural resources. All too familiar examples include soil degradation and erosion following on the removal of vegetation cover by forest clearance and over-grazing, and expensive, 'prestige' projects such as dams, which displace the local population, have negative environmental effects, and generally deliver less benefit than promised.[9]

By contrast, ecodevelopment seeks to manage the impact of human activity upon the natural environment by the application of ecological criteria to development projects. Each ecologically defined region, which may centre on a river basin or mountain region, will be closely examined for what that region has to offer in the way of natural and human resources. This in itself may involve crossing different conventional boundaries and harmonizing previously separate activities and interests. A programme of development is then devised that is specially suited to the needs and character of that region. Further, it is intended that all programmes for development be worked out and implemented with the fullest participation of the local inhabitants. Against the usual top-down pattern of decision making common to orthodox, centralized development planning, ecodevelopment encourages a bottom-up, decentralized approach, making the most of local know-how:

> ...*[ecodevelopment emphasizes] the capacity of people themselves to invent and generate new resources and techniques, to increase their capacity to absorb them, and to put them to socially beneficial use,* to take a measure of command over the economy, and to generate their own way of life[10] [my emphasis].

Ecodevelopment therefore begins with the existing local resources and seeks to build upon and maximize those resources for the direct benefit of the local population. It stresses interdependence over dependence and quality of life over gross national product.

CHOOSING TECHNOLOGY

Though it evolved separately, the concept of appropriate technology is central to ecodevelopment policy and practice. Inspired by E. F. Schumacher's 'economics as though people mattered',[11] its proponents emphasize the value and dignity of human labour in the choice of technology for development projects. Cultural context and scale – usually meaning small scale – are all important in this view, which also rejects the still common belief held in the South as well as in the North, that technology is somehow value free:

> *The idea of appropriate technology is derived as much from a vision of a diversified society, of self-reliant and prosperous homes and communities, as it is from technology per se. Just building a few small-scale technology demonstration projects will not accomplish the broader goal of a more human technology.* The idea of appropriate technology

challenges the existing order of things, especially the values of centralized government, institutions and industries[12] [my emphasis].

17.2.
Low cost, wind-powered electricity generator. From Brenda and Robert Vale, *The Self-Sufficient House*, 1980.

Schumacher himself coined the related term 'intermediate technology' in 1963 after a visit to India, with the express purpose of encouraging the small-scale technologies suited to village life which Mahatma Gandhi had advocated. As the name implies, intermediate technologies are designed to fill the gap between capital intensive and unsuitable imported technologies, and inexpensive but often inefficient traditional technologies. Typically, they are: low in capital costs; use local materials wherever possible; are labour intensive; small scale, easily understood and easily produced by people without high levels of education; involve decentralized renewable resources, such as wind power, solar energy, etc., and are flexible so that they can continue to be used or adapted to fit changing circumstances. As with ecodevelopment, most applications have been in the rural areas the approach was mainly conceived for, and focus on agriculture, small-scale manufacturing, shelter and infrastructure support.[13] Effective projects are in place throughout the developing world, backed by a growing army of specialist groups such as Schumacher's own creation, the UK-based Intermediate Technology Development Group.[14]

The pattern of self-build housing for the poorest sectors of both urban and rural populations lends itself readily to appropriate technology solutions, based on the use of unskilled labour, affordable and accessible materials.[15] Global networks of both governmental and non-governmental organizations (NGOs), combine to exchange information and expertise on a vast range of projects, involving anything from a handful to tens of thousands of families.[16] Inevitably, increasing pressures on scarce economic and physical resources, especially urban land, also place a continuing emphasis on the importance of non-architectural factors, such as problems of land tenure, legal aid, financing, infrastructure and sanitation. There are many exemplary projects to

17.3.
Squatter housing, Ankara, Turkey. Photo: Chris Abel.

17.4.
Surabaya Kampung Improvement Programme with the Surabaya Institute of Technology, Surabaya, Indonesia, 1981. Improvement scheme for squatter settlements provides surfaced pathways, drainage systems and clean water supplies, as well as structural improvements to homes. View of completed section of Kampung Kebalen. Courtesy of the Aga Khan Award for Architecture.

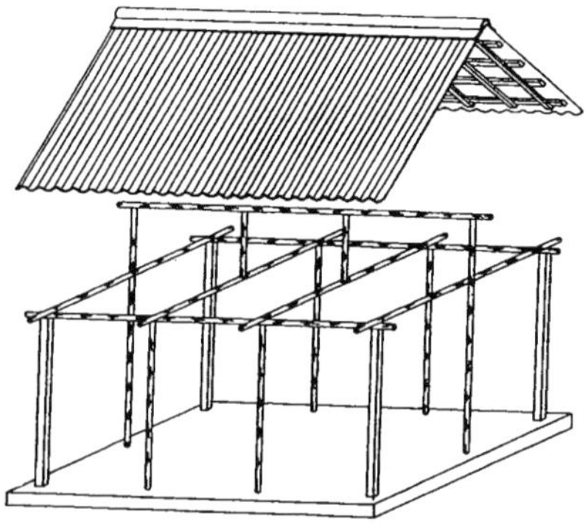

17.5a.
Basic shelter 'kit' designed and funded by the Grameen Bank, a non-profit making organization. Courtesy of the Aga Khan Award for Architecture.

17.5b.
Housing by Grameen Bank. The provision of relatively sound shelter in turn provides a vital base for the growth of cottage industries. Courtesy of the Aga Khan Award for Architecture.

choose from, but the Grameen Bank (a cooperative, non-governmental organization) Housing Programme in Bangladesh is noteworthy not only for its cheap, do-it-yourself basic shelter 'kit', but also for its unusually liberal banking policy in making low cost credit available to its impoverished clients (84% of whom are women) to finance construction.[17] So far, hundreds of thousands of landless rural Bangladeshes have benefited from the scheme, which is widely studied and imitated in other developing countries.

Beyond intermediate applications of this sort, in its broadest sense appropriate technology refers more to an attitude to the way we choose and evaluate the use of a particular technology, rather than to any specific type or level of technology. Murray Bookchin,[18] for example, cautions against making pre-emptive value judgements concerning specific technologies, especially advanced technologies:

...there is no such word as 'Technology' that presides over all social conditions and relations; there are different technologies and attitudes toward technology, some of which are indispensable to restoring the balance (between humanity and nature), others of which have contributed profoundly to its destruction. What humanity needs is not the wholesale discarding of advanced technologies, but a sifting, indeed a further development of technology along ecological principles that will contribute to a new harmonization of society and the natural world[19] [my emphasis].

Within this broader interpretation of appropriate technology, there is considerable potential for what has been called combined technology, meaning a hybrid integration of sophisticated technological innovation and traditional knowledge.[20] So far this has been limited to the application of techniques of waste disposal and energy production, but it is also conceivable that information technologies will enter into the picture as costs continue to fall. This applies especially to ecodevelopment projects, where such technologies are essential for data collection and analysis and could encourage decentralized decision making.

Other appropriate applications for advanced technologies may be found in local industrial sectors as part of a balanced development strategy for self-sufficiency. Automated production technologies, for example, are presently undergoing radical change.[21] The new computer-controlled systems are both highly flexible and specially geared to small batch production; an important feature normally associated with intermediate technologies. Capital outlay can therefore be amortized over a greater range and variety of products, including building components, than was previously possible with rigid, mass-production systems. Present patterns of mass consumption have so far limited the impact of these new technologies to non-essential product variety and options. The same technologies, however, can be directed to improving product performance through custom-made design, making them more suitable for developing countries with limited capital and locally specific and varied product needs.

Also at the cutting edge, the use of information technologies to monitor and control a building's environmental performance under changing climatic conditions[22] heralds a new relationship between machine and nature of the sort envisaged by Bookchin and others. It is no coincidence that, like the new computerized production systems, these cybernetic, or adaptive, technologies are themselves modelled on the adaptive principles of living systems.[23]

REGIONAL ARCHITECTURE

As with ecodevelopment and appropriate technology, contemporary regionalism in architecture represents a rejection of previously dominant international movements, in favour of emphasizing regional building forms and environmental conditions.[24] Seen in the light of centre-periphery theory, the International Style and related Western movements can be understood as an outcome of the same neo-colonial domination of peripheral cultures by the centre, producing its own cultural side-effects in displacing local forms of building. The search for more sympathetic forms of architecture expressive of regional identities can therefore be interpreted as a variation of those cultural movements in developing countries that demand changes in the world economic order.

In rural areas, housing forms and settlement patterns based on traditional models may be suitable for a wide range of income levels. The traditional, timber-framed Malay house, for example, offers many 'modern' features and 'near-perfect solutions to the control of climate, multifunctional use of space, flexibility in design and a sophisticated prefabricated system to extend the house with the growing needs of the family'.[25] The 'A' frame houses designed by Yousef B. Mangunwijaya for the Kampung Kali Cho-De development in Yogyakarta, Indonesia, show how similar approaches can be used for low cost housing in the tropics.[26] In other parts of the developing world, Hassan Fathy's experiments with traditional forms of sun-dried, mud-brick construction have inspired numerous similar projects suited to arid climates.[27] Both traditions may also be adapted for a wide range of small-scale building types, both traditional and contemporary, such as mosques, shops and schools, which are needed for a rural community.[28] In the same vein, the Muhanna brothers in Syria have exploited local building materials and techniques refined by computer analysis to produce a simple but elegant stone building system for schools, houses and other single-storey buildings.[29]

17.6a
'A' frame house, Yogyakarta, Indonesia. Architect: Yousef B. Mangunwijaya. Courtesy of the Aga Khan Award for Architecture.

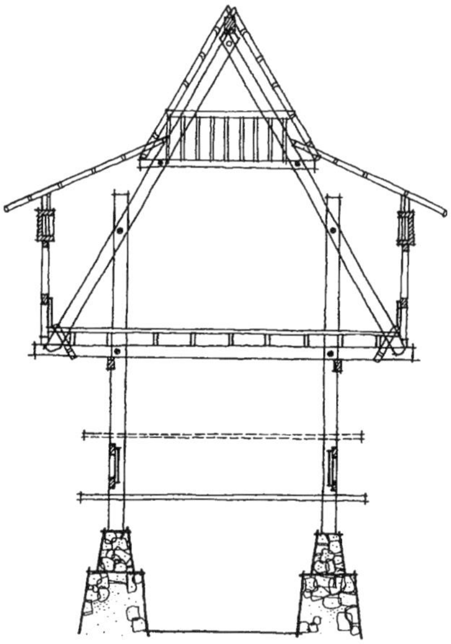

17.6b
'A' frame house. Architect: Yousef B. Mangunwijaya. From Steele, 1992.

Regional architecture becomes more problematic, however, when it comes to more recent urban building types, for which traditional architecture does not offer such clear models. Most of the types that now characterize cities in the developing world were originally imported from elsewhere as either part of the colonial era, or of later development patterns. It seems unlikely, however, that any changes in development strategy, or in the economic order between North and South, will affect this trend. Essentially, modern building types such as universities, hospitals, government buildings, offices and hotels and so forth are the outcome of growing complexity in the social order of an evolving society. As an alternative to rigid, centralized planning, decentralization is itself a policy for handling social complexity in a more flexible and rational fashion.[30] While it may reduce the need for large-scale or high-rise solutions, it will not do away with the important functions these buildings perform.

Nevertheless, if universal building types are unavoidable, they can still be adapted to local climatic, site and social conditions. Elements of traditional form may also be incorporated, if these can be shaped to the new purpose. A few foreign as well as local architects have demonstrated exceptional skill in producing a hybrid regional architecture of this kind that reflects both modern and traditional influences.[31] Inevitably, some of the best works are high-cost projects, since their architects were purposefully commissioned to design buildings which not only fulfilled

17.7.
Architect's own house, New Gourna village, near Luxor, Egypt, 1948. The entire village was designed and built in mud brick as a demonstration of the contemporary value and relevance of indigenous construction methods. Architect: Hassan Fathy. Photo: Glyn Halls.

17.8.
Diplomatic Club, Diplomatic Quarter, Riyadh, 1985. Architect: Omrania with Frei Otto. Courtesy of the Aga Khan Award for Architecture.

17.9.
Thammasat University, near Bangkok, 1985–6 (Phase I). The master plan with its axial planning and elaborate system of drainage channels and lakes is based on the ancient temple-city of Angkor Thom, Cambodia. The raised form of the main teaching blocks is also based on regional practice and provides shaded open-air spaces for learning, dining and recreation. Architect: Sumet Jumsai. Photo: Chris Abel.

their functional programmes, but which also represented the cultural aspirations of their state or private clients. Projects in this category include the Ministry of Foreign Affairs in Riyadh, by Henning Larsen,[32] and Omrania's Diplomatic Club,[33] also in Riyadh, both of which incorporate Pan-Islamic spatial features. Other architects have developed a regionalism based primarily on a low energy strategy and response to the local climate, combined with a judicious mix of modern and traditional materials and technologies. Sumet Jumsai's Thammasat University,[34] near Bangkok, Bimal Hasmukh C. Patel's Entrepreneurship Development Institute of India[35] in Ahmedabad and Payette Associates' Aga Khan University and Hospital[36] in Karachi, all proffer valuable models of this kind with potentially wide applications.

IMPLEMENTATION

Sound though it may be in principle, advocates of ecodevelopment concede that serious problems of both a methodological and political character hamper implementation. Such problems may occur in data collection and analysis, or in persuading central planning authorities and other vested interests in the status quo, to yield control over planning decisions to disadvantaged local populations. Likewise, the institutions and techniques necessary for public participation are usually lacking, and have to be created on the spot. The theoretical requirement for local homogeneity and self-sufficiency is also difficult to maintain in the face of existing economic and cultural structures, which frequently transgress ecologically defined regions. Such problems become especially apparent if similar approaches are to be applied to urbanized regions, which are anything but homogeneous or self-contained. The scale of national development needed and the allocation of scarce resources will also require a continuing high level of central planning. Unavoidably, compromises have to be made, and conceptual and practical goals adapted to cope with on-the-ground realities. Increasingly, emphasis is now placed more on heterogeneous development patterns at the regional level, and on the need for grass-roots representation to mediate between central authorities and local populations.[37]

While complete self-sufficiency may not be practicable, it may be significantly increased through the diligent application of appropriate technologies. The widespread success of such projects can be attributed partly to the economic logic of the approach, which becomes more apparent daily as conditions in the developing world deteriorate, but also to the relative ease of implementation. Since the approach is orientated to small scale, highly practical projects with an easily appreciable payoff, it can be applied to most situations of need, without entailing either the complex surveys or local homogenizing efforts which ecodevelopment policy stipulates. Appropriate technology and self-build approaches can also help to alleviate the shelter problems of the urban poor, whose ranks are continually being swollen by new waves of migrants fleeing even worse situations in the countryside.[38] In the long run, however, only new rural development policies along the lines of ecodevelopment are likely to stem the flow. The fate of developing world cities is as much bound up with that of the rural areas as the fate of the South is bound up with that of the North.

Though examples of high quality, regional architecture proliferate – in the North now as well as in the South – they remain a tiny proportion of the total built environment; a significant indication of alternative possibilities, but an indication only. The vast amount of 'normal' architecture remains a prisoner of the same narrow range of global cultural values and remotely controlled systems of production which characterize international consumerism. Any change towards a normative regionalism, therefore, depends on equivalent changes in production systems, such as the localized methods of production which characterize ecodevelopment and appropriate technology.

Finally, it should be stressed that cultural exchange can be equally positive as well as negative, and has been responsible for the most creative as well as regressive forms of culture, including regional forms of architecture.[39] It is not cultural exchange *per se* that is at fault, but rather the unequal political and economic basis for current international forms of exchange. The need to increase economic self-sufficiency should not therefore obscure the need to encourage the free and creative exchange of ideas across borders, including the transfer of appropriate technologies and other relevant innovations.

A CULTURAL TYPOLOGY

Ecodevelopment, appropriate technology, and regional architecture all represent significant movements toward cultural emancipation and social devolution, away from Western domination, toward relatively autonomous regional cultures. Each, however, is dependent on the others for wider implementation and success. Ecodevelopment, for example, requires both appropriate technological and built solutions in order to translate principles into environmental results. From the other

	Traditional Culture	*Colonial Culture*	*Consumer Culture*	*Eco-culture*
Technological era	Pre-industrial (craft-based)	Early industrial (machine-based)	Late industrial (automation- and information-based)	Post-industrial (computer- and network-based)
Cultural differentiation	Homogeneous (highly integrated and localized)	Heterogeneous (exposure to secondary cultures)	Homogeneous (West is best)	Heterogeneous (based on reciprocal cultural exchanges)
External communication	Limited and slow (local trade and migrations)	Global but slow (sea and overland)	Global and speedy (air and telecommunications)	Global and instantaneous (near universal network access)
Level of innovation	Tradition governs all (rate of change difficult to record)	Sporadic leaps (when officially sanctioned)	Continuous but centralized (concentration of research and benefits in North)	Continuous and decentralized (global dissemination of research and benefits)
Social roles	Specialized and stable (life-long)	Specialized but changeable (promotion/overseas postings, etc.)	Specialized but changeable (promotion, redundancy/retraining, etc.)	Multiple roles based on changing skills and continuous education/training
Decision structures	Generally hierarchic and patriarchic, with notable exceptions (i.e., Malay peasant society)	Hierarchic and patriarchic (dependent relations between colonies and metropolitan centre)	Corporate and patriarchic (modified by democratic and market-led systems) dominated by short-term goals	Participatory, with mix of global and local 'bottom up' structures, based on gender equality and sustainable goals
Production systems	Autonomous, self-sufficient (small surplus) and labour intensive	Centralized (large surpluses for export) with both capital and labour intensive sectors	Centralized mass-production (capital and energy intensive) for mass-consumption	Decentralized, flexible manufacturing systems (intermediate to advanced technologies)
Settlement patterns	Rural and village-based	Urban and rural (sharp differentiation between cities and country)	Predominantly urban or suburban in the North and urban/rural in the South	Predominantly urban or 'exurban' based on balanced public/private transportation
Built forms	Isomorphic with social form and climate	Mix of functional and hybrid forms (products of cultural exchange) partly shaped by climate	Ambiguous/flexible forms independent of climate	Customized for place, purpose and climate

Table 17.1

end of the scale, regional architecture requires both ecologically sensitive development policies and appropriate technologies in order to turn an exemplary movement into a normative building pattern. Taken together, these movements comprise the core elements of a decentred global culture in-the-making, which, though incomplete, may be set against present Western ethnocentric cultural forms as a positive alternative.

These emergent alternative forms of development may be grouped under the name *eco-culture*, in contrast to the *consumer culture* represented by the Western-dominated, corporate-run society which presently holds sway. Both these contemporary culture-forms may in turn be set within a wider historical perspective by the addition of two further categories: *traditional culture* and *colonial culture*. The complete typology therefore comprises four cultural types, summarized in Table 17.1 to emphasize the relations between different forms of architecture and different forms of economic and cultural development.

It will be seen that homogeneity is a defining characteristic mainly of both the first and third cultural types, though it may also exist at a local level for the last type. However, the internal homogeneity characteristic of traditional cultures, which may otherwise vary greatly, represents a vastly different form of integration from the global homogeneity characteristic of consumer culture. From this point of view, consumer culture represents a regressive trend, which may be useful for the purposes of centralized control of international commerce, but depletes regional populations, and the world at large, of diverse and irreplaceable cultural resources. To adopt an ecological metaphor: orthodox development presents just as much a danger to the store of human knowledge contained within these 'cultural gene-banks', as it does to nature's own gene-banks.

Paradoxically, by comparison with present development patterns, colonial culture appears as a relatively complex global evolution, in which different cultures coexisted without severe loss of character,[40] albeit still under conditions of domination from the centre. The last type, eco-culture, suggests a further and more positive evolution toward global complexity, based on complementary regional and international cultures, free from domination. It shares ecological values similar to those of traditional cultures, and while the same degree of self-sufficiency may not be achievable, it marks a significant movement in the direction of cultural diversity and equity.

NEW RATIONALITY

In turn, it will be apparent from the preceding discussion that any possibility of a normative eco-culture being realized in the South depends heavily on equivalent structural and cultural changes in the North, in order that the required resources and energies can be released and the appropriate production systems created. At best, the prospects are mixed. The more pessimistic observers suggest we may already have entered a new and even more severe phase in North–South relations, a process of 'super-exploitation', by which the North seeks to solve its present economic problems by further drastic expansion into, and control of, the economic resources of the South.[41]

Real change, if it comes, is most likely to be forced on the North by the self-destructive consequences of its own actions. Belatedly, even Northern planners and economists are coming to realize that the long-term global environmental effects of more of the same economic policies are as damaging for the North as for the South. Despite the disappointing outcomes, the Earth Summit marked a new level of governmental and public awareness of the complex interrelations between problems of development, poverty, and environmental degradation.[42] Hampered though it is by present constraints, ecodevelopment and related concepts of sustainable development are perhaps most effective as 'heuristic instruments', stimulating new ways of thinking about development.[43] As such, they are already encouraging changes in strategic habits of thought amongst development agencies, away from rigid central planning and capital intensive projects, toward flexible planning, more attention to rural development, and pragmatic, ecologically sensitive projects.[44]

Equivalent cultural changes, though tentative, are also now emerging in the North. Originating out of the green politics of the 1960s and 1970s, realistic strategies have been posited for moving toward an ecological society,[45] or its complement, a 'conserver society',[46] offering similar development strategies applicable to Northern industrialized and urbanized regions. The growing, energy-conscious green architecture movement[47] in the North is further evidence of the seriousness with which many, if by no means all, Northern planners and designers are taking their environmental responsibilities. Parallel proposals are also now emerging for sustainable, or green cities, based on decentralized patterns of production and consumption, mixed land use, improved public transport and community control over local affairs. Ideally, new settlement patterns would be comprised of dispersed networks of pedestrianized urban villages, providing for local work, residence and commerce, but interlinked by regional transport with similar urban subcentres and special facilities.[48] Aside from their relevance to Northern regions, many of these ideas may also be usefully applied to the more developed and urbanized regions of the South.

These and other innovative developments offer some hope that Northern decision makers may yet take the wider political and economic actions needed to make ecodevelopment in both North and South a working reality. The more the global environmental crisis worsens, the more these devolutionary concepts will come to be seen, not so much as the work of eccentric radical thinkers, but for what they are: a new rationality for global development.

18 ASIAN URBAN FUTURES

Based on a paper presented to the Asia Design Forum No. 9, Kuala Lumpur, June 13–14, 1998.

While students of urban growth and form in the West have long enjoyed the benefit of well-established bodies of theoretical and empirical knowledge, comparable studies in the developing world lag behind what often seems like an uncontrollable speed of events. With the prospect already looming of more Asian megacities of 20 to 30 million population early in the next century, the statistics are frightening in themselves.[1] The difficulty for planners and other decision makers, however, lies not just with the rate or even the vast scale of urban development, but with the lack of appropriate models equivalent to Western theoretical tools which might help to make sense of these extraordinary phenomena, and, hopefully, to prescribe solutions to the enormous problems they raise.[2] The temptation in these circumstances for developing world theorists to reach for Western urban models to explain or prescribe for essentially different historical or contemporary situations, coupled with the widespread lack of open or critical debate of current urban programmes, only worsens matters.

18.1.
Hong Kong. Shortage of building land and population migrations from mainland China helped create Asia's most dense megacity. Photo: Chris Abel.

Any conscious effort by Asian urbanists to break out of this impasse and create an alternative approach to planning and design born of their own cultures and histories, if only in part, is therefore to be greatly welcomed. The following discussion traces and compares the principal ideas and urban projects of four Asian architect-planners, one Indian, one Malaysian and two Singaporeans, who in their different ways are all striving for appropriate solutions to some of the most intractable problems in their regions. All but one are better known outside their own countries for their architecture than for their urban works, yet their collective contribution is vital to the debate on development planning and urbanization. All of them take as their starting points the colonial histories of the cities in which they live and practise, which have long since outgrown their historical structures and boundaries. All find inspiration to a greater or lesser extent in ecological models of sustainable development, and in the multicultural history and diversity of their respective regions. All also attempt to confront the huge scale of urban population growth in Asia and the consequent problems of high densities and inadequate infrastructures. Aside from recognition of these common origins and problems, however, there are considerable differences as well as similarities in approach, according to the respective interests of each thinker, and the economic and cultural resources available within his area of focus. Neither can any of their models be described as purely indigenous or Asian, but are rather a composite of Western and Eastern ideas and values, reflecting a continuous process of cross-cultural exchange carried over from earlier periods. This in itself suggests a rejection of simplistic solutions and a willingness to deal with the world as it is, in contrast to some of the more extreme ideological positions which have characterized urban planning and design in the past.

CHARLES CORREA AND THE NEW BOMBAY PLAN

Social and structural imbalances

A renowned architect and RIBA Gold Medal winner, Charles Correa has been engaged in the planning of the Bombay city region since the early 1960s, involving some of the most severe problems of urban development and social inequality in Asia. His ideas and projects are therefore especially relevant to the less developed and underdeveloped regions of South Asia, and also to parts of East Asia, such as mainland China and both the Indonesian and Philippine archipelagos.[3]

For Correa, the most urgent problems to be resolved centre on the social and structural imbalances resulting from the migration to the cities of the rural poor in search of work, whose population daily swells the squatter settlements surrounding the older and more affluent urban centres. Like John Turner and other advocates of the urban poor,[4] Correa sees positive as well as negative aspects in their epic struggle for survival, and in their attempts to create a better life for themselves and their families out of the most extreme conditions of hardship and minimal resources. He also acknowledges their contribution in relieving socio-economic pressures on the countryside, which can no longer sustain the population growth.

Nevertheless, while demographic adjustments from rural-based to industrialized economies may be inevitable, they place an unbearable strain on older cities and their outmoded infrastructures, which are unable to cope with the massive influx of population. Taking a broader view, the only viable long-term solution, Correa reasons, is a national policy of rural regeneration through land reform and economic support for villages to help stem and control the outward tide, coupled with urban and industrial decentralization aimed at shifting the burden of economic growth toward the newer, and more numerous, medium sized cities. These would soak up as much rural–urban migration as possible within their own regions, diverting it away from the larger overcrowded cities. He concedes that progress in India on the first, politically sensitive policy, with its echoes of Gandhi's earlier call for similar reforms at the village level, is slow.[5] The latter shift, however, thanks to government incentives, is already happening throughout India, where cities of 100,000 to 1 million are now growing faster than the older metropolitan centres. Nevertheless, while redistributing much of the national pressure for growth, it still leaves the larger cities with the accumulated problems of decades of uncontrolled expansion and extreme contrasts between urban rich and poor.

Founded by the British owned East India Company as a trading post in the seventeenth century, Bombay is typical of these older, former colonial cities. Now India's main financial centre, most of the commercial growth and new workplaces have been concentrated along with the government and other colonial-era buildings in the original harbour breakwater. As the city has expanded northwards along the two main railway lines and roads leading into the centre, so have the distances between it and the newer residential suburbs and main squatter areas increased, creating a barely passable bottleneck as rich and poor struggle daily into work. Unable to afford any kind of accommodation within the city itself or to find any closer shelter, countless casual workers choose instead to sleep near to their workplace wherever they can, on streets or stairways or any other available nook or cranny.

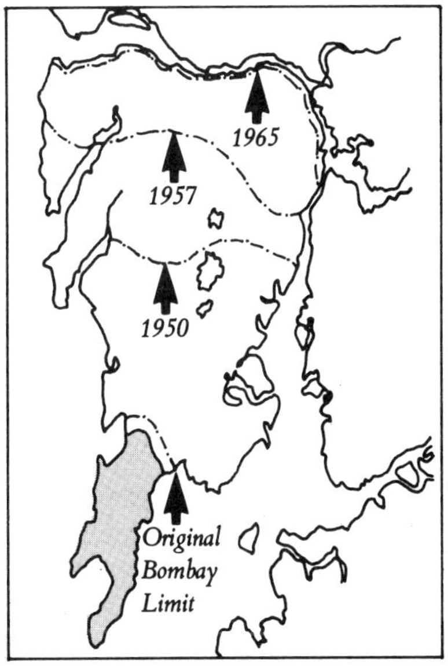

Bombay: Municipal Limits

18.2.
Bombay. Location plan showing historical expansion of municipal boundaries. From Correa, 1989.

A matter of density

Correa argues that the provision of additional squatter areas, even with local infrastructure support – the so-called 'sites and services' approach supported by many activists[6] – does little good if the new sites are located, as they generally tend to be, on vacant land remote from employment centres or public transport. Individual factories set up close by also bring little benefit, and invariably take advantage of the squatters' lack of choice by offering unacceptable wages and conditions. Raising densities even further along the lines of Hong Kong or Singapore was also out of the question, since the cost of subsidizing high rise dwellings for the poor on the scale needed was beyond the means of India's relatively less developed economy. Rejecting the Western Modernist orthodoxy of the times, he concluded there was no architectural 'fix' for Bombay's or India's problems. The solution would have to be found elsewhere:

For too long have we struggled for answers when from the beginning the question has been wrongly formulated in the first place. The problem of housing the vast majority of our people is not one of miracle building materials or construction technologies; it is primarily a matter of density, of re-establishing land-use allocations.[7]

Polycentred city

Correa deduced that the best strategy for Bombay was to establish a completely new city on undeveloped land where new centres of employment and residential areas could grow together in tandem. By the early Sixties a new industrial belt and second port was already well established on the other side of the harbour bay, joined by new bridge and rail links to the old city. In 1964 Correa and two colleagues, Pravina Meta and Shirish Patel, proposed consolidating these and other developments by restructuring Bombay and diverting further commercial growth across the water into a second, new city centre. Other centres of work and residential neighborhoods would be built on land to be purchased by the government, creating a 'polycentred city' stretching right around the bay. In 1970 the government accepted their proposals, setting aside 55,000 acres for the new city, to be called New Bombay, and asked Correa to assist in its planning and design.

Correa's primary aim was that all sectors of the population should prosper from the development, a concern that was carried over both into the structure plan and into his model housing projects. A committed advocate of low rise high density settlements, Correa argues that, aside from the additional costs of high rise housing in construction materials and maintenance, the amount of land saved over that taken up by terraced housing and other compact forms was, contrary to common belief, relatively small.[8] More than that, traditional Asian building types such as the dual function shophouses of East Asia and elsewhere allowed for a richer mixture of functions and the kind of small-scale economic activities vital to the poorer sectors, as well as to the life and character of the city. A hierarchy of public transport and urban nodes was devised, with low rise but dense settlements strung out like strings of beads along bus lines. These feed in turn into the Mass Rapid Transit system connecting up the main nodes, which stretch out linear fashion in three directions along the coasts and waterways of the bay, joining together at the new commercial centre. The principal urban activities and workplaces are gathered around these transport interchanges, bringing them within easy reach of the entire population.

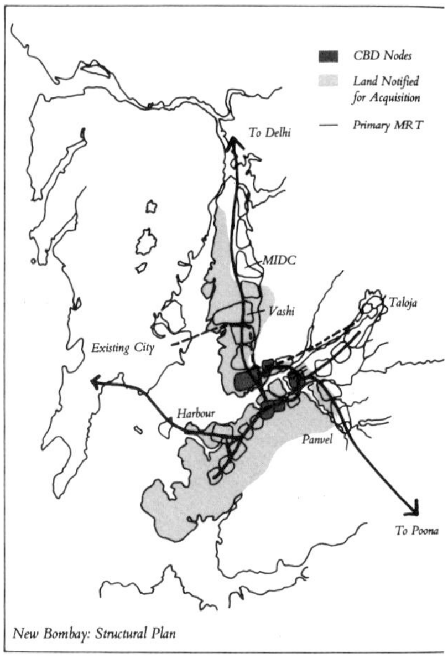

18.3.
New Bombay. Structural plan. From Correa, 1989.

Egalitarian programme

The egalitarian nature of Correa's social programme comes most clearly into focus, however, in his model 'incremental' housing complex for mixed income groups at Belapur, a district of New Bombay close to the main centre, completed in the mid-Eighties.[9] One of Correa's main criticisms of high rise housing patterns is that they entrench existing class and income barriers, separating people by land-use and space as well as differences in wealth. At Belapur Correa mixed different plot sizes together in low rise high density clusters so that people of widely

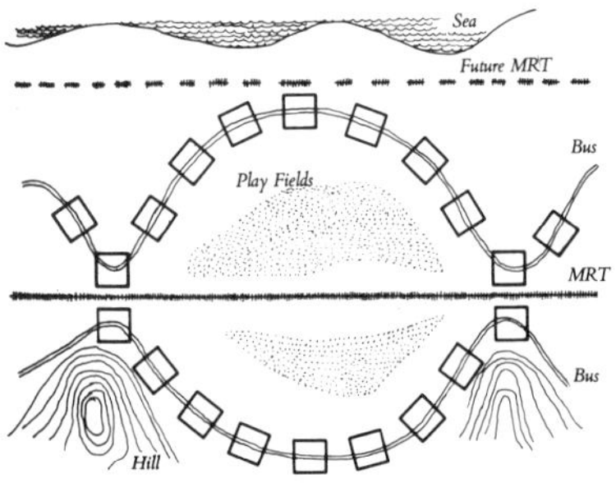

18.4.
New Bombay. Concept diagram showing integrated pattern of settlements and public transport systems. From Correa, 1989.

18.5.
'Incremental' housing at Belapur, New Bombay. Architect: Charles Correa.

disparate income groups would be able to build their own houses, each according to their individual means and desires, yet living side by side, much as they do in traditional housing clusters all over the world. For the detailed design, Correa took as his model the courtyard houses of the villages of South India, with their multifunctional, 'open-to-sky' spaces. Protected boundary conditions between each plot ensure privacy and allow each dwelling to grow independently of its neighbors. A hierarchy of shared open spaces from small to larger clusters helps to create a sense of place and to locate each dwelling within the larger settlement. The same hierachy of spaces provides opportunities for social intercourse at different levels of the community, connecting all the way up through the transport interchanges and larger urban nodes to the main city centres.

In 1991, the State Government Corporation in charge of developing New Bombay asked Correa to produce a detailed land-use plan and urban design guidelines for the new city centre at Ulwe, together with 1000 demonstration housing units for a wide range of anticipated income groups. Embracing the full breadth of environmental issues, from management of the rainfall catchment areas to detailed studies of the Central Business District, the project logically completes Correa's model of sustainable urban development. As with his incremental housing strategy, the medium sized city blocks forming the CBD are broken down into various sized plots and elements, offering both large and small investors equal opportunities to develop their own sections independently of their neighbours. Comprehensive but flexible design guidelines based on regional urban patterns ensure overall unity of the development, including covered arcades along the main street fronts. Moderate height limits and wide gaps in between block segments also encourage air movement across the interior courts; an important consideration in Bombay's subtropical climate. By the mid-Nineties New Bombay had grown into a thriving city of over a million population, less than the target figure of 2 million (the government has not yet moved to the new city as Correa had hoped it would) but already attracting growth away from the old city.

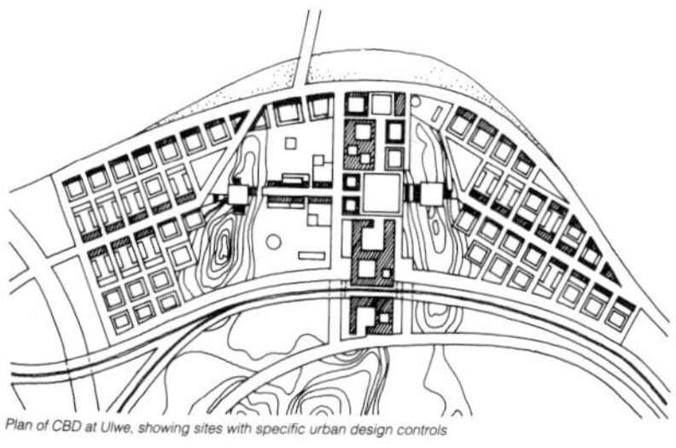

18.6a.
New Bombay. Plan of city centre at Ulwe. From Correa, 1996.

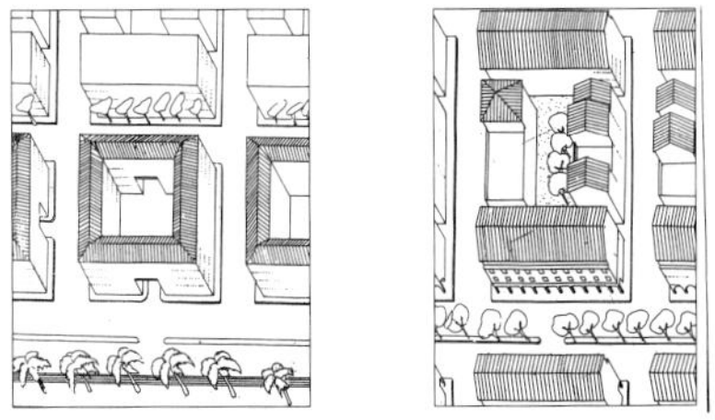

18.6b.
City centre at Ulwe. Block typologies allow for both small and large investors. From Correa, 1996.

KEN YEANG AND THE BIOCLIMATIC CITY

Vernacular models

Best known as the innovative designer of the 'tropical skyscraper' as a distinctive building form, Ken Yeang's urban theories spring from the same 'bioclimatic' principles as those which shape his architecture.[10] Settlement patterns, like individual buildings, he contends, should be accommodated to the natural landscape and biosphere and respond to the local climate and its cycles. Inspired by the tropical vernacular architecture of his native Malaysia, Yeang has generally avoided any direct imitation of local forms, abstracting the relevant lessons for climate control and adapting traditional techniques for modern needs and building types. To these original sources he has added progressively elaborate analytical methods of building performance and energy efficiency to deal with increasingly complex and varied building programmes.[11]

18.7.
Bioclimatic skyscraper. New HQ for Malaysia's UMNO political party is situated amongst terraced shophouses in Georgetown, Penang Island. Architect: Hamzah and Yeang.

Like Correa, Yeang's early thinking on urban design was strongly influenced by the compact urban patterns and covered ways of the shophouses of Kuala Lumpur and other Asian cities and towns. For similar reasons he also generally favours high urban densities, since they make for more efficient transport systems and infrastructures and therefore less energy use. Unlike Correa, however, Yeang has few reservations about the tower type, recognizing the commercial as well as other pressures in favour of the tall buildings his practice focuses on. Nevertheless, while accepting the type in principle, he is strongly critical of conventional design approaches to tall structures in Malaysia which ignore locality, and in the wasteful land-use patterns they generally create. Usually set well back from the streetfront in large plots formerly occupied by colonial villas, they contribute nothing to the streetside, which is further broken up by numerous access roads and separate parking lots. What is needed, he argues, is a way of integrating modern tall buildings into a denser and more diverse urban pattern, which would restore the streetwalks to the pedestrian. In his writings on the 'tropical verandah city', he abstracts the traditional idea of the covered shophouse arcade or 'verandahway', ingeniously converting it into an 'urban organizing principle', linking buildings together through a system of arcaded pedestrian pathways. Noting, like Correa, that former colonial building types employed the same principle of covered walkways at street level, he suggests the new verandahways would provide both shelter from the tropical sun and rainstorms and a unifying urban element at street level to tie together all the buildings of different shapes and sizes immediately behind. The same covered ways could be used to access public parking structures, which could be discreetly tucked away above and below ground within the general building mass. Thus infrastructure, climate control and urban aesthetics could be resolved with the same device, providing all the attractions of a busy streetlife that the original shophouse arcades provided and enhancing the tropical character of the city.

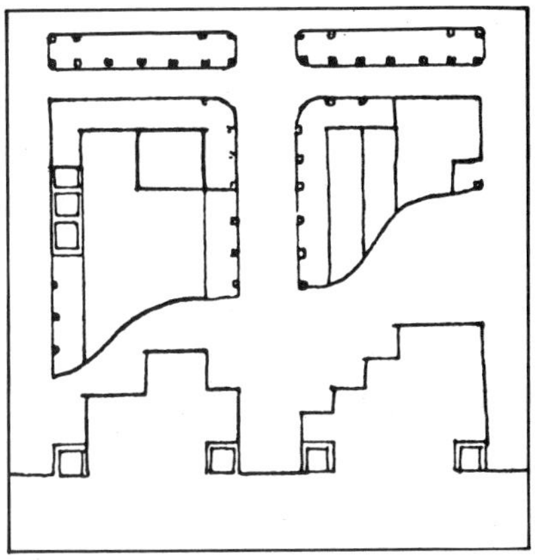

18.8.
The verandahway as 'urban organizing principle'. Plan and sectional diagram. From Yeang, 1986.

As well as drawing inspiration from vernacular building, Yeang also refers to the metaphor of the 'tropical urban garden' in suggesting how nature can be introduced into the heart of Southeast Asian cities in a way which both further strengthens their tropical identity and helps modify the microclimate. The Western approach to urban landscaping in dense cities, he notes, focuses attention on the use of reserved open spaces such as squares and parks. While Yeang encourages the development of suitably planted open spaces and any natural features, he proposes that Asian designers should go further and take full advantage of the fast-growing and luxuriant tropical vegitation, making use of every terrace and roof space to create a continuous urban greenery. This would help shade buildings, soak up greenhouse gases, and generally raise human spirits, complementing the role of more conventional parks and squares.

Living organism

The development of Yeang's ideas on urban design has gone hand-in-hand with the evolution of his built and unbuilt high rise projects. For the last decade, beginning with the landmark Menara Mesiniaga Building,[12] his tower designs for the tropics – now including Vietnam and other countries in the region – have become a virtual microcosm of the 'bioclimatic city': experimental platforms and metaphors for ideas with wider urban implications. Thus the ever larger, well planted 'skycourts' all his towers feature now take on the function and character of public or semi-public open spaces – urban meeting places in the sky equivalent to earth-bound squares – breaking up the building mass and providing accessible recreational spaces for the occupants. Describing his tower project for Hanoi, Yeang even likens the external scenic lifts taking passengers up and down between heavily planted terraces to travellers along one of that city's French-style boulevards. On a more practical level, Yeang has extended the use of similar techniques of climate and wind control which he has used to cool and ventilate his individual towers, to do the same for the spaces between buildings at street level, so that several structures act dynamically in consort to modify the urban micro-climate. Using cybernetic terminology, he envisions the future bioclimatic city as a living organism, a 'wind channelling and cooling apparatus' serving the needs of its occupants the way the human body behaves:

The bioclimatic city reacts like the human body to changes in its environment. As the body maintains its organic stability, for example by cooling via its extremities and by its homeostatic systems, so can the tropical city employ cooling layers and use the principles of homeostasis to maintain levels of comfort.[13]

Architects' duties are similarly defined and enlarged, encompassing not just the internal comfort conditions of their own buildings, but also the environmental effects they have on surrounding structures and spaces:

In the bioclimatic city, the role of the architect is to identify and design new structures, devices and spaces to protect and enhance climatically the local urban environment, meeting criteria to improve existing layers

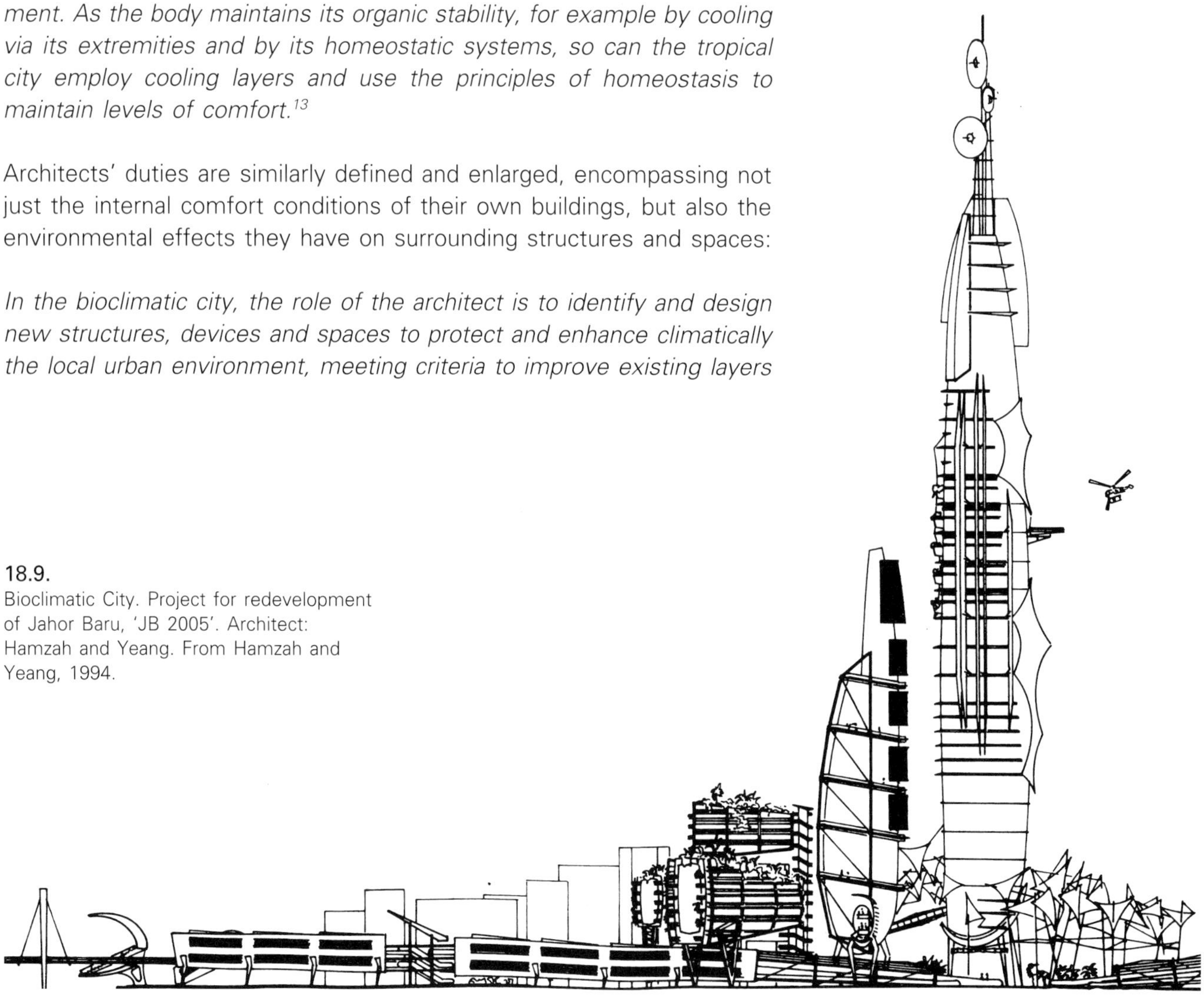

18.9.
Bioclimatic City. Project for redevelopment of Jahor Baru, 'JB 2005'. Architect: Hamzah and Yeang. From Hamzah and Yeang, 1994.

of bioclimatic control. Thus additional layers are assigned a co-ordinated form according to the city's needs as it grows and changes, allowing a three-dimensional superimposition and layering to take place over existing layers, cooling and shading the living organism of the city.[14]

In his most recent urban design projects, Yeang's buildings present a Gaudiesque collection of large and smaller tower forms, freely hung with shading tensile canopies or bound with spiralling terraces and walkways, broken here and there by completely open levels revealing the skeletal structure within. The more Yeang explores the relations between buildings and climate, the more they seem to take on the exotic character of the tropical nature they respond to.

TAY KHENG SOON AND THE TROPICAL MEGACITY

Outspoken critic

A native Singaporean and articulate critic of his country's orthodox planning methods and approaches to urban design, Tay Kheng Soon[15] sees little gain in the developing world's continued reliance on Western concepts and consultants:

Today we have new industrial estates, public housing estates, and free-trade-zones, but they are modified from their northern models. There were adaptations in the developing countries but no basic review. Thus today we have megacities in the tropics but have yet to realize the potentials of tropical living in cities because there has not been any basic review of the inherited town-planning doctrines and concepts...nothing intrinsic has come out of city planning in the tropics thus far.[16]

Tay's outspokeness earned him early notoriety with the conservative Singapore authorities. Discouraged as a young architect from exploring alternatives to the state's high-rise housing strategies, Tay moved to Kuala Lumpur in 1974 where he found the official response more sympathetic to his ideas. There he designed and built two experimental low rise high density housing projects for low income groups, demonstrating, as Correa was doing elsewhere, that compact housing could be provided at considerably less cost than comparable high rise solutions. In what was to become a typical pattern, Tay's designs necessitated major changes to the colonial era building regulations, which were then still based on conventional British practice.

Alternative strategies

More than a decade later, having returned to Singapore to establish his present office, Akitek Tengarra, Tay found himself attacking official policy from a different viewpoint. By the mid-Eighties the population of the small island state had grown to 2.6 million and was forcast to grow to 3.2 million by 2015. Anticipating a possible still larger increase of 1 million over the same period, Tay argued that if the government persisted in its established policy of distributing population expansions around the island in yet more new towns, the result would be irreparable harm to what was left of the natural environment. Reversing his earlier stance on housing densities, he argued in favour of a radical policy of raising densities in existing urban centres, especially in Singapore city itself, concentrating the increase on available undeveloped land and at the same time reducing the need for additional infrastructure.

Whilst he was sharpening his thoughts on urban strategy, Tay built a number of building projects with a distinctly urban character, using his architecture, like Yeang, to explore broader ideas on the built environment. He had also become concerned over the same period at the official calls, particularly in neighbouring Malaysia, for a national architectural identity, seeing them as a politically motivated and potentially divisive stamp of a singular ethnic identity upon what was essentially a multicultural region. Like Yeang, he argued instead for a modern architecture rooted in the tropical environment itself, which all Southeast Asians shared. In his larger projects of the time, like the Institute of Technical Education at Bishan[17] and the Serangoon Gardens Country Club, Tay exploited the balmy climate, turning the spaces in between the separate elements into open gardens or naturally ventilated, covered meeting places. Other climate-control devices were developed over the same years in what Tay has described as his personal search for a 'tropical design language', eventually leading him back along the same path towards his urban projects and concerns.

Urban workshop

In 1988 Tay ran an urban workshop on The Intelligent Tropical City with Robert Powell, an architecture teacher at the National University of Singapore. Two years earlier Tay had participated in the international competition at Kawasaki in Japan for an Advanced Information City, a theme and project which he saw as highly relevant to Singapore, which was then already heavily investing in information technology. The student workshop was an attempt at bringing together Tay's responses

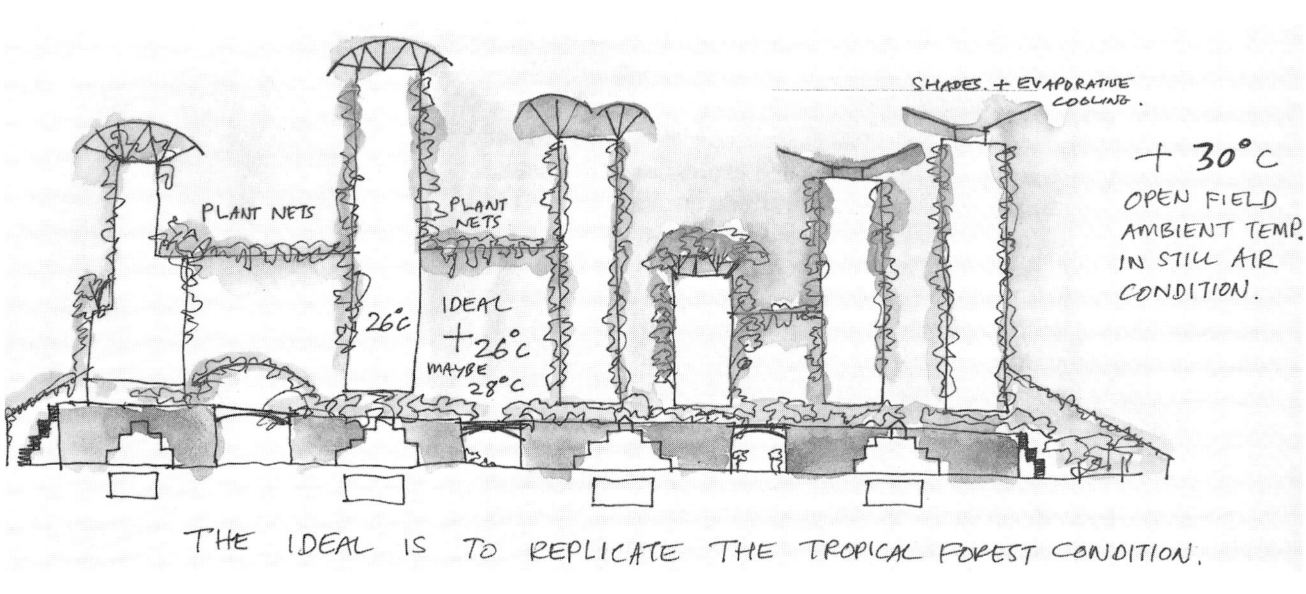

18.10.
Project for The Intelligent Tropical City. Concept sketch. From Tay, 1989.

to these developments, together with his ideas on Singapore's expansion and the specific problems of urban design in the tropics.

The workshop team proposed developing the reclaimed land adjacent to Singapore's Marina Bay into a high density, mixed use city sector, housing half the expected population increase of 1 million. At a gross plot ratio of 12.5:1, the density of building and the pattern of vertical stratification into different functions strongly resembles that of Hong Kong, a relatively chaotic model previously eschewed by Singapore's planners.[18] Much like that megacity, Tay envisages the project as a kind of 'giant shophouse', with the inhabitants all living in residential towers directly over the lower commercial and civic activities. Constrained by Singapore's strict zoning laws – boundaries Tay was reluctant to cross – the functional mix excluded the kinds of IT industries Tay would have liked to have. He proposed instead that specific IT-oriented departments of the university be re-sited to the new district, along the lines of the IT campus city proposed at Kawasaki. Aside from the sheer density, the most striking aspect of the project is the handling of the different levels and their interconnections. 'Plant nets' between the towers would shade the lower levels and streets below, while the roofs of the bottom structures would be connected together by bridges, creating another level of open public spaces to serve the communities living above. Solar and rainwater collectors suspended from the tower tops would provide more shade as well as energy and evaporative cooling systems would be used to further lower the temperatures inside and outside the buildings below. The entire complex, claims Tay, could be likened to the upper canopies and layered micro-climatic structure of a tropical forest.

Test of reality

A year later, in a significant move to open up the planning process to the private sector, the Urban Redevelopment Authority (URA) invited Tay to draw up a scheme for the development of 72 hectares in the Kampong Bugis district, situated at the confluence of two rivers close to the city centre. Tay treated the exercise as an opportunity to put the ideas coming out of the workshop to the test of reality, considerably modifying them in the process. Aside from the more detailed and varied building studies, now liberally hung with vertical landscaping, the major evolution in the new project is in the reduction in building density to an overall plot ratio of 4.5:1, still higher than the 2.8:1 net density required

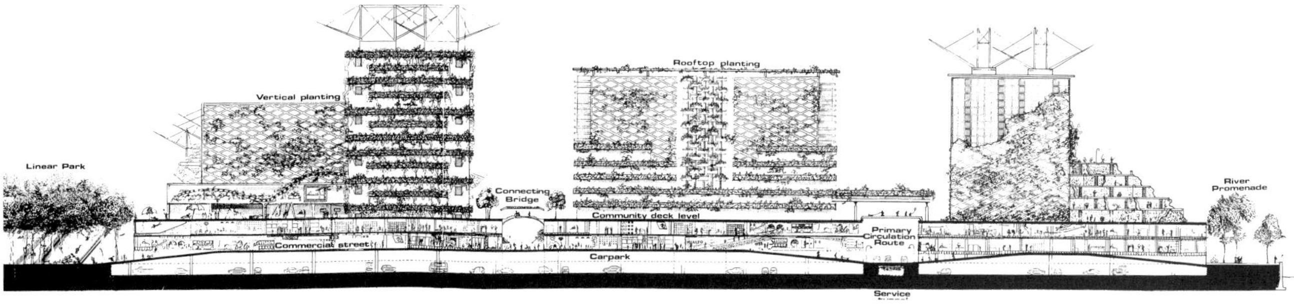

18.11.
Project for redevelopment of Kampong Bugis district, Singapore. Section. Architect: Akitek Tengarra.

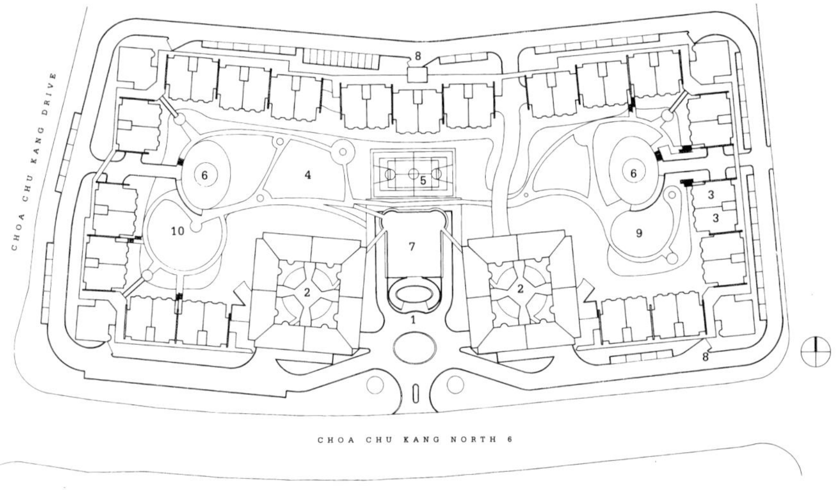

18.12.
Housing complex for HDB at Choa Chu Kang, Singapore. Plan. Architect: Akitek Tengarra.

1 Entrance court
2 18-storey blocks
3 Perimeter housing
4 Landscaped open space
5 Basketball court
6 Community pavilion
7 Viewing deck
8 Perimeter access road
9 Children's play area
10 Fitness area

of Singapore's new towns, but relatively modest compared to the earlier proposals. The resulting impression is of a still crowded, but vibrant and livable tropical metropole befitting Singapore's status and location in the region. Nevertheless, for all its attractions and Tay's efforts to render his ideas into practical proposals, the planning authorities finally deemed the scheme too radical, deciding in favour of a conventional, low rise high density scheme by Singapore's own state professionals.

More recently, Tay gained a small but potentially important victory for his ideas with his competition-winning housing complex for the Singapore Housing and Development Board (HDB) at Choa Chu Kang, completed in 1997. Despite presenting the highest tender, Tay's scheme was praised for its innovative manipulation of block depth and morphology, allowing an increase in the plot ratio from the required minimum of 2.8:1 to 3:1. Similar modest but effective design approaches, argues Tay, could be used to raise the figure still more to 3.5:1, which if generally adopted as the rule would significantly increase housing densities in Singapore without detriment to environmental quality. Current projects abroad, including masterplans in China and low income housing in the Philippines, offer further challenging tests for Tay's ideas in new and more varied contexts.

LIU THAI KER AND THE CONSTELLATION CITY

Singapore experience

The most experienced planner in the group, Liu Thai Ker has played a key role in shaping the physical development and urban character of Singapore. As head of the HDB from 1969–89, Liu oversaw the building of over half a million dwelling units in one of East Asia's largest and longest-running state housing programmes. The following three years he led the URA, where he spearheaded major revisions to the Singapore Concept Plan, the state's blueprint for the future. Since then he has continued to exert an influence over regional development from private practice with Raglan Squire and Partners (RSP), one of Singapore's oldest firms, and is consultant planner to Beijing and many other cities throughout China and Asia.[19]

18.13.
Tampines North Community Centre, Singapore. Private architects now share work with state architects in new towns. Architect: William Lim Associates.

Responding to criticism of Singapore's earlier uniform high rise housing and derivative planning policies, Liu points to the increasing variety of architecture and urban design in Singapore's new towns, in which private firms like Tay's now play an increasing role.[20] These and other changes have helped the new towns evolve from glorified housing estates modelled on European lines to relatively self-contained and diversified small cities of up to 300,000 population. Partly influenced by his Singapore experience and partly by his new responsibilities in China and elsewhere, a wider evolution is also apparent in Liu's thinking on urban structure, now increasingly focused on the special problems of Asia's megacities. For Liu, as for Correa, the way ahead for Asian planners lies in a radical restructuring of large cities, breaking up existing conglomerations centred on historic cores and decentralizing future growth points and CBDs to create what he calls the 'constellation city'. While recognizing the economic and cultural benefits of very large urban concentrations and the range of choices they afford, Liu argues that, above a certain size – he tentatively suggests around 3 million – difficulties of access and other problems outweigh the advantages to the point where an acceptable quality of life, and even basic urban functions, are no longer sustainable. The limiting figure is only an approximation, and even well-planned and smaller Singapore, he contends, has its problems:

Despite the gallant efforts by the government to provide excellent public transportation and road networks as well as to discourage private car ownership; despite efforts to decentralize CBD functions into the outlying areas, road traffic congestion in the central area continues to intensify.[21]

As Liu admits, despite raising the population of Singapore's new towns and offering numerous incentives to decentralize, increasing numbers of commercial and other workers apparently still prefer to wade through all the obstacles to do business in the original city, if not to live there. The implication is that, while there may be a maximum size to any conurbation limiting the quality of life, there is a no less important lower limit of size below which it becomes difficult if not impossible to attract commercial and other functions vital to the economic well-being of a city.

Clusters of cities

It might be thought that such observations support Tay's proposed strategy of reversing the process of decentralization and increasing densities within the city boundaries. However, Liu draws a different conclusion: 'In hindsight, the decentralization efforts could have been bolder'.[22] If anything, he implies, Singapore's planners should have gone for fewer and larger new urban centres, offering sufficient and diverse attractions to compete more successfully with the main city.

With a current total population of 3 million and a maximum desirable population set out in the Concept Plan of 4 million at year 'X' (meaning whatever year that figure is achieved in, whether 40 or 80 years hence), Liu comments that Singapore 'can hardly call itself a megacity'.[23] Nevertheless, he believes the city state, with its multiple urban nodes all connected up by its efficient Mass Rapid Transit system, offers valuable lessons for larger conurbations. While the nodes themselves might be presently undersized, the basic idea of linked centres was, and is, he suggests, the right solution. Looking to the future, the new Concept Plan drawn up by Liu projects a more concentrated system of larger regional urban centres of half a million to 800,000 population each, virtually turning Singapore into a model constellation city, albeit a smaller-scale one than Liu envisages elsewhere.[24] Based on these lessons, he posits a more general lower

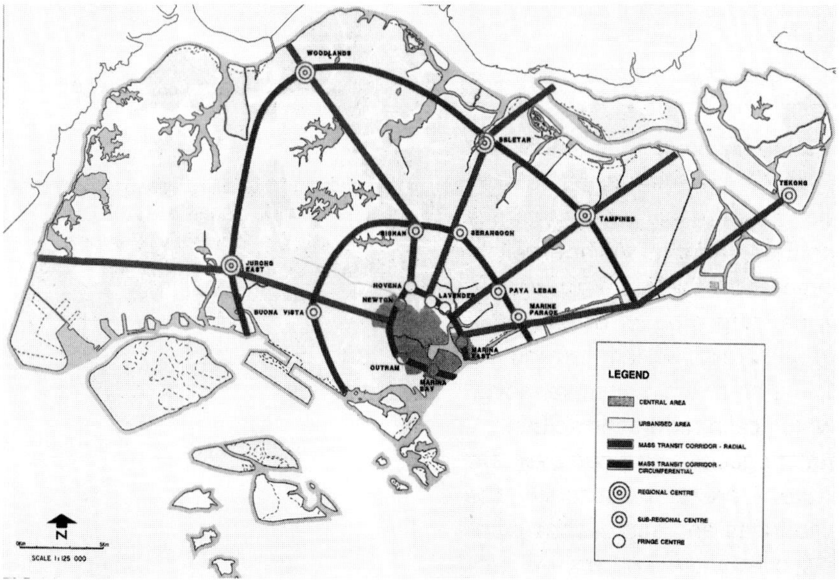

18.14.
Concept Plan, Singapore. Diagrammatic plan showing 'constellation' of regional centres distributed along MRT system. From Urban Redevelopment Authority, 1991.

population limit for a self-sufficient urban centre at 1.5 million, within a linked system of like centres:

The ideal situation is to enjoy the benefits of megacities without the associated problems...One possibility to realize this is to organize a major metropolis into a constellation city. Such a city is comprised of a cluster of self-sufficient cities of 1.5 to 3 million people, spaced (at least) 30–50 kilometres but not more than 100 kilometres apart from one another. Each city functions independently on a day to day basis, and yet related to one another in terms of special cultural, scientific and commercial synergy. All the cities can have more or less equal status, or one of them can be dominant, depending on the historical background...[25]

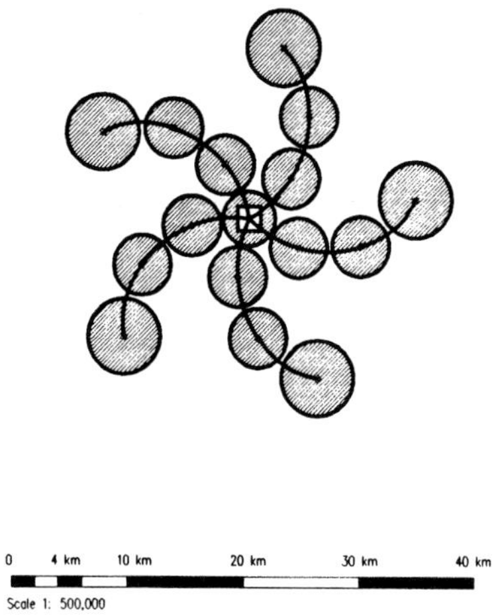

18.15a.
Constellation City. Diagram showing city of 2.5–4 million people consisting of new towns of 150,000–400,000 people. Concept drawing by Liu Thai Ker.

Liu points to the cluster of small and medium sized cities in the western part of Germany which includes Bonn, Cologne, Düsseldorf and Frankfurt, as a relevant example of urban structuring. While each has its own separate identity, a dense and efficient network of autobahns and commuter trains enables them to function essentially as one urban unit. Why not, Liu asks, take advantage of today's rapid rail and other transportation systems and create similar clusters of cities? Asian megacities, he adds, already contain many competing commercial nodes, though distributed in such a way that they often undermine each other. However, if the commercial centres were to be located in a more rational fashion and properly sized accordingly, then they could work together instead as a system, each complementing the other in a network of related functions. If each city was also separated from the others by green belts and the distances between them were kept within the recommended limits, then access could be further enhanced to every centre and to nature at the same time. Such an urban structure, Liu suggests, would offer all the economic and cultural advantages that very large conurbations normally have, but in a more harmonious and sustainable way.

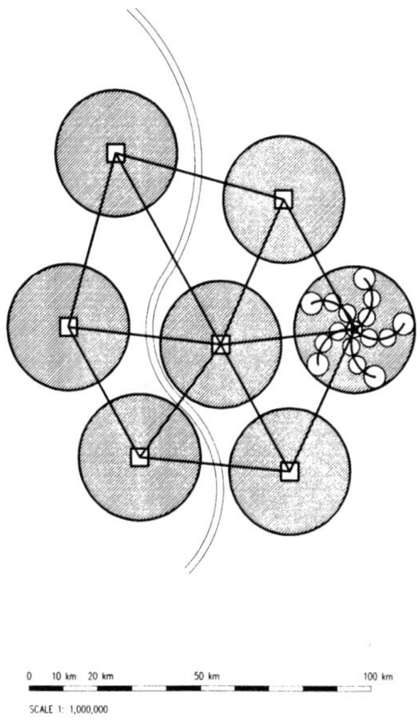

18.15b.
Constellation City. Diagram showing city of 12–20 million people consisting of smaller cities of 2.5–4 million people. Concept drawing by Liu Thai Ker.

TOWARD THE DEVELOPMENT CITY

Dominant force for change

What is striking about all these diverse ideas and projects is the extent to which the four thinkers confidently embrace a scale and complexity of human development which would have daunted earlier generations of architects and planners, from West or East. Another Asian intellectual, the Thai architect Sumet Jumsai, even goes so far as to suggest that the megacity, problems and all, is a defining product or aspect of contemporary Asian culture, and the ingenuity with which commuters and dwellers alike cope with their situtation is as much a positive indication of indigenous creativity as anything which calls for drastic solution.[26] Jumsai's view may be a benign one, but megacities – what they are and what they foretell of the urban future – are unquestionably the dominant force for change in Asia, and the ideas and approaches of all four architect-planners are shaped by this overwhelming fact, no less than the thinking of Western architect-planners was shaped earlier by the unavoidable fact of mass ownership of the automobile, and the uncontrollable popular choices that entailed.

The convergence of any of these leading environmentalists around common solutions, if only at the most general levels of planning, is therefore of some importance. An endemic feature of the development of Asian cities, both large and small, is the way growth invariably – Singapore excepted – precedes infrastructure, which then has to be inserted at a later date at considerable extra cost. The emphasis Correa and Liu place upon the necessity for integrated heterarchies[27] of public transportation and urban form is the structural bedrock upon which all else they propose stands. Tightly linked by road, rail, bus, bridge and ferry, Old Bombay and New Bombay could well be described as a constellation city, albeit an imbalanced one, as many future constellations are likely to be. Tay has also proposed his own inter-regional constellation, similarly linked across both water and land, by which the city of Singapore would be networked together with those of neighbouring Johore state on the southern tip of Malaysia, and Riau province in Sumatra on the north western end of the Indonesian archipelago.[28] Current political and economic differences between all three states, aggravated by the recent financial crisis, make any imminent integration of this sort highly implausible. In the longer run, however, Tay's proposed strategy contains much good sense and portends the likely pattern of future regional co-operation and development.

Parallel urban cultures

Nevertheless, whilst there is broad agreement on strategy, there are considerable differences in urban form and detail. Given the confusions

18.16.
Dispersed high rise city. Kuala Lumpur CBD in background. View from top of 310 metre high Telekom Tower during construction (see Fig. 18.19). Photo: Chris Abel.

and competing influences of post-colonial development, this can only be expected. Yeang, for example, identifies several types of Asian cities, each with its own morphology: 'ancient cities' like Beijing and Tokyo which have been modernized; 'post-colonial cities' like Kuala Lumpur and Singapore whose morphology was shaped by their colonial past; 'non-colonized cities' like Bangkok; 'dormitory cities' like Petaling Jaya ('PJ') in Malaysia and Saitama in Japan; 'instant cities' or 'new towns' like Shenzhen in China; and 'transitional cities', which includes squatter settlements and other non-formal habitations. Finally, he lists the media-based 'virtual cities', comprised of telecommunications systems, which can exist anywhere in the world.[29]

Useful as they are, such typologies obscure an even more complex reality, which is that Asia's megacities generally include most of these urban types within the same area, each tied to the others in overlapping and ambiguous ways and each offering its own parallel urban culture, distinct from but not separate from all the rest. The wildly varying shape of the most recent developments and projects only confuses matters still further. Malaysia's new federal capital, Putrajaya, is consciously planned as a modern garden city, while its new parliament centre – astonishingly for such a symbolic venture – mimics the historic colonial buildings in Kuala Lumpur. Part of Malaysia's ambitious plan for a Multimedia Supercorridor or 'cybercity' stretching between the capital and the new international airport 50 kilometres away, Putrajaya's function and location also qualify it as a key hub in the future virtual city, which is designed to qualify the country as a major player in the global IT industry.[30] The relatively spontaneous clusters of commercial and apartment buildings around the outer fringes of most Asian cities are even more difficult to categorize. Neither low rise low density garden city, nor high rise high density CBD – both Western concepts in origin – these unevenly distributed settlements are more accurately described as components of a 'dispersed high rise city',[31] an altogether different urban form, reflecting both market forces and the chaotic energy of Asia's urbanization process. In the futuristic category, there is 'KL Linear City', otherwise known as 'Giga World', also in Kuala Lumpur, an Archigram-inspired megastructure project bestriding the capital's main river.[32] Postponed for now and probably doomed by the recent financial crisis, the imaginative scheme adds yet another, if questionable, prototypical city form to Asian planners' and architects' growing repertoire. Last but not least, there are Sir Norman Foster's 840 metre high Millennium Tower project for Tokyo, and its smaller variant, the 'M' Tower, also shelved for now.[33] The more Asia's megacities grow, the more likely it seems that vertical townships like these will move off the computer screen into reality.

Given the profusion of urban histories and of both old and new models, the attention given by all four architect-planners to climate and ecology as a primary shaper of urban form offers the prospect of both a unifying and relatively neutral theme which conveniently bridges potentially fractious issues of ethnic and cultural identity. There is also general agreement on the need for firm but flexible urban design guidelines of one kind or another, ensuring, in the case of Yeang's schema, the control of the urban microclimate in addition to enhancement of the streetsides. Whilst these are positive results in themselves, no definitive model of

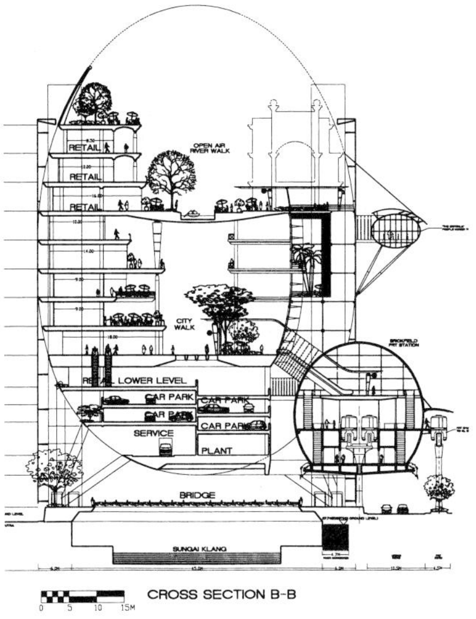

18.17.
KL Linear City, Kuala Lumpur. Section of main structure spanning Klang River. From Original Scope Sdn. Bhd., 1996.

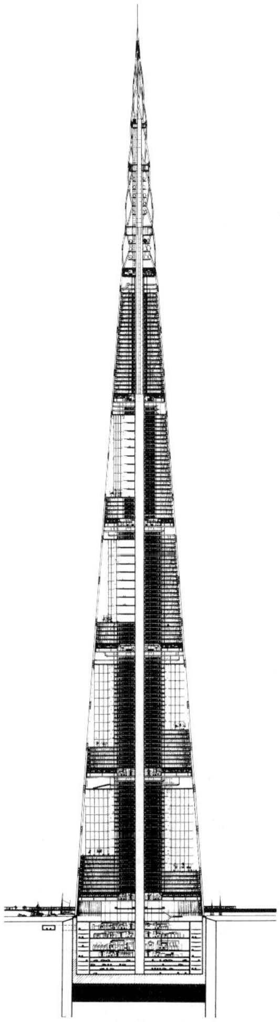

18.18.
Millennium Tower project, Tokyo. Section. Architect: Foster and Partners.

the tropical city as such has yet been presented, raising the question whether 'one model fits all' is feasible or even desirable, even for specific climatic regions. What is offered instead at this stage are important fragments, such as the reinterpretation of the verandahway as a key element of urban design, of an incomplete vision. There are also serious contradictions amongst the proposals, some easily resolved, some less so. It is doubtful, for example, that any useful purpose is served by complicating an already uncertain concept with the description '*intelligent* tropical city' – meaning that IT has somehow shaped the concept if not the form – when the same description is used for such totally different urban designs as an ultra high density scheme for Singapore and Malaysia's low density cybercity.

Responses to climate

Similar questions are raised regarding the actual, as opposed to the assumed, effectiveness of proposed responses to climatic factors. For example, in his writings Tay cites research into the heat island or 'canyon effect' of Malaysian city centres, compared with lower temperatures in an open landscape and still cooler temperatures within the tropical forest. Given the still higher urban densities Tay favours it is doubtful whether evaporative cooling or any other proposed measures would be sufficient to counter such a large effect, which even at present densities produces differences between forest and city centre of as much as 8 to 10°C. Vertical landscaping, whilst attractive in theory, also carries severe maintenance and cost penalities[34] which also rule it out as a general solution, except possibly for the most wealthy clients and cities. In short, the ultra high density, high rise city and the *tropical* city, meaning one that is genuinely shaped by the climate, may be fundamentally incompatible concepts.

The clear influence of Lionel March's seminal studies on urban morphology[35] on most of these architect-planners' thinking – Liu Thai Ker being the sole exception – may be partly to blame here. March demonstrated that the same volume of structure may be provided by building around a site's perimeter in a low rise high density pattern as is normally provided by a single tower standing in the middle of the same site. However, in promoting the former historic European pattern, March gave no consideration at all to the impact of different climatic conditions upon the two building forms. While the enclosed, courtyard pattern is most effective in hot-arid climates, and to a lesser extent in temperate and subtropical regions, exactly the reverse is true of building in the hot-humid tropics, where the free-standing building, whether *kampong* house, villa or tower, is the better solution for continuous natural ventilation (the shophouse pattern admired by Correa and Yeang was imported by Chinese settlers into the tropics and is rarely more than two stories high, punctuated by ventilating yards[36]). For the same reasons, the higher the perimeter structure, which restricts air movement across the site, the more the climatic advantage goes to the free-standing tower.

Seen in this light, the sporadic clusters of towers which exemplify the dispersed high rise city may make better sense in the tropics, if only from a purely climatic viewpoint, minimizing the heat island effect and maximizing the benefits of cooling air movements. Singapore's much criticized Modernist new towns, with their widely spaced high rise blocks interspersed by mature and easily maintained landscaping – what Liu also describes as 'the tropical garden city', or more poetically, 'the garden in the city and the city in the garden'[37] – may also be re-evaluated for similar reasons, as a sound if repetitive solution to a sustainable micro-climate in tropical cities. As much as Correa generally prefers the low rise high density solution in India for economic and social reasons, he allows that the tower type meets a given need for upper income housing and commerce and includes appropriate clusters in the city centre and subcentres in his New Bombay plan. He also made an early and significant contribution himself to bioclimatic high rise design with his 1983 Kanchanjunga Apartments in the old city, which remain an exemplar of the type. In addition to Yeang's work, other leading Southeast Asian architects such as Hijjas Kasturi and Jimmy Lim are also now pushing the frontiers of high rise design in their own region, creating completely new tower forms bedecked with large and open hanging gardens, which could only function properly in the tropics.

Fortunately, the debate over the relative climatic suitability and energy efficiency of one settlement pattern or building form over another looks set to be radically transformed, and much for the better, with the increasing use of the new battery of computer simulation techniques. Already in regular service by Yeang's practice, the availability of such relatively low cost procedures, which have even been used by architecture students elsewhere,[38] now obliges every practitioner or theorist to put his or her designs to a simulated test of performance before trying them out in the real world, when it is too late or too expensive to change anything. The same advances may also eventually produce more concrete and potentially fruitful interrelations between information technology and the future shape of the tropical city.

18.19.
Telekom Tower, Kuala Lumpur. Model. Architect: Hijjas Kasturi Associates.

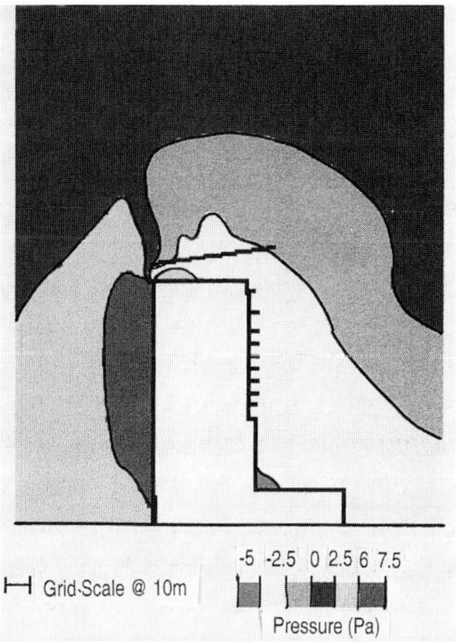

18.20.
Computer simulation of wind-flow around UMNO tower. Architect: Hamzah and Yeang.

Economic and social focus

The four architect-planners differ most, however, in how each deals with the complex economic and social issues associated with Asia's megacities, and the special needs of different sectors of the population. Partly due perhaps to the different professional backgrounds of the four, a clear division exists between the broader concerns and works of the two most experienced planners, Correa and Liu, and the more architectural and design centred concerns and works of Yeang and Tay. While Yeang's earlier schemes for a verandah city suggest more accommodating urban patterns, his most recent and technologically advanced projects for the bioclimatic city, exciting as they are, convey a more exclusive image. It is difficult to see, for example, how lower income groups fit into either these projects or Tay's equally ambitious schemes, other than as commuters from more affordable residential areas. This may be acceptable for prosperous Singapore and Japan, but hardly presents a general model for the rest of Asia. By contrast, Correa's and Liu's proven record of urban planning indicates a more pragmatic approach to the provision of employment centres and affordable housing, without which no urban scheme is viable, 'green' or not. Both Correa and Liu also see planning and urban design primarily as engines of economic and social development, which the physical and spatial form of the city must ultimately serve. Both are also in broad agreement on macro-planning policies and decentralization strategies, using different terminologies – 'polycentred city' and 'constellation city' – for similar, if not identical solutions.

Significant differences, however, exist in Correa's and Liu's approaches elsewhere, most especially in their respective attitudes towards the mixing of activities and social groups and the alternative settlement patterns and building types each approach calls for. Whereas Singapore's strict, Western-style zoning and new town policies are generally designed to segregate workplaces from residential areas,[39] New Bombay's plan and settlement patterns are purposefully designed to mesh both together, wherever the scale and type of economic activity permits. Correa's complex land-use policies and incremental building schemes, for example, not only encourage social integration, but are also intended to generate employment in the informal or 'bazaar economy', which he sees as an essential component of the larger Asian urban economy, along with the more advanced commercial centres. For Correa, not only the transportation system and distribution of housing, commerce and industry, but also the pattern, fabric and maintenance of the city itself are treated as an integral part of the urban economy. The variety of building types, construction techniques and materials, are accordingly designed to maximize participation at the smallest scale of operation, down to the individual craftsman, entrepeneur or self-builder, and not just favour the largest construction firms, as is usually the case with official projects.

To appreciate the full scope and meaning of Correa's achievement it is useful to recall just how narrowly the scope for urban planning and design has previously been defined, most especially where borrowed Western models are involved. Commenting on Le Corbusier's plan for Chandigarh, the new capital of the Punjab whose 50th birthday was recently celebrated by architectural pilgrims from around the world, the British planner Peter Hall offers the following devasting observations:

The relationship between streets and buildings is totally European, and is laid down without regard for the fierce north-Indian climate or for Indian ways of life. There is a total failure to produce built forms that could aid social organization or social integration; the sections fail to function as neighborhoods. The city is heavily segregated by income and civil service rank, recalling La Ville contemporaine*; there are different densities for different social groups, resulting in a planned class segregation.*[40]

Given the now familiar preoccupation of Le Corbusier and other early Modernist architect-planners with formal and geometric concepts, the apparent 'blindness' of the Chandigarh plan to local social and cultural complexities, let alone the rigours of the Indian climate, no longer surprises. However, while ecological or bioclimatic models may address the latter blind spot, there is a danger, which both Yeang's and Tay's schemes illustrate to some extent, that the bioclimatic or tropical city, like the 'city of monuments' Hall describes Chandigarh as, is a one-dimensional or one-theme model, no less blind than previous one-dimensional models to all the other economic, social and cultural factors which go to make up a living city.

This is not to underestimate the importance of ecological and climatic considerations, which grow more urgent by the day, or of Yeang's and Tay's architectural innovations. But if the ecological model is to be applied at the urban scale, then either it needs to be integrated with other more comprehensive models of development, or else it needs to be broadened itself to assimilate the same considerations.[41] It is in this respect that Correa's multi-dimensional approach is most effective. Correa's settlement patterns and selection of local building types are consciously devised with their economic and social impact in mind, no less than their suitability to Bombay's subtropical climate. Most important, in making purposeful and generous provision for the bazaar economy alongside other sectors – which now include Bombay's famous legions of software writers – Correa also implicity takes on board the structural parallelism or so-called 'dual economy' which distinguishes Asian cities from Western cities, with all of the cultural complexities and regional eccentricities which go with it.[42]

Unplanned and planned development

Correa's stress on the economic and social aspects of urban planning and design does not exclude the formal or symbolic aspects which have preoccupied, and still preoccupy, most other designers, but rather puts them into proper perspective. As an architect, Correa has produced superlative monumental buildings of great spatial intricacy and depth of meaning, as well as more humble structures; a depth of meaning, moreover, that arises directly out of his native Indian culture.[43] He has also demonstrated, at New Bagalkot township and elsewhere, that he can produce urban plans with multiple levels of symbolic interpretation, taking in both his social concerns as well as more abstract meanings. This and the clear focus on economic and social development – and equal opportunity moreover – sets his schema apart from either the spatial and formal models planners and urban designers are historically accustomed to, or any of the other new models they are in the process of learning to use.

Such considerations and priorities point towards a new model of city planning and design more directly suited to Asia's developing societies, which may appropriately be called the 'development city'. This model, which is based upon a positive strategy for equitable development, may be contrasted in summary with the main negative features of Asia's unplanned megacities, as follows:

The unplanned megacity

(i) ...is typified by a lack of strategic and forward planning and mostly random patterns of growth.

(ii) ...has large-scale, destructive and health-endangering effects on the natural environment and micro-climate.

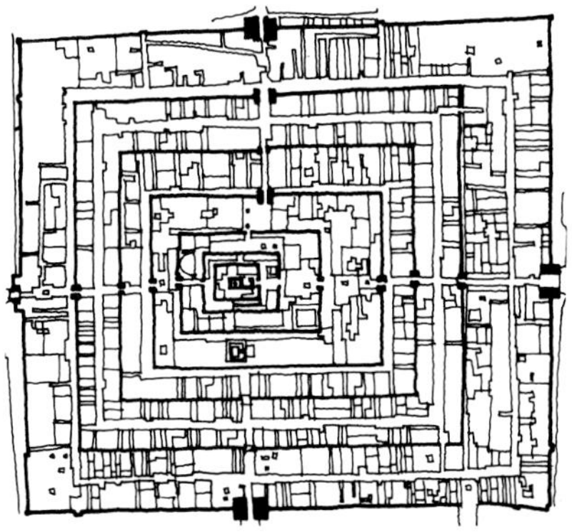

18.21a.
Plan of the ancient holy city of Srirangam, India. From Correa, 1996.

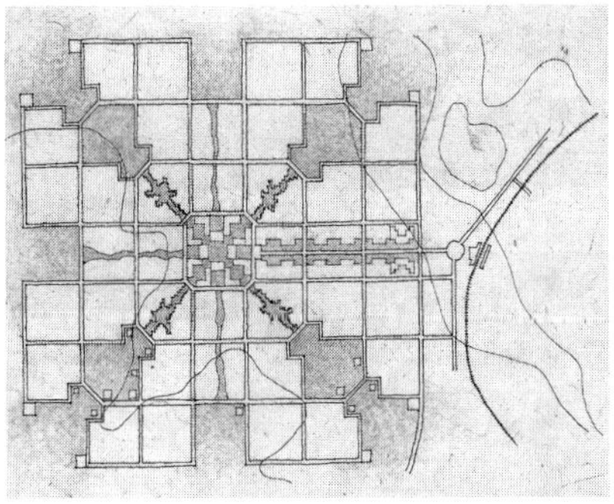

18.21b.
New Bagalkot, India. Plan of new township is oriented along four cardinal directions similar to metaphysical structure of Srirangam. From Correa, 1996.

(iii) ...is a wasteful user of human resources as well as land, energy, rainwater and other natural resources.
(iv) ...places most of its population out of reach with nature.
(v) ...is composed of several distinct and parallel urban forms and cultures, partly historical or traditional and partly modern, whose interconnections are arbitrary and limited.
(vi) ...has a hierarchical or radial structure and growth pattern, increasing pressures on the original centre and limiting direct communications between subcentres.
(vii) ...grows faster and far ahead of its infrastructure, which is always inadequate to its needs.
(viii) ...maximizes distances between residential and employment centres for the majority of the population, resulting in increased travel time and pressure on congested transportation systems.
(ix) ...forces its newest immigrants and lowest income groups to settle on the periphery, socially isolated and remote from the main employment centres.
(x) ...restricts social integration and segregates the general population by settlement patterns and housing types differentiated according to income and social class.
(xi) ...has an insufficient variety of building types with different price structures to meet population needs, restricting upward social and economic mobility.
(xii) ...restricts access to urban amenities due to lack of adequate and affordable public transportation.
(xiii) ...has several large and competing commercial centres which are unevenly located and poorly interconnected.
(xiv) ...concentrates building construction in the hands of the largest firms.
(xv) ...restricts small-scale commercial and other private initiatives by the lack of affordable space in the right places.
(xvi) ...has inadequate or poorly enforced urban design guidelines and building regulations.
(xvii)...is characterized by great extremes of wealth and poverty dictating access to employment, educational and cultural opportunities.

The planned 'development city'

(i) ...is typified by long-term planning and strategically controlled growth patterns.
(ii) ...has large but sustainable effects on the natural environment and micro-climate.
(iii) ...makes the most of human resources and is a large but efficient user of land, energy, rainwater and other natural resources.
(iv) ...distributes its population in such a manner that most are within easy reach of green belts.
(v) ...is composed of several distinct and parallel urban forms and cultures, partly historical or traditional and partly modern, whose interconnections are multiplied and diverse.
(vi) ...has a heterarchical structure and growth pattern comprising constellations of small and larger cities, with direct and efficient communications between city centres.

(vii) ...*grows with its infrastructure, which is planned ahead of other activities.*

(viii) ...*minimizes distances between residential areas and employment centres, which are distributed evenly throughout the constellation, including local small-scale industries.*

(ix) ...*distributes its newest immigrants and lowest income groups evenly throughout the constellation through the use of positive land-use and housing policies.*

(x) ...*encourages social integration through the use of mixed settlement patterns and housing types, covering a wide range of income groups and social classes.*

(xi) ...*encourages upward social and economic mobility through incremental design strategies, from self-build housing to flexible apartment and commercial buildings.*

(xii) ...*facilitates access to urban amenities through evenly distributed and affordable systems of public transportation.*

(xiii) ...*has several large and evenly distributed commercial centres offering maximum consumer choice.*

(xiv) ...*encourages incremental building methods and low-cost construction techniques involving small firms and entrepeneurs.*

(xv) ...*facilitates small-scale commercial and other private initiatives through the use of mixed-use land policies and incremental block design.*

(xvi) ...*enforces sustainable urban design guidelines and building regulations to ensure efficient use of energy and natural resources and socially beneficial building patterns.*

(xvii)...*is characterized by equal employment, educational and cultural opportunities.*

While the complete development city has yet to be built in its entirety, most of the above features have already been or are in the process of being implemented in one form or another, either in New Bombay or in Singapore if not elsewhere. Though the more extreme versions of laissez-faire development are rejected, neither does the model represent any kind of return to old style, rigid physical master-planning. The development city's heterarchical structure of well-connected and evenly distributed nodes and functions comprises an essentially flexible strategy for growth and change, encouraging individual and entrepeneurial initiatives and allowing for the unexpected but inevitable problems in the distribution of resources and functions. Similarly, the incremental design policies and guidelines which underpin much of the physical fabric of the city allow considerable room for participation and interpretation by both professionals and non-professionals. Most important of all, the strong focus on economic and social development suggests a radical and overdue break with the geometric and formal models which have diverted architect-planners in the past, offering lessons for megacities in other parts of the developing world as well as Asia. Having been on the receiving end of Western influence for so long, it would not be surprising if the innovative works and ideas of the four Asian urbanists discussed here were eventually seen to represent the beginnings of a genuine non-Western school of urbanism, joining more familiar architectural initiatives.

NOTES AND REFERENCES

CHAPTER 1

1. Wilson, R. (1967). 'Annual report January 1984: Ideal Building Corporation'. *Architectural Design*, Vol. XXXVII, No. 4, pp. 158–159.

2. Galbraith, J. K. (1966). 'The Reith Lectures, 1 – The new industrial state'. *The Listener*, 17 November, pp. 711–714. The same lectures were subsequently published in Galbraith, J. K. (1967). *The New Industrial State*. A Mentor Book.

3. Kahn, H. and Wiener, A. J. (1967). 'The next thirty-three years: a framework for speculation'. *Daedalus*, Vol. 96, No. 3. pp. 705–732. Quote from p. 712.

4. Jencks, C. (1969). 'Pop-non pop 2'. *Architectural Association Quarterly*, Vol. 1, No. 2, pp. 56–74.

5. See, for example, Int. Council for Building Research, Studies and Documentation-CIB, eds (1966). *Towards Industrialized Building: Proceedings of the Third CIB Congress, Copenhagen, 1965*, Elsevier.

6. Scholfield, P. H. (1958). *The Theory of Proportion in Architecture*. Cambridge University Press, p. 6.

7. Ehrenkrantz, E. D. (1956). *Modular Number Pattern*. Alec Tiranti.

8. Eden, J. F. (1967). 'Metrology and the module'. *Architectural Design*, Vol. XXXVII, No. 3, pp. 148–150.

9. Eden, J. F. (1967), p. 149.

10. Eden, J. F. (1967), p. 150.

11. Prouvé, J. (1965). 'L'habitation de notre epoque'. *Arena*, Vol. 81, No. 897, pp. 128–129. Also Prouvé, J. (1966). 'Address delivered at the symposium of the Union Internationale des Architectes, held in Delft, The Netherlands, on 6th–13th September 1964'. In Int. Council for Building Research, Studies and Documentation-CIB, eds (1966).

12. Prouvé, J. (1966), p. 95.

13. Woolard, F. G. (1952). 'The advent of automatic transfer machines and mechanisms'. *Mechanical Handling*, Vol. 39, No. 5, pp. 207–215. Also Woolard, F. G. (1957). 'Automation and the designer'. *Engineering Designer*, March, pp. 11–15.

14. Ballinger, H. A. (1968). 'Machines with arms'. *Science Journal*, Vol. 4, No. 10, pp. 58–65.

15. Brewer, R. (1964). 'Where numerical control stands in industry today'. *New Scientist*, Vol. 22, No. 397, pp. 794–797. Also Iredale, R. (1968). 'Putting artisans on tape'. *New Scientist*, Vol. 37, No. 584, pp. 353–355.

16. Williamson, D. T. N. (1967). 'New wave in manufacturing'. *American Machinist*, 11 September, pp. 143–154. Also Williamson, D. T. N. (1968). 'A better way of making things'. *Science Journal*, Vol. 4, No. 6, pp. 53–59.

17. Beer, S. (1962). 'Towards the cybernetic factory'. In *Principles of Self-Organization* (Von Foerster H. and Zopf, Jr., G. W. eds) pp. 25–89, Pergamon Press.

18. Beer, S. (1962), p. 28.

19. Beer, S. (1962), p. 27.

20. Beer, S. (1968). 'Machines that control machines'. *Science Journal*, Vol. 4, No. 10, pp. 89–94. Also Beer, S. (1967). *Cybernetics and Management*. The English Universities Press.

21. Abel, C. (1969a). 'A comeback for universal man?' *Architectural Design*, Vol. XXXIX, No. 3, pp. 124–125.

CHAPTER 2

1. Archigram, like the general public, identified advanced production technology with mass production, hence their images of repetitive living modules or cells. More flexible, computerized production methods were, however, already emerging which were to rapidly outdate their vision of a machine-based future architecture. See Chapter 1.

2. Webber, M. M. (1964). 'The urban place and the nonplace urban realm'. In *Explorations into Urban Structure* (Webber M. M., et al., eds) pp. 79–153, University of Pennsylvania Press. Also Webber, M. M. (1968). 'The post-city age'. *Daedalus*, Vol. 97, No. 4, pp. 1093–1099.

3. Foley, D. (1964). 'An approach to metropolitan spatial structure'. In Webber, M. M., et al., eds (1964), pp. 21–78.

4. McLuhan, M. (1964). *Understanding Media*. Routledge and Kegan Paul. Also Pierce, J. R. (1967). 'Communication'. *Science Journal*, Vol. 3, No. 10, pp. 77–81.

5. Gottman, J. (1961). *Megalopolis*. MIT Press. Also Gottman, J. ed. (1967). *Geographers Look at Urban Sprawl*. Wiley and Sons. Also Hall, P. (1966). *The World Cities*. World University Library.

6. Ashby, W. R. (1964). *An Introduction to Cybernetics*. Methuen. Also Weiner, N. (1968). *The Human Use of Human Beings*. Sphere Books.

7. Bertalanffy, L. von (1968). *General System Theory*. George Braziller. Also Miller, J. G. (1965). 'Living systems: Basic concepts'. *Behavioural Science*, Vol. 10, No. 3, pp. 193–237.

8. Hall, A. D. (1962). *A Methodology for Systems Engineering*. D. Van Nostrand.

9. It was noted by G. E. Shannon that the statistical measure of the negative of entropy is the same as that for information. See Shannon, G. E. and Weaver, W. (1949). *The Mathematical Theory of Communication*. University of Illinois Press.

10. Bertalanffy, L. von (1950). 'The theory of open systems in physics and biology'. *Science*, 13 January, Vol. 111, pp. 23–29.

11. Bertalanffy, L. von (1950), p. 26.

12. Rapoport, A. (1953). 'What is information?' *Synthese*, Vol. 9, August, pp. 157–73. The evolution of living systems typically involves what have been described as deviation-amplifying processes, i.e. processes that exhibit positive feedback. For example, the deviation-amplifying mutual causal process between mutations and the environment; interspecific deviation–amplification and its effects; preference for above-average members for mating amplifying above-average qualities in the species and the effects of inbreeding. It has also been suggested that the increase in internal structuredness and inhomogeneity in the growth of a city is against the Second Law of Thermodynamics. See Maruyama, M. (1963). 'The second cybernetics: deviation amplifying mutual causal processes'. *American Scientist*, Vol. 51, pp. 164–179.

13. Ashby, W. R. (1962). 'Principles of the self-organizing system'. In *Principles of Self-Organization* (Von Foerster, H. and Zopf, Jr., G. W. eds) pp. 255–278, Pergamon Press.

14. Ashby, W. R. (1960). *Design for a Brain.* Wiley.

15. Ashby, W. R. (1962), p. 265.

16. Ashby, W. R. (1964), p. 207. According to Ashby's Law of Requisite Variety, given a game with two players R and D, the variety in the outcomes of D's moves can be decreased only by a corresponding increase in the variety of R's moves.

17. Ashby, R. (1962).

18. Beer, S. (1962). 'Toward the cybernetic factory'. In Von Foerster, H. and Zopf, Jr., G. W. (1962), pp. 25–89.

19. Beer, S. (1962), p. 25.

20. Alonso, W. (1964). 'Location theory'. In *Regional Development and Planning* (Friedman, J. and Alonso, W. eds) pp. 78–106, The MIT Press.

21. Berry, B. (1964). 'Cities as systems within systems of cities'. In Friedman, J. and Alonso, W., eds (1964), pp. 116–137.

22. Etzioni argues that if urban components are highly heterogeneous, a large degree of organizational segregation may be necessary for them to act as a system at all. Segregation or dispersion of subsystems into duplicate or multiple components may also make a system less vulnerable to trauma. See Etzioni, A. (1962). 'The dialectics of supranational unification'. *American Political Science Review*, Vol. 56, pp. 927–935.

23. Webber, M. M. (1964).

24. Chapin, Jr., F. S. and Hightower, H. C. (1965). 'Household activity patterns and land use'. *Journal of the American Institute of Planners*, Vol. 31, No. 3, pp. 222–231.

25. Gans, H. (1962). *The Urban Villagers*. Free Press of Glencoe.

26. Gans, H. (1967). *The Levittowners*. Pantheon Books. See also March, L. (1967). 'Homes beyond the fringe'. *RIBA Journal*, Vol. 74, No. 8, pp. 334–337.

27. Cultural prejudice may be at least partly responsible for the widespread antipathy to dispersed cities like Los Angeles. See Worthington, J. (1967). 'What's wrong with the American city is that we view it through European eyes'. *Arena*, March, Vol. 82, No. 910, pp. 210–213.

28. Smith, R. A. (1965). 'Los Angeles, prototype of Supercity'. *Fortune*, Vol. LXXI, No. 3, pp. 99–101; 200; 202; 207–208; 210; 212.

29. Reuben Lovret, of the LA city planning staff, quoted in Smith, R. A. (1965), p. 200.

30. Lindblom, C. E. (1959). 'The science of "muddling through"'. *Public Administration Review*, Vol. 19, No. 2, pp. 79–88. Also Chapin, S. (1963). *Urban Land Use Planning.* University of Illinois Press.

CHAPTER 3

1. Barbour, I. G. (1974). *Myths, Models and Paradigms.* Harper and Row.

2. It was Ernst Cassirer's belief, espoused in his 'philosophy of symbolic forms', that the major forms of human culture had each evolved according to its own distinct purpose: 'Man's outstanding characteristic, his distinguishing mark, is not his metaphysical or physical nature – but his work. It is this work, it is the system of human activities, which defines and determines the circle of "humanity". Language, myth, religion, art, science, history are the constituents, the various sectors of this circle...it is the basic function of speech, of myth, of art, of religion that we must seek far behind their innumerable shapes and utterances, and that

in the last analysis we must attempt to trace back to a common origin.' See Cassirer, E. (1962). *An Essay on Man.* Yale University Press. p. 68. Also Cassirer, E. (1955). *The Philosophy of Symbolic Forms.* Yale University Press.

3. Archer, B. (1968). 'Extracts from the structure of the design process'. Unpublished paper, Royal College of Art.

4. Berlin, I. (1976). *Vico and Herder.* Random House.

5. Berlin, I. (1976), p. 10.

6. Steiner, G. (1975). *After Babel.* Oxford University Press.

7. Berlin, I. (1976), p. 153.

8. Herder expressed his sensitivity to place throughout his writings. For example, 'One must enter the time, the place, the entire history (of a people); one must "feel oneself (sich einfuhlen) into everything"'. Quoted in Berlin, I. (1976), p. 186.

9. Blumer, H. (1969). *Symbolic Interactionism.* Prentice-Hall. Also Meltzer, B. N., Petras, J. W. and Reynolds, L. T. (1975). *Symbolic Interactionism.* Routledge and Kegan Paul.

10. Mead, G. H. (1934). *Mind, Self and Society.* University of Chicago Press.

11. Blumer, H. (1969).

12. Flavell, J. H. (1963). *The Developmental Psychology of Jean Piaget.* Van Nostrand Reinhold.

13. Pask, G. (1976). *Conversation Theory.* Elsevier.

14. Laing, R. D., Phillipson, H. and Lee, A. R. (1966). *Interpersonal Perception.* Tavistock Publications.

15. Kelly, G. (1963). *A Theory of Personality.* W. W. Norton.

16. Goffman, E. (1967). *Interaction Ritual.* Doubleday.

17. Kuhn, T. S. (1962). *The Structure of Scientific Revolutions.* University of Chicago Press.

18. Feyerabend, P. (1975). *Against Method.* Verso.

19. Whorf, B. L. (1956). *Language Thought & Reality.* The MIT Press.

20. See Chapter 7.

21. Proshansky, H. M. (1976). 'Environmental psychology and the real world'. *American Psychologist,* Vol. 31, No. 4, pp. 303–310.

22. Proshansky, H. M. (1976), p. 309.

23. Proshansky, H. M. (1976), p. 310.

24. Negroponte, N. (1975). *Soft Architecture Machines.* The MIT Press.

25. Abel, C. (1975a). 'Instructional simulation of client construct systems'. Paper presented to the 1975 Architectural Psychology Conference, University of Sheffield. A brief note on ARCHITRAINER is included in Negroponte, N. (1975), pp. 112–113. For an introduction to the educational rationale underlying the use of simulation techniques in higher education generally, see Armstrong, R. H. R. and Taylor, J. L., eds (1970). *Instructional Simulation Systems in Higher Education.* Cambridge Institute of Education.

26. The meaning of the word 'empathy' as used here accords with Hans-George Gadamer's hermeneutics of interpretation. According to Gadamer, the hermeneutical perspective rejects both the complete or partial neutrality of role ascribed to the interpreter by objectivists and extreme relativists, and posits in their place a dialectical process of exchange which brings forth into the account the interpreter's own background as well as the culture of the subject under study. Thus the act of interpretation or empathy in the 'hermeneutical situation' always entails a process of mediation between differing world views – the interpreter's and the subject's – which leaves neither unchanged. See Gadamer, H. J. (1976). *Philosophical Hermeneutics.* University of California Press.

27. According to Kelly, all personal constructs have a dimensional character, defined by the extreme cases of similarity and contrast. Based on this idea, Kelly devised the repertory grid technique to record how a subject uses his or her own range of constructs applicable to a given situation, and to translate this pattern of use into numerical data for statistical analysis. See Kelly, G. A. (1963). Also Bannister, D. (1970). *Perspectives in Personal Construct Theory*. Academic Press. Also Fransella, F. and Bannister, D. (1977). *A Manual for Repertory Grid Technique*. Academic Press.

28. Abel, C. (1975a).

29. Abel, C. (1975b). 'A note on the direct elicitation of construct links'. Research monograph, Portsmouth Polytechnic.

30. Kelly, G. A. (1963). p. 95.

31. For example, see Bieri, J. (1955). 'Cognitive complexity-simplicity and predictive behaviour'. *Journal of Abnormal Social Psychology*, Vol. 51, pp. 263–268. Also Crockett, W. H. (1965). 'Cognitive complexity and impression formation'. In *Progress in Experimental Personality Research*, Vol. 2 (Maher, B. A., ed) pp. 47–90, Academic Press. Also Adams-Webber, J. R. (1969). 'Cognitive complexity and sociality'. *British Journal of Social and Clinical Psychology*, Vol. 8, pp. 211–216. Also Adams-Webber, J. R. (1970). 'Actual structure and potential chaos: relational aspects of progressive variations within a personal construct system'. In Bannister, D., ed (1970).

32. Abel, C. (1976). 'Landscape studies project: Portsmouth Polytechnic/Hampshire County Council'. Report to the Centre for Educational Research and Innovation of the OECD, June, 1976.

33. Using the Bieri measure of differentiation. See Bieri, J. (1955). Although the sample was a small one, analysis of the results supports the main hypothesis, i.e. the more complex the subject's own construct system the greater the skill exhibited in predicting other persons' constructs. Abel, C. (1976).

CHAPTER 4

1. Heskett, J. (1980). *Industrial Design*. Oxford University Press.

2. Banham, R. (1960). *Theory and Design in the Machine Age*. The Architectural Press.

3. Quoted in Banham, R. (1960), p. 281.

4. Abel, C. (1966). 'Ulm HfG, Department of Building'. *Arena*, Vol. 82, No. 905, pp. 88–90.

5. See Chapter 1.

6. Gropius, W. (1964). '1926: principles of Bauhaus production (Dessau)'. In *Programs and Manifestos of Twentieth Century Architecture* (U. Conrads, ed). pp. 95–97, The MIT Press. Quote from p. 96.

7. See Chapter 1.

8. Abel, C. (1986a). 'A building for the Pacific Century'. *The Architectural Review*, Vol. CLXXIX, No. 1070, pp. 54–61.

9. See Chapter 1.

10. Feigenbaum, L. (1986). 'Advances in computer science and technology'. Unpublished lectures given at the National University of Singapore, 24–25 March.

11. See, for example, Beer, S. (1967). *Cybernetics and Management*. The English Universities Press.

12. For a general survey, see Giraud, C. ed (1986). *CAD and Robotics in Architecture and Construction: Proceedings of the Joint International Conference at Marseilles, 25–27 June*. Hermes Publishing.

13. Suzuki, S., Yoshida, T. and Veno, T. (1986). 'Construction robots in Japan'. Paper presented at The Second Century of the Skyscraper: Third Int. Conf. of the Council on Tall Buildings and Urban Habitat, Chicago, 6–10 January.

14. For an account of the pros and cons of using robots in industry generally, see Froehlich, L. (1981). 'Robots to the rescue' *Datamation*, January, Vol. 27, No. 1, pp. 84–96.

15. Abel, C. (1986a).

CHAPTER 5

1. For overviews of related movements, see Johnson, P. and Wigley, M., eds (1988). *Deconstructivist Architecture*. The Museum of Modern Art. Papadakis, A. C., ed (1988). *Deconstruction in Architecture*. Architectural Design Profile No. 72. Lynn, G., ed (1993). *Folding in Architecture*. Architectural Design Profile No. 102.

2. For a typical contemporary response, see Manser, J. (1995). 'Hadid bemuses New Yorkers'. *Building Design*, No. 1207, 10 February, p. 17. The current obsession with graphical representation as an end in itself can be traced back to the 1970s and the early works of the so-called 'New York Five' architects, who, according to Colin Rowe, '...sometimes seem to regard buildings as an excuse for drawing rather than drawings as an excuse for building'. Rowe, C. (1975). *Five Architects: Eisenman, Graves, Gwathmey, Hejduk, Meier*. Oxford University Press, p. 8.

3. A strong connection has been drawn between the deconstructionist philosophy and criticism of Jacques Derrida and the work of Bernard Tschumi and other architects. For example, see Benjamin, A. (1988). 'Derrida, architecture and philosophy'. In Papadekis, A. C., ed. (1988), pp. 8–11. It should also be noted, however, that the same architects are frequently described as deconstruct***ivists***, implying their work is at least partly, and probably mainly, influenced by sources from within architectural culture. See, for example, Johnson, P. and Wigley, M., eds (1988).

4. Jencks, C. (1995). *The Architecture of the Jumping Universe*. Academy Editions.

5. The so-called ENIAC is generally acknowledged as the first electronic computer. Developed at the University of Pennsylvania, it became operational in December 1945. The room-sized machine weighed over thirty tonnes and contained 18,800 vacuum tubes. See Goldstine, H. H. (1972). *The Computer from Pascal to von Neumann*. Princeton University Press.

6. Weiner, N. (1948). *Cybernetics*. The MIT Press. For other key early works see Von Foerster, H. and Zopf, Jr., G. W. eds (1962).

7. Turbayne, T. M. (1971). *The Myth of Metaphor*. University of South Carolina Press.

8. Landau, R. (1968). *New Directions in British Architecture*. Studio Vista.

9. Conway, D., guest ed (1969). 'What did they do for their theses? What are they doing now?' *Architectural Design*, Vol. XXXIX, No. 3, pp. 129–164.

10. Abel, C. (1969b). 'Mobile learning stations'. *Architectural Design*, Vol. XXXIX, No. 3, p. 151.

11. Friedman, Y. (1975). *Toward a Scientific Architecture*. The MIT Press.

12. Negroponte, N. (1970). *The Architecture Machine*. The MIT Press.

13. Negroponte, N. (1975).

14. For key early works, see Feigenbaum, E. A. and Feldman, J. (1963). *Computers and Thought*. McGraw-Hill.

15. Pask, G. (1975). 'Aspects of machine intelligence'. In Negroponte, N. (1975), pp. 6–31.

16. See Chapters 1 and 2. Also Luggen, W. W. (1991). *Flexible Manufacturing Cells and Systems*. Prentice-Hall.

17. Abel, C. (1968). 'Evolutionary planning'. *Architectural Design*, Vol. XXXVIII, No. 12, pp. 563–564. See also Chapter 2.

18. Abel, C. (1969b), p. 151.

19. Landau, R., guest ed (1969). 'Despite popular demand...AD is thinking about architecture and planning'. *Architectural Design*, Vol. XXXIX, No. 9, pp. 478–514. Landau, R., guest ed (1972). 'Complexity'. *Architectural Design*, Vol. XXXXII, No. 10, pp. 608–647. The following two issues of *Architectural Design* also contained related articles on complexity which could not be included in the 1972 special issue.

20. Quoted by Landau, R. (1972), p. 608, from Kohl, H. (1965). *The Age of Complexity*. Menor Books.

21. Abel, C. (1991). *Renault Centre: Norman Foster*. Architecture Design and Technology Press.

22. Abel, C. (1989). 'From hard to soft machines'. In *Norman Foster*, Vol. 3 (I. Lambot, ed) pp. 10–19, Watermark.

23. Kerr, P. (1995). *Gridiron*. Chatto & Windus.

24. Campagno, A. (1995). *Intelligent Glass Façades*. Artemis. Also Harrison, A. (1994). 'Intelligence quotient: smart tips for smart buildings'. *Architecture Today*, No. 46, March, pp. 34–41. Also Pepchinski, M. (1995). 'The building breathes'. *Architectural Record*, No. 10, pp. 70–71.

25. Davies, M. (1994). 'Changes in the rules'. In *Visions for the Future*, Architectural Design Profile No. 104, pp. 20–23. Quote from p. 23.

26. Fisher, N. (1993). 'Construction as a manufacturing process'. Inaugural lecture at the University of Reading, Tuesday 18 May.

27. For virtual prototyping and its effects on collaborative work patterns see Bricken, M. (1994). 'Virtual worlds: no interface to design'. In *Cyberspace: First Steps* (M. Benedikt, ed), pp. 363–382. Also Barrett, T. and Pruitt, S. (1994). 'Corporate virtual space'. In Benedikt, M. ed. (1994), pp. 383–409. For rapid prototyping see Dickens, P. M. (1994). 'Rapid prototyping – the ultimate in automation'. *Journal of Assembly Automation*, Vol. 14, No. 2, pp. 10–13. Also Dickens, P. M. (1992). 'Rapid prototyping'. Unpublished paper, Institution of Mechanical Engineers Seminar on Rapid Prototyping Systems, 18 December, London.

28. 'Smart materials', like 'smart systems', generally refer to materials and technologies which are designed to sense changes in their environment and are able to respond to those changes by an adaptation of their own properties or organization. See Antonelli, P. (1995). *Mutant Materials in Contemporary Design*. The Museum of Modern Art. Also Sheenan, T. (1996). 'The smart option'. *Building Design*, No. 1267, 31 May, p. 28.

29. Negroponte, N. (1995). *Being Digital*. Hodder & Stoughton, p. 181.

30. Kelly, K. (1994). *Out of Control*. Fourth Estate.

31. Among other emergent changes, extravagant claims are made for the democratizing effects of computer networks. See, for example, Katz, J. (1995). 'The age of Paine'. *Wired*, Vol. 1, No. 1, pp. 64–69.

32. Lawrence, A. (1995). 'Agents of the Net'. *New Scientist*, 15 July, No. 1986, pp. 34–37.

33. Seaman, B. (1995). 'The future is already here'. *Time Special Issue: Welcome to Cyberspace*, spring, pp. 30–33.

34. Hinssen, P. (1995), 'Life in the digital city'. *Wired*, Vol. 1, No. 1, pp. 53–55.

35. Cypergurus such as William Mitchell argue that computer networks may

soon displace the functions of many traditional urban building types. While Mitchell simplifies his case by ignoring all of the symbolic content of building types and much of their social significance, there seems little doubt that the computer revolution will have considerable and probably irreversible effects on conventional patterns of work and communication. See Mitchell, W. J. (1995). *City of Bits*. The MIT Press.

36. In the 'Poetry of Desolation', the architects call for an '... architecture of sudden death on the pavement. Death from a ribcage pierced by a steering shaft.' Co-op Himmelblau (1983). *Architecture is Now*. Rizzoli, p. 115. Just what such an aesthetic might mean is amply demonstrated in the architects' projects of the late 1970s, such as the 'Vector' and 'Hot Flat' projects, both of which show buildings 'speared' by giant spikes.

37. Rattenbury, K. (1995). 'In glorious technicolour'. *Building Design*, No. 1205, 27 January, pp. 12–14. Quote from p. 12.

38. Tschumi, B. (1988). 'Parc de la Villette, Paris'. In Papadakis, A. C. ed. (1988), pp. 33–39.

39. Benjamin, A. (1993). *Re-working Eisenman*. Academy Editions/Ernst & Sohn.

40. Johnson, P. and Wigley, M., eds (1988).

41. Erickson, B. (1995). 'The rules of transformation'. *Building Design*, No. 1208, 17 February, p. 19.

42. Erickson, B. (1995), p. 19.

43. Jencks, C. (1995), p. 79.

44. Zucchi, B. (1992). *Giancarlo de Carlo*. Butterworth Architecture.

45. Collymore, R. (1994). *The Architecture of Ralph Erskine*. Academy Editions.

46. Kroll, L. (1986). *The Architecture of Complexity*. B. T. Batsford.

47. Allen, G., Lyndon, D. and Moore, C. (1974). *The Place of Houses*. Holt, Rinehart and Winston.

48. Zucchi, B. (1992), p. 26.

49. For details, see Miles, H. (1992). 'Process and product'. *The Architectural Review*, Vol. CXC, No. 1141, pp. 25–29.

50. Porphyrios, D. (1979). 'Heterotopia: a study in the ordering sensibility of the work of Alvar Aalto'. In *Alvar Aalto* (Architectural Monographs 4) pp. 8–19, Academy Editions.

51. See Chapters 4 and 9.

52. Sudjic, D. (1994). *The Architecture of Richard Rogers*. Fourth Estate and Wordsearch.

53. Pawley, M. (1993). *Future Systems: The Story of Tomorrow*. Phaidon.

54. Yeang, K. (1995). *Bioclimatic Skyscrapers*. Artemis. Also see Chapter 15.

55. Inoue, M. (1985). *Space in Japanese Architecture*. Weatherhill.

56. For detailed studies, see Jones, P. B. (1978). *Hans Scharoun*. Gordon Fraser.

57. For details, see Jones, P. B. (1988). 'University Library, Eichstatt, West Germany'. *The Architectural Review*, Vol. CLXXXIII, No. 1093, pp. 28–40.

58. (1990). *Tadao Ando*. Architectural Monographs 14. Academy Editions/St Martin's Press.

59. Abel, C. (1996). 'Space, place and the net: metaphorical extensions of mind and body'. Paper presented to the *Design Dialogue II: A Meeting of Metaphors*, University College London, 17 May.

CHAPTER 6

1. For critical evaluations of the state of architectural education on both sides

of the Atlantic, see the special issue (1989), *The Architectural Review*, Vol. CLXXXV. No. 1109, pp. 23–87. Also Crosbie, M. J. (1995). 'The schools: how they're failing the profession'. *Progressive Architecture*, September, pp. 47–51, pp. 94, 96. The latter article refers to several studies commissioned in the US documenting widespread professional dissatisfaction with the quality and skills of architecture graduates.

2. Abel, C. (1995). 'Globalism and the regional response: educational foundations'. In *Educating Architects* (Pearce, M. and Toy, M., eds), pp. 80–87. Academy Editions.

3. Abel, C. (1966). op. cit. See also Chapter 4.

4. Hesket J. (1980). *Industrial Design*. Oxford University Press.

5. Stringer, P. (1970). 'Architecture as education'. *RIBA Journal*, Vol. 77, No. 1, pp. 19–22.

6. See Chapters 4 and 5.

7. For a detailed study, see Abel, C. (1991). *Renault Centre: Norman Foster*. Architecture Design and Technology Press.

8. Muir, T. and Rance, B., eds (1995). *Collaborative Practice in the Built Environment*. E. and F. N. Spon.

9. Educational foundations for the studio programme included undergraduate theory lectures by the author on architecture in different parts of the world, including Southeast Asia, where projects were focused. An optional series of lectures titled 'Architecture and Production' organized by the author was also available on a wide range of innovative production systems, from self-build to robots and rapid prototyping.

10. The stereotypical idea of scientific method which shaped orthodox Modernist thinking before and after the war has since been heavily revised in favour of more liberal interpretations. See Chapter 3. Also Abel, C. (1982). 'The case for anarchy in design research'. In *Changing Design* (Evans, B., Powell, J. and Talbot, R., eds), pp. 295–302. John Wiley & Sons.

11. The value of exemplary works in education and practice is discussed in Chapters 9 and 11.

12. Ken Yeang supplied the brief for the 'tropical tower' project and also advised Nottingham students during visits to the UK. For the evolution of the regional tower type, including examples of Yeang's work, see Chapter 15.

13. A brief for a secondary school project sited in Singapore was supplied by Phan Pit Li of the Public Works Department.

14. Brian Ford now heads Brian Ford & Associates, London. Other visiting staff on the Design Research Studio were Pierre Balosso (1995) and Mark Hewitt (1996). Regular tutorial assistance for both the DRS and the Bio-Tech Architecture Workshop was also provided by Nottingham staff members: John Chilton (structures); John Whittle (environmental services) and David Nicholson-Cole (computing).

15. Relevant theory courses given by the author included: 'Outside Architecture'; 'New Paradigms in Modern Architecture'; and 'Theory and Criticism of Modern Architecture'.

16. See also Abel, C., *Bio-Tech Architecture: Design and Production in the 21st Century*, Architectural Press, forthcoming.

17. Phil Dickens, formerly of the Innovative Manufacturing Centre (IMC), and Chris Rudd, of the Composites Institute, both lent vital support, including research staff and production facilities, to the Workshop.

18. See Hall, A. (1996). 'Heralding the intelligent wall'. *Building Design*, March 22, p. 20.

19. A regular optional course on 'Computer modelling and presentation' taught by David Nicholson-Cole ran concurrently with the Workshop. Students taking

this course were able to receive separate grades for CAD and multimedia work produced for Workshop projects.

20. The term 'virtual practice' was coined by the author at the same time as 'Bio-Tech architecture' (see note 16). It denotes a computer and network based design practice where the main focus of collaborative effort between designers and consultants is the development of a virtual prototype of the design. The same virtual prototype also functions as the primary communications medium between the various parties involved, who may be geographically distributed and who may also change from project to project, according to the nature of the task.

21. A 'virtual prototype' may or may not involve virtual reality technologies, according to whether visual or physical properties are being simulated. Both types were developed in the Bio-Tech Architecture Workshop, according to the nature of the projects concerned.

22. The heart of the Reality Centre consists of a Silicon Graphics, Infinite Reality super-computer. Interactive controls allow users to control views from any angle and to 'fly through' simulated scenarios projected onto a cinema-sized curved screen, thus doing away with cumbersome headsets.

23. Former CIMI Operations Manager Richard Petheram and research associate Kim Wiesman both assisted with the final presentation at the Reality Centre, which included taking students' Web pages directly off the Internet, or else taking displays from linkups with students' own computers.

24. For further information on CIMI and its architectural services contact: Simon.Hart@nott.ac.uk. See also website: http://www.cimi.nottingham.ac.uk/.

25. Successful projects include an Interbuild '97 virtual reality exhibition on façade engineering in collaboration with Ove Arup Partnership.

CHAPTER 7

1. Watkin, D. (1977). *Morality and Architecture.* Clarendon Press.

2. See Chapter 3.

3. See Chapter 8.

4. Quoted in Hester, M. B. (1967) *The Meaning of Poetic Metaphor.* Mouton & Co., p. 136.

5. Hester, M. B. (1967).

6. Hester, M. B. (1967), p. 137.

7. Koestler, A. (1964). *The Act of Creation.* Macmillan.

8. Quoted in Koestler, A. (1964), p. 126.

9. Quoted in Koestler, A. (1964), p. 140.

10. Notably Kuhn, T. S. (1962). Also Harre, R. (1972). *The Philosophies of Science.* Oxford University Press. Also Barbour, I. G. (1974).

11. Leatherdale, W. H. (1974). *The Role of Analogy, Model and Metaphor in Science.* North Holland/American Elsevier.

12. See, for example, Jencks, C. and Baird, G. (1969). *Meaning in Architecture.* George Braziller. Also Bonta, J. P. (1979). *Architecture and its Interpretation.* Rizzoli. The above authors, like most writers in the field, base their approaches mainly on structuralist theories of language. See Chapter 12 for a critique of this approach. For a general introduction to semiotics and its relation to structuralism, see Hawkes, T. (1977). *Structuralism and Semiotics.* Methuen & Co.

13. The idea of a purposive culture-form centred around a distinctive cultural function derives from Ernst Cassirer. See Cassirer, E. (1978). See also Chapter 3, Note 2.

14. For relativism in other fields, see Mandelbaum, M. (1967). *The Problem of Historical Knowledge.* Harper and Row. Also Aron, R. (1959). 'Relativism in history'.

In *The Philosophy of History in Our Time* (Meyerhoff, H., ed), pp. 152–161. Doubleday. Also Kaplan, D. and Manners, R. A. (1972). *Culture Theory*. Prentice-Hall.

15. Mandelbaum, D. G., ed (1929). *Selected Writings of Edward Sapir*. University of California Press.

16. Caroll, J. B. (1956). *Language Thought & Reality: Selected Writings of Benjamin Lee Whorf*. The MIT Press.

17. Caroll, J. B. (1956), p. 134.

18. Caroll, J. B. (1956). Also Waters, F. (1963). *Book of the Hopi*. Ballantine Books.

19. Wittgenstein, L. (3rd Ed 1958). *Philosophical Investigations*. Macmillan Publishing. Also Van Peursen, C. A. (1970). *Ludwig Wittgenstein*. E. P. Dutton. For an account of Wittgenstein's broader impact on the social sciences, see Winch, P. (1958). *The Idea of a Social Science and its Relation to Philosophy*. Routledge and Kegan Paul.

20. Wittgenstein, L. (1958).

21. Barbour, I. G. (1974), p. 127.

22. It was Wittgenstein's aim in his later work to clarify the social basis, grounded in human language, of the forms of human understanding in particular kinds of contexts – what he called 'forms of life'. According to Peter Winch, Wittgenstein had the effect of giving new meaning to the problems of epistemology, and to its relations with the more specialized branches of philosophical activity. As it is usually defined, epistemology is concerned with 'the general conditions under which it is possible to speak of understanding'. However, redefined in the light of Wittgenstein's work: '...whereas the philosophies of science, of art, of history, etc., will have the task of elucidating the peculiar natures of those forms of life called "science", art, etc., epistemology will try to elucidate what is involved in the notion of a form of life as such'. Winch, P. (1958), pp. 40–41. For a related approach to art history based on Wittgenstein's philosophy, see Wollheim, R. (1975). *Art and its Objects*. Penguin Books.

23. Popper, K. R. (1970). 'Normal science and its dangers'. In *Criticism and the Growth of Knowledge* (Lakatos, I. and Musgrave, A., eds), pp. 51–58, Cambridge University Press.

24. Carroll, J. B. (1956).

25. It is taken here that Wittgenstein's idea of a language game and his related concept of a 'form of life' are compatible with the concept of functionally centred culture-forms discussed elsewhere. See Chapters 3 and 12.

26. For related discussions of language and social behaviour, see Bernstein, B. (1970). *Class, Codes, and Control*, Vol. 1. Routledge and Kegan Paul. Also Howell, R. W. and Vetter, H. J. (1976). *Language in Behaviour*. Human Sciences Press. Also Gregory, M. and Carroll, S. (1978). *Language and Situation*. Routledge and Kegan Paul.

27. Kuhn, T. S. (1962).

28. Zevi, B. (1949). *Towards an Organic Architecture*. Faber and Faber. Also (1978). *The Modern Language of Architecture*. University of Washington Press.

29. Jones, P. B. (1978). 'Organic versus classic'. *Architectural Association Quarterly*, Vol. 10, No. 1, pp. 10–20.

30. Zevi's polemic frequently borders on hysteria, and even homophobia: 'Symmetry = a spasmodic need for security, fear of flexibility, indetermination, relativity, and growth – in short, fear of living. The schizophrenic cannot bear the temporal aspect of living. To keep his anguish under control, he requires immobility. Classicism is the architecture of conformist schizophrenia. Symmetry = passivity or, in Freudian terms, homosexuality. This is explained by pschoanalysts. *Homo*logous parts instead of *hetero*nymous parts'. Zevi, B. (1978), p. 17.

31. Greenhalgh, M. (1978). *The Classical Tradition in Art*. Duckworth.

32. Jones, P. B. (1978).

33. Jones, P. B. (1978), p. 12.

34. Kuhne, G. (1969). 'Pure form'. *Architectural Design*, Vol. XXXIX, No. 2, pp. 89–90.

35. It is significant that proponents of both schools refer to their preferred styles as 'languages'. See Zevi, B. (1978). Also Summerson, J. (1963). *The Classical Language of Architecture*. The MIT Press.

36. For details, see Jones, P. B. (1978). *Hans Scharoun*. Gordon Fraser.

37. Barbour, I. (1974). *Myths, Models, and Paradigms*. Harper and Row.

38. See, for example, Bonta, J. P. (1979). *Architecture and its Interpretation*. Rizzoli. Also Cohen, L. Z. (1980). 'A sensible analysis of language and meaning in architecture'. *Design Methods and Theories*, Vol. 14, No. 2, pp. 58–65.

39. Collins, P. (1980). 'The language analogy in architecture'. Introductory address to the *68th Annual Meeting of American Collegiate Schools of Architecture*, San Antonio, 19–22 April.

40. Barbour, I. (1974).

41. Harre, R. (1972). *The Philosophies of Science*. Oxford University Press.

42. Turbayne, C. (1962). *The Myth of Metaphor*. Yale University Press.

43. Barbour, I. (1974).

44. Harre, R. (1972).

45. Collins, P. (1965). *Changing Ideals in Modern Architecture*. Faber and Faber. Also Steadman, P. (1979). *The Evolution of Designs*. Cambridge University Press.

46. Collins, P. (1965).

CHAPTER 8

1. Before Kant, philosophers generally held that all concepts derived directly from observations and experience of 'reality' and were independent of any human preconceptions. In challenging this essentially passive view of human perception, Kant wrote: 'Hitherto it has been assumed that all our knowledge must conform to objects. But all attempts to ascertain anything about them *a priori* by concepts, and thus to extend our knowledge, came to nothing on this assumption. Let us try then, whether we may not make better progress in the tasks of metaphysics if we assume that *objects must conform to our knowledge*' (my emphasis). Quoted in Coplestone, S. J. (1959). Vol. 6, Part II, p. 20. Kant likened his reversal of human perception to that proposed by Copernicus, equivalent to a complete reversal of former cosmologies. However, no doubt anticipating criticisms of extreme relativism, Coplestone points out that: 'Kant's "Copernican revolution" does not imply the view that reality can be reduced to the human mind and its ideas... What he is suggesting is that we cannot know things, that they cannot be objects of knowledge for us, except insofar as they are subjected to certain *a priori* conditions of knowledge on the part of the subject'. Coplestone, S. J. (1959). Vol. 6, Part II, pp. 20–21. It is this so-called 'active model of man' that has subsequently prevailed in post-war thinking in both philosophy and the social sciences. See Chapters 3, 7, 9 and 11.

2. Quoted in Hester, M. B. (1967), p. 14. See also Ross, W. D, ed (1959). *The Works of Aristotle*. The Clarendon Press.

3. Quoted in Hester, M. B. (1967), p. 14.

4. Hester, M. B. (1967).

5. Berggren, D. (1962). 'The use and abuse of metaphor, I'. *The Review of Metaphysics*, Vol. 16, No. 12, pp. 243–244.

6. Scully, Jr., V., (1960). *Frank Lloyd Wright*. Mayflower, p. 31.

7. Scully, Jr., V., (1961). *Modern Architecture*. George Braziller/Prentice-Hall, p. 23.

8. Writing on Mendelsohn's early sketches, of which his Einstein Tower drawing is the most famous, A. Whittick comments that 'In many of the sketches the sense of the building as a machine fulfilling its purpose is very strong, and the emphasis of character is given as it is in the flowing lines of the more beautiful of modern transport vehicles'. Whittick, A. (1940). *Eric Mendelsohn*. Faber and Faber, p. 45.

9. Jencks, C. (1974). 'A semantic analysis of Stirling's Olivetti Centre Wing'. *Architectural Association Quarterly*, Vol. 6, No. 2, pp. 13–15. See also Jencks, C. (1975). 'The rise of Post Modern architecture'. *Architectural Association Quarterly*, Vol. 7, No. 4, pp. 3–14.

10. Jencks, C. (1974), p. 14.

11. Jencks, C. (1974), p. 14.

12. It is unclear from Jencks's text whether or not the 'professional' comments were the outcome of interviews or hypothetical responses concocted by Jencks himself. If it was the latter case then clearly that would answer the question posed here.

13. While the Opera House is commonly likened to a sailboat, Utzon himself specifically alludes to images of waves as the primary source of inspiration: 'The character, the style, has developed from a series of shapes in combination, all with the characteristics of water, waves – waves within waves – the wave that breaks, foams, etc.' Quoted in Giedion, S. (1967, 5th Ed). *Space, Time and Architecture*. Harvard University Press, p. 674. Images of oriental architecture – umbrella roofs hovering over empty platforms – as represented in other study sketches, provided another potent source for the design.

14. Jencks, C. (1977). *The Language of Post-Modern Architecture*. Academy Editions.

15. Schon, D. (1963). *The Displacement of Concepts*. Tavistock Publications.

16. Quoted in Schon, D. (1963), p. 36.

17. Schon, D. (1963), p. 192.

18. Schon, D. (1963), p. 51.

19. Banham, R. (1965). 'A clip-on architecture'. *Architectural Design*, Vol. 35, No. 11, pp. 534–535. Quote from p. 535.

CHAPTER 9

1. Alexander, C. (1964). *Notes on the Synthesis of Form*. Harvard University Press.

2. Jacobson, M. (1971). 'Max Jacobson interviews Christopher Alexander'. *Architectural Design*, Vol. XLII, No. 12, pp. 768–770. For a further critique of Alexander's approach, see Abel, C. (1972). 'Cultures as complex wholes'. *Architectural Design*, Vol. XXXXII, No. 12, pp. 774–776.

3. The uncritical manner in which orthodox Modernists were trained and thereafter adhered to preferred formulae is ample evidence of the influence of unselfconscious architectural norms in this century. The same might also be said, however, of any dominant and socially sanctioned design approach at other points in time in Western modern history. This, it may be argued, is the downside of tacit knowing, and needs to be balanced by other approaches.

4. Polanyi, M. (1966). *The Tacit Dimension*. Doubleday. Also (1958). *Personal Knowledge*. The University of Chicago Press.

5. Polanyi, M. (1966), p. 4.

6. Polanyi, M. (1966), p. 10.

7. In stressing the importance of indwelling or empathy Polanyi acknowledges the related ideas of Wilhelm Dilthey. See Hodges, H. A., ed (1944). *Wilhelm Dilthey*. Oxford University Press. Similar parallels may be found in the work of Johann Gottfried Herder and Hans-George Gadamer. See Chapter 3.

8. Polanyi, M. (1966), pp. 15–16.

9. Polanyi, M. (1966), p. 16.

10. Kuhn, T. S. (1962). *The Structure of Scientific Revolutions*. University of Chicago Press.

11. The project was introduced by Ruslan Khalid to the 3rd Year Studio Programme at Portsmouth Polytechnic School of Architecture in 1975. It was recast into the present form by the author as 3rd Year Coordinator in the following year after Khalid left the School. Since the experiment was begun accounts have been published of similar exercises in other schools. See Simmons, G. B. (1978). 'Analogy in design: studio teaching models'. *Journal of Architectural Education*, Vol. 31, No. 3, pp. 18–20.

12. The approach was inspired partly by the work of G. H. Mead and the significance he attached to 'taking the role of the other' in human communication. Support for a related approach to education generally is also given by P. H. Hirst, who explains: 'All knowledge involves the use of symbols and the making of judgements in ways that cannot be expressed in words and can only be learnt in a tradition. Accordingly, the business of acquiring knowledge of any form is therefore to a greater or lesser extent something that cannot be done simply by solitary study of the symbolic expressions of knowledge, *it must be learnt from a master on the job*' (my emphasis). Hirst, P. H. (1975). 'Liberal education and the nature of knowledge'. In *The Philosophy of Education* (Peters, R. S., ed) pp. 87–111, Oxford University Press.

13. Stringer, P. (1970). 'Architecture as education'. *RIBA Journal*, Vol. 77, No. 1, pp. 19–22.

14. Abel, C. (1981). 'Liberal education, architecture and human science'. Paper presented to *EDRA 12*, Environ. Design Res. Assoc. Conf., Iowa State University, 20–26 April.

15. For a broad survey of alternative teaching methods and techniques, see Cross, K. P. (1979). *Accent on Learning*. Jossey-Bass.

CHAPTER 10

1. Venturi, R. (1966). *Complexity and Contradiction in Architecture*. The Museum of Modern Art.

2. Venturi, R. (1966), p. 22.

3. Venturi, R. (1966), p. 22.

4. Geddes, R. L., quoted in Venturi, R. (1966), p. 20.

5. Venturi, R. (1966), p. 20.

6. Venturi, R. (1966), p. 22.

7. Rossi, A. (1982). *The Architecture of the City*. The MIT Press.

8. Krier, L. (1978). 'Urban transformations'. *Architectural Design*, Vol. 48, No. 4, pp. 218–221. Krier, R. (1979). *Urban Space*. Rizzoli.

9. Jencks, C. (1977).

10. Scruton, R. (1979). *The Aesthetics of Architecture*. Princeton University Press.

11. Watkin, D. (1977).

12. Banham, R. (1981). *Design by Choice*. Academy Editions.

13. Quoted from P. Sparke's introduction to Banham's essay, 'Stocktaking', in Banham, R. (1981), p. 48.

14. Quoted from P. Sparke's introduction to Banham's essay, 'Stocktaking', in Banham, R. (1981), p. 48.

15. Kuhn, T. S. (1962).

16. Capra, F. (1975). *The Tao of Physics*. Fontana/Collins.

17. Capra, F. (1975), p. 20.

18. Capra, F. (1975), pp. 133–134.

19. Capra, F. (1975).

20. Von Bertalanffy, L. (1968).

21. Lovelock, J. (1979). *Gaia*. Oxford University Press.

22. Kelly, G. (1963).

23. See Chapters 3 and 7.

24. Kelly, G. (1963).

25. See Chapter 8. Also Abel, C. (1988a). 'Analogical models in architecture and urban design'. *Journal of the Faculty of Architecture, Middle East Technical University*, Vol. 8, No. 2, pp. 161–188.

26. Rowe, C. (1976). *The Mathematics of the Ideal Villa*. The MIT Press.

27. See Chapter 7.

28. Popper, K. (1959). *The Logic of Scientific Discovery*. Hutchinson.

29. Wollheim, R. (1968). Also Gombrich, E. H. (1963). *Meditations on a Hobby Horse*. Phaidon.

30. Hughes, R. (1981). *The Shock of the New*. Alfred A. Knopf.

31. Chapter 6, p. 82.

32. Abel, C. (1982). 'The case for anarchy in design research'. In Evans, B., Powell, J. and Talbot, R. eds (1982), pp. 295–302.

33. See Chapter 7.

34. See Chapter 9.

35. See Chapter 14.

36. See Chapters 1 and 4.

37. Capra, F. (1975).

38. Turbayne, C. M. (1971).

39. McHarg, I. L. (1969). *Design with Nature*. Doubleday/Natural History Press.

40. Ehrenfeld, D. W. (1972). *Conserving Life on Earth*. Oxford University Press.

41. Abel, C. (1988a). 'Modern architecture in the Second Machine Age'. *Architecture and Urbanism*, No. 5, pp. 11–22. Also Abel, C. (1989). 'From hard to soft machines'. In *Norman Foster*, Vol. 3 (Lambot, I., ed), pp. 10–19. Also Chapter 1 and Chapter 5.

42. Kuran, A. (1987). *Sinan*. Institute of Turkish Studies/ADA Press Publishers.

43. Kuban, D. (1987). 'The style of Sinan's domed structures'. *Muqarnas*, Vol. 4, pp. 72–97.

44. Kuban, D. (1987), p. 74.

45. Kuban, D. (1987), p. 93.

46. Arik, M. O. (1985). *Turkish Art & Architecture*. Turkish Historical Society Press, p. 153.

47. Arik, M. O. (1985), p. 152.

48. Violett le Duc, quoted in Collins, P. (1965). *Changing Ideals in Modern Architecture*. Faber and Faber, p. 214.

49. Erzen, J. (1989). 'Sinan as anti-classicist'. *Muqarnas*, Vol. 5, pp. 70–85.

50. Lambot, I. (ed) (1989). *Norman Foster*, Vols. 2 and 3. Watermark.

51. Banham, R. (1981), p. 80.

52. Banham, R. (1981), p. 80.

53. Lambot, I. ed (1989).

54. Abel, C. (1986b). 'Modern architecture in the Second Machine Age'. *Architecture and Urbanism*, No. 5, pp. 11–22.

55. Piano, R. (1989). *Renzo Piano.* Rizzoli.

56. Piano, R. (1989), p. 224.

57. Venturi, R. (1966), p. 23.

58. Ryle, G. (1949). *The Concept of Mind.* Barnes and Noble.

CHAPTER 11

1. See Chapters 7 and 8.

2. Koestler, A. (1964).

3. Schon, D. (1963).

4. Kuhn, T. S. (1962).

5. Kubler, G. (1962). *The Shape of Time.* Yale University Press.

6. Masterman, M. (1970). 'The nature of a paradigm'. In *Criticism and the Growth of Knowledge* (Lakatos, I., and Musgrave, A., eds), pp. 59–89. Cambridge University Press.

7. Popper, K. (1959).

8. Feyerabend, P. (1975).

9. Masterman, M. (1970), p. 66.

10. Kuhn, T. S. (1977). *The Essential Tension.* University of Chicago Press.

11. Kuhn, T. S. (1977), p. 305.

12. Kuhn, T. S. (1977), p. 306.

13. Kuhn, T. S. (1977), p. 297–298.

14. Kuhn, T. S. (1977), p. 298.

15. Kuhn, T. S. (1962).

16. Kubler, G. (1962).

17. Thompson, D'Arcy (1966). *On Growth and Form.* Cambridge University Press.

18. Kubler, G. (1962), p. 34.

19. Kubler, G. (1962), p. 69.

20. Kubler, G. (1962), p. 58.

21. Brodsky, J. (1980). 'Continuity and discontinuity in style: a problem in art historical methodology'. *Journal of Aesthetics and Art Criticism*, Vol. 39, No. 1, pp. 28–37.

22. Brodsky, J. (1980), p. 33.

23. Kubler, G. (1940). *The Religious Architecture of New Mexico.* University of New Mexico Press.

24. Kubler, G. (1940), p. xii.

25. Kubler, G. (1940), p. 139.

26. Kubler, G. (1962), p. 70.

27. Rowe, C. (1976). *The Mathematics of the Ideal Villa and Other Essays.* The MIT Press. While Rowe's comparison of Corbusier and Palladio appears convincing, P. H. Schofield suggests that such likenesses as exist between the architects' works appear to be accidental, and that the proportional systems used by each architect are actually quite different. See Schofield, P. H. (1958).

28. See Chapter 7.

29. Rowe, C. (1976).

30. See Chapters 9, 14 and 15.

31. Koestler, A. (1964).

32. Schon, D. (1963).

CHAPTER 12

1. For example, see Zevi, B. (1957). *Architecture as Space.* Horizon Press.

2. See Chapter 7.

3. Lynch, K. (1960). *The Image of the City.* The MIT Press.

4. Stea, D. (1974). 'Architecture in the head: cognitive mapping'. In *Designing for Human Behaviour* (Lang, J., Burnette, C., Moleski, W., and Vachon, D., eds) pp. 157–168, Halsted Press. Also Downs, R. and Stea, D. (1977). *Maps in Minds.* Harper and Row.

5. Canter, D. (1977). *The Psychology of Place.* St Martin's Press.

6. Rapaport, A. (1968). 'The personal element in housing: an argument for open-ended design'. *RIBA Journal*, Vol. 75, No. 7, pp. 300–307.

7. Turner, J. (1976). *Housing by People.* Pantheon Books.

8. Appleyard, D. (1979). 'Home'. *Architectural Association Quarterly*, Vol. 11, No. 3, pp. 4–20.

9. Erikson, E. H. (1968). *Identity Youth and Crisis.* W. W. Norton.

10. Cooper, C. (1974). 'The house as symbol of the self'. In Lang, J. et al. eds (1974) pp. 130–146. Halstead Press.

11. Tuan, Yi-Fu. (1977). *Space and Place.* Edward Arnold.

12. Norberg-Schulz, C. (1980). *Genius Loci.* Rizzoli.

13. The following includes the relevant writings, including the key essay, 'Building Dwelling Thinking'. Heidegger, M. (1977). *Basic Writings.* Harper and Row.

14. Norberg-Schulz, C. (1980), p. 21.

15. Norberg-Schulz, C. (1980), p. 23.

16. Merleau-Ponty, M. (1962). *Phenomenology of Perception.* Routledge and Kegan Paul, p. vii.

17. Jencks, C. (1980). 'The architectural sign'. In *Signs, Symbols, and Architecture* (Broadbent, G., Bunt, R., and Jencks, C., eds) pp. 71–118, John Wiley & Sons.

18. Jencks, C. (1980), pp. 72–73.

19. Jencks, C. (1980), p. 74.

20. Eco, U. (1980). 'Function and sign: the semiotics of architecture'. In Broadbent, G., Bunt, R. and Jencks, C., eds (1980), pp. 11–69.

21. Eco, U. (1980), p. 39.

22. See Chapter 7.

23. Steiner, G. (1975).

24. Steiner, G. (1975), p. 24.

25. Chomsky, N. (1965). *Aspects of the Theory of Syntax*. Cambridge.

26. See, for example, Greene, J. (1969). 'Lessons from Chomsky'. *Architectural Design*, Vol. XXXIX, No. 9, pp. 489–490. Also Broadbent, G. (1980). 'The deep structures of architecture'. In Broadbent, G., Bunt, R. and Jencks, C., eds. (1980), pp. 119–168.

27. Steiner, G. (1975), p. 100.

28. Steiner, G. (1975), p. 101.

29. Steiner, G. (1975), p. 98.

30. See Chapter 7.

31. Steiner, G. (1975), p. 87.

32. Steiner, G. (1975), p. 87.

33. Steiner, G. (1975), p. 94.

34. Steiner, G. (1975), pp. 87–88.

35. Steiner, G. (1975), p. 473.

36. Jencks, C. (1977).

37. Wittgenstein, L. (1958). See also Chapter 7.

38. Wittgenstein, L. (1958).

39. Norberg-Schulz, C. (1980).

40. See also Chapters 12 and 13.

41. Pask, G. (1976).

42. Mead, G. H. (1934).

43. Blumer, H. (1969).

44. In conversation with the author.

CHAPTER 13

1. Lim, J. Y. (1981). 'The traditional Malay house – a forgotten housing alternative'. Presented at the *Seminar on Appropriate Technology, Culture and Lifestyle in Development, Universiti Sains Malaysia, Penang, 3–7 November.* Also Wan, B. (1984). 'The Malay house: learning from its elements, rules and changes'. In *Design and Society, Vol. 1, Proc. of the Design and Society Section of the Int. Conf. on Design Policy, Royal College of Art, London, 20–23 July, 1982* (Langdon, R. and Cross, N., eds) pp. 28–33, The Design Council.

2. Osborne, M. (1979). *Southeast Asia.* George Allen & Unwin/Heinemann Educational Books (Asia). Also Kuchiba, M., Tsubouchi, Y. and Maeda, N. (1979). *Three Malay Villages: A Sociology of Paddy Growers in West Malaysia.* University of Hawaii Press. Also Winstedt, R. (1947). *The Malays: A Cultural History.* Routledge and Kegan Paul.

3. See Chapter 7.

4. The term is used here in the sense of Parfit, D. (1979). 'Personal identity'. In *Philosophy As It Is* (Honderich, T., and Burnyeat, M., eds) pp. 183–211, Pelican Books. Parfit uses the term to distinguish between the logical relations of identity, which are all-or-nothing, and the more ambiguous relations which matter in the survival of personal identity.

5. Ackerman, J. (1966). *Palladio.* Penguin Books. Also Canova, A. (1981). *Palladio: Catalogue of Photographic Exhibition.* Edizioni Canova Treviso.

6. Murray, P. (1978). *The Architecture of the Italian Renaissance*. Schocken Books.

7. Summerson, J. (1953). *Architecture in Britain: 1530–1830*. Penguin Books.

8. The social system underpinning the shophouse is typical of the so-called 'bazaar economies', or surviving pre-industrial segments of the economies of developing countries. See McGee, T. G. (1971). *The Urbanization Process in the Third World*. G. Bell & Sons.

9. Tang, C. A. and Yeo, K. H. (1976). 'Old row houses of Peninsula Malaysia'. *Majallah Akitek*, Vol. 2, June, pp. 22–28. Also in the same journal, Emrick, M. (1976). 'Vanishing Kuala Lumpur: The Shophouse', pp. 29–36.

10. Summerson, J. (1963). p. 52.

11. Summerson, J. (1963).

12. Grube, E. J. (1978). 'What is Islamic architecture?' In *Architecture of the Islamic World* (G. Michell, ed), pp. 10–14, William Morrow.

13. Whitstone, D. (1982). *Colonialism, the PWD, and Early Kuala Lumpur*. Unpublished thesis, Polytechnic Central London.

14. Whitstone, D. (1982), p. 46.

15. Grube, E. J. (1978), p. 10.

16. Ackerman, J. (1966).

17. Whitstone, D. (1982).

18. See Chapter 7.

19. The position taken here on the ambiguous relations between built and social form contrasts with that taken by Christopher Alexander, who favours a close fit concomitant with the logical concept of identity. See Alexander, C. (1964). For a related critique, see Tomas, L. (1982). 'In defense of misfit'. In *Changing Design* (Evans, B., Powell, J., and Talbot, R., eds) pp. 311–324.

20. For a detailed sociological critique of the same housing complex see Abraham, C. E. R. (1979). 'Impact of low-cost housing on the employment and social structure of urban communities'. In *Public and Private Housing in Malaysia* (Tan, S. H. and Hamzah, S., eds), pp. 209–266, Heinemann Educational Books (Asia).

21. Abel, C. (1982). 'Living in a hybrid world 1: the evolution of cultural identities in the developing nations'. *Design Studies*, Vol. 3, No. 3, pp. 127–132. This paper formed the first part of a two-part series of papers on 'Living in a hybrid world', the second of which is reproduced here.

22. The British administration's strategy in colonial Malaya was to disturb local traditions as little as possible and to maintain at least a façade of local autonomy through working with the Sultans. See Tan, D. E. (1975). *A Portrait of Malaysia and Singapore*. Oxford University Press. Despite this, the acquisition of Western values and lifestyles by the Western educated élite eventually served to push the post-independence leadership inexorably in the direction of their former colonial masters.

23. Abel, C. (1982).

24. Many such experiments have been inspired by Schumacher, E. F. (1973). *Small is Beautiful*. Harper and Row.

25. For typical examples of the approach, see The Mahadevapura Team (1979). 'The Mahadevapura ecodevelopment project'. *Ecodevelopment News*, No. 11, pp. 3–11. Also in the same journal, Bredariol, C. S. (1979). 'Ecodevelopment in urban areas of the State of Rio de Janeiro', pp. 12–20. See also Idris, S. M. (1984). 'A framework for design policies in Third World development'. In Langdon, R. and Cross, N., eds (1984), pp. 22–27. See also Chapter 17.

CHAPTER 14

1. Rudofsky, B. (1964). *Architecture Without Architects*. Museum of Modern Art.

2. Alexander, C. (1964).

3. Talib, K. (1984). *Shelter in Saudi Arabia*. Academy Editions/St. Martin's Press.

4. Wardi, P. S. (1981). 'The Malay house'. *Mimar*, No. 2, pp. 55–63.

5. Prijotomo, J. (1984). *Ideas and Forms of Javanese Architecture*. Gadjah Mada University Press. Also Nasir, A. H. (1984). *Mosques of Peninsula Malaysia*. Berita Publishing.

6. MacDonald, W. L. (1976). *The Pantheon*. Allen Lane.

7. A number of scholars have confirmed that the Great Mosque at Damascus, a key model for later mosque architecture, was built on the remains of a Roman pagan temple. See Creswell, K. A. C. (1958). *A Short Account of Early Muslim Architecture*. Lebanon Bookshop. For general histories, see Kuban, D. (1974). *Muslim Religious Architecture*. E. J. Brill. Also Hoag, D. (1977). *Islamic Architecture*. Harry N. Abrams. Also Rivoira, C. T. (1918). *Moslem Architecture*. Oxford University Press.

8. Wolters, O. W. (1982). *History, Culture, and Region in Southeast Asian Perspectives*. Institute of Southeast Asian Studies.

9. For a description of Simla and other colonial settlement patterns, see Morris, J. et al. (1986). *Architecture of the British Empire*. Weidenfeld and Nicolson. Also King, A. D. (1976). *Colonial Urban Development*. Routledge and Kegan Paul.

10. The term 'series' is used here in the sense of Kubler, G. (1962). See also Chapters 11 and 17. Similar cross-cultural exchanges of a consistent nature are evident in the former Dutch East Indies. See Jessup, H. (1984). 'The Dutch colonial villa, Indonesia'. *Mimar*, No. 13, pp. 35–42.

11. The history of Southeast Asian culture has been accurately described in terms of the assimilation of one imported culture after another, each new culture-form being 'localized' to help create the hybrid culture-forms which characterize the region. See Wolters, O. W. (1982). The history of the colonial architecture of the region conforms with this perspective.

12. See Chapter 13.

13. The new tolerance and enthusiasm for colonial architecture was clearly expressed at two conferences on architectural and urban conservation in the region: Strategy for Conservation, held by the Heritage of Malaysia Trust, 6–7 May 1986, Kuala Lumpur, and The Int. Conf. on Urban Conservation and Planning, held by the Malaysian Institute of Architects, 23–24 June 1986, Penang.

14. Parfit, D. (1979), pp. 183–211. Parfit describes continuities of behaviour in terms of 'relations of degree' (See Chapter 13), which is an elegant formulation but is adumbrated here by the broader concept of 'relations of analogy', which is more effective in dealing with problems of change and creativity. See also Chapters 7 and 8.

15. Kubler, G. (1962). See also Chapters 10 and 16.

16. See Chapters 7 and 11.

17. The term 'purified identity' was coined by Richard Sennett to refer to the flight of Americans from the complexities and competing identities of urban life. Sennett, R. (1970). *The Uses of Disorder*. Vintage Books. It is used here in a similar fashion to describe architects' preferences for idealized indigenous architectural images rather than deal with the complexities of cross-cultural exchange.

18. It is no coincidence that Johannes Itten's Basic Course at the Bauhaus owed much to kindergarten theory. See Cross, A. (1983). 'The educational background to the Bauhaus'. *Design Studies*, Vol. 4, No. 1, pp. 43–52.

19. Taylor, B. B. (1986). *Geoffrey Bawa*. A Mimar Book. Also Jayawardene, S. (1986). 'Bawa: a contribution to cultural regeneration'. *Mimar*, No. 19, pp. 47–67.

20. Gurstein, P. (1984). 'Traditional Chinese shophouses of Peninsula Malaysia'. *UIA-International Architect*, No. 6, pp. 22–23. See also Chapter 13.

21. Banham, R. and Suzuki, H. (1985). *Contemporary Architecture of Japan, 1958–84*. The Architectural Press.

22. Abel, C. (1986a).

23. Taylor, B. B. (1984). *Charles Correa*. Concept Media.

24. England and England (1969). 'Four tourist hotels'. *The Architectural Review*, Vol. CXLVI, No. 869, pp. 52–56. Also in the same journal, England, R. 'Vernacular to modern', pp. 45–48. Also Knevitt, C. (1983). *Connections*. Lund Humphries.

25. Hoag, D. (1977). Also Michell, G., ed (1978).

26. Sabra, A. I. (1983). 'The exact sciences'. In *The Genius of Arab Civilization*, pp. 147–169. Eurabia.

27. Abel, C. (1985). 'Henning Larsen's hybrid masterpiece'. *The Architectural Review*, Vol. CLXXVIII, No. 1061, pp. 30–39.

28. For details, see Cantacuzino, S., ed (1985). *Architecture in Continuity*. Aga Khan Award for Architecture.

29. See Chapter 15.

30. Al-Hathloul, S. A., Al-Hussayen, M. A. and Shuaibi, A. M. (1975). *Urban Land Utilization Case Study: Riyadh, Saudi Arabia*. Urban Settlement Design Program, MIT.

31. For details, see Cantacuzino, S., ed (1985).

32. For Fathy's work, see Richards, J. M., Serageldin, I. and Rastorfer, D. (1985). *Hassan Fathy*. Concept Media/The Architectural Press.

33. Abel, C. (1986c). 'Work of El-Wakil'. *The Architectural Review*, Vol. CLXXX, No. 1077, pp. 52–60.

34. Mozhan Khadem. 'The architecture of the Aga Khan University and the Aga Khan University Hospital, Karachi, Pakistan: a summary statement'. Unpublished consultative paper by Payette Associates. Undated.

CHAPTER 15

1. The term 'prime objects' as used here, together with 'series' and other associated concepts, derives from Kubler, G. (1962). *The Shape of Time*. Yale University Press. See also Chapter 11.

2. Frampton, K. (1981). *Modern Architecture 1851–1919*. GA Document, Special Issue 2. The interior has featured in a number of Hollywood movies, notably in the 1982 cult sci-fi hit, *Bladerunner*.

3. For a detailed description of the building's environmental systems and other innovations, see Banham, R. (1969). *The Architecture of the Well-tempered Environment*. The Architectural Press.

4. Spaeth, D. (1985). *Mies van der Rohe*. The Architectural Press.

5. For details, see Khan, H. (1985). 'National Commercial Bank, Jeddah'. *Mimar*, No. 16, pp. 36–41.

6. For a comparative analysis of these buildings, together with other works by the same architects, see Sudjic, D. (1986). *New Architecture: Foster, Rogers, Stirling*. Royal Academy of Arts. For a detailed analysis of the Hongkong and Shanghai Bank, see Abel, C. (1986). See also Chapter 4.

7. For details, see Coomber, M. (1991). 'State of the Ark'. *Building*, 1 March, pp. 40–44. Also Duffy, F. (1992). 'Office Cultures'. *Architects Journal*, 10 June, pp. 28–37.

8. For details, see Richards, I. (1993). 'Tropic tower'. *The Architectural Review*, Vol. CXCII, No. 1152, pp. 26–31.

9. For an account of the architect's approach, see Yeang, K. (1995).

10. For details, see Farrelly, E. M. (1991). 'Capita Centre'. *The Architectural Review*, Vol. CLXXXIX, No. 1134, pp. 49–54.

11. For details, see Papadakis, A., ed (1992). *Foster Associates: Recent Works*. Architectural Monographs No. 20, Academy Editions/St Martin's Press.

12. For details, see Toy, M., ed (1995). *Reaching for the Skies*. Architectural Design Profile No. 116.

CHAPTER 16

1. Walters, O. W. (1982). See also Chapter 13.

2. King, A. D. (1976).

3. Prior to the British colonial settlements, historic urban development was concentrated exclusively in the port city of Malacca. See Kow, L. H. (1978). *The Evolution of the Urban System in Malaya*. University of Malaya Press.

4. McGee, T. G. (1967). *The Southeast Asian City*. G. Bell and Sons. Also McGee, T. G. (1971). Also O' Connor, R. A. (1983). *A Theory of Indigenous Southeast Asian Urbanism*. Institute of Southeast Asian Studies.

5. Sullivan, M. (1985). *Can Survive, La: Cottage Industries in High-rise Singapore*. Graham Brash.

6. Thompson, W. I. (1985). *Pacific Shift*. Sierra Club Books. For a more recent and detailed comparative economic analysis, see OECD (1992). *Long-Term Prospects for the World Economy*. Organization for Economic Co-operation and Development.

7. Hall, S. (1991). 'The local and the global: globalization and ethnicity'. In *Culture Globalization and the World System* (A. D. King, ed), pp. 19–39. Macmillan.

8. Naisbitt, J. (1994). *Global Paradox*. Nicholas Brealey Publishing.

9. From the subtitle to Naisbitt, J. (1994).

10. See Chapters 2 and 5.

11. For popular accounts, see Prigogine, I and Stengers, I. (1985). *Order Out Of Chaos*. Flamingo. Also Gleick, J. (1993). *Chaos*. Abacus. Also Lewin, R. (1993). *Complexity*. Phoenix.

12. See Chapter 2.

13. See Chapters 13 and 14. Also Abel, C. guest ed (1994). 'Southeast Asia'. *The Architectural Review*, Vol. CXCVI, No. 1171, pp. 26–86.

14. See, for example, Yeang, K. (1986). *The Tropical Verandah City*. Asia Publications. Also Tay, K. S. and Powell, R. (1991). 'The intelligent tropical city'. *Singapore Institute of Architects Journal*, Nov./Dec., pp. 32–37. Also Awang, A. B. H. (1992). 'Kuala Lumpur – towards becoming an intelligent city'. *Majallah Akitek*, Sept./Oct., pp. 63–67.

CHAPTER 17

1. Galtung, J., Heiestad, T. and Ruge, E. (1979). *On the Decline and Fall of Empires: The Roman Empire and Western Imperialism Compared*. HSDRGPID-1/UNUP-53, The United Nations University.

2. It should be noted that, while new centres of power have emerged in the East, economic imbalances between developed and developing countries are still generally increasing. See note 3.

3. For example, Bernstein, H., ed (1973). *Underdevelopment and Development*. Penguin Books. Also Chng, N., ed (1977). *Questioning Development in Southeast Asia*. Select Books. Also Clements, K. P. *From Left to Right in Development Theory*. Occasional Paper No. 61, Institute of Southeast Asian Studies. Also George, S. (1988). *A Fate Worse Than Debt*. Penguin Books. Also Rist, G. (1979). *Development Theories in the Social Looking Glass: Some Reflections from Theories to 'Development'*. HSDRGPID-4/UNUP-56, United Nations University. Also Trainer, T. (1989). *Developed to Death*. Green Print.

4. For details of the critical situation in the Malay Peninsula, see CAP (1982). *Development and the Environmental Crisis*. Consumers' Association of Penang.

5. A broad international consensus has existed since the mid 1980s on the dangers of continuing current rates of 'greenhouse gas' emissions: 'After reviewing the latest evidence on the greenhouse effect in October 1985 at a meeting in Villach, Austria, organized by the World Meteorological Organization (WMO), the UN Environment Programme (UNEP), and the International Council of Scientific Unions (ICSU), scientists from 29 industrialized and developing countries concluded that climate change must be considered a "plausible and serious probability"'. See World Commission on Environment and Development (1987). *Our Common Future*. Oxford University Press, p. 175.

6. UNEP (1976). *Ecodevelopment*. UNEP/GC/80, United Nations Environment Programme.

7. The Brundtland Commission, chaired by Gro Harlem Brundtland, defines sustainable development as '...development that meets the needs of the present without compromising the ability of future generations to meet their own needs'. World Commission on Environment and Development (1987), p. 43. The concept has a much longer history, however, and is closely associated with the work of the International Institute for Environment and Development founded by Barbara Ward in 1972. See Holmberg, J. ed (1992). *Policies for a Small Planet*. Earthscan.

8. UNEP (1976), p. 1.

9. Bartelmus, P. (1986). *Environment and Development*. Allen and Unwin.

10. UNEP (1976), p. 2.

11. From the subtitle to Schumacher, E. F. (1973).

12. Clark, W. (1976). 'Big and/or little? Search is on for the right technology'. *Smithsonian Magazine*, p. 55.

13. Darrow, K. and Saxenian, M. (1986). *Appropriate Technology Sourcebook*. Volunteers in Asia. Also Bender, T. (1977). *Rainbook: Resources in Appropriate Technology*. Schocken Books.

14. McRobie, G. (1982). *Small is Possible*. Abacus.

15. Ward, P., ed (1982). *Self-Help Housing*. Mansell Publishing. Also Turner, J. (1976).

16. Abel, C. (1993). 'An architect for the poor'. In *Companion to Architectural Thought* (Farmer, B. and Louw, H., eds), pp. 56–58, Routledge. Also in the same volume: Anzorena, J. (1993). 'Informal housing and the barefoot architect', pp. 59–62.

17. Holod, R. and Rastorfer, D. (1983). *Architecture and Community*. The Aga Khan Award for Architecture/Islamic Publications.

18. Bookchin, M. (1980). *Toward an Ecological Society*. Black Rose Books. Also Bookchin, M. (1974). 'Liberatory technology'. In *Man-Made Futures* (Cross, N., Elliot, D. and Roy, R., eds) pp. 320–332, Hutchinson/The Open University Press.

19. Bookchin, M. (1980), p. 37.

20. Bartelmus, P. (1986).

21. See Chapters 1 and 4.

22. Vincent, G. and Peacock, J. (1985). *The Automated Building*. The Architectural Press.

23. See Chapter 5.

24. See Chapter 13.

25. Lim, J. Y. (1987). *The Malay House*. Institute Masyarakat, p. 4.

26. For details, see Steele, J., ed (1992). *Architecture for a Changing World*. The Aga Khan Award for Architecture/Academy Editions.

27. Fathy, H. (1973). *Architecture for the Poor*. The University of Chicago Press.

28. For example, see Noweir, S. (1982). 'Weisa Wasef's Museum, Harania'. *Mimar*, No. 5. pp. 50–3. Also the Association for the Development of Traditional African Urbanism and Architecture (ADAUA) (1983). 'Building toward community'. *Mimar*, No. 7, pp. 35–51. Also El-Miniawys (1983). 'Maader Village, M'sila'. *Mimar*, No. 8, pp. 9–11.

29. For details, see Steele, J., ed (1992).

30. See Chapters 2 and 15.

31. See Chapter 13. Also Abel, C. (1988). 'Model and metaphor in the design of new building types in Saudi Arabia'. In *Theories and Principles of Design in the Architecture of Islamic Societies* (Sevccenko, M. B., ed) pp. 169–184, The Aga Khan Program for Islamic Architecture.

32. Abel, C. (1985). See also Chapter 14.

33. For details, see Curtis, W. (1986). 'Diplomatic Club, Riyadh'. *Mimar*, No. 21, pp. 20–25.

34. For details, see Jumsai, S. (1986). 'Thammasat University New Campus, Rangsit'. *Mimar*, No. 20, pp. 34–42.

35. For details, see Steele, J., ed (1992).

36. Abel, C. (1989). 'The Aga Khan University and Hospital complex: a critical appraisal'. *Atrium*, No. 6, pp. 24–31. Also Payette, T. M. (1988). 'Designing the Aga Khan Medical Complex'. In Sevccenko, M. B. ed (1988). pp. 161–168. See also Chapter 14.

37. Bartelmus, P. (1986).

38. Ghosh, P. K., ed (1984). *Urban Development in the Third World*. Greenwood Press.

39. See Chapters 12 and 13.

40. It should be stressed that this is a comparative statement regarding a contentious issue. For a contrary view of the negative effects of colonialism on regional architecture see Mumtaz, K. K. (1985). *Architecture in Pakistan*. A Mimar Book.

41. Frank, A. G. (1978). 'Superexploitation in the Third World'. *Two Thirds*, Vol. 1, No. 2, pp. 15–28.

42. For a summary of the main issues at stake, see Third World Network, eds (1992). *Earth Summit Briefings*. Third World Network. Also Strong, M. F. (1992). 'The challenge of environment and development'. *Journal of the World Food Programme*, No. 20, April–June. pp. 17–20.

43. Bartelmus, P. (1986).

44. Amongst relevant World Bank initiatives, the Global Environmental Facility (GEF) was set up in 1990 to help safeguard '...the global commons with the specific objectives of protecting the ozone layer, limiting emissions of greenhouse gases, protecting biodiversity and reducing pollution of international

waters'. Holmberg, J. ed (1992), p. 298. Global programmes such as the GEF are in turn supported by regional programmes aimed at the preservation of shared heritages and managing common resources. See, for example, the World Bank/The European Investment Bank (1990). *The Environmental Program for the Mediterranean.* The World Bank.

45. Bookchin, M. (1980).

46. Valaskakis, K., et al (1979). *The Conserver Society.* Harper and Row.

47. Vale, B. and Vale, R. (1991). *Green Architecture.* Thames and Hudson.

48. Vale, B. and Vale, R. (1991). Also Kelbaugh, D., ed (1989). *The Pedestrian Pocket Book.* Princeton Architectural Press.

CHAPTER 18

1. Between 1970 and 1990 the number of cities worldwide of over 5 million population grew from 8 to 31, of which 21 were situated in Asia. The largest of these, Greater Tokyo, already has a population of 30 million. It is predicted that by 2020 more will have populations of over 30 million and that over half of Asia's total population will be urbanized, or more than double the figure of 23% in 1970. See Liu, T. H. (1997). 'From megacity to constellation city: towards sustainable Asian cities'. Paper presented to the *Conference on India, Southeast Asia and the United States: New Opportunities for Understanding and Cooperation*, 30 January–1 February, Singapore.

2. For a history of the most influential Western urban theories and models, see Hall, P. (1988). *Cities of Tomorrow.* Blackwell.

3. The following summary is based on Correa, C. (1980). 'New Bombay'. *Process*, No. 20, pp. 108–118; Correa, C. (1989). *The New Landscape: Urbanization in the 3rd World.* Mimar/Butterworth Architecture; and Correa C. (1996). *Charles Correa.* Thames and Hudson.

4. Turner J. (1976) op. cit. For an overview of self-build housing and the 'informal sector', see Ward, P. ed (1982) op. cit. For regular reports by activists on related works and projects, see *SELAVIP Newsletter: Journal of Low-Income Housing in Asia and the World.* Pagtambaya Foundation, Inc. E-mail: pagtamba@durian.usc.edu.ph

5. For a summary of the origins and growth of Gandhi's rural reforms, see Ramachandran and Gupta, D. K. (1952). 'The village industries movement'. In *The Economics of Peace: The Cause and the Man.* (George, S.K. ed) pp. 225–236. Wardha M. P., Gram Udyog, Akhil Bharat Sarva Seva Sangh. While middle and upper income groups have generally benefited from India's economic development, the rural poor targeted by Gandhi's village reform movement have made relatively little progress since independence and have even fallen further behind in recent years. See Ainger, K. I. (1999). 'The meek fight for their inheritance'. *Guardian Weekly*, February 21, p. 23.

6. For an introduction, see Goethert, R. (1985). 'Sites and services'. *The Architectural Review*, Vol. CLXXVIII, No. 1062, pp. 28–31. See also, Anzorena, E. J. (1996). 'New approaches in the Orangi Pilot Project (OPP)'. *SELAVIP Newsletter*, April, pp. 59–62.

7. Correa, C. (1989). p. 46.

8. Based on contemporary British studies in the 1960s for Hook New Town, Correa argues that the majority of land required for urban development is given over to non-housing purposes, such as industry, commerce and infrastructure. Consequently any lowering of housing densities has a relatively small impact on the total amount of land required for towns or cities of the same population.

9. See also, Correa, C. (1985). 'The new landscape'. *Mimar 17*, pp. 34–40. It is useful to compare Correa's relatively open-ended approach with Christopher Alexander's earlier and less successful Mexicali cluster housing project, which

was based on Alexander's own domed construction system. A main reason for the project's failure was that the domed design limited construction to one storey, preventing any upward expansion – normally the main direction of growth and change for low cost or informal housing on compact plots. For a critical analysis, see Fromm, D. (1985). 'Mexicali patterns'. *The Architectural Review*, Vol. CLXXVIII, No. 1062, pp. 55–58.

10. The following summary is based on Yeang, K. (1986) op. cit.; Hamzah and Yeang (1994). *Bioclimatic Skyscrapers*. Ellipsis; Yeang, K. (1996). *The Skyscraper Bioclimatically Considered*. Academy Editions: Yeang, K. (1998a). The Malaysian city of the future: some physical planning and urban design ideas'. *Architecture Malaysia*, Vol. 10, No. 2, pp. 70–75; and Yeang, K. (1998b). 'Designing the green skyscraper'. *Building Research and Information*, Vol. 26, No. 2, pp. 122–141.

11. For a recent example of Yeang's approach and techniques, see Schaik, L. Van (1998). 'Big chill'. *RIBA International*, May, pp. 6–11.

12. See also Chapter 15.

13. Hamzah and Yeang (1994). p. 135.

14. Hamzah and Yeang (1994). p. 135.

15. The following summary is based on Tay, K. S. (1989). *Mega-Cities in the Tropics: Towards an Architectural Agenda for the Future*. Institute of Southeast Asian Studies; Tay, K. S. and Powell, R. (1991) op. cit.; Tay, K. S., Powell, R. and Chua, B. H. (1991). 'Planning the city in the tropics: the intensified nodal strategy'. *Singapore Institute of Architects Journal*, January/February, pp. 21–31; and Powell, R. (1997). *Line Edge and Shade: The Search for a Design Language in Tropical Asia*. Page One.

16. Tay, K. S. (1989), pp. 3–4.

17. See also Chapter 16.

18. For a discussion of Hong Kong's unique urban character and mixed land use patterns, see Tao, H. (1980). 'Hong Kong: a city prospers without a plan'. *Process*, No. 20, pp. 84–88.

19. The following summary is based on, Liu, T. K. (1988). 'Overview of urban development and public housing in Singapore'. Paper presented to the *Workshop on Housing and Urban Development*, 20–23 September, Singapore; Liu, T. K. (1991a). 'Landscaping Singapore'. Paper presented to the *1991 Eastern Regional Conference of the International Federation of Landscape Architects*, 31 May to 2 June, Singapore; Liu, T. K. (1991b). 'Implementing the Concept Plan'. Paper presented to the *City Trans-Asia 1991 Conference*, 17 September, Singapore; Liu, T. K. (1992). 'Public housing in Singapore: an architectural portrait'. Paper presented to the *Housing Design 2000 Conference*, 24–25 September, Singapore; Liu, T. K. (1996). 'Asian cities at the crossroads'. Paper presented to the *International Conference on Asia: Redefining the City*, 18–20 October, Tokyo; and Liu, T. K. (1997) op. cit. See also Lim, W. S. W. (1983). 'Public housing and community development: the Singapore experience'. *Mimar 7*, pp. 20–34; Wong, K. W. and Yeh, S. H. K. eds (1985). *Housing a Nation: 25 Years of Public Housing in Singapore*. Maruzen Asia; and Building and Social Housing Foundation (1993). *Cities of the Future: Successful Housing Solutions in Singapore and Surabaya*. Building and Social Housing Foundation.

20. For another example of a local private practice at work in Singapore's new towns see, Abel, C. (1994). 'Community collage'. *The Architectural Review*, Vol. CXCVI, No. 1171, pp. 62–67.

21. Liu, T. K. (1997), p. 12.

22. Liu, T. K. (1997), p. 14.

23. Liu, T. K. (1997), p. 16.

24. Liu, T. K. (1991b). Also, Urban Redevelopment Authority (1991). *Living the Next Lap: Towards a Tropical City of Excellence*. Urban Redevelopment Authority.

25. Liu, T. K. (1997). p. 14.

26. Jumsai, S. (1994). 'Bangkok and East Asian Megacities'. Paper presented to the *OECD-Australia Conference on Cities and the New Global Economy*, Melbourne.

27. Correa specifically describes both his land-use schemes and transportation plans in terms of structural 'hierarchies'. Nevertheless, the polycentred plan of New Bombay as well as the complex mix of land-use functions are more accurately described in terms of heterarchical structures, similar to those described by Christopher Alexander in his analyses of 'natural' as opposed to planned cities. Alexander, C. (1965). 'A city is not a tree'. *Architectural Forum*, Vol. 122, No. 1, pp. 58–62, and No. 2, pp. 58–61. See also Chapters 2 and 3.

28. Powell, R. (1997).

29. Yeang, K. (1998a).

30. Jacques, M. (1997). 'Malaysia takes a leap into future'. *Guardian Weekly*, 6 April, p. 23; and Fuller, T. (1997). 'Malaysia's wired "Supercorridor"'. *International Herald Tribune*, 15–16 November, pp. 1 and 6. For a discussion of the Malaysian government's development plans, of which the Supercorridor is a key part, see Hamid, A. S. A. ed (1993). *Malaysia's Vision 2020*. Pelanduk Publications.

31. Abel, C. 'Architecture in the Pacific Age'. In *Public Places in Asia Pacific Cities: Current Issues and Strategies* (Pu, M. ed). University of Hawaii Press, forthcoming.

32. Original Scope Sdn. Bhd. (1996). *Giga World: KL Linear City*. Urban and Architectural Design Statement prepared for KL Linear City Sdn. Bhd. The editors (1997). 'A new record for Kuala Lumpur? The world's longest complex'. *Architectural Record*, February, p. 30.

33. Abel, C. 'Millennium Tower, Japan'. In *Norman Foster: Complete Works Vol. III* (Jenkins, D. ed). Norman Foster and Partners, forthcoming. Abel, C. 'M-Tower project'. In *Norman Foster: Complete Works Vol. III*. ibid.

34. Tay, K. S. (1989).

35. Martin, L. and March, L. eds (1972). *Urban Space and Structures*. Cambridge University Press.

36. See Chapter 13.

37. Liu, T. K. (1991a). p. 2.

38. See Chapter 6.

39. While the official policy is to segregate urban functions, cottage industries continue to flourish in Singapore, wherever entrepreneurs can find space to work. See Chapter 16.

40. Hall, P. (1988). p. 214.

41. See Chapter 17.

42. See Chapter 16.

43. Correa, C. (1996).

INDEX

Page numbers in italics refer to illustrations.

'A' frame houses, 204, *204*
Aalto, Alvar, 64, 115
Abel, Chris, viii–x
Abstract design, 48, 58, 60, 61, 114
Advanced Information City, 220–1
Advanced technology, *see* technology
Aga Khan University and Hospital (Payette Associates), Karachi, 176, *176*, 177, 206
Akitek Tengarra, *196*, 219, 220
Alexander, Christopher, vii, 106
Amsterdam, Digital City, 56–7
Analogy (analogical thinking), ix–x, xii, 19, 31, 81–4, 89, 95–6, 102–3, 112, 115, 119, 120, 133, 137
  alternative use of, 144
  in architecture, 83–4
  functions of, 81–3
  negative, 95
  neutral, 95, 96
  positive, 95
  psycho-social, 141
  relations of, 169
  skycourts, 188
  see also biological models; language analogy
Ando, Tadao, Chapel on Mount Rokko, Kobe, 66–7, *66*
Andrew, John, 18
Ankara (Turkey), *201*
Appleyard, David, 141
Arabian Peninsula, 163
Archer, Bruce, 27
Archigram, vii, 15, 18, 104–5
Architects:
  cognitive profile of, 35, 36
  computer-based program for dialogue with client, 33–6
  empathy of, 34
  learning by example, 121
  and manufacturing, 37–47 *passim*
  open approach by, 62–4
  pseudo-complexities and sham images, 58–62
  regional culture, 195
  role of, 48, 50
  self-taught in regional traditions, xiii, 170
  simulation techniques used by, 57
  social role of, 35
Architectural Association (AA) School of Architecture, London, 50
Architectural Design (*AD*) vii–viii, 51
Architectural games, 113
Architectural theory, viii, ix, x, xii, 48, 51
Architecture Machine Group, 50
ARCHITRAINER computer game, 33–6, *33*
Aristotle, 97
Art, 29, 120, 133–4
Artefacts, 150
  as exemplars, 133–5, 137
  paradigms, 132
Artificial intelligence (AI), 43, 50
Artists, intuitive, 120
Arts and Crafts Movement, 37
Arup, Ove *see* Ove Arup Partnership
Ashby, Ross, 20
Asia, xiv, 193–4
  cities, 192–3, 227
  urban futures, 211–34
Ateliers One and Ten, *54*, 72
Athens (Greece), museum beneath the Acropolis, 127
Atomists, 117
Automation, 7, 11, 21, 203
  computerized, 43–5
Autonomy, *see* relative autonomy

Badran, Rasem, 175
Bali, 165
Bangladesh, Grameen Bank Housing Programme, 202, *202*
Banham, Reyner, vii, 4, 105, 116–17, 125
Barbour, Ian, 95, 96
Barcelona (Spain), Casa Milá (Gaudi), 98, *99*, 100
Barragan, Luis, 171
Batch production, 7–8, 9, 12
Battle McCarthy (engineers), 69, 70
Bauhaus School, vii, 37, 68, 69, 77, 169–70
Bawa, Geoffrey, 170
Beehah Group, 175
Beer, Stafford, 10–11, 12, 21
Behnisch, Gunter, University Library, Eichstatt, *65*, 66
Belapur, New Bombay (India), 214–15, *214*
Belief systems, 88–95
Berggren, D., 98
Berlin (Germany):
  Free University, 15, *17*, 18
  Glass Skyscraper project (Mies van der Rohe), 180, *180*, 189
  IBA Social Housing, 60
  National Gallery (Mies van der Rohe), *90*, 91–3, *91*, *92*, 137
  Philharmonie (Scharoun), 66, 93–4, *93*, *94*
Berlin, Isaiah, 28, 29, 30
Bertalanffy, Ludwig von, 20, 118
Bio-Tech architecture, *63*, 64, 71–7
Bio-Tech Architecture Workshop, xiii, 71–4, 76, 77
Bioclimatic city, 215–19, *229*, *231*
Biographical approach, 134, 135
Biological models (analogies), xi, 19–20, 50, 71, 76, 96, 134, 195
Bishan (Singapore), Institute of Education (Tenggara II), *196*, 220
Blacksburg Electronic Village, Virginia, 56
Blumer, Herbert, 30–1, 149

Bohr, Niels, *118*
Bombay (India):
  Kanchanjunga Apartments, 229
  New Bombay, 212–15, 226, 229, 230, 231, 233
Bookchin, Murray, 203
Brodsky, Joyce, 135, 137
Brown, S. J., 102
Brown, Scott, *115*
Buddhism, 117, 118
Buddhist architecture, 171
Buffalo (USA), Larkin Company Office Building (Wright), 178–9, *179*
Building industry, 3–14, 38–9, 42
Building materials, local, 135–6, 204, 230
  adobe brick, 136
  mud-brick, 163, *164*
  timber-framing, 195, 196
Bunshaft, Gordon:
  Lever House, New York (for SOM), 180, *180*
  National Commercial Bank (for SOM), Jeddah, 174, *181*, 182, *182*
Burlington, Lord, Chiswick House, 154, *154*, *155*

Cairo (Egypt), 163, 175
Cameron Highlands, nr Kuala Lumpur, Tudor-style inn, *167*
Candilis Josic Woods, 15, *17*
Capra, Fritjof, 117, 118, 119, 121
Capsule Homes Tower, Folkestone, *105*
Cardwell, Simon, 73
Carlo, Giancarlo de, 63
Centre and periphery, 198–9
Chalk, Warren, 104, *105*
Cham Ltd, 57
Chandigarh (India), 230, 231
Chernikhov, 66, *136*
Chicago (USA):
  Crown Hall (Mies van der Rohe), *137*
  New York Life Building (Jennie and Mundie), *178*
  tall buildings, 178
Chinese-built shophouses, 155, *155*, 170, 190, 192, 228
Chinese immigrants, 165, 191–2
Chinese style tiled stairways, 165, *165*
Chinese symbols of *t'ai-chi*, 118, *118*
Chiswick House (Lord Burlington), 154, *154*, *155*
Chomsky, Noam, 145, 146
CIMI *see under* Nottingham, University
Cities:
  as aircraft carrier metaphor, 103–4
  Asian, 192–3, 227
  bioclimatic city, 215–19, 229, 231
  computer infrastructures, 50
  constellation city, 223, 224–5, *224*, *226*, 230
  cybercity, 55–7, 227
  decentralization of, 18
  developing, 207
  development city, xiv, 231, 232–3
  dispersed (urban dispersal), 18, 21, 51, 174, 227, *227*, 228–9
  fortified, 18, *18*
  green, 210
  ideal city, 15, *18*
  megacities, 211, *211*, 225, 229, 231–2
  and orientation, 141
  polycentred city, 213–14, 230
  self-organizing, 25–6, 36
  urban growth simulated, 62
  virtual city, 227
  see also Plug-in City; urban architecture and planning
Classical architecture, 90–3, 136, 152, 153, 155–6, 183
Clients:
  dialogue with architects, 33–4, 77
  identity of, 90
  as own architects, 50
Climate, 71, 77, 90, 121, 175
  arid, 204, 228
  climate control devices, 187, 203, 217, 218
  Malaysia, 151–4, 155, 159, 204
  office buildings, 188, 189
  skycourts, 182
  tropical, 151–4, 155, 159, 166, 195–6, 204, 206, 215, 217, 218, 219–22, 227, 228–31
  water use, 176
Co-op Himmelblau, 58, *58*
Cognition, self-conscious and unself-conscious, 111
Cognitive complexity, 31, 35, 36
Cognitive mapping, 141
Cognitive profiles, *35*, 36
Colonial architecture (colonialism), x, 135–6, 149, *149*, 158, 159, 161, 166–8, 198–9, 208, 209
Communication theory, 134
Communications skills, 70, 73
Community architecture, 113
Community-based networks, 56
Complementary themes, 117–22, 124–9
Complexities, ix, 19–20, 48–67
  complexity theory, xiv, 60, 195
  cultural, 188
  pseudo-complexities:
    sham images, 62
    superimpositions, 57–61
Computational fluid dynamics (CFD) program, 73, *73*, 76
Computer-aided design (CAD), 43–5, 50, 51, 53, *55*, 57, 69, 71, *72*, *73*, 74
Computer-aided manufacture (CAM), 43
Computers, 48–51, 58
  ARCHITRAINER computer game, 33–6, *33*
  computer-based design, 69–77
  computer-based media studies xiii–xiv
  computer-based production, viii, 11–12, 13, 38, 41, 42–3, 121, 194, 203
  computerized automation, 43–5
  computerized building management systems, 52, *52*
  networks, 55
  self-learning, 49
  Sim City simulation game, 62
  simulation techniques, 229, *229*
Concepts, *see* constructs
Constellation city, 223, 224–5, *224*, *226*, 230
Construction Industry 'Superhighway Initiative', 57
Constructivists, Russian, 66
Constructs:
  defined, 118–19
  polar (bi-polar) concepts, 118, 119–22
  related, 119–22
Consumer culture, 208–9
Continuity and discontinuity, 135–7, 188
Conversations, theory of, 149
Cook, Peter, vii, *16*
Cooper, Clare, 141
Copcutt, Geoffrey, *18*
Correa, Charles, vii, 171, 212–15, 226, 229–30, 231
  New Bagalkot, India, 231, *231*
Cosham, IBM Advance Head Office (Foster Associates), *39*
Craddock, Paul, 73
Craft manufacture, 37–47, 121
Creativity, 87, 112, 113, 134, 137, 170
Critical relativism, xii, 31, 86–7, 120
Criticism (architectural), xii, 84, 89, 120
  by analogy, 31–2, 88, 89, 93
  and metaphor, 98–101, 102
  partisan, 89–93
Critics, 143
Cross-cultural effects, 163–6
Cross-cultural exchange, 212
Cuba, Bacardi Corporation Headquarters, 92

Cultural complexity, 188–9
Cultural differentiation, 208
Cultural diversity, 199
Cultural exchange, 121, 136, 149, 166, 207
Cultural identities, 77, 169
Cultural innovation (identity), 159–60
Cultural typology, 207–9
Culture-forms (forms of life), xii, 84, 86, 88, 89, 144, 148–9, 150, 169, 177
  hybrid, 152, 154, 158, 159, 160, 162
  interaction of, 154
Cumbernauld New Town, 15, *18*
Cupples Building Products, 41–3, *41*, *42*
Customized building production, ix, 52–5, 76, 77
Cutlery Factory for David Mellor (Hopkins), Derbys, *126*, 127
Cybercity, 55–7, 227
Cybernetics, 10–12, 13, 19, 21, 37, 43, 49, 50, 51, 121, 149, 203, 218
Cyberspace, 56, 67

Damascus, Great Mosque, *166*
Darwin, Charles, 82, 83
Davies, Mike, 53
Decentralization, 21–5, 204, 208, 212
Deconstructionists, ix, 67
Descartes, Rene, 28, 117
Design
  development, 39–41
  explicit, 109, 112, 113
  learning to, 109–12, 120–1
  rational, 120
  self-conscious and unself-conscious, 106, 111, 113, 119, 120–1
Design methods movement, 27–36
Design Research Studio (DRS), Nottingham University, xiii, 69–71, 72, 75
Design studio projects, 109–10
Design studios, 68–9, 111
Designers, 37, 38
  and industrialized production, 3–7, 14
  rational and romantic, 120
Developing countries, 198–210
Development city, xiv, 231, 232–3
Dialogue, open approach, 62–4
Disciplinary matrix, 132–3
Dispersed cities (urban dispersal), 18, 21, 51, 174
Dispersed high rise city, 227, *227*, 228–9
Doshi, Balkrishna, vii
DP Architects, *54*
Durer, Albrecht, *18*

Eco, Umberto, 143–4, 145, 148
Eco-culture, x, xiv, 208–9
Ecodevelopment, 162, 199–200, 203, 206, 207, 209–10
Ecology, xii, 118, 121, 151, 152, 199–200, 210, 227, 230–1
Ecosystems, 199–200
Eden, J. F., 6
Edo (Japan), Shoin Style Datè residence, *64*
Education (architectural), xiii, 68–9, 77, 111–13, 120–1, 148, 169–70, 171–3, 195
  new model of design education, 69–77
Ehrenkrantz, Ezra, 5
Eichstatt (Germany), University Library (Behnisch), *65*
Eisenman, Peter, 60, *61*
El Jem (Tunisia), Colosseum, *167*
El-Wakil, Abdelwahed, 175–6, *176*, 177
Electricity generator, wind powered, *201*
Empathy, concept of, 30, 34
Empirical constructs (concepts), 32, 120
Energy conservation, 189, 195
England, Richard, 171, *171*
Entropy, 19, 20
Environment, 13, 18, 20–1, 22, 51
  crisis, 195
  environmental dialogues between architect and client, 32–4
  smart materials responding to, 55
  urban, 15–26
EPR Architects, 72
Erikson, Erik, 141
Erskine, Ralph, 63
  Ark, London, 184–5, *185*
Eva Jiricna Architects, 72
Evaluation, 88, 90, 91 2
Evolutionary processes (metaphor), xii, 18, 19, 25–6, 103, 134
Exemplars, 120–1, 132, 133, 137
Experimentation, ix, 50, 125, 127, 129
  man–machine dialogue, 50–1
Expressionism, 29

FastCad, *57*
Fathy, Hassan, 175, 204, *205*
Feyerabend, Paul, 31–2, 132
Flexible production techniques xi, 42–3, 52, 71, 77, 194
Foley, Donald, 15
Folk architecture, 163
Folkestone
  Capsule Homes Tower, *105*
  International Exhibition of Experimental Architecture, *5*

Ford, Brian, 70
Form
  flirtation with, 115–16
  and style, 148–9
Fortified cities, 18, *18*
Foster, Sir Norman (Foster Associates), 69, 124–5, 129
  Century Tower, Tokyo, 125, *125*
  Commerze Bank, Frankfurt, 188, *188*
  Hongkong and Shanghai Bank, 39–43, 45, *46*, 52, *54*, 170–1, 183–4, *184*
  IBM Advance Head Office, Cosham, *39*
  Millennium Tower project, Tokyo, 227, *227*
  Renault Centre, Swindon, 52, *52*, *53*
  Stansted Airport Terminal, 125, *126*
  Willis Faber and Dumas Head Office, Ipswich, *124*, 125, *125*
Frampton, Kenneth, ix
Frankfurt (Germany)
  Commerze Bank (Foster Associates), 188, *188*
  Rebstockpark near (Eisenman), 60, *61*
Free form management, 13
Friedman, Yona, 50, 57, 62
Fuller, Buckminster, 105
Future Systems, 64, 127

Galbraith, John Kenneth, 3, 7, 10
Gans, Herbert, 23
Gaudi, Antoni, Casa Milá, Barcelona, 98, *99*, 100
General systems theory (GST), viii, 19, 20, 51, 118
Georgetown, Penang (Malaysia), 193, *193*
  Komtar Tower, *161*
  'Rifle Range' housing estate, 160–1, *160*
  shophouses, 155–6, *155*
  villas, 152–4, *153*, 156, 159
Ghaia theory, 118
Gharghur village (Malta), *142*
Glass architecture, 125, 180, *180*, 182
Global eco-culture, 198–210
  centre and periphery, 198–9
Global village, 18, 169
Globalization, xii, 190–7
Goffman, Erving, 31
Grameen Bank Housing Programme, Bangladesh, 202, *202*
Graves, Michael, *147*
Green architecture, 125–9, 210; *see also* eco-culture
Green movement, 162
Greene, David, vii

Gröninger Museum (Holland), 58, *58*
Gropius, Walter, 37, 38, 42, 68
Gunton, Martin, 73

Hadid, Saha, Peak Club, 60–1, *61*
Hagia Sophia, *see* Istanbul
Hall, Andrew, 73
Hall, Arthur D., 19
Hall, Peter, 230, 231
Hamzah and Yeang 70, *186*, 187, *189*, *216*, *218*, *229*; *see also* Yeang, Ken
Hanging balconies, 163, *164*
Hanoi, 218
Harper, Cliff, *49*
Heidegger, Martin, 141, 142
Herder, Johann Gottfried, 27–30, 31
Herron, Ron, vii
Heterotropic planning technique, 64
High rise buildings, 229
  towers by Yeang, 217–19
High rise cities, dispersed, 227, *227*, 228–9
High rise housing, 160–1, 213, 214, 223
High rise office buildings, 178–89
High-Tech, 45, 64
Hindu-Javanese temple, 165
Hinduism, 117, 165
Hollein, Hans, 'Aircraft Carrier City', 103–4, *104*
Hong Kong, *211*, 213, 221
  Peak Club (Hadid), 60–1, *61*
Hongkong and Shanghai Bank (Foster Associates), 39–43, 45, *46*, 52, *54*, 170–1, 183–4, *184*
Hopkins, Michael, *126*, 127
Housing
  'A' frame houses, 204, *204*
  incremental housing, 214–15, *214*, 230
  mass housing systems, 38
  'open-ended' design, 141
  prototypes, 37–8
  self-build, 141, 201, 202, *202*, 207, 215
  see also Malaysia
Houston (USA), Menil Collection Museum (Piano Workshop), *127*, 129
Human science and culture, 27–30, 34, 144
  new paradigm, 30–2
  role of indwelling, 108
Hybrid architecture, 114, 116, 121, 129, 151–62, 191, 204

IB movement, 5, 6, 7
Ideal city, 15, *18*
Identities
  of architecture, ix, xii, 34, 141–50
    'architecture as identity', 141, 149
  cultural, 77, 169
  individual and social, 77
Imported cultures, 191–2
Incremental building, 214–15, *214*, 230, 233
Indeterminant forms of architecture, 50
India, 168, 171, 212, 213, 215, 229
Indonesia, 165, 212
Industrialized production, 3–14, 68, 121
  cybernetic factory, 10–12
  management, 12–13
  team assembly, 12–13
  variable production, 7–10, 46
Indwelling, 107–9, 110, 113
Information technologies, xiii, 18, 50, 52, 193, 194, 203
  advanced, 71
  in Singapore, 220
  and the tropical city, 229
Information theory, 51, 134
Innovation, 87, 208
  radical, 134, 135, 137
  by Sinan, 122–4
  and tradition, 131–7
Intelligent buildings, 53, 64, 121
Intelligent environments, 50
Intelligent Systems Solutions Ltd, *54*
Intelligent Tropical City, 196–7, 220, *220*, 228
Intermediate technology *see* technology
Intermediate Technology Development Group, 201
International Exhibition of Experimental Architecture, Folkestone, *5*
International Style, 137, 170, 204
Internet, 55–6, 62, 67, 74
Intuitive concepts, 120
Ipswich (Suffolk), Willis Faber and Dumas Head Office (Foster Associates), *124*, 125, *125*
Islam, 165
Islamic architecture, 152, 156, 157–9, 166, 168, 171–4, 176, 177
Istanbul (Turkey), 163, *164*
  Hagia Sophia, 122
  Suleymaniye Mosque, 122, *123*
Itten, Johannes, 68

Jahor Baru, *218*
Japan, 45, 55, 125, 170–1, 229
  architecture, 65–6
  house (Utzon), *101*
  Shoin Style, *64*, 65
  space concepts, 64–7
  Sukiya Style, 65, 114
Java, Great Mosque, 165, *165*
Jeddah (Saudi Arabia)
  Haj Terminal (SOM), *173*, 174, 177
  hanging balconies, 163, *164*
  National Commercial Bank (Bunshaft for SOM), 174, *181*, 182, *182*, 187, 188–9
  Rewais Mosque (El-Wakil), 176, *176*
Jencks, Charles, ix, 62, 100–1, 102, 115, 143, 144, 145, 148
Jennie and Mundie, *178*
Johnson, Philip, 137, 148
  Seagram Building, New York, 182–3, *183*
Jones, Peter Blundell, 90, 91–2, 93, 94–5
Jumsai, Sumet, 225
  Thammasat University, 206, *206*
Just-In-Time production, 55

Kahn, Louis, 115, 171
kampong houses, 151–2, 228
Kampulan Akitek Group, 170
Kansai International Airport Terminal (Piano Workshop), Osaka, *127*, *128*, 129
Kaplicky, Jan, 127
Karachi (Pakistan), 176, *176*, 177, 206
Kasturi, Hijjas, 229
Kelly, George, 31, 34–5, 118–19
Kelly, Kevin, 55
Kepler, Johannes, 82, 87
Khadem, Moshan, 176
Kikutake, Kiyonori, Sky House, *171*
Kipnis, Jeffrey, 62
Knowledge (architectural), xii, 28–9, 81, 83, 84, 88, 106–13, 121, 137, 148
  Cartesian model of, 28, 30
  indwelling (bodily experience), 107–9
  tacit knowing, 106–7
  theory of, 28, 110
Knowledge-based engineering (KBE) system, 53, 57
Kobe (Japan), Chapel on Mount Rokko (Ando), *66*
Koenigsberger, Otto, vii
Koestler, Arthur, 82, 83, 87, 131, 137
Koolhaas, Rem, 62
Koski, Solomon and Ruthven, 72
Krier, Leon and Rob, 115
Kroll, Lucien, 63
Kuala Lumpur (Malaysia), 158–9, 168, 190–1, *191*, 192, 193, *198*
  FMS Railway Headquarters, 158, *168*
  General Post Office, 158
  High Court Building, 158, *159*
  high rise city, *227*
  Hitechniaga Corporation (Hamzah and Yeang), 188, *189*

KL Linear City, 227, *227*
Menara Mesiniaga Building (Hamzah and Yeang), *186*, 187
MIMOS, *194*
MRT system, 197
Peter Eu House, *197*
Public Works Department (PWD), 157, 158
Selangor State Secretariat (former), 157, *157*
shophouses, 217
Walian House, *170*
Kubler, George, 131, 133–6, 137
Kuhn, Thomas, viii, xii, 31–2, 108, 109, 131–3, 136, 137

Laing, R. D., 31, 34
Landau, Royston, 51
Lang, Fritz, *Metropolis* (film), *49*, 103
Language analogy (linguistic analogy), x, 81–96, 141, 143–4
comparison of architectural languages, 88–9
language cultures, 89
linguistic theory, 84–8
critical relativism, xii, 31, 86–7, 120
language games, ix, xii, 85–6, 89
relative autonomy, 87–8, 144
relativism, 84–5
as metaphor, 103
monadist (relativist) view, 145, 146, 148
partisan criticism, 89–93
strong thesis of relativism, 86
style and form, 148–9
theory of, 87, 144
universalist view, 144–8
Larsen, Henning, Ministry of Foreign Affairs, Riyadh, *172*, 173–4, 177, 206
Le Corbusier, vii, 115, 119, 137, 171
plan for Chandigarh, 230
Ronchamp chapel, *103*, 176
Leaker, D. R., *18*
Leonidove, 66, *66*
Lim, Jimmy, 170, *197*, 229
Lim (William) Associates, *223*
Lindblom, Charles E., 25–6
Linguistic relativism 28, 31, 84–5; *see also* language analogy
Literary references, 98
Literary theory, 48, 60
Liu Thai Ker, 222–5, 226, 228, 229–30
constellation city, 223, 224, *226*, 230
Localization, versus globalization, xii, 190–7
Loggias, 158–9
London, *54*
Architectural Association (AA) School of Architecture, 50
Tropical Architecture Department, vii
Ark (Erskine), 184–5, *185*
Lloyd's HQ (Rogers), 52, *53*, 183–4, *184*
National Gallery, Sainsbury Wing extension, *115*
Long Island, Nassau County, *24*
Lord's cricket ground (Hopkins), 127
Los Angeles, 23, *24*, 25, *25*, 51
Bradbury Building (Wyman), 178, *179*
Lovelock, James, 118
Lynch, Kevin, 141, 143

McCarthy, Chris, 70
Machine Age
First Machine Age, 49, 119, 121
Second Machine Age, 45, 121
Machine production, *see* industrialized production
Madison (USA), Unitarian Church (Wright), 98, *99*, 100
Mahoud, Wassim Ben, El Hafsia Quarter, Medina, 174–5, *174*
Malaysia, x, 151–62, 168, 170, 193, 195, 197, 228
Chinese shophouses, 155, *155*, 170, 190, 228
hill stations, 166, *167*
house-on-stilts, 151–2, *151*, 165, 166, 168, 169
houses, 204
'hybrid' houses in Malacca State, 165, *165*
villas, 152–4, 156, 159–60, 166
see also Georgetown; Kuala Lumpur
Malmo (Sweden), housing development (Waldhor), 64
Malta, *142*, 171
Festaval Tourist Village, *171*
Mangunwijaya, Yousef B., 204, *204*
Manosa, Francisco, 170
Manufacturing technologies
computer-aided, 43, 45
craft and industry, 37–47
see also industrialized production; mass production; robots
March, Lionel, 228
Mass production, viii, 3–14 *passim*, 69, 77, 105, 161, 208
flow-line method of assembly, 12
team assembly, 12–13
Massachusetts Institute of Technology, 33, 50
Mead, George Herbert, 30, 149
Mechanical Age, 100
Mechanical universe, 117
Mechanistic construct, 121
Megacities, 211, *211*, 225, 229, 231–2
Megastructures, 15, 18, 50, 183, 187, 188, 227
Mendelsohn, Erich, Einstein Tower, Potsdam, 98, *99*, 100
Meta, Pravina, 213
Metaphors, ix, 67, 81, 82, 95, 97–105, 141
in architectural criticism, 98–101
'architecture as identity', 141, 149
definitions, 97–8
dynamic and creative role of, 102–3
isolated pictorial, 98, 101, 103
negative, 100, 101
new architectural concepts, 103–5
ornamental view, 97–8
positive, 100, 101
rational view, 97–8, 102
structural, 98, 100
textural, 98
Meurer, Bernd, *38*
Mexico, 134
Mies van der Rohe, 137, *137*, 182, 184
Brick Country House project, *137*
Crown Hall, Chicago, *137*
Glass Skyscraper project, Berlin, 180, *180*
Glass Tower project, Germany, *180*
New National Gallery, Berlin, *90*, 91–3, *91*, *92*
Seagram Building, New York, 182–3, *183*
Mind
mind-body dualism, 117, 129–30
theory of, 149–50
transformations of, 149
Mission architecture, 135–6, *135*
Mobile Learning Stations, 50, *50*
Models, 132, 133, 188
dynamic, 133–6
see also biological models; exemplars; language analogy
Modern architecture, and neo-colonialism, 160–2
Modern cultures, 106
Modern Movement, vii, 42, 47, 105, 116, 123, 136–7
Modernism (Modernists), 7, 45, 46, 48, 66, 81, 114–15, 116, 129, 130, 163, 174, 182, 195
Modernity, 114–30 *passim*
Modular coordination, 4–5, 6
Molins Machine Company, 10, *10*
Montreal Expo, Habitat (Safdie), 15
Moore, Charles, 63, 171
Morris, William, 37
Mosques, 122, *123*, 165–6, *165*, *166*, 169, 176, *176*, 177, 191

Motel units (Schein), *5*
Muhanna brothers, 204

Nature, 49, 60, 64, 83, 118, 121, 129, 217
  and the atomists, 117
NCB Building, *see* Jeddah, National Commercial Bank
Negroponte, Nicholas, 50, 55, 62
Neo-classicism, 64, 92, 137, 182
Neo-colonial architecture, 161–2
New Bagalkot (India), 231, *231*
New Bombay, *see* Bombay
New Gourna village (Egypt), *205*
New Mexico, 135–6
New towns, 15
New Training Centre for Olivetti (Stirling), in Hampshire (UK), 100–1, *100*
New York (USA):
  Lever House (Bunshaft for SOM), 180, *180*, 182, 188
  Seagram Building (Mies van der Rohe with Johnson), 182–3, *183*
New York State (USA), Westchester County, *16*
Newton, Isaac, 117, 121
Non-governmental organizations (NGOs), 201, 202
Non-Linear Systems, 12
Norberg-Schulz, Christian, 141, 143, 144, 148, 149
Norman, A. C., 157, 158, 159, *159*
Nottingham:
  Cyberpub, *56*
  Inland Revenue HQ (Rogers), *63*
  University
    Centre for Industrial and Medical Informatics (CIMI), 75, 76
    Design Research Studio, xiii, 69–71, 72, 75
    rapid prototyping, *55*, 73

Objectivism, xii, 120
Office buildings, 52, 178–89
Ohio (USA), Columbus Convention Centre (Eisenman), 60, *61*
Olivetti New Training Centre (Stirling) in Hampshire, 100–1, *100*
Omrania, Diplomatic Club, Riyadh, *205*, 206
Opposites, 117–22
Organic architecture and systems (analogy), 19, 48–9, 90, 91, 92, 93, 94–5
  and mechanistic systems, 121
Ottoman architecture, 122
  hanging balconies, 163
Ove Arup Partnership, 73, 76

Pacific region, 45, 193–4, 195–7
Palladio, Andrea, 119, 137, 153–4, *153*, *155*, 156, 159–60, 166
  Vicenza Basilica, 158, *158*
  Villa Cornaro, 153–4, *153*
Paradigms, viii, xii, 109–10, 112, 133
  alternative, 199–200
  meaning of, 131–2
  'new paradigm' human science, 30–2
Paris (France), Parc de la Villette (Tschumi), 58, *58*, *59*, 60
Pask, Gordon, 31, 51, 149
Patel, Bimal Hasmukh C., 206
Patel, Shirish, 213
Payette Associates, Aga Khan University and Hospital, Karachi, 176, *176*, 177, 206
Penang (Malaysia):
  colonial villa *167*; *see also* Georgetown
  Malay house-on-stilts, 151–2, *151*, 165, 166, 168, 169
Personal construct theory, 31, 34–6, 118–19
Personal identity formation, 141
Petaling Jaya (Malaysia), *69*, 227
Philippines, 170, 212, 222
PHOENICS CFD program, 57
Piaget, Jean, 31
Piano, Renzo (Piano Workshop), 46, 127, 129
  Kansai International Airport Terminal, *127*, *128*, 129
  Menil Collection Museum, Houston, *127*, 129
Pidgeon, Monica vii–viii
Place (place identity), 30, 32, 34, 46, 69, 71, 77, 90, 113, 141, 143, 148, 162
Plug-in City project (Archigram), vii, 15, *16*, 18, 104–5
Pluralism, 29
Polanyi, Michael, 106–9, 110, 111, 112
Popper, Karl, 86–7, 132
Populism, 29
Portland, Oregon (USA), Public Services Building (Graves), *147*
Postmodernism, ix, 48, 114, 129, 130, *147*, 148
Potsdam (Germany), Einstein Tower (Mendelsohn), 98, *99*, 100
Powell, Robert, 220
Price, Cedric, vii, 50
Prime objects, 134–5, 178–89
Project drawings, 48
Proshansky, Harold, 32
Prototype development and manufacture, 71, 73, 74
Prouvé, Jean, 6–7, *7*

Purpose, of architecture, 69, 71, 77, 92, 143, 144
Putrajaya (Malaysia), 227

Ranchos de Taos, *136*
Rapaport, Anatol, 141
Rapid prototyping, 55, *55*, 73, *73*, 75, 77
Rational architecture, ix, 120
Reading University, 53
Ready-made components, 39, 45
Rebstockpark (Germany), scheme by Eisenman, 60, *61*
Regional architecture (regionalism), xii, ix, x, 46, 64, 90, 113, 114, 121, 162, 163–77, 198, 203–6, 207, 208
  cross-cultural effects, 163–6
Relations of degree, 152
Relative autonomy, 87–8, 144
Relativism, 31, 84–5, 119, 120
  critical relativism, xii, 31, 86–7, 120
  extreme relativism, vii, 31
  relativists, 145, 146–8
  strong thesis of relativism, 86
Religion, 89, 165
  Eastern, 117–18
Renaissance architecture, 155, 156, 158
Renault Centre (Foster Associates), Swindon, 52, *52*, *53*
Responsive architecture, 45–6, 71, 90
Responsive technologies, 77
Richard Rogers Partnership 53, *and see* Rogers, Richard
Riyadh (Saudi Arabia), *173*, 175, *175*
  Diplomatic Club (Omrania with Frei Otto), *205*, 206
  Ministry of Foreign Affairs (Larsen), *172*, 173–4, 177, 206
Robots, 8–9, *9*, 41, *42*, 44–5, *44*, 121
Rogers, Richard (Richard Rogers Partnership)
  Inland Revenue HQ, Nottingham, *63*, 64
  Lloyd's HQ, London, 52, *53*, 183–4, *184*
Roman architecture, 156, 166, *167*
Romantic designers, 120
Rome (Italy), Pantheon, 166
Rossi, Aldo, 115
Russian Constructivists and Suprematists, 66
Ryle, Gilbert, 129–30

Saarinen, Eero, 137
  TWA airport terminal, 101
Safdie, Moshe, 15
Santa Barbara Mission, *149*

Santa Fe, New Mexico, Church of Cristo Rey, *135*
Sapir, Edward, 84
Satellite navigation systems, 56
Saudi Arabia 173–4
central Nejd area, 163, *164*
see also Jeddah; Riyadh
Scharoun, Hans, 66, 93–4
Schein, Ionel, *5*
Schiedhelm, Manfred, *17*
Schocken, Hillel, *103*
Schon, Donald, 102–3, 131, 137
Schools of architecture, 38, 68, 75, 76, 112
Schumacher, E. F., 200, 201
Science, xi, 19–20, 51, 108–9, 112, 115, 116, 119, 123
and analogy, 82–3
and design method, 27–36
empirical and intuitive, 120
exemplars of, 120–1
and Kuhn, 132–3
language, 89
new science and design method, 27–36
Scruton, Roger, 115
Scully, Vincent, 98, 100
Seidler, Harry, Capita Centre, Sydney, *187*, 188
Self-build housing, 141, 201, 202, *202*, 207, 215
Self-build services, 57, *57*
Self-conscious and unself-conscious concepts, 120–1
cognition, 111
design, 106, 111, 113, 119, 120–1
Self-organizing systems, xi, xii, xiv, 20–1, 25–6, 36, 49, 51, 55, 56, 76, 195
Self-regulating city, 197
Self-regulating 'intelligent building', 53
Self-sufficiency, 206–7
Semiotics, viii, 100, 102
Sham images, 62
Shophouses, 155, *155*, 170, 190, 214, 217, 228
Sikuya Style (Japanese), 114
Sim City (computer simulation game), 62
Simla (Malaysia), 166
Simulations, 57, 70, *70*, 71, 73–4, 75
Sinan ibn Abdulmennan, 122–4
Singapore, 170, 190–2, 193, *193*, 195, 197, 213, 226, 227, 228, 229, 233
Arts Centre, *54*
Choa Chu Kang, 222, *222*
DRS projects, 70, *70*
Dynasty Hotel, *170*
Kampong Bugis district, 221–2, *221*
Liu Thai Ker (planner) and the constellation city, 222–5
Mass Rapid Transit system, 56, 197, 224, *224*
new towns, 229, 230
Tampines North Community Centre (William Lim Associates), *223*
Tay Kheng Soon (architect), 219–22
villas, 166
Skidmore Owings and Merrill (SOM)
Haj Terminal, Jeddah Airport, *173*, 174, 177
Lever House, New York, 180, *180*
National Commercial Bank, Jeddah, 174, *181*, 182, *182*, 187, 188–9
Skycourts, 182, 187, 188, 218
Smart materials, 55, 76
Smart tools, 41–3, 52
Social forms of housing, 151–2, 156, 158, 159, 208
Sousse (Tunisia), courtyard house, *158*
Southeast Asia, 165–6, 191, 195–7
Sovkino Film Studios project (Leonidove), *66*
Spooner, E. C., 157, 158
Sri Lanka, 170
Srirangam (India), *231*
Stack effects, 71
Standardization, 3, 4–5, 6, 7, 13, 38, 77, 114, 121, 161
Stansted Airport Terminal (Foster Associates), 125, *126*
Steiner, George, 145–6, 147, 148, 149
Stirling, James, New Training Centre for Olivetti, 100–1, *100*
Stress analysis tests, 73–4
Strong, Maurice F., 199
Studio design projects, 109–10, 111–12, 113
Styles of architecture, 148–9
Stylistic categories, 114–15
Sullivan, Louis, 178
Summerson, John, 156
Superimposition (superposition), 58, 60, 62
Suprematists, Russian, 66
Surabaya (Indonesia), *202*
Swindon, Renault Centre (Foster Associates), 52, *52*, *53*
Sydney (Australia)
Capita Centre (Seidler), 187, *187*, 188
Opera House (Utzon), 101, *101*
Syria, 204
Systems design movement *see* design methods movement

Tacit knowing, ix, 106–7
in learning design, 106–13
Taj Mahal, Agra (India), *172*, 174
Takenaka, *44*
Tange, Kenzo, 175
Tay Kheng Soon, 219–22, 226, 229, 230–1
Technology, xi, xiii, 21, 116, 119
advanced, 125, 127, 129, 203
appropriate/intermediate, 200–3, 207, 208
combined, 203
innovations, 183
modern and traditional, 123, 124–5, 127, 129
Thammasat University (Jumsai), nr Bangkok, 206, *206*
Tokyo (Japan)
Century Tower (Foster Associates), 125, *125*
Millennium Tower project (Foster), 227, *227*
Nunotani Headquaters (Eisenman), 60
Sky House, Bunkyo-ku (Kikutake), *171*
Toronto (Canada), Scarborough College (Andrew), 18
Tradition, 114, 116–17, 119–22, 124–5, 129, 130, 208, 209
building types and materials, 170
and innovation, 131–7
traditional cultures, 151
Transformations of mind, 149
Tropical architecture, 195–7, 215, 217
graduate programme, 69, 70, 71, 72
see also climate; Kuala Lumpur; Singapore
Tropical city, 196, 228–9, 231
Tschumi, Bernard, Parc de la Villette, 58, *58*, *59*, 60
Tuan, Yi-Fu, 141
Tunis, El Hafsia Quarter (Wassim Ben Mahoud), 174–5, *174*
Turner, John, vii, 141
TWA airport terminal (Saarinen), 101

Ulm (Germany), Hochschule für Gestaltung, vii, 37, *38*, 68, 69
Universal building types, 121, 204
Universalists, 144–8
Urban architecture and planning, xiv, 36, 115
Asian, 211–34
chaos or self-organization, 15–26
in cyberspace, 56–7
decentralization, xii, 18, 21–5
dispersal, 21, 51
fragmentation of urban structure, 18–19, 21, 26
modern and traditional building types, 204–6
responses to changing context, 174–5
urban conservation, 192

Urban architecture and planning (*cont.*)
urban cultures, 226–8
urban growth simulated, 62
urban oasis, 177
urban theory, 15
USA, vii, 177
decentralization and centralization, 21–5
New Frontier, 56
Utzon, Jorn
Japanese house, *101*
Sydney Opera House, 101, *101*

Variable production, 7–10, 46
Venetian window, 155–6
Venturi, Robert, ix, 114, 115, *115*, 116, 129
Verandahways, 217, *217*, 228
Vicenza (Italy)
Basilica (Palladio), 158, *158*
Villa Almerico, 154
Vico, Giovanni Batista, 27–30, 31
Vienna (Austria), 58
Villa Cornaro, nr Padua, 153–4, *153*
Villas, 152–4, 156, 159–60, 166, *167*, 168, 169, 175, 228
Virtual cities, 227
Virtual practice, 57, 73
Virtual prototyping, 53, 55, 72, 73–4, 75, 77
Virtual reality, 53, *54*, 55, *72*, 74, 75, 77
Virtual workplaces, 77

Waldhor, Ivo, 64
Watkin, David, 81, 84, 88, 93, 116
Ways of being, 149–50
Webber, Melvin, 15, 22
Whorf, Benjamin, 31, 84–5, 86, 87, 146
Wilford (Michael) and Partners, *54*
Williamson, D. T. N., 10
Wilson, L. Hugh, *18*
Wilson, Raymond, 3, 4
Wind-tunnel tests, 70, *70*, 71
Windsor, Connecticut, *22*
Wittgenstein, Ludwig, 85–6, 87, 146, 147, 148, 149
World architectures, 156–62
Wright, Frank Lloyd, 66, 184, 189
Larkin Company Office Building, Buffalo, 178–9, *179*
Unitarian Church, Madison, 98, *99*, 100
Wyman, George H., Bradbury Building, Los Angeles, 178, *179*

Yeang, Ken, 64, 70, 215–19, 227, 229, *229*, 230–1
Hitechniaga Corporation, Kuala Lumpur, 188, *189*
Yogyakarta (Indonesia), 204, *204*

Zevi, Bruno, ix, 90